Eye for Talent

Eye for Talent

*Interviews with
Veteran Baseball Scouts*

EDITED BY P.J. DRAGSETH
Foreword by Lenny Yochim

McFarland & Company, Inc., Publishers
Jefferson, North Carolina, and London

This work contains information derived from content and/or data owned
or licensed by the Society for American Baseball Research, Inc. (SABR),
and is published with the permission of SABR.

LIBRARY OF CONGRESS CATALOGUING-IN-PUBLICATION DATA

Eye for talent : interviews with veteran baseball scouts /
edited by P.J. Dragseth ; Foreword by Lenny Yochim.
p. cm.
Includes bibliographical references and index.

ISBN 978-0-7864-4361-1
softcover: 50# alkaline paper ∞

1. Baseball scouts — United States — Biography.
2. Baseball — United States — History.
I. Dragseth, P.J.
GV865.T88E94   2010
796.3570922 — dc22   2009039030
[B]

British Library cataloguing data are available

©2010 P.J. Dragseth. All rights reserved

*No part of this book may be reproduced or transmitted in any form
or by any means, electronic or mechanical, including photocopying
or recording, or by any information storage and retrieval system,
without permission in writing from the publisher.*

Cover photograph ©2010 Shutterstock

Manufactured in the United States of America

*McFarland & Company, Inc., Publishers
Box 611, Jefferson, North Carolina 28640
www.mcfarlandpub.com*

To Dad for taking me out to the ballgame, Sal Taormina and the San Francisco Seals for sparking my passion, the Chicago Cubs for all the memories, the scouts without whom none of it would have been possible, and especially to my husband Rich who has always been my rock.

Acknowledgments

Work on this book spanned eight years and wouldn't have happened without help from many people. This was a labor of love for the game and these scouts who dedicated so much to it.

Thank you to those who chronicled the experiences and contributions of the earliest scouts so the rest of us could pick up where they left off and continue forward.

Thank you to the Society for American Baseball Research (SABR). Your efforts on behalf of preserving baseball history are inspirational to fellow members like me and to fans everywhere. I look forward to joining your research ranks soon.

To Roberta Mazur, president of the Baseball Scout of the Year Awards Program, whose work on behalf of the scouts is deeply appreciated. The programs from all the award banquets that you sent left me speechless. Thank you.

To Jim Cummins, former editor and publisher of *The Baseball Scout: A Newsletter For and About Scouting*, thank you for sending some my way.

To Fred McAlister, a scout who helped put me in touch with many in this book, and who was always available to assist, thank you. I could always hear the smile in your voice over the phone. And a special thank you to Patty.

To the scouts who were kind enough to share their stories, who stuck with it when they were tired or unwell, but were determined to contribute, thank you.

To my family, thanks for understanding my passion and encouraging me to enjoy it.

Table of Contents

Acknowledgments vi
Foreword by Lenny Yochim 1
Preface 3
Introduction 5

THE INTERVIEWS

Hugh Alexander	19	Al LaMacchia	128
Dick Egan	29	George Genovese	144
Jerry Gardner	41	Julian Mock	160
Jethro "Jeth" McIntyre	52	Fred McAlister	171
Ellis Clary	62	Gib Bodet	187
Dick Wilson	74	Phil Rizzo	199
Gene "Junior" Thompson	106	Cecil Espy	207
Bobby Mattick	116	Bob Harrison	221
		George Digby	231

Bibliography 235
Index 237

Foreword
by Lenny Yochim

I was exposed to professional baseball very early. I was born four blocks from Pelican Stadium, home of the New Orleans Pelicans Double A classification in the Southern Association in 1928. My brother Ray preceded me, being born in 1922. He signed a contract with the Cardinals and the Pelicans in 1941 and I signed with the Pelicans in the fall of 1946.

My career lasted ten seasons mixed in with four years of Winter League ball in Venezuela. I was a left-handed pitcher. Ray and I both reached the majors, Ray with the Cardinals and I with the Pirates. The honeymoon didn't last long enough for either one of us. We both played with and against some great major leaguers, some hall of famers and some not so hall of famers.

Somewhere along the way after my last season as a player in 1956, I was approached by a scout with the Chicago Cubs, Tom "Shaky" Cain. He asked me if I would be interested in a job as a Bird Dog, recommending players with major league potential, and I accepted. That fall at a baseball clinic I attended as an instructor, Colonel CB "Buster" Mills, a scout with the Kansas City Athletics, asked if I was interested in the same position helping him. I said I was, but I wanted some money for gas, ticket admission, and a cola and a hot dog. He agreed. That lasted three seasons. In 1962 Buster went to work with the Yankees leaving his scouting job open. Hank Peters, scouting director of the Athletics, offered me the job and I accepted. My territory was Louisiana, Mississippi, half of Texas, and Arkansas. That August I was fired along with six or seven others. I was stunned. I took a job in sales with the Jackson Brewing Company and went back to work with Buster and the Yankees. In the fall of 1965 the Pirates offered me a job covering Louisiana, Mississippi, Texas, Oklahoma, and Arkansas. I accepted. For thirty-seven years my employer was the Pittsburgh Pirates. First I was a territorial scout. I then became a national crosschecker, a major league scout, special assistant to the general manager, and lastly senior advisor/player personnel. All those titles meant the same thing. I WAS A SCOUT and very proud of the title. I truly loved my job. The Pirates had great people up and down the employee roster. When "Whitey" Lockman, my dear friend with the Marlins, heard of my promotion he said he hoped that I got a better raise for the same title than he did. I said, "No, it was the same as yours. ZERO."

The scouts that were interviewed for this book are well known and thought of highly by their peers and I can't say enough about their qualifications. In my position as national crosschecker for the Pirates I was spread out all over the United States and I would see these scouts throughout my travels. We would visit with each other and break bread on occasions. I learned from the likes of Howie Haak, Jerry Gardner, George Digby (my legion coach in New Orleans), scouts Milt Bolling, Al LaMacchia, Hugh Alexander, and Fred McAlister. Our free agent areas were similar. They didn't work by the clock and they were diggers for information to get a leg up in getting their player drafted. They were tough competitors and they would fight to get their player drafted.

It is time that scouts are being recognized with books documenting their signings and achievements. There is a canned phrase overused and abused by all the clubs in baseball: "Scouting is the backbone of an organization." As scouts are well aware, they are not actually treated as the backbone, but maybe a little lower. There are a couple of organizations who have stepped up to help scouts in their time of need—the Scout of the Year Program honoring their achievements in scouting, and the Baseball Scouts Foundation lending their financial support to assist a scout in need. I know that to be true because they have been assisting a scout I recommended as needing help. This is independent of MLB.

On the flip side of scouting, often funny things occur. I was cross checking at the time one of Carlton Keller's players was drafting down the line. This was perhaps twenty or twenty-five years ago. I won't mention the town; it could give away the name. We were negotiating with him and his attorney (family). After spending a couple of hours eating out, the player suggested he take us on a tour of the city. Carlton drove while I was in the front passenger seat, and from the rear the player says, "Turn here, then turn here" and we were going down the boulevard. I noticed that we were cruising in front of the new car dealerships and our prospect was pointing out the cars he liked. I said, "We need to look at some of the used car lots. We don't have new car money." You could have heard a pin drop.

The purpose of a scout is to find and procure talent for major league clubs. They wage a verbal war selling their opinion to the scouting director and the general manager that a certain player will be a star in the major leagues. Case in point: I live in the New Orleans area. On the west bank of the Mississippi River there is a small town by the name of Gretna. One hundred years ago Mel Thomas Ott was born there. As a seventeen-year-old high school graduate, Ott was signed by the New York Giants on the recommendation of a friend of manager John McGraw. The rest is history. Ott never played a game in the minor leagues, had a twenty-two year major league career, was a Hall of Famer and was the first National League player with more than 500 home runs, had a .304 lifetime average, and his records are numerous.

The story goes that Mel Ott was recommended to Manager McGraw by Harry Williams, owner of a lumber company and semi-pro club in New Orleans. It is believed that Williams, a friend of McGraw's, was also one of the manager's many bird dogs. With Harrison's letter of introduction in hand, Ott made his way to the Polo Grounds and a tryout for McGraw. That the rest, as they say, is history points to the need for this book by P.J. Dragseth. Most fans and historians are missing out on an important, and sometimes fascinating, part of the story. Without the amateur and pro scouts there to give history that first nudge, how many memorable major league careers might never have been?

Lenny Yochim played ten years in the majors and scouted for several teams before retiring in 2002. During his career he received numerous awards, including Scout of the Year, Midwest, in 1994.

Preface

My baseball journey began on a warm Sunday afternoon in 1953 when I was eight years old. Dad took my kid brother and me to our first ballgame at beautiful Seals Stadium in San Francisco between the Seals and Hollywood Stars in the Pacific Coast League during those final years when all eight teams in the league actually played on the Pacific Coast.

Before that day baseball was just one of the games the neighborhood kids played in the schoolyard, third favorite on my list behind dodgeball and kickball. But that was a long time ago in the Bay Area where I grew up in the small town of Martinez, the birthplace of Joe DiMaggio.

I followed the Seals game by game with announcer Don Klein on KSFO radio, kept box scores, collected the *San Francisco Chronicle* green sheets (sports pages), and made scrapbooks on every player. It kept me quite busy for the next four and a half seasons. Dad took us to home games on Sundays and sometimes to away games in Sacramento. It was a time when the only game on television was the "Saturday Game of the Week," colorfully described by a character named Dizzy Dean. Everything changed, of course, at the end of the 1957 season, when the New York Giants and Brooklyn Dodgers moved west. My young mind saw the whole thing as a disaster while everyone around me called it progress. To me the final insult happened when the Giants occupied Seals Stadium during their first season while Candlestick Park was under construction.

Life went on. And baseball went on, but without me. I just couldn't bring myself to become a Giants fan. High school, college, marriage, and two small children later, baseball beckoned me back. At that time the only MLB team carried on our cable network was the New York Mets. As it happened, that was 1969, the year of the Amazing Mets. What a ride! I was hooked all over again. When we moved for a new employment opportunity in 1970, the cable scenario was the same, but this time the team was the Chicago Cubs. Today the family has grown into three generations of Cubs fans.

Things changed for my life when my first baseball hero and friend, former Seals player Sal Taormina, died suddenly. When the Giants arrived in 1958, he worked for them as a coach with their minor league team in Phoenix, Arizona. He scolded me constantly, saying, "Get with the program. The Giants are the Bay Area team now." Later, when he was the head baseball coach of the Santa Clara Broncos, he continued his tirade every time we went to see his team play. Sal loved baseball, especially mentoring young players. One of his success stories was Willie McCovey.

Shocked and saddened by his death, I contemplated writing a book that would help young ballplayers, one I was sure he would have written if he'd had more time. I talked with his old Seals teammates Ken Aspromonte and Nini Tornay, and they encouraged me. The result was *Go Pro Baseball Wise*. The book included interviews with more than

200 members from all levels of the baseball community — rookies, active and retired minor and major league players, managers, player development personnel, scouts and scouting directors, general managers, and members of the Baseball Hall of Fame. They discussed elements of their own careers and offered tips and guidance to youngsters dreaming the baseball dream and their parents. In preparation for the book, I spent an entire season with a team of rookies in the Northwest League and worked with players from every club in the league, and then followed them to instructional league in Arizona in the fall and back again for spring training. The next eight years were spent traveling as I followed their careers while they scattered to ballparks and leagues throughout the country.

That adventure also included my first encounters with the scouts. They heard about my project and approached me during batting practice one night offering their help. It seems silly now, but at the time I didn't know much about them or what they did other than they wore interesting hats and carried clipboards and stop watches. They told lots of stories about this player and that, encouraged my questions, educated me with copies of scouting reports, and referred me to others in the game. During my travels we ran into each other in ballparks here and there.

A few of us kept in closer touch. Meanwhile, I started doing some research in order to write an article about scouts but was frustrated by the range of information available, which was basically nothing to very little. How could that be when their stories are a unique piece of baseball history? After ranting and raving to baseball friends about the situation, word got out, and one day a couple of years later I received a large packet in the mail from one of the oldest scouts, Dick Wilson, whom I'd met while working on *Go Pro Baseball Wise*. It was his hand-written recollections of his life in baseball as a player and scout. He attached a note that read, "This is for you just in case you ever want to do a book about scouts."

That was another beginning.

The scouts in this book are the veterans who are becoming a vanishing breed. They're among the most respected men in the business for all their contributions to the game. Most have a minimum of forty years in scouting; some have even more. Two others, now retired, are younger but have more than twenty-five years under their belts. I asked everyone to share his player background because, after all, that was where they got their "scout training." It also demonstrates their tenacious commitment to the game and their determination to make it their life's work.

In the interviews that follow, they remember the players signed and the ones who got away, the details of "the chase," stories about Branch Rickey and Jackie Robinson, ways their jobs changed over the years because of the draft, the Major League Scouting Bureau, expansion, and other changes they've witnessed during their careers.

Records listing players signed by these scouts cite only those who reached the major leagues. Signed players whose careers were cut short by injuries, who were released along the way for whatever reason, or who had long and successful minor league careers without making it to the major leagues are not included.

To express my gratitude to these unforgettable men for their generosity of spirit is inadequate. They have my profound respect individually and as a group. Meeting them and working with them will always remain a highlight in my life-long baseball experience. Sadly, some have passed away since our interviews. Their memories are preserved here as part of the history of the game they loved.

Introduction

"Baseball is a game of adjustments" is one of the most overused phrases in professional baseball, usually referring to player performances. But it goes deeper. The game is a revolving door of constant and never-ending adjustments to financial changes and dilemmas of its own making. Despite all the bumps and potholes in the road, baseball keeps on keeping on for better or worse. Addicted fans stay tuned to see what happens next and cheer for their favorites. Meanwhile, the media focuses on players, agents, corporate owners, illicit performance-enhancing drugs, and money, big money. Often unseen and frequently forgotten in this milieu is the invisible cog in the machine, the scouts.

The older veteran scouts are a vanishing breed. They have been called the foundation of the game, the backbone of baseball, the ones who put the teams and the talent in touch, the traveling salesmen, the million-mile men, the ivory hunters, and the baseball prophets. All these phrases are cliché, but they're accurate.

In order to understand how the scouts fit into the overall scheme of things, we must take a brief look at the history of professional baseball. The changes from 1846, when Daniel "Doc" Adams, president of the New York Knickerbockers, revised and codified some of the most recognizable features of the modern game (90 feet between bases, nine innings, nine players to a side), to the mega-industry we know today have been an evolutionary roller coaster.

Initially, there was only one league, the National Base Ball Players Association, comprised of twenty-two teams that grew to sixty-two by the start of the Civil War. Internal bickering, financial losses, and declining attendance due to gambling and rowdyism among players and fans alike finally led to the league's dissolution. Historians have referred to letters written by soldiers on both sides of the Mason-Dixon Line during the Civil War describing how they played baseball whenever possible. Some even mentioned instances in which ballgames were suspended because their camps were under attack or the baseball itself was captured by the enemy.

In 1876, Chicago White Stockings owner William Hulbert and others formed the National League of Professional Base Ball Clubs featuring eight charter members: the Chicago White Stockings, New York Mutuals, Philadelphia Athletics, Hartford Dark Blues, St. Louis Brown Stockings, Boston Red Caps, Louisville Grays, and Cincinnati Reds. The short-lived Players League, formed in 1890 by John Montgomery Ward and populated by many stars who jumped from the National League, lasted only one season. After its demise the wayward players were welcomed back to their former teams.

By 1901 Ban Johnson, president of the eight-year-old Western League, a minor league, was frustrated and angry about losing his best players to the National League. He believed his only recourse was to start the American League with himself as president, a position he held until 1927. The eight charter teams were the Baltimore Orioles, Boston Somersets, Chicago White Stockings, Cleveland Blues, Detroit Tigers, Milwaukee Brewers, Philadelphia Athletics, and Washington Nationals. This formation was followed by a three-season "rebellion" in the mid–1910s called the Federal League. After the upstarts' demise, it seemed things would finally stabilize with two major leagues, both east of the Mississippi River, dividing the fan base and the profits.

Throughout the alignments and realignments of teams and leagues, the game was played at the minor and major league levels. Players were bought and sold at the discretion of team owners on an as-needed basis to fill rosters or replace injured players. Some worked their way up the ladder to the major league level. Men already in the game, such as players, managers, and even umpires, kept an eye out for good young players and reported their findings in hopes of getting a small bonus if the prospects were signed at a higher level. In the 1880s and 1890s, Cap Anson, the legendary Chicago player and manager, preferred to scout players on his own and was quite successful. He purchased such prominent players as George Gore, Abner Dalrymple, Jake Stenzel, Billy Sunday, Joe Wilhoit, and two future Hall of Famers in Clark Griffith and Hugh Duffy. Eventually, clubs used watchers and bird dogs, men who were not full-time employees, to watch games and find players.

Larry Sutton (1858–1944) was a printer and proofreader at the *Newark Eagle Star* newspaper who moonlighted as an umpire in the late 1870s in Oswego, New York. As an arbiter he was able to compare and evaluate the best players and make recommendations to the Brooklyn Robins. More than thirty years later, in 1909, he was finally put on the Robins' payroll, and today is considered the first paid full-time scout in professional baseball. Descriptions of him have Sutton as a big and somewhat humorless man who always carried an umbrella regardless of the weather.

Despite his reputation as a serious evaluator of players, Sutton was also known as a man with unique superstitions, including a preference for light-haired players because he said they held up better in the summer heat. It was said that his territory was limited only by his imagination and his budget for traveling expenses.

Sutton signed more than forty players who played in the big leagues, including Zack Wheat, Dazzy Vance, and Casey Stengel. When the Robins won the pennant in 1916 before losing the World Series to Boston in five games, Sutton had signed eleven players on that team for a total bonus of $14,500. He scouted professionally for more than thirty years, all but three with Brooklyn. When he retired from the game due to ill health, he returned to his job at the *Newark Eagle Star*.

A contemporary of Larry Sutton, Timothy Paul, a.k.a. "TP" or "Ted," Sullivan (1851–1929) is often forgotten in the ledgers of baseball history even though he was out there at the same time, but doing the job differently. Whereas Sutton recommended players to the Robins prior to 1909, Sullivan was signing players himself for teams in leagues he founded.

Dubbed "best hustler of them all" by the *Sporting Weekly Journal,* published in Philadelphia at the turn of the twentieth century, Sullivan was a businessman and promoter whose business was powered by his love of baseball, and he didn't limit himself to scouting. His contributions to the game are many. He began in 1874 when he left St. Mary's College in Kansas, and, as early as 1876 he formed his first team, Sullivan's Alerts, soon followed by the Dubuque Rabbits, where he signed his college chum, Charles Comiskey, to his first baseball contract to play third base.

Over the next fifty years, he served baseball as a team owner, league organizer and president, business manager, field manager at both the major and minor league levels, crosschecker, and international promoter. He established or co-founded such leagues as the Northwest League in Iowa and Illinois, which included his Dubuque Rabbits (1879), the Western League and the Southern League (1885), the Connecticut State League (1893), the New Jersey League (1897), the Atlantic League (1900) and the new South Atlantic League (1904), reorganized the Texas League (1902), and was a member of the consortium that established the American League in 1903. Throughout this time he was an independent scout who traveled first by covered wagon and later by train, finding and signing hundreds of players for these ventures.

Sullivan also did "managing rescues" of several minor league teams, but his feisty and hard-nosed style sometimes backfired when his teams did so well the leagues folded. One example occurred in 1902 when, as substitute manager, he led the Texas League Corsicans to the pennant, 28½ games ahead of the pack, and then helped reorganize the league when it collapsed. He also did managerial stints in the major leagues with the Washington Senators and Pittsburgh Pirates.

From 1901–1908 his primary focus was on scouting when he scouted for the Reds, Phillies, Cubs and White Sox, but the understanding was that he was not limited to any one of the teams. He then worked exclusively for Charles Comiskey's White Sox from 1909–1920.

Over the years he found many players who wound up on different major league teams. Every one of them was born in the nineteenth century. These players and the year they first appeared in a major league game include: Cliff Blankenship, 1905, Reds; Joe Burke, 1890, Cardinals; Clarence Currie, 1902, Reds; John Dolan, 1890, Reds; Chick Gandil, 1910, White Sox; Jake Gettman, 1897, Senators; William "Dummy" Hoy, 1888, Senators; Johnny Kling, 1900, Cubs; Arlie Latham, 1883, Cardinals; Orval Overall, 1905, Reds; Billy "Bunker" Rhines, 1890, Red Stockings; Ray Schalk, 1912, White Sox; Bert Sincock, 1905, Reds; George Stovall, 1904, Cleveland; Sammy Strang, 1896, Cubs; Ben Tincup, 1914, Phillies; Buck Weaver, 1912, White Sox; Walt Wilmot, Senators, 1888; Henry Wilson, 1898, Orioles; and Charlie "Hoss" Radbourn, 1880, Buffalo, who pitched his way into the Baseball Hall of Fame.

Sullivan spent his latter years traveling back and forth to Europe promoting the game, sending American players to tryouts, and writing about his adventures. His most-noted book was one he'd written in 1903 titled *Humorous Stories on the Ball Field*. Throughout his life he never slowed down and always had another baseball innovation up his sleeve.

From the late 1920s to the late 1930s a few scouts appeared on the horizon here and there with teams that could afford one, and by World War II a few teams had scouting departments consisting of two or three scouts. At the war's conclusion, the need for and value of professional scouts was finally recognized as the best way to remain competitive in the hunt for talent. At last the scouting profession was recognized as an official part of Major League Baseball.

Back in their day, the order of things was simple. Becoming a scout was the result of a lifelong process that began the first time they held a baseball. From the childhood days of sandlot ball through their final professional at-bats, their love of the game and the skills needed to scout were learned as players and honed with experience.

Today the game is inundated with specialists, from hitting instructors to pitching coaches to fielding coordinators, just to name a few. Scouting also has become more refined and specialized. The scouts' job descriptions are divided into two general categories, named for the type of baseball players they cover: amateur and professional.

Amateur scouts evaluate players in amateur baseball. They go to high schools, junior colleges, four-year colleges, American Legion games, showcases and elsewhere looking for players who still have amateur status. Most are full-time area scouts assigned to a specified geographic territory, which requires them to spend considerable time on the road. Others cover Latin America and the Pacific Rim. Those classified as part-time area scouts usually work in the most populated areas, or on special assignments from the organization. Even though they have limited duties, they work throughout the year.

Full-timers and part-timers alike depend on the volunteer services of local people throughout their areas known as bird dogs, who point out talent for the scouts to evaluate. As George Genovese explained, "It's always smart for scouts to cultivate people in their areas. I always did. Call them bird dogs or associates or whatever, but scouts pay attention to what they say because they're people hanging around locally in the area and they are well apprised of what's going on there. If they told me they liked a certain kid, I always took the time to go and see him. In fact, some of them are so good that I've gotten them started in full-time jobs in baseball."

Another group of amateur scouts is the Major League Scouting Bureau, created in 1974 to help minimize scouting costs. The bureau consists of a group of scouts who work for Major League Baseball as a whole rather than for specific organizations. Their reports are electronically submitted to all thirty clubs, who use the information any way they deem appropriate.

Professional scouts cover professional baseball, players already playing for pay. Within their assigned areas they evaluate professional players of all organizations at all levels of the game. Their information helps organizations make decisions regarding trades, releases, promotions, and the like. Many only cover the big leagues and are called **major league scouts**.

Advance scouts, used primarily at the major league level, travel ahead of their teams to see future opponents a week or two in advance of a series to gather data on pitching and hitting tendencies, possible injuries, and other pertinent information. Services they provide have made the differences in successful trades as well as winning pennants, World Series rings and more.

Near the top of the hierarchy in every organization is an elite corps of between two to four more experienced scouts called **crosscheckers**. They oversee and evaluate reports of both the amateur and professional scouts by providing another set of eyes and an additional opinion. For instance, if scouts in Florida and California say they have amateur players at shortstop with all the tools and the best speed they have ever seen, the crosschecker will see each player in game situations and submit his opinions. Among their other responsibilities, crosscheckers assist the scouting department in compiling the draft list that ranks the players available, beginning with the best.

Perhaps the smallest category is that of **scouting consultants,** usually older scouts highly respected for their experience, judgment, and insight, who work closely with the scouting director and general manager.

While the specifics of each scouting role differ, the goals are always the same. As fans focus on the present season and look to the past with reverence, scouts always look to the future as they scour the United States, Latin America, and the Pacific Rim. They don't wear uniforms. They seek no glory, no fame. They don't garner star-sized salaries or have groupies asking for autographs. Instead, they prefer to remain anonymous, even elusive, in order to do their jobs. Though most are former players, few made it to the major leagues, but don't let that fool you. They know how the game is played. They've done it all as players, player-managers, coaches, scouting directors, general managers, or all of the above. They know how to spot and evaluate talent, always with an eye to the continuity of the game.

Throughout their careers money has been the catalyst for changes that impacted the business of baseball and the way they do their jobs. The never-ending demands for more money made the game itself a "game of adjustments." The scouts here were involved with and impacted by many of them: Branch Rickey, always ahead of his time, developed the farm system as we know it today and encouraged the initial opening of Mexico and the Latin American countries by MLB scouts; the need for financial parity among teams that resulted in the "bonus baby" system in the 1950s and then the draft in 1965; the establishment of the Major League Scouting Bureau only nine years later, in 1974; the seeds of expansion that brought the number of major league teams from sixteen to thirty between the early 1960s and late 1990s; astronomical signing bonuses and salaries brought about by arbitration and agents; and, experiments with corporate ownership. As baseball adapted and adjusted, for good or bad, the scouts did likewise, although they unanimously agree that the draft was a big mistake. Instead of fixing or adjusting baseball's financial woes, it magnified and exacerbated the situation.

By the end of World War II, the writing was on the wall in Major League Baseball. Large market teams, such as the New York Yankees, New York Giants, and the Boston Red Sox, controlled the acquisition of the best players by simply outbidding small market teams, which led to a lack of parity on the field. Fans of the small market clubs knew year after year that their team couldn't afford the best players and had no chance at winning the pennant.

One of the early attempts to level the playing field was the Bonus Rule that lasted from 1947–1965. It was designed to limit rich teams with deep farm systems from continued domination and prevent the escalation of signing bonus dollars spent on young amateurs. It stated simply that any amateur signed for a bonus of more than $4,000 had to be placed on the major league roster immediately and could not be sent to the minor leagues for a minimum of one season.

But this, too, added to the financial quagmire for two reasons. Some of the rich teams that didn't mind the costs bid against each other for those players, which increased bonuses to as much as $50,000 or more. Perhaps even worse was the effect on the young players who spent their first pro season on a big league bench instead of minor league player development programs; in some cases, careers were stunted or ruined. Although the players signed under this rule were given the derogatory nickname of "bonus babies" because of their youth, many of them went on to successful major league careers, and others like Harmon Killebrew and Sandy Koufax went to the Baseball Hall of Fame.

As a result of the bonus rule, more than ever professional baseball had become a bottom-heavy see-saw controlled by large market teams, which left the small market teams dangling in the air. Something more had to be done. Finally, in 1965, baseball made what many see as its biggest adjustment when the draft was instituted as a two-with-one-blow measure to control costs and level the playing field.

Actually, the process initially involved three annual drafts. The largest and most significant to clubs and amateur players, the June draft, centered on eligible high school graduates and college students who were either twenty-one years old or had completed their senior year. A secondary phase draft was held in January to accommodate high school and college players who graduated in the winter. Third draft was held in August for amateurs who played in the amateur summer leagues. In 1986, both the January and August phases were eliminated. Once again economics was the underlying reason for the change with fewer drafts each year meaning fewer signing bonuses, which converted to money saved.

The rules and guidelines established in 1965 regulated the ways scouts are allowed to interact with players before and after the draft, which forever changed the way they did their jobs. Nevertheless, the essentials of scouting remained the same. In their quests, they continued to spend the bulk of their professional lives on the road scanning their territories. They saw nothing unusual about driving all night from one game to another or many hundreds of miles in a week to cover as many as three or four games in a single day. They continued to put pressure on themselves to find the talent as a matter of personal pride. But the similarity to the old ways ended there. A new word — "signability" — was created to define ways in which scouts could determine if drafted players would sign even though discussing money specifics with them or their families was prohibited.

George Kissell retired from a seventy-year baseball career with the St. Louis Cardinals in 2007. He was a staunch Branch Rickey man who served in many capacities, including minor league player and player-manager, major league coach, scout, director of player development, major league assistant under Red Schoendienst for seven seasons, spring training instructor, and senior field coordinator of player development. He loved to tell the story of how he signed and the amount of his signing bonus to make the point about how things have changed in the game.

> I signed out of a tryout camp in 1939 in Rochester, New York. Of course, there was no draft then. I was on the eleventh infield. My number was 385, so you can see how many people were out there that day. There were only two of us signed. One was Ted Wilkes, who became a good relief pitcher for the Cardinals in the 1940s, and me.
>
> I played shortstop, and my tryout consisted of them hitting five balls to me in the hole at short. Then they told me to run from home to first. Then they told me to take a seat in the bleachers. And that was the extent of it. I sat there maybe an hour to an hour and a half and thought I'd been eliminated. So I was getting ready to go home when one guy called me over.
>
> The scout who signed me was Pop Kelchner. He asked me how old I was and I told him, nineteen. He asked if I'd come down there by myself, and I said that I'd come with my dad. He told me to go get my dad, and I did, and he talked to both of us together. He asked my father if he wanted me to play ball and my dad said yes. He asked if they could sign me today and my dad said yes.
>
> Pop Kelchner asked me to go figure up our expenses for that day. We drove about a hundred-five miles, plus overnight at a guest house on the way, so our expenses were about $19.80. He gave me a twenty dollar bill and said, "Congratulations. Sign here." And that's the way I got signed. Right there on the spot! He told me to keep the twenty cents change, and I always tell folks that was my signing bonus. Twenty cents!

The first fifty-five years of scouting, the "Pre-Draft Era," could possibly be compared to the frontier days of the Old West when it was every man for himself. Scouts considered every available player as a challenge to be met and a prize to be won. Competition with other scouts was the name of the game, and they loved it. One example is an old Baltimore scout, Al Kubski, who was reputed to be one of the most tenacious of all. Other scouts knew they'd have to act fast if Kubski was in the hunt for a player they had seen but not yet signed. It's said that he waited outside youngsters' homes and watched other scouts come and go. When the last one left, he knocked on the door, announced himself, and said he'd top any and all offers if the boy would sign on the spot. Although he was slowed by draft rules, he managed to sign another nineteen players who played in the major leagues over the next thirty years.

Thirteen-year American League first baseman Eddie Robinson went on to a long and impressive executive career in the game. He held such positions as scouting director/director of player development with Baltimore, Houston, and Kansas City. He was assistant general manager with Atlanta, general manager for the Texas Rangers, and executive vice president/general manager and special assistant to owner George Steinbrenner of the New York Yankees. He remembers the impact of the draft on the scouts. He explained:

When Eddie Robinson retired as a player, Baltimore manager Paul Richards gave him his start as a scout, and he wound up as director of player development. Later he was a ground floor scout with the Houston Colt .45s/Astros during franchise building for the expansion team. He served as director of player development with Houston, Kansas City, Atlanta, and the Texas Rangers, where he also served as GM. SABR credits him with signing Jerry Adair and Ron Darling, and he was involved in signing and the development of Joe Niekro, Larry Dierker, Jimmy Wynn, and others (Eddie Robinson Collection).

Well, they'd been talking about having a draft for awhile as they felt they had to do something with these clubs bidding against each other. So I think the reason for the draft was to give everybody a fair shake and then only one club, the one who drafted the player, would have the rights to negotiate with him. This was supposed to keep the costs down.

I think the draft changed the way things were done entirely. Scouts were better and more competitive before the draft came in. For instance, before the draft, a scout would find a player, not say anything about him, and when he graduated from high school, sometimes he could sign the player without anybody else knowing about him. And he might be a pretty good player. But when the draft came in, everybody knew about all the good players and scouting became more of a fraternity, and there got to be a scouting combine right away. Some scouts had a tendency to follow what their peers had to say rather than have their own opinions. That's always been the case. Some scouts have the real ability to judge talent. Others want to be scouts but they have a tendency, I think, to lean on other scouts' opinions. Every scout knows if he's a good scout or not. All these guys need to do is look back at the players they've recommended over the last two or three years and see what's happened to them.

After I stopped playing I was always in the front office and never really worked at the ground level with young players and their families. But I could see how my scouts were before the draft and how they had to be afterward. They all adapted to the way things were done because of the draft. They all had their tricks, as I call their strong points. Some are good signers and some aren't. That's where I came in. Once we depended on the scout and his judgment and drafted the player, then we'd go in there and try to sign him for as little as we could.

Further adjustments were made nine years later when the Major League Scouting Bureau was established in 1974. Owned and operated by Major League Baseball with the same hierarchy as any scouting department, it employs an average of thirty-five qualified and experienced scouts who cover specified territories throughout the United States. They submit their scouting reports to the bureau, which then electronically transmits them to all thirty clubs. This has been controversial from its inception because organizational scouts and bureau scouts have different functions. Bureau scouts make generalized reports for organizations to screen, and then teams send their scouts to evaluate players in which they're interested. Many scouts, like former Detroit pitcher Kevin Saucier, have spent their careers with the bureau and many have won multiple awards for scouting excellence, like former major league shortstop Lennie Merullo. Over the years the bureau has expanded its services by operating an average of one hundred tryout camps every season throughout the country.

Scouts note that whenever there's any kind of financial stress on an organization, the first thing it does to tighten its fiscal belt is decrease the size of its scouting department. "Scouts are always the first to go," they say. Eddie Robinson remembered the man probably most notorious for cutting his scouting department, Athletics owner Charlie Finley.

When I was his scouting director at Kansas City, Charlie and I got along fine. Working with him was okay. He was a successful businessman, like so many of them, except he owned the team by himself. He was a little hard-headed. He thought he knew how to do it. And he didn't make many mistakes. His big mistake was that he was stubborn, kind of like that big mule he carried around. Charlie knew he was successful because he did things his own way and was willing to take chances. He was very close to his money and led a very small operating staff and an extremely small scouting staff. Later on, after he got out from under my direction, he kind of went crazy and cut the entire scouting staff.

As early as the late 1940s when the need for some kind of regulatory procedure was needed, and throughout the period when plans for some kind of a draft were being formulated, Branch Rickey, again ahead of his time, saw the onslaught of the coming storm and began sending scouts into Mexico and Latin America to look for young players who would not fall under the umbrella of the anticipated draft rules. Men like George Genovese, Howie Haak, and Joe Cambria were among the leaders in the effort.

Joe Cambria, a longtime friend of Calvin Griffith, was signed to scout for the Washington Senators in Cuba. Cambria was probably the most successful of his era, credited with signing as many as four hundred players. The Senators needed inexpensive players to remain solvent as an organization and competitive as a team, and Cambria's efforts are credited with saving the Senators from bankruptcy.

For "Papa Joe," as he was known there, the one that got away is one of the most memorable. That player was an ambitious pitcher who asked to be signed so he could go to the United States to play in Washington for the Senators. Cambria told him he didn't have a major league arm and thought that was the end of it. According to legend, Ruben Amaro felt the face of world history could be different today if Cambria would have remembered that some pitchers mature late. By the late 1940s the pitcher had developed a wicked curveball, and in 1949 a scout from the New York Giants offered him a five thousand-dollar contract. To his surprise, the player turned him down, which was unheard of in those days because of the poverty in the region. But by then the pitcher, Fidel Castro, was interested in politics and didn't want to leave Cuba.

Eddie Robinson, a first baseman from Paris, Texas, played in the American League from 1942–1957, with 1943–45 in the military. He was a member of the 1948 world champion Cleveland Indians, and later spent 1954–55 and part of 1956 with the New York Yankees (Eddie Robinson collection).

Today every organization has scouts in the Pacific Rim, the Latin countries, and even Australia. There are famous baseball academies with player development programs where youngsters live in dormitories sponsored by such organizations as the Dodgers and others. Youngsters in those areas are not subject to the draft rules like American players. For instance, there's no education requirement for them, they don't have to go through the draft, and they often sign for a fraction of the bonuses sought by American players. Today more than twenty percent of all major league players come from the Latin American countries. Major League Baseball experimented with a draft in the Dominican Republic in

1985 but sloppy records and poor administration that resulted in players being signed by more than one club resulted in early failure. Currently there's talk about some kind of a world-wide draft in the future.

Expansion is remembered as the best time in the life of the scouts who were called upon to help in the birth of the new major league clubs. It not only offered unprecedented challenges, but also created additional scouting jobs in each of the new organizations. The ever-present flip side is the controversy over whether or not talent at the major league level is watered down while many youngsters have been pushed to the big leagues before they're ready.

Al LaMacchia, a scout for more than fifty years and counting, explained, "Another change besides the draft that happened during my career was the major league expansion. Bobby Mattick and I had the good fortune to be the first scouts hired by the Toronto Blue Jays the year before the team took the field, and it was an exciting time for us. A really wonderful opportunity for a scout."

During their tenure, scouts observed the trend that saw teams go from family-owned businesses to corporate ownership, yet another attempt to alleviate skyrocketing operating costs. For instance, the Wrigley family sold the Chicago Cubs to the *Chicago Tribune* in 1981, and they were for sale again in 2008. The O'Malley family sold the Dodgers to Rupert Murdoch's NewsCorp in 1998, and the team was later sold to developer Frank McCourt in 2004. In 1992 the Seattle Mariners were purchased by Nintendo. The Gene Autry-owned Los Angeles Angels went to Disney, and then in 2003 were purchased by Arturo Moreno. The Atlanta Braves were bought by Liberty Media in 2006. The argument rages on about whether or not this is good for the game.

Meanwhile, the longtime scouts feel caught in the middle and adamantly believe it's bad for scouting. They witnessed the arrival of a new breed of younger scouts on the scene whom the veterans describe as company men rather than baseball men. Many of the newcomers didn't learn the ins and outs of scouting by years of playing the game. In fact, many have never played baseball at any professional level. The veterans describe this new breed as "baseball's bureaucrats." While the veterans consider themselves baseball men with an eye on talent and an allegiance to the game, by definition the eye of the bureaucrats must always be on the bottom line. The old clipboards have been replaced with laptops. Their work ethic includes heavy reliance on the Major League Scouting Bureau rather than their own scouting instincts and skills. Sadly for them, the old scouting methods and pride involved in finding talent have different meanings now. But it's not their fault. In this new era of corporate ownership and outrageous salaries, they work with different job descriptions.

One of the major complaints about the new corporate owners was the propensity to "clean house" and replace front office staff and scouting departments with untrained people, many of whom via nepotism and other "creative" hiring practices. Many took crash courses operated by their organizations or found on the Internet where the only requisite for admittance was the price of tuition. It didn't take long to note this training was inadequate. In essence, the new scouts didn't know how to scout!

But things improved. The Major League Scouting Bureau Development Program, started in the 1980s, evolved into a comprehensive educational clinic for scouts and other front office employees who must be sponsored by a major league organization in order to participate. Their success rate has been demonstrated by the professional progress of its graduates who became area scouts, scouting supervisors, scouting directors and farm directors. White Sox General Manager Kenny Williams and Kansas City Royals Assistant GM Muzzy Williams are among its graduates.

"Everybody wants to be a scout and watch ballgames every day," the scouts all say laughingly. The fact that it happens pounds home the point that their expertise is not recognized. While fans watch games, scouts watch players, intricate things about players that fans don't even realize or recognize. A scout of nearly thirty-five years sent what he described as a short list of some things that must be noticed and noted by them. He quickly explained that it's only a small sample of what scouts look for and report on.

Position players: He should be a run and throw type athlete. There's much to see when looking at a hitter, such as how he approaches the plate. How does he hold the bat? Does he "wrap" the bat? Does he hit from a flat bat position? Is his stance open, closed, or straight away? How does he hold the bat, choked up at the handle? Are his hands spread apart or close together? How does he start the bat? Is the bat long or short? Does he turn the top-hand handle over quickly or does he drag his hands through the zone and slow down his bat speed? Does the ball jump off the barrel of the bat? Does he have an inside-out swing? Does the bat have lift with over-the-fence power? Can he drive the ball into the gaps? Is he a corner player? Will he hit for power on a championship club? When it involves a high profile college or high school player, seeing him the day before a game in a workout during batting practice, taking ground balls, and seeing his overall demeanor and how he handles himself prior to his game performance is always helpful.

Pitchers: Hard throwing pitchers with good arm extension and good balance and follow-through are preferred. The radar gun is used to correlate the MPH with the fastball, curveball, and changeup to the letter grade of the pitch on the report. With a pitcher with an above-average fastball, look at his overall delivery, the arm angle, and the way he holds the fastball. You know when you see a pitcher who has an above-average fastball. For me, I like to see the four-seam rising fastball most hitters fear because of the movement up in the zone, and the curve with the twelve-to-six break and good downward plane with good snap and hard rotation. The change is a good off-speed pitch, which keeps the hitter off balance, with great deception, a good "out" pitch when used effectively. How does the pitcher hold base runners on? Average release time with runners on is 1.50 seconds for the right-hander and 1.60 seconds for the left-hander. Anything below the norm was a base stolen on the catcher. Anything above the norm was a base stolen on the pitcher. Does he like to pitch inside and brush hitters off the plate? Is he a good fielder coming off the mound?

George Genovese remembered how things were when he began scouting in the early fifties.

Scouts go through a lot that the fans know nothing about. I recall one election day in Caracas. Lou Johnson was there, too. Men in cars with brooms tied to the bumpers were on all the roads, sweeping them. It seems terrorists littered the roads, dirt roads remember, with nails to keep people from driving to vote. And when we flew from area to area in Mexico, it was taking our life in our hands. The planes were old and dilapidated to say the least. Once we took off in a small plane, and when we landed I was sitting in a different seat and couldn't remember how I'd gotten there! The stewardess explained that the plane hit an air pocket and dropped 5,000 feet. My seat belt was broken, and I flew out of my seat, hit my head on the ceiling, got knocked out, and landed in a seat across the aisle. I was the lucky one. Two other guys didn't have seat belts at all.

Back in their day when players retired and expressed an interest in scouting, one of the organizations for which they had played asked them to scout in this territory or that. It was a matter of "a word and a handshake." For example, Cleveland rookie outfielder Hugh Alexander's promising playing career ended suddenly before it began in 1937. He explained, "The GM from Cleveland called me, then wrote me a letter in January of '38, about five weeks after the accident, and said, 'I want you to come to New Orleans and stay about ten days with me personally and I'm going to give you a little training. I want you at the ballpark with me every morning when we work out and we'll talk about those ballplayers.' And we did. Then he said, 'Now you're ready to go, scout.'" From there Alexander went on to the longest scouting career on record, almost sixty-five years.

The relationship of scouts and the dreaded agents historically resembles oil and water. To them the words "agent" and "Boras," the most successful agent of them all, are synonymous. When agents first appeared on the scene, some scouts said their organizations wanted them to ask prospective draft picks who their agents would be. When the answer was Scott Boras, the organization wouldn't draft the player because of the money Boras demanded. Today there are several agents certified via an extremely comprehensive screening process, and the players are more informed about when and how to get one. But the scouts say agents are a major cause of baseball's financial woes.

Professional baseball, with all its ups and downs, changes and adjustments, corrections and over-corrections, has another issue that has not been addressed. The scouts are the only faction of the game not represented in the Baseball Hall of Fame in Cooperstown, New York. It's considered an insult the scouts don't understand. They say they've been told for the last thirty-plus years that there are "plans" for their inclusion, but nothing has gone beyond the talking stage during that time. The people at the Hall say it's a matter of money. The scouts remain puzzled, skeptical of what they perceive as deliberately empty promises, and angry.

While they wait, the Scout of the Year Award Program was founded in 1984 by three longtime scouts — Tony Pacheco, Jim Russo, and Hugh Alexander. The annual award recognizes excellence in scouting and is given to one scout in each of the three areas of the country: West Coast, Midwest, and East Coast. The scouts are nominated and elected by their peers. Eligible scouts have at least twenty years of full-time scouting experience at any level. An annual awards banquet is held to honor the winners as well as to raise money to help defray the costs of their place of honor in the Hall of Fame at Cooperstown ... some day.

In 2005 the Professional Baseball Scouts Wall of Fame at the new Richmond County Bank Ballpark in Staten Island, home of the Yankees team in the New York-Penn League, was dedicated as a celebration of veteran scouts. Located along the right field concourse and now called Pinstripe Alley, the area has bronze plaques with the likeness and brief baseball profile of each of its inductees. Some of the inductees include Cesar Presbott, John Hagemann, Billy Blitzer, Gil Bassetti, Ralph DiLullo, Roland Hemond, and Herb Stein.

There's no shortage of awards and honors for scouts. Every organization selects its own scout of the year. There are awards for excellence and dedication named after those who have demonstrated those traits in their careers, such as the Roland Hemond Award, the George Genovese Award, the Al LaMacchia Award, the Bobby Mattick Award, among others.

More recently, the Goldklang Group, a sports entertainment, consulting, and management firm that owns and operates six minor league baseball teams, in conjunction with the Topps Company, Inc., established the Professional Baseball Scouts Hall of Fame in 2008. The first twelve scouts inducted in its inaugural year included John Tumminia of the Chicago White Sox, Tom Giordano of the Texas Rangers, Tom Kotchman of the Los Angeles Angels, Rudy Santin of the San Francisco Giants, Lennie Merullo of the Major League Scouting Bureau, Buzz Bowers of the Boston Red Sox, Lon Joyce of the Los Angeles Dodgers, Donny Rowland of the New York Yankees, Brad Sloan of the Los Angeles Dodgers, Art Stewart of the Kansas City Royals, Phil Rizzo of the Los Angeles Dodgers, and Hep Cronin of the Atlanta Braves. These twelve scouts collectively represent nearly six hundred years of professional scouting.

Hugh Alexander

(1917–2000)

Alexander became baseball's youngest scout at age twenty and scouted the longest, more than sixty-two years while working with the Cleveland Indians, Chicago White Sox, Brooklyn/Los Angeles Dodgers, Philadelphia Phillies, and Chicago Cubs. According to his own recollections, he was the twenty-fourth scout in baseball history.

Although scouting was Plan B for him, he made the most of it. The tall, confident, graceful athlete with flaming red hair played one full season of minor league baseball with the Cleveland Indians, and eighty games into the second season, 1937, he was promoted to the major league team. He appeared in seven games and recorded one hit in eleven trips to the plate. Everyone expected the five-tool player to become a major league slugger and a big star.

Unfortunately, he was never able to reach his full potential because he lost his left hand in an off-season accident the following December.

His tenacity served him well during his recovery, and the Indians invited him to become a scout. He approached scouting with the same assuredness that he approached playing. His long career began in 1938. However, by 1965 "Uncle Hughie," as he was then known, was discouraged when he felt the new draft rules restricted his style and success. He turned from amateur scouting to major league scouting for the rest of his career, although he continued to sign an amateur player here and there.

The first player he ever signed, pitcher Allie Reynolds, had a stellar career that many say should have earned him a place in Cooperstown. History credits Alexander with signing more than sixty players who played in the major leagues. Among them SABR lists Dale Mitchell, Carl Warwick, Frank Howard, Bart Shirley, Tommy Dean, Don Sutton, Billy Graharkewitz, Bill Russell, Doyle Alexander, Ron Cey, Steve Garvey, Davey Lopes, Tom Paciorek, and Marty Bystrom.

From 1983–86 he was the player personnel advisor/special assistant to the general manager for the Phillies, and he spent seven years of his tenure with the Cubs as special player consultant/special assistant to the GM.

Hugh Alexander was full of advice. The last thing he told me was to pass this tip to new scouts who come along: "Don't ever drive straight through from a game in Texarkana, Texas, to a game the next day in El Paso. It's 927 miles!"

Hugh Alexander was the recipient of the Scout of the Year Award, East Coast, in 1996.

Let me give you a little bit of my life. I'm a Southern boy, born in Buffalo, Missouri, but reared in Seminole, Oklahoma. Most of my youth was spent playing lots of sports. It'll probably sound like I'm bragging, but please don't take it that way. I was really some kind of an athlete. My hair was flame red, and I was a big old kid, over six-feet tall and 185 pounds at seventeen years old. I was a four letterman at Seminole Oklahoma High School.

In 1935 I ran in the Olympic trials for the '36 Olympics in Germany. When they asked me to try out, I told them my sports were football and baseball. Well, they kind of pressured me and I finally said, "Okay." And I ran real good. I ran about a 9.8 60-yard dash. The world's record at that time was 9.6. They told me if I were the state winner, I'd be picked to run in the Olympics. In those trials I ran it in 9 (flat), as well as Jesse Owens, who became the world's champion. Well, to make a long story short, I told them that if I get a chance to sign and play baseball before the Olympics come, that's exactly what I'm going to do. Then they finally let me withdraw.

But I could really play that football. I mean really play it good. I was a running back, because I could run so fast. Anyway, I recall one game when we beat the other club 75-nothing and I scored six touchdowns and gained five hundred and five yards in that game! That was a standing record for quite some years, but it was broken.

Hugh Alexander began scouting in 1939 for the Cleveland Indians when he was just twenty years old after an accident prematurely ended his promising major league career. "Uncle Hughie," as he was known by his protégés and peers, scouted close to sixty-five years (courtesy Scout of the Year Program).

But anyway, along came the Cleveland ball club and they saw me play on a real good semi-pro club. We won the state championship. But there wasn't any scout then, remember. So we played a team out of Tulsa, Oklahoma. We played them a doubleheader on the Fourth of July in my town of Seminole, Oklahoma. I hit four home runs in those two ballgames.

In about a week, Mr. Cy Slapnicka, who was working for the Indians, came and said he wanted to see me play that Sunday. So what I wanted to do, well, I was a pretty sharp old country boy and let word out that if I was asked, I was going to sign. It wasn't until later, after I'd signed, that I found out that the manager of the Tulsa team was a bird dog scout for Cleveland, old Larkin Bailey.

Anyway, Mr. Slapnicka offered me a thousand dollars to sign and asked me to report for spring training with the big team. He kind of found me by accident and stuck with me and signed me, sorta illegally at the time, but I didn't know it. There's a long story that goes with that thousand, but suffice it to say that he tried to beat me out of it, but eventually he paid.

So I went all the way through spring training. He really liked me and I liked him. So during spring training we'd get together in his room and talk a lot. Anyway, then they sent me to Fargo, North Dakota, to the Northern League. It was a good league. I hit .385, 39 home runs, made all-star center fielder. And I remember I was only 18 years old.

So then I went back home and worked in the oil fields to make some money. In those days all players had to make money in the off-season to survive. Anyway, I went to my second-year spring training and this time they sent me to Springfield, Ohio. Another real good league. I played 80 ballgames in center field. I hit .349 with 30 home runs. Then I went to the big leagues in my second pro season. It was August 15, 1937. My roommate was Bob Feller. They put us together because we were about the same age. I think I was six months older, or he was.

Later I asked Mr. Slap, as I called him, why he didn't just bring me up to the big leagues at the beginning of that second season. He laughed and told me it was because they just wanted to see if I was really that good.

I was real good. I mean I could hit them real good, throw real good from center field. I was a good fielder, and I was a good hitter with a lot of power, and I could run like hell. They called me a complete player. I mean I had all five tools. We'll never know what I could've become because I had the accident and I knew my career as a player was finished.

It occurred on December 6, 1937. What happened was this. I was working on this oil well with three or four roust-abouts and they were on a well about two to three hundred yards away, way out in the woods in the middle of nowhere. They hollered at me and asked me to start this really big engine we needed to do everything. They knew I'd started it before. It was a pistol to start but sometimes I got lucky, so I told them I'd try. So I rolled up my sleeves to do that.

Meanwhile, those guys left and went down to another well. So I was there by myself and I'm cranking on that thing, and cranking and cranking. I didn't pay any attention to the big gears under the thing down on the ground, one bigger one and one smaller one. They were huge! They were kind of scary. I saw the cover for those gears on the ground because somebody took them off. They should have been left on. Anyway, I cranked and I cranked and it spit and sputtered and when I reached for the throttle, which was directly above those gears, it caught my shirt sleeve and I couldn't tear myself free and there goes my hand — right through those gears!

Luckily it didn't bleed that much because the gears kind of sealed it all together. I immediately got a big pair of pliars and made a tourniquet. Then I proceeded to walk about a quarter of a mile to a path that led me to a house down there. A lady was home and she took me to the edge of town. There were only two doctors. One was Dr. Jones and the other was a full-blooded Cherokee Indian who was known as a good country doctor. I knew him and interrupted him with a patient to tell him about my hand. He took very good care but explained that it couldn't be repaired. So he made it a clean amputation at the wrist. My anesthetic was a pint of whiskey which he said to drink down as fast as I could. He found a little morphia and between the two we got the job done. And that was it.

I knew that was the finish of Hugh Alexander as an athlete. My little mother really helped and made me do the right thing. I was only 20 years old at that time.

Anyway, the GM from Cleveland called me, then wrote me a letter in January of '38, about five weeks after the accident, and said, "I want you to come to New Orleans and stay about ten days with me personally and I'm going to give you a little training. I want you at the ballpark with me every morning when we workout and we'll talk about those ballplayers." And we did. Then he said, "Now you're ready to go, scout."

So, in 1938, I began my career as a scout with a salary of $3,000 a year. It was nearing the end of the Depression and we could live on that. Remember now, at that time paid scouts were a new thing and there were only 23 others in all of baseball when I began. The Yankees had three, Detroit had three, the Cardinals had three, but the rest of the clubs had one or none. Cleveland had one before me, Bill Bradley, and I was made number two. They just couldn't afford scouts.

The teams without official scouts had to buy their players off independent teams. Of course, back then, everything was independent teams, Class D, Class C, Class B, then there's A, AA, and AAA. All those clubs were independent clubs, not like now where they're all affiliated with the big leagues. And they would just sign ballplayers in their area. They had tryouts and so on and so forth in order to see players to sign. But in all of that word got out about players, and I learned to follow that around. It was so easy in those days. There were so many ballplayers and so few scouts. All we had to do was show up at ballparks and sign players.

The territory he assigned me was something else. He said, "I want you to scout all the way from Nevin, Oklahoma, which is almost in the middle of the United States, but you'll start at the edge of Canada and go all the way to Mexico. It was a plot on the map about 40–50 miles wide. He said to check the newspapers and pal around with anybody that might tell you where there's a ballplayer. I did, and my scouting career was on its way. I scouted for Cleveland for the next fourteen years.

The first player I signed was that big Indian pitcher, Allie Reynolds, a right-handed kid. We didn't call the boss much back in those days, but when I saw this guy I sent him a telegram and said I found an Indian pitcher who could throw real hard.

He then called me and asked, "How much does he want?"

"He told me he'd play for a thousand dollars," I told him.

"A thousand dollars?" he screamed.

"He wants a thousand dollars or he's going to go play football with the New York Giants," I answered.

He said, "But we don't give bonuses."

And I explained that we were going to have to if we wanted to get this guy. "He could certainly be another Jim Thorpe, I know that," I told him.

The boss said, "Now wait a minute, you're young as a scout and all that."

"Yes, but I just played ball last year and I never saw a pitcher in the whole American League who could throw as hard as this guy, except maybe Bob Feller. Actually, I'd put him in the same class as Bob Feller."

He paused, then said, "Okay, I believe you, Hughie, so go sign him."

So for that thousand dollars he won almost 200 major league ballgames for the Indians and Yankees.

In 1939, I was out in Western Oklahoma when I found another good player. They had a good semipro team in Clinton, a little town about 90 miles west of Oklahoma City, and I heard about that time. It was a little bitty town and had a very small ballpark. They played on Saturday and Sunday. So I went there and checked into the hotel. All those little towns in those days had one hotel. No such thing as a motel. I asked the clerk if he knew a fella named Joe Gore.

"I sure do," he said. Joe Gore was pretty famous in those parts. He was a pretty fine player but never went pro ... just played semipro, but he had some age on him and so on and so forth. He told me Joe Gore "works in a beer joint down that way about two blocks." So I walked down there to the beer tavern. There wasn't a soul in there except for one heavy-set guy. I asked if he was Joe Gore and he said, "I sure am. Who are you?" I told him and we talked a little bit. Then he said, "I know where there's a good player." He said, "I'll tell you who he is if you'll give me some money."

"I'll tell you what," I said, "I'll go see him, and if I don't sign him there's no deal. But if I do sign him, I'll give you seventy-five dollars."

"You're on," he said. "His name is Dale Mitchell." I checked him out, signed him too, and he wound up playing left field for Cleveland for ten years and had a career batting average over three hundred.

He sent me to a little bitty town of about 38 people about 20 miles away where Mitchell lived. I found his mother. His father got killed. So I talked to her and she said, "He's going to play a ballgame Sunday at the next town over." Most of those little places don't exist any more. So I go over there and watch Dale Miller play. He hit three home runs and a single. He was big and strong but he couldn't throw very good, so I explained that he'd have to play left field.

By '39 I knew a little bit about scouting, but didn't know anything in '38. Just didn't know anything. What happened? Well, in scouting, experience and a good mentor make a lot of difference. And I learned one thing and it's now a famous saying of my own. When I'd see a ballplayer, from my second year of scouting till now even 60 years later, I still do this. Back when I was an area scout, when I see a ballplayer that I think could be a pretty good prospect, I'd get in my car and I'd start driving to the next place and say to myself, "Okay, Hughie, break him down. Break down the ability tool by tool. And I'd say to myself, "Well, he's got an average big league arm. He's probably a little bit below average runner with the stopwatch put on him. But he can swing the bat with power and that means one thing: I'm going to sign him."

During those early years I used to travel 60,000 miles a year because I covered that big area of Oklahoma, Texas, Louisiana, Arkansas, Mississippi for 33 years. All total I covered over two million miles driving. A lot of talent comes from those areas still because it's warm and they have long seasons.

One thing I'll never forget if I live to be a hundred years old is 1965 was when the draft started. Prior to that I was probably the best scout in baseball. But I didn't know how to handle the draft and neither did people who ran the big league clubs. They didn't know what the hell to do. But anyway, I'd come up with some pretty good ballplayers, especially considering the kind of territory I covered. We struggled with the procedure of the whole thing. Just because we scouted the guy and did all the footwork and preparation didn't mean we were going to sign the guy. It was tough.

There was no doubt the draft had to come in, no doubt about it because the clubs with money overshadowed all others. Clubs like the Yankees, the Boston Red Sox, St.

Louis, Cleveland, and a couple others. When you got into competition for players with those ball clubs, you lose. Can't win. So coming up with the draft was an attempt to level the playing field, so to speak.

But the draft's a bad deal because the club that doesn't have any money, they still can't win because they can't get the players to sign. Good players now are at a premium. I mean here's a little high school boy who's 17 years old and getting a five to eight million dollar bonus just to sign. Even the kid who can't play too good, well, he'll get $750,000 and he could be a number ten, eleven or twelve. That's a lot of players drafted before him and he still requires that kind of money. I'll tell you, it's really out of reason.

Years later when I went to the Phillies from the Dodgers to help Dallas Green, I sat down with Bob Carpenter, the owner and his son. I told them I was interested in coming over there and helping Dallas Green and Paul Owens. Owens was going to be the GM and I knew that. I told them, "But if you tie my hands, I don't want the job. I don't want any part of it. You got to open the purse strings and give me some money and I'll recommend the ballplayers and you can draft them."

See, what the draft did directly to the scouts was change the whole way we went about our business. The dollar figures started climbing to a point where the players didn't want the $50,000–100,000 bonuses, which used to be considered big signing bonuses. Once the draft came in, they started turning down that money and went to college.

I used to say I'd bet my right hand that someday somebody is going to take this to court because it's a violation of somebody's rights, it seems to me. I mean the scout really likes a player, and I mean really likes him, but he doesn't have a chance to sign him because the organization can't afford the bonus money. The draft itself drove me out of free agent scouting. I said to myself, "I just got to get out of this. This isn't working for me." I haven't done free agent scouting since '68. I remained with the Dodgers and became a major league scout.

Here's exactly how that happened. In 1965 and '66, I didn't do very good in the new system. By 1967, I'd been with the Dodgers eleven or twelve years, and to make a long story short, I was in Fort Worth, Texas, and was talking to scouting director Al Campanis the day before the draft. I said, "Al, I got nine players in for the draft. Nine good high school and college players who, in my opinion, have the abilities to become good prospects. And those ballplayers will go real early. We got the number 23 draft pick and if you don't take one of mine, then all the work I've done this spring will go by the wayside. I'm telling ya, I know this."

"Well, I'll do the best I can," he said, "but there's lot of good players." I told him firmly that mine were good, too.

"The problem," he said, "is that by the time they get down to number 23, there could be none of these players left. And there's nothing either one of us could do about it." He told me he'd call me at the hotel after it was done.

He called and said, "I've got some bad news. I couldn't get you any players. Not even one of yours." He tried to make me feel better by saying the fact that they were all gone validated my good judgment. But I was mad.

So I said, "Well, okay. Call me at home." I'd moved to Florida by then, hadn't been home since February, and I had had enough for that season. He told me to go ahead and go home and rest for a few days. I got into the car and drove 1,200 miles straight to get home. Did a lot of thinking on that ride.

See, the thing was, we all knew something like the Draft had to come in. There's no doubt about it because the clubs with money overshadowed all others. Clubs like the Yankees, the Boston Red Sox, St. Louis, Cleveland, and a couple others. When you got into competition for players with those ballclubs, you lose. Can't win. So coming up with the Draft was an attempt to level the playing field so to speak.

But that Draft's a bad deal because the club that doesn't have any money, they still can't win because they can't get the players to sign. Good players now are at a premium. I mean here's a little high school boy who's 17 years old and getting a five to eight million dollar bonus just to sign. Even the kid who can't play too good, well, he'll get $750,000 and he could be a number ten-eleven or twelve. That's a lot of players drafted before him and he still requires that kind of money. I'll tell ya, it's really out of reason.

What it did directly to the scouts was change the whole way we went about our business. The dollar figures on players started climbing to a point where the players didn't want the $50–100,000 dollar bonuses which used to be considered big signing bonuses. Once the draft came in they started turning down that money and went to college.

So I finally decided, "I can't win. There's just no way in the world I can win with this kind of a draft." And by that time I was a pretty sharp scout. So there was only one thing for me to do and that's change jobs and go with the pro deal.

So you can say that the Draft itself drove me out of free agent scouting. I said to myself, "I just got to get out of this. This isn't working for me." I haven't done free agent scouting since '68.

So I remained with the Dodgers and became one of their big league scouts until 1982. Before the draft I signed Davey Lopes and Billy Russell and several more. [He worked with John Keenan in both of those signings.] There was a whole lot more but my memory isn't what it used to be.

Another thing I did while with the Dodgers was break in new scouts. I probably broke in more scouts than anyone else in the game. Of course, there were bird dogs and guys like that, but teams knew they were going to need us if they wanted to compete.

The thing you got to remember in this is that these men [I trained] weren't necessarily young, just new to scouting. And in those days I was considered one of the best free agent scouts in baseball. It started one day when I was talking to Fresco Thompson, the farm director for the Dodgers, when we were still in Brooklyn. It was in 1955 or '56 because we left there after '57. Anyway, I said, "Fresco, I got a good idea."

And he said, "What you got, Hughie?"

I said, "You got four full-time scouts who are living up here in New York, Pennsylvania, and New Jersey, don't you?"

He said we had three plus one good part-time man. I told him I'd like to have those three scouts. I said, "You pay them a salary right now but they don't do anything until April, do they?" And he nodded in agreement.

"So," I said, "why don't you send them down to me in Texas because I start in late February and I have to run my tail off to try to see those ballplayers?"

He thought that was a good idea and he sent three scouts to meet me in Waco, Texas. I had a meeting scheduled for them and we began scouting those players. It lasted about three years and nobody else did it. And we had a lot of good times, too.

This actually involved quite a few scouts. Let me think a minute. I can't remember them in any sort of order, but there was Ellis Clary, Al LaMacchia, Donnie Williams,

Doug Gassaway and lots more. And later I was the first man to bring in a northern scout to Texas in the spring to help out the head scout in that area. It was Fred McAlister. He's a good man. Anyway, we immediately got together in Waco, Texas. When Freddie came down, he introduced himself. I knew him a little bit as a ballplayer. And he said, "Can you help me?"

And I told him I could but, "If you don't follow what I say, then I don't want any part of you. You're young and you don't know it all." And he became a real good scout for a long time. He signed a lot of very good players, including Brian Jordan. Then he served as the director of scouting for St. Louis. I think he's an advance scout or a consultant or something like that these days.

Anyway, I told Al LaMacchia the same thing. "If you double-cross me, I'll just walk away from you." So I really helped them and they all still remember it, too.

Then Johnny Hudson, a scout for the Giants, he was in spring training and said, "That Hugh Alexander did something that's really a good thing for baseball and we ought to do it." Then everybody started sending scouts into Texas and Florida. These guys were on salary anyway so why not put them to some use for the organization? So you come into Florida now during spring training and in California and Texas, and you may run into 50 scouts around those ballparks, I mean full-time scouts. They're trying to dig up players for the man in charge of that area.

Starting in 1983, the Phillies made me the deal of being assistant GM, second in command of the whole shooting match. I did everything over there. I broke the salary limit. The Phillies gave me $150,000 a year and that was absolutely unheard of in those days. Most others in my position were making around $65,000–70,000 at that time. But I was worth it because I knew ballplayers and I could make deals.

I did a lot of trades over there and some newspaper writer started calling me "the Minister of Trade" after I got Bake McBride from the Cardinals in '77. In another deal the GM from the Cardinals called me and said, " Hughie, would you be interested in Steve Carlton?"

I said, "Well, yeah, I think so." Now he was only a minor league pitcher in Oklahoma at that time.

He said, "Augie Busch got mad at Carlton in spring training and told me to get rid of him. I tried to talk him out of it because Carlton's too good a prospect, but he still wanted him gone."

We gave them a good pitcher, Rick Wise, but not as good as Carlton was. [Actually, records show Carlton had pitched for the St. Louis Cardinals since 1967, and the trade for Rick Wise happened after the 1971 season.]

I signed quite a few others, but my memory's not real good anymore. Altogether I signed about 60 ballplayers, as best I can remember, who played in the big leagues. Several of them played real good, some pretty good, and others couldn't play too good. But they still played in the big leagues.

But no matter how successful a scout is, there's always the story about the player who got away, the one he couldn't sign. And I have mine. Since I'm from Oklahoma, one of my friends there gave me the name of a young athlete getting ready to graduate from Commerce High School. He said the kid was playing on some sort of semi-pro team because his high school didn't even have a baseball team. But they did have a football team and he was quite a football player, at least until he got hurt. I had written his name down on a piece of paper and put it in my car thinking I'd try to see him play. But when I learned that he had bad knees, well, I just tore up that paper and threw it away. He did end up playing a little baseball. Ever hear of Mickey Mantle?

Did you know about the ring I wear? Well, in 1987 when I left the Phillies, Dallas Green, a very good man, I raised him, kept telling me, "I'll go to Chicago as the president and GM if you'll go with me."

I told him, "I don't want to do that. I just signed a five-year contract and don't want to break it."

Then he said, "But I need you. I need you." Well, he broke me down and I said I'd try to break the contract with the Phillies. They let it happen without too much squawk and I went to the Chicago Cubs. That was shortly after the 1986 season. In February, he told me, "Come to spring training with me and help me out. You won't have to do any scouting. We'll just talk. I want you to help me out."

I went and sat with him every day and we went to dinner every night. One night at one of those fancy restaurants for dinner, there was five, six, seven people with us, all having drinks and what not, and pretty soon Dallas says to me, "Hey, Hughie, what are you going to be doing on July the tenth of this year?"

"Come on, Dallas," I laughed, "this is only February! I don't know what the hell I'm going to be doing, but I know what July the tenth is. It's my birthday."

He said, "Do you know what? I'm going to do something that's never been done

After a long hot day at the ballpark during the dog days of August in 1991, three longtime friends get together to plan where they will go for a relaxing dinner. (Left to right) Hugh Alexander, scouting consultant — Cubs, Marty Keough, national crosschecker — Cardinals, and Fred McAlister, scouting director — Cardinals, always discuss "what's what" in baseball when they have time for a get-together (Fred McAlister collection).

before. I'm going to have a Hugh Alexander Day in Chicago." He had a wonderful ring made up, a big huge ring like a Super Bowl-type ring with lots of diamonds and everything.

What really happened that night was a celebration of my fiftieth year in baseball. There were 35,000 people there and we were playing the Dodgers. All those Dodger players I'd signed were in the dugout, especially Lasorda. I walked to the mound to throw the first ball to home plate and Tommy hollered, "You'll never make it to home plate, Uncle Hughie!"

I said, "Well, we'll find out." I laughed, because what they didn't know was that Charlie Hart and I had gone out on the field at nine that morning and I'd warmed up in the bullpen for about 20 minutes. "Well, I can make it now," I told myself. They gave me a great big gold and silver trophy that weighed something like 35 pounds, and we had a big party that night. I still wear the ring every day next to my World Series ring. I don't flaunt it, but it's a good conversation piece.

Let's make a long story short concerning me and the Cubs. The first deal I made for Dallas was for a pitcher, I forget his name, but his dad was a big league pitcher. Anyway, I traded him to the Yankees for three players and four million dollars. The three guys were all prospects but never got to the big leagues. Before it happened, I told Dallas what I had in mind, and he said, "You can't make that trade." I told him what they offered us and he turned me loose to make the deal.

The Cubs is the only club I ever scouted for that's a loser. When I was with Cleveland years ago, they were winners and took the Series in '48. Then I went to the White Sox, working under Frank Lane, and we finished second four years in a row behind the Yankees. We couldn't beat the Yankees. Nobody could. Then I went to the Dodgers and got five World Series rings. Then I went to Philadelphia and took a club that couldn't beat anybody and the first thing you know, in '75, '76, '77, '78, four years in a row, we won the division and (later) played in two World Series. We won one and lost the other. And then I came to the Cubs because I wanted to help Dallas Green because he's really like a son to me. He's got a son, John, and I took John under my wing and signed him with the Cubs. He played minor league ball for three years. He was an average pitcher. And then I taught him everything I know and he became a scout.

Since I went to Chicago, I've worked for almost fifteen years with the title of special consultant, a title rigged up by Dallas. And here it is, I've been scouting sixty-two years and it's amazing to me that I could be as lucky as I've been. I'm so well respected in any major league or minor league ballpark anywhere in the country. Back when I had scouted about 40 years, I said to myself, "I'm going to set a record that nobody will ever come close to." And I'm doing year number 62. I've slowed down but still counting. Baseball has been very good to me.

Dick Egan

(1937–)

Egan began his fifty-first year in professional baseball in 2008 as special assistant to the GM/baseball operations with the Detroit Tigers. In a nutshell, he has been a minor league player and manager, major league pitcher, one of the first scouts signed by the Major League Scouting Bureau, a major league pitching coach, a scout and national crosschecker for the Padres, Rangers, and Tigers, and he worked with the expansion Florida Marlins during their inception.

He's credited with signing only one amateur player, Bob Patterson, during his brief stint with the San Diego Padres, because the majority of his amateur scouting was spent with the bureau. Later, he had much to do with the careers of Kevin Brown, Robb Nen, Craig Counsell, and others. Egan always stuck by the players he believed in and became their advocates, even when they were at the major league level. For instance, he was a pitching coordinator for the Texas Rangers when young left-hander Kenny Rogers was drafted out of high school in 1982. Dick Egan supervised his development.

Years later, in 2005, when Egan was a professional scout for the Tigers, he noted that Rogers was a free agent. When others thought Rogers was "done," as they say in the game, Egan checked him out and convinced Tigers GM David Dombrowski to sign him. As it turned out, Rogers was a crucial player in their 2006 World Series appearance.

In February 2008, Egan was a key factor when the Tigers traded for injured right-hander Armando Galarraga and relief pitcher Francisco Cruceta with Texas. Egan and the rest of the staff worked with Galarraga and he responded with a 12–6 record. Some say Cruceta was one of his "mistakes" because he developed control problems early and was sent to Toledo, the Tigers' AAA club. Egan stands by him and hopes to see him back at the major league level. Time will tell.

All in all, Dick Egan is known as a good judge of talent, a man with dependable baseball instincts, and a good sense of humor. He describes himself as an aggressive scout who isn't afraid to make mistakes, but not too many.

Dick Egan wrote the following on a large notepad and sent to me for this book.

Baseball was my only love. Even when I was in high school and junior college, I simply assumed I'd play pro baseball.

After the 1957 season at Diablo Valley Junior College, I only knew two scouts. One was a bird dog for Detroit named Ray Robb, who drove me to Stockton, California, to a Class C independent club. Roy Partee was the manager. I was a left-handed hitting first baseman and a left-handed pitcher. My Stockton workout consisted of throwing a very inconsistent batting practice stint and a horrible batting practice as a hitter. I drove home very discouraged.

A day later Tony Robello, a scout with the New York Yankees, drove me to Modesto. We attended the Modesto Relays track meet, stayed overnight, then drove to Visalia the next day. It was very hot and my workout before the Modesto at Visalia game was great! I had good stuff in BP and good control.

At bat I hit the ball hard consistently. After hitting I was called to the bullpen and threw to manager Dee Phillips. I was throwing all out and he called for me to turn it loose. I already was! Not a good sign. On the drive home to Pleasant Hill, California, Tony offered me a contract in Fort Lauderdale (Class D) as an outfielder.

Being very naïve, I suggested that Stockton had offered me $500 and $250 per month. He said that was no problem and he would do better. Of course, that wasn't true. I'd not talked money with Roy Partee. All I knew for sure was Class C was better than Class D and I'd never played in the outfield. So I called Roy Partee to ask if he had interest. He said yes. Could I come to Stockton tomorrow?

In his cubbyhole office around 1 PM he was already in uniform. And sitting there he offered me $10 a day. Not the smartest student, but I easily figured that to be $300 a month. I signed. No bonus. The contract was for $150 per month with $150 under the table. That was a pretty common practice back then.

That night in my pro debut, I struck out as a pinch-hitter to end the game.

My 1957 summer in Stockton was not very impressive. I went 1–4 and had a high ERA. My highlights of a mediocre career are few and far between. At the end of the 1957 split season, I'd been released before 90 games to preserve my rookie status after I'd agreed to come back in 1958.

Spring came. I'd heard nothing, so I called Roy Partee in San Francisco. He said we'd all been released, and he'd lost his job, too. St. Louis bought the Stockton club. So I called Ray Robb again and he called Bernie DeViveiros, the Detroit scout who was in Florida for spring training. Bernie sent me a contract for $300 a month and I went to Lakeland, Florida, to make a Class D team in Erie, Pennsylvania, in the New York-Penn League.

After a second full year in 1959 with Class D Montgomery in the Florida League, where I'd done good and we won the pennant, I was assigned to Birmingham, AA, Southern League. Eddie Glennon owned and operated that team, the Barons, like the guy in the movie, *The Natural*. He wanted to win, and while they were affiliated with Detroit, he was one of the last aggressive GMs.

I needed to make more money and had sent back two contracts while working in a grocery store in Danville, California, and time was running out. I'd asked for $750 a month but decided I wouldn't accept less than $500. With only five days left before spring training, Eddie called me at the grocery store. The boss was a bit put out that I'd had a long distance personal call at the store, but he relieved me at the cash register.

"Hello, Egan. You're a tough Irishman. This is Eddie Glennon calling. What do you want to play for the Birmingham Barons?"

Now, I've already proved what a financial wizard I was, so I said, "I can't sign for less than $500."

"Of course," he said. "And if you stay with us 45 days, I'll give you your $750."

I got sent to another AA club at the end of spring training, and then to a Class A club just before Opening Day. I never accomplished much success in the major leagues, but I loved it! Still do to an extent, but today the animals are running the zoo and it's not the same. In the '60s we were slaves, but we got paid for what we did or didn't do. There were no multi-year contracts and no huge bonuses.

In 1965, the year I was traded to St. Louis before spring training, I was to find out about the bonus rule. In those days, if you got over $4,000 you had to stay on the major league club. I thought I had a lock on a spot with them. Some luck! They had a few kids with money contracts, including a big skinny left-handed pitcher named Steve Carlton and a right-handed pitcher named Nelson Briles. Can you believe it? They sent me to AAA for those guys?

I got revenge. In 1967 my only major league win was against St. Louis as they went on to win the pennant. I was with the Los Angeles Dodgers that year, my last as a player. To sum it up, I pitched my first game in the major leagues with the Detroit Tigers in 1963. I stayed with them in 1964, then went to the Angels in 1966, and finished with the Dodgers in 1967. My record was less than the one I'd dreamed about. I appeared in seventy-four games, pitched about a hundred innings, and had a high ERA, something over five. Against that one win against St. Louis I had two losses and compiled two saves. Obviously I wasn't making any plans to be called by the Baseball Hall of Fame!

A sense of humor was always one of Dick Egan's mainstays. On January 2, 1965, when the Tigers traded him to the Cardinals for Glen Hobbie and Bob Lipski shortly before spring training, he thought he had a lock on a spot. But that's when he learned about the bonus rule. He remembered, "Some luck! They had a few kids with money contracts, including a big skinny LHP named Carlton and a RHP named Nelson Briles. Can you believe it? They sent me to AAA for those guys" (Dick Wilson collection).

After working in the gaming business dealing craps and roulette at Lake Tahoe, Nevada, I finally got back into baseball. I was signed to be a bird dog, non-salaried, with the California Angels and had no clue what I was doing. My contact scouts were Dick Hanlon and Jim Miller. They didn't like any of my recommendations. That was 1973. In 1974 I went to work with the original Major League Scouting Bureau for $500 a month plus expenses with a territory of northern Nevada only.

The late Jim Wilson ran the original Major League Scouting Bureau and he was great. Very knowledgeable and very far-sighted. He started video work and a lot of the ideas that are now routine in scouting. I learned fast and got promoted to a full area in 1976. Bruce Hurst, who was Boston's number one pick, was my first big name. But as an MLSB scout, I didn't sign them, I just reported on them. With the MLSB, we were always under the gun financially. We got as high as twenty clubs one year, but as low as ten or twelve clubs, too. Membership was not mandatory in those years.

Wilson had organizational meetings where we were taught consistency and we talked baseball. We were tested and quizzed, and we were not bad as a group until our better scouts started leaving.

Significant to my development were Sandy Johnson and Dick Bogard. The grading system we used with the bureau is almost industry-wide now. Two to eight, with eight being high or best.

Later, as a crosschecker with the bureau, I graded Bo Jackson even though his fielding tools didn't stand out. I also hesitated to recommend Barry Bonds as a "can't miss" prospect despite his obvious tools because he seldom hustled. I was too old fashioned and still am to a degree. Makeup meant a lot and I didn't and wouldn't accept less than 100 percent all the time. Bo I could project. But Bonds, well, I never thought he worked hard enough to be as good as he could be.

Scouting with a system of numbers to grade all of a player's tools and then formulate that into an overall grade became the ranking system we used. Today most clubs use the number system, but not all use the OFP (overall future potential) as the final ranking criteria. The idea was to rank all players in order of how good they would eventually be. Nobody has ever been that smart and I doubt that anyone will ever be, but as a scout you have to rank them in some kind of preferential order.

Ideally, area scouts and their associate scouts, the helpers or bird dogs, scout small areas. Regional crosscheckers see and give a second opinion on their players. National crosscheckers go all over and see the highest-ranking players, thereby adding a third report. The scouting director usually sees the best guys, too, but his reports don't get factored into building or compiling a final preferential list.

The bureau, which tried to represent all clubs and all types of needs, was simply a computerized list. In the bureau we had the same scouting alignment — scout, regional and national crosscheckers — and by computerizing the graded reports, they offered all clubs the final bureau preferential lists.

Each club does the same thing, but most clubs are able to build their lists with specific priorities. Some clubs may be infield rich and lack pitching or speed. That club's list will be different than some others who have different needs. Before the draft scouts were more selective and had to not only evaluate a player, but had to sell himself and his organization. He had to develop a trusting relationship. Scouts in those days would have fairly short lists and were always at the games of a select few.

Nowadays even the area scouts are dealing in quantity and large lists, especially with the bureau providing a quantity of names, as area scouts are directed to scout them, too. They are also younger and less experienced. Many young scouts today have limited professional backgrounds. They are no less motivated, but the "feel" for a player may be different. Scouts used to jot down notes on anything because they had a simplistic method of selection. With the advent of the draft, there are forms that each organization uses to put this player on paper or, more recently, into a computer.

Although scouting itself is not a high-paying job, the money involved for the players is probably the biggest change and is a huge reason why scouting is getting more and more complicated. Because signing bonuses are reaching higher numbers, the risk of a mistake is critical. Now the tools (arm, speed, batting, pitching, etc.) are still the same to identify talent, but today we're involved in makeup evaluations, injury-risk factors, medical reports, and most unpredictable, the prospect's signability.

Today most kids say they will sign. They say, "Yes, I'll sign for the market value." But the agents and advisors and access to other bonus units have made that "yes" answer loaded with uncertainties. Quite often a team ends up paying more, much more, than they originally planned to spend. Then they blame the pressure of the media or they won't admit they made a miscalculation.

I would not begrudge this insane money upfront if these players were more dedicated to earning it. However, if they get big money, the tendency is to rush their progress and accept less than desired progress. In the process we restrict playing time for some kids who are less touted!

With the Marlins we have a few examples. John Lynch was a pitcher at Stanford. We gave him a lot of money in 1992 but agreed to let him play his senior year in football. He banged up his shoulder and didn't pitch well in 1993. Then he quit and went to the NFL. We goofed by paying him in advance and/or by letting him play football. Then we took Josh Booty number one in 1994. We brought him out of football at LSU, and maybe the story will be okay, but in actuality, the family and agent lied about the terms it would take and we gave in. Until a scouting director and GM step up and say "no" and don't give in to these situations, they will continue to happen. The players, on the other hand, face enormous pressure to prove they are worth such contracts. But maybe, because they are prepaid, few of them have the motivation or dedication.

The draft itself creates problems for the organization that has limited financial resources. The way we do it to avoid mistakes is expensive. We spend a lot of money creating a preferred list and then we draft too many players each year. In my opinion, we deal in quantity to justify the rising costs of scouting, and we are inclined to take extra players hoping to catch lightning in a bottle. But that method creates an annual turnover of players who don't get a good or complete chance to develop. We have fewer farm teams with fewer jobs to fill, but now we draft more players than ever.

There is not equal accountability for the whole system. Scouting is an inexact science. But quantity over quality does not work! For example, when I signed in 1957, organizations had seven to fourteen farm teams. In today's world, I'd have been released or maybe rushed upwards too fast. It takes awhile to fully develop players. We don't always allow that to happen now. Colleges have to win, so they can't develop players, either. Immediate production is the standard in college.

I want to get back to today's scouting procedures. Forming an accurate preferred list is very hard. With the idea of crosscheckers being your best and highest-paid scouts, teams have a tendency to rely on crosscheckers over area scouts. That is absurd for the most part. For example, a young athlete is growing up fast between his sophomore and senior years in high school. Area scouts have noticed this kid, gotten to know him and his family, and watched his rate of progress. They like his potential a lot. As a senior in high school, he is just emerging from the growth spurt. As a sophomore he was 5'10", grew to 6'1" as a junior, and stands 6'4" as a senior.

The crosschecker comes in for one or two games tops and sees an interesting but gangling kid. Awkwardness is tough to overlook, and even tougher for the kids. As a result, the crosschecker grades this boy considerably lower than the area guy. And on the final list, this boy is a fifth-round type instead of a second-to-third-round type. The area guy usually doesn't get him because he has less experience or less voice in the final matter.

The system creates this problem, just as it does in player development. Both scouting and coaching are low-paid areas of the major league organization. In order to keep good people, we make the better scouts crosscheckers in order to pay them more, and the better coaches and managers are promoted to the higher levels, such as Double-A, Triple-A and the major leagues.

In reality the best scouts should be the area guys whose responsibilities include signability, makeup and other factors. And the best coaches and managers should be with the youngest players who need the most instruction. In my early years, 1957–1961, I was coached by veterans, former major league players, coaches and managers. Most scouts in those days had done it all: played, coached, and managed.

As of 1997, the scouting trend is beginning to lean more to foreign countries and especially to professional scouts. Because of free agency, more organizations are spending more time and money scouting other organizations. Because of trades and free agency, organizations are a more certain way of upgrading your own club. Foreign countries—Latin America and recently the Orient—are heavily scouted and in some cases less expensive bonus wise.

I went to the Florida Marlins' expansion draft in 1992 and have to put this experience at the top of my baseball career. We only had one year to see the entire industry, unlike Arizona and Tampa Bay in '96 and '97. David Dombrowski organized our efforts and it was a monumental effort. I scouted free agents through the June draft while a few teams of scouts were scouting major league organizations. Their reports came in and we started to create a list of players we liked. I was assigned all AA and AAA pitchers in all organizations as a pitching crosschecker. I did report on a few positive players, but for the most part I was out scouting four months and then we began meeting and putting together a list — a preferred list, first by organizations, then by position, and eventually overall preferential. The magnitude of this one-year operation was ten-fold more intense and exciting as any June draft. As has been documented, all that work comes down to a final result of 30-some players. These players, in turn, become value to either keep or trade. Coupled with a few free agent signs, we had 50-to-60 players in our system. For example, we picked a veteran left-handed pitcher from one club and traded him for two young prospects. We did this a lot. Our on-the-field success was less impressive early on, but our overall organizational strength has been built up to among the industry's best.

During the expansion process, each organization has to do a lot of the same work. First, they have to know and evaluate their own players, and at the same time, be aware of other organizations' value when trades become available. This surge of pro scouting has stayed with us, not only because of the Marlins' success and the eventual Tampa Bay and Arizona expansion, but because of rising free agent bonuses, and major league baseball leaders seem to be determined to reduce the cost and size of scouting and player development. So more and more clubs have formed separate scouting divisions, dividing the process between evaluating professional and amateur players.

While I'm on the subject of the draft, the January phase of the draft was never cost efficient. Most January draftees waited until June to sign or had to be redrafted. But it definitely made for better scouts. The effort it took to scout junior college kids who often played against college teams each fall season gave scouts a better knowledge of their players and schools, and overall made them more efficient. After the January draft was dropped, the talent level in junior colleges went down some. Now it's working back up, but the best baseball kids are still going to four-year schools. Today many scouts do far less work in the fall. There is less urgency and less required work.

Let me tell you some of the differences in scouting with the new breed of young scouts, young scouting directors, and even young GMs. There is an expression, "He can play," which has far less meaning than in the old days. Tools are tools and that won't change, but there are players like Pete Rose who can play but their tools don't grade out exceptionally high by today's criteria. Ozzie Smith was another, and Mark Lemke and Craig Counsell.

Now when a scout says "he can play," he has to convince the bosses on paper. And this is an example of the new lack of feel for the game. It isn't enough for a scout to just have a "gut feel" for a prospect any more because the risk of mistakes is meaningful due to the high bonus prices. Therefore, I guess all the forms and grades, all the tools graded out, are now a means of justification in case a mistake is made. Even if you do draft a player, there has to be justification for the huge bonus. The result is equal blame or equal credit, but not equal accountability.

As a rule crosscheckers don't sign any players, and of the many drafts and trades I've been involved with, there are a few more memorable names that come to mind. During our expansion draft I was adamant about obtaining Charlie Hough and Robb Nen. Hough for his leadership, and Nen for his potential. We got Hough and he was great for two years before injury forced him to retire. Nen was protected but we got him in a trade with Kurt Miller later. I liked Miller, but Nen turned out to be super! During our meetings, my comment was something to the effect that, "Get Nen and if he's not a starter within two years, fire me!" They remembered, but luckily I was right. I also lobbied for Bobby Witt and Kevin Brown, among others. We acquired both and eventually traded both, but they proved their value.

My favorite player, though, has to be Craig Counsell. During the summer of 1997 I was scouting the Pacific Coast League for Florida and just happened to be in Colorado Springs at the time I got urgent calls from David Dombrowski. He asked me if I thought Counsell could play second base for us. I said, "Yes," and we got him two days later. Without him the Marlins would not have won the pennant or the World Series.

What makes this special is that he is not a big tools guy. I had him graded out as "fringe with high interest because he can play." He is an old-fashioned baseball player! He can play because his intangibles — traits like hustle, aggressiveness and makeup — put him up there with guys like Mark Lemke. We grade fringe as a role player, a guy who can help a club but is usually not a regular every day guy.

So, when asked "Can he play for us now?" and I said yes to that, my grade didn't make sense. I told them that he was going to be fine, that he was better than fringe, and to make the deal. For some reason, in his case I never hesitated. Probably because I thought he could play! Just instincts and experiences a scout has from remembering similar type guys who help a club win despite just marginal tools. Lucky for me, I was right again.

The future of scouting is vague, but I think there will always be a need. Because of computers, fax machines and other modern modes of communication like voice mail and email, the young college-type guys will become a bigger factor. Old dinosaurs like me will have to scuffle to keep a job. I do okay on the laptop and desk computer because my wife is computer literate and has guided me to the novice level.

Professional scouts, those who scout professional players, will continue to play a larger role. The decision makers of baseball are toying with the idea that includes complex baseball for all first-year players. I reject the validity of that idea but it may happen. In other words, all college and high school guys, except the few premier prospects, will play and be scouted from the spring training complexes. This would eliminate the need and expense to scout the whole world of amateur baseball like we do now. Or at least not as extensively as we do now. The almighty dollar is the bottom line factor here.

Another new idea is to move the draft to late summer and limit the draft to far fewer rounds. This makes more sense. High school and college schedules are so compacted now it's hard to be accurate before early June. And too many times players won't sign quickly enough to play in June. This forces us to draft quantity as opposed to quality.

The better summer programs, like Cape Cod, Alaska, and other college-level leagues, will be better stocked as well as American Legion, Babe Ruth, Connie Mack and other high school-age leagues. This second season scouting will let us fine-tune our draft lists and the high turnover rate in the low minor leagues should be lessened.

Scouting will survive and the best scouting staffs will reap the rewards. But bottom line budgets are still the biggest weak spot. Owners today can't control their dollar waste at the major league level, but they can and do scrimp at the scouting and player development levels. As an industry, scouting is cheap labor. Most area scouts still earn near poverty levels plus expenses, which are strictly monitored. Crosscheckers and major league scouts are paid more but still earn way less than major league rookie players.

The life of a good area scout, which is the backbone of a good organization, is spent in a car, marginally rated motels, and a lot of fast food stops. There are long hours in a car between games trying to dodge weather and other problems and still find time to get on the phone soliciting pitching rotations, game times, make-up dates and other information. Most of this info has to be passed on to their bosses and a crosschecker by entering the info in the computer, uploading to the office, and still trying to sleep. That's not to mention the needs of the wife and kids that some scouts are always behind on.

An area scout's car is loaded with cold weather gear, file boxes of new and old reports and schedules, their clothes and workout gear. Many travel with coolers to carry snacks. Many have cell phones and pagers to go with their scout cards so they can get notes during games, and maybe luxury items like a folding chair and seat cushion.

Crosscheckers are supposed to have it made. We only carry a suitcase, carry-on size usually, a computer case, and all the paperwork items needed to keep track of all their scouts. Most of our time is spent on the telephone finding out who's playing where and when, including backup games in case of bad weather, and making reservations, usually two or three different flights and car rentals to match. Hotels are a problem if you don't know exactly which game you'll end up attending.

Weather problems, pitching rotations — we usually see a pitcher over a position player — and directions to and from the airport are the first and last thing we do each day. Time becomes a huge enemy. Getting home occasionally, having regular meals and sleep are last on the list.

On top of the loneliness of the job, it's a thankless job for the most part. No matter how hard you work, how well organized you are, you are still at the mercy of the draft.

Even the best scouts don't get most of their players. Nobody knows how well you did your job unless you sign a player, and then it's three-to-five years before you can tell if he makes good. Long hours, low pay, and very little gratification from the major league level, the people you are working for.

Here's an example. A scout got three players in the June draft. One player wanted a big bonus and was a high pick. The club paid it. The second player and third player were not as highly rated, but both were needed to fill out minor league rosters. The boss calls. He wants me to sign players two and three. I tell him that he gave me $25,000 and $20,000, respectively, and they won't sign unless we up it to $35,000 and $25,000.

"Do you like them enough?" the boss asks me.

"Yes."

"Okay, give it to them."

So, after a five-minute phone call, we gave away an extra $15,000. Now that's in mid–June. Four to five months later the same scout gets his contract for next year with a token raise. He calls the same boss. "I need to get a better raise. I've worked hard and have a baby on the way."

Boss says, "Whoa. We just can't afford to spend that kind of money at this time." This happens every year with most organizations and a lot of scouts.

Why can't baseball's brain trust figure out the obvious lack of public interest in the June draft? Why not allow clubs to trade picks? One excuse is the complex contracts players have. Whose fault is that? Dumb. Dumb. Poor marketing.

I forgot to mention about my playing days. As a scout we all talk at clinics or speak to public service groups. I like to ask my audience who the greatest home run hitter is. Hank Aaron is the easy answer. Well, I can't claim Hall of Fame stats, but I struck Aaron out every time I faced him! Hopefully someone usually asks, "How many times did you face him?" The answer: once.

As a member of the 1967 Los Angeles Dodgers, my catcher, John Roseboro, once told me about Hank, saying that the only time he was likely to lose concentration was if he thought a pitcher was cheating. I threw a spitter occasionally, which I never considered cheating because I never was warned or caught. Anyway, with one strike I threw Aaron a spitter he fouled off into Roseboro. The ball landed in front of the plate and was still glistening wet. Aaron starts screaming and pointing. The ump comes out, picks it up and says, "It must have hit Rosey in the mask," threw it back hard, and there I was with two strikes on Hank Aaron, who was mad at me. So, whenever in doubt, go with your best pitch. I cranked up my best fastball and he missed it! KO!

Once in spring training when I was with Detroit, in 1963, I think, I faced Mickey Mantle and got him out easily with a fastball away. At Detroit early in the season I faced him again. I can remember looking in from the mound and his bat looked so big, so menacing that I could see no pitch that he couldn't hit hard. When in doubt, so I threw my best fastball. Mantle hit a laser beam past my right knee. Being a left-handed pitcher, all I did was turn my head, and my shortstop, Dick McAuliffe, hadn't even twitched and my center fielder was already starting to go to one knee to catch this one-hop line drive. Okay, Mantle gets a single to center field. I stood on the mound and thought about what would have happened if that ball would have hit me. My legs were actually shaking with the realization that I'd have been on crutches for sure.

Once Frank Howard hit a ball off me to my shortstop, Jim Fregosi, who caught it chest-high for an out. But it was hit so hard it literally lifted Jim off the ground and put him on his butt a few feet behind his position! He brought the ball back to me with a request: "Please warn us infielders the next time you throw that pitch!"

Another time Jim Gentile of Baltimore hit a homer off me to the peak of the third deck roof in Detroit. My right fielder, Al Kaline, barely moved, but turned and caught the rebounding homer ball and tossed it to Jerry Lumpe with a comment. Jerry was a nice, quiet man. He never fooled around. He was just a good professional. Anyway, he brought the ball to me and said, "I thought you'd like to keep this ball. It's flat on one side!"

And then there is Willie Mays. In 1966 spring training I struck out Mays but the ball got by my catcher. Mays was on first base, but I was out there gloating to myself. As I got set to take my sign, it's just natural for a left-handed pitcher to see first base. I was stunned and paralyzed. I didn't have a good move to first base anyway, so I just let out a cussword and stepped off. Mays instantly retreated, laughing. I'm out there trying to make this team in spring training and I'd never seen a lead like that and I'd never had Willie Mays on first base before, either. When I finally got back onto the rubber and looked to first base, Mays was no more than ten inches off and in his high squeaky voice he says, "Is this better?" Superstar versus struggling wannabe!

In 1967 I went to the Dodgers and faced Mays during the regular season

Dick Egan, a left-handed pitcher with Dodgers, warming up before a game against the Chicago Cubs at Wrigley Field in 1967 during his fourth and final major league season. He was thirty years old and not ready to leave the game. He continued by learning scouting with Jim Wilson at the Major League Scouting Bureau. Today, more than forty years later, he is with the Detroit Tigers as special assistant to GM David Dombrowski (Dick Wilson collection).

games, and I can't remember ever getting him out. Popped him up to left field once in Candlestick. Al Ferrara, my left fielder, took off backwards but the ball fell in for a two-bagger. I'd been told that Mister Mays never forgets. Don't ever try the same pitch in the same at-bat if you fool him. Well, this one night in San Francisco I threw him a slider down and in, which he missed. Strike one. Then I threw a spitter he missed. Strike two. And when the ball came back to me it was still soaking wet. I never acquired Gaylord Perry's finesse. So I just used the same load and fired it up there. Thirty years later it was a hell of a spitter: low, hard, late bottom-out sink. It really was a good spitter in 1967, too, but I'd been warned and forgot. Mays hit a bullet right by my ear. I turned to see my center fielder, Willie Davis, tap his glove and I remember thinking, "At least I finally got him out!"

Wrong! Simultaneously Davis turned to watch this ball just keep going up and up and out into the San Francisco Bay. He crushed that spitter and I was behind the mound cussing him as he passed second base. His high voice came back, "I hit the dry side of that SOB!" Obviously I had a brief and undistinguished major league career.

Most scouts can relate travel nightmares. Once on a Western Airlines flight out of Salt Lake City to Sheridan, Wyoming, there were three of us in the front row of coach. Tom Gamboa and Jesse Flores, Jr., and I were on our way to an American Legion tourney. Jesse was in front of Tom and I was on the left side of the aisle. Shortly after taken off, Jesse was turned around in conversation and the plane rolled over, right wing to the ground. As we plummeted I saw Jesse's eyes open wide. I'm sure he saw us the same way! I looked to my right over a woman's shoulder and out the window and all I could see was treetops coming right at us. The pilot leveled us quickly and we climbed back up to normal altitude. Then he came on the loud speaker to apologize for the excitement, and explained that we were almost hit by another aircraft. As they resumed service, Gamboa asked the stewardess, "How close were we to that other plane?"

The stewardess never paused and answered, "The pilot told me he didn't know. He had his eyes shut!" Great feeling!

As a player for Spokane (the Dodgers' Triple-A farm club in the Pacific Coast League), we were en route from Tulsa to Indianapolis on a DC-3. I was asleep. I woke up looking out the right-side window and the motor was idle. The prop wasn't turning. We'd lost oil pressure and were going down. Fortunately, we were right above Joplin, Missouri. We landed safely, then spent five hours playing pepper at this little, tiny airport on a small lawn while we waited for another plane.

During my first year with Stockton (California League, Class A ball), our bus was stopped for two hours because road crews were working on Highway 80 in preparation for the 1960 Winter Olympics at Lake Tahoe. Rather than just sit there, Jim Johnson, a former Atlanta scout, and I decided to walk and let the bus pick us up as they let westbound traffic go through. We'd walked about twenty minutes and passed a lot of construction in the Donner Pass area. We heard this big truck blowing his air horn, so finally I turned to see why. It turned out to be a water truck and he soaked us head to toe as he passed by. At 2 AM high in the Sierras, it's cold. And when you're soaked to the bone, it's really cold. Our teammates had quite a laugh when they picked us up about twenty minutes later.

People always want to know about tryout camps. They used to be a frequently used means of identifying follows or prospects. Within the Major League Scouting Bureau, it was a rule and still is to have camps at hard-to-reach sites. Inner-city sites are important. Today most clubs have a few but not many. Today's kids, especially those with talent, are less inclined to tryout en masse. Maybe the national attention paid to bonuses paid to drafted players has had an adverse effect. But today many kids lack that "just give me a chance" attitude.

Clubs today use invitational workouts quite often to keep the talent pool more consistent. It's easier to organize and far less work on the field. It's very hard to give an objective and fair chance to a group that is large and mostly non-talented.

Once in Utah, as an area scout with the bureau, I had an open camp in Ogden. We had 220 signers and were completely overwhelmed. Late morning, as the signups were near completion, an old Cadillac towing a horse trailer full of household goods rolled into the parking lot. This guy gets out, he was at least 30 years old and all cowboy. He had a beautiful wife, old Levi's, and even older glove and cleats. They came over and said, "We saw your ad in the paper. I'm moving to California, but I've always wanted this opportunity."

Despite an age limit of 15 to 25 in our ad, I said, "Okay." This guy stayed all day, survived all cuts and did all right. He not only hit from both sides and doubled off the opposite wall, but he ranged among the best arms and ran okay. At the conclusion he even demonstrated arm strength with each arm. When I tried to explain the scouting bureau policy regarding his age, he cut me off saying he was not looking to get signed or even offered another tryout. He simply never had this chance and wanted to do it before they went to California. So he thanked us and drove off.

Once scouting a game at BYU, a lady in the stands observed my radar gun and quizzed me about velocities and scouting. She proceeded to tell me that her husband was a softball pitcher who could throw harder than the players on the field. I finally gave in and carried my gun on the grass behind the stands and gave this guy a chance to prove it. Now major league average on the JUGS gun is 89–90. This guy never broke 75 and was furious, but thanked me for my time. His wife didn't say anything else.

Individual workouts during and after the high school and college seasons are still used a lot. They are still the topic of controversy each year. Once in the early 1980s it was rumored a certain scout from the Big Red Machine worked out some of South Florida's top high school players the day before the high school all-star game. Therefore, most were too tired to showcase well for the rest of us at the big event. In 1991, a scout in the Northwest worked out a previously injured high school player who was just coming off his injury. Although he'd been cleared by the doctor to play, he ended up disabled again. Unfortunately, that's all part of the game, too.

I guess you could say my career has come full circle. I was signed by the Tigers, and after doing many things with them and other organizations, I'm back with them. All in all, looking back at my life in baseball, it's been a good one. Of course, it's not over yet. I'm still out there and still loving every single day of it.

Jerry Gardner

(1920–2006)

Like so many of his peers he played baseball during a unique era of our national history. He started during the final years of the Depression, had his playing career interrupted by World War II, and returned to a time of growth and experimentation in the minor leagues when they were classified as D, C, B, A, AA, and AAA. It was a time of growth when many new minor leagues appeared throughout the country, and playing in them was definitely a lesson in geography. Instability was a characteristic of many of them because teams frequently jumped from league to league or simply went bust. This fact coupled with the lack of money and poor management meant many leagues were short lived.

It was a time when informal salary caps and tight budgets existed, and, to save money, most of these teams assigned players the job of player-manager, and as they got older, several stayed on as managers. For many of the veteran scouts, that was the normal transition to their next phase in the game—scouting. Jerry Gardner's player-manager and managerial history is a perfect example. He began managing in the Sunset League, first with the Anaheim Valencias in 1947, and then with the Anaheim/San Bernardino Valencias in 1948 when the team moved. He spent two seasons in the KITTY League with the Mayfield Clothiers. He found himself managing the Burlington-Graham Pirates in the Carolina League in 1952, and then the Visalia Stars in the California League in 1953. The Phoenix Stars of the Arizona–Texas League employed his services in 1954–55.

That was the end of a time when the dream of playing baseball, "getting rich in the big leagues," and playing on TV didn't exist. Back then most players weren't motivated by money or fame; they played baseball for the love of it. For them playing the game they loved was a privilege.

When Jerry Gardner began to scout, the influence of television and the impact of the westward movement of the New York Giants and the Brooklyn Dodgers had changed the baseball landscape. His grandson, now a San Francisco attorney, told me he learned about baseball and about life by going with his grandfather on his baseball jobs in the summers.

Jerry Gardner was the recipient of the Scout of the Year Award, West Coast, in 1994.

I never played very high. I played '39, '40, '41, '42, and then went in the service until the winter of '45, and didn't play again until 1947. In fact, I was going to play in

'46 but broke my knee and sat out the season that year. Then they weren't going to pay me enough to support my family. So I really got back in it because I got the job managing over here where I live.

I was signed out of a tryout camp in 1938 in Riverside, California, by the St. Louis Cardinals. Branch Rickey and several other scouts were involved. They had several scouts there and we stayed for three days.

I was a catcher, number 450-something. They put a number on each guy's back and that tells you how many guys we had out there. What we'd do was go out and take hitting practice and everything else, then they'd make up teams and we'd play actual games. We had problems because it rained a lot. So they would get the field ready to go and we would continue wherever we were and it would rain again and so on.

It rained on and off, so we had problems. At that time they signed two of their teams out of that camp. One of them was Albuquerque in the Arizona-Texas League, and the other was Midland in the West Texas–New Mexico League. They signed two complete teams out of there and they both won the pennants that year. Isn't that something?

At night we sat down in the hotel lobby and waited for scouts who ran the camp to come down so we could get some information from them about which players they were going to sign. The scout who talked to me over there and signed me was a guy by the name of Bob Hughes.

It really was a memorable experience. They just had so many kids show up that wanted to play baseball. We were not hard to find. We were all starving to death because of the Depression, so we were more than happy to play for whatever they offered. We were all young men just trying to get jobs and I don't think anybody got any kind of signing bonus. I got seventy-five dollars a month. Then I got a job driving the team bus, too, which brought my salary up to a hundred a month, which I thought was pretty good. Of course, it didn't take much to get by. I got lunch for twenty-five or thirty cents, and they provided lodging on the road, and we got to play.

I played and managed with the Anaheim Valencias in the Sunset League that they had just created in '47. Some of the other teams were the El Centro Imperials, the Las Vegas Wranglers, the Ontario Orioles, the Reno Silver Sox, and the Riverside Dons. It was an unstable league, teams came and went every season, and it only lasted three seasons. When it folded some of the teams moved to the Arizona-Texas League. As player-manager I made enough so I could support my family. I had a wife and one child.

It was a professional team. The league had four teams in California — Ontario, Anaheim, Riverside, and El Centro — and there were two teams in Nevada, one in Reno and the other in Las Vegas. That's as best I can remember anyway. It could be explained in today's terms as a kind of rookie baseball, maybe a step below the California League.

When I went in the service, Branch Rickey left my contract on the table of Sacramento of the Pacific Coast League, and when I got out, we all belonged to Sacramento. But the Cardinals had sold that club to a local businessman in Sacramento. Only some of the players were left on the Sacramento club and I was one of them. When I returned, I didn't go back to that club. I went up there in '48 for a few days but they had some mix-up and I had to leave and go up to the Western International League, which was a B league in Wenatchee, Washington. I played up there for awhile, too. In '49 I was a catcher in San Diego, mostly in the bullpen.

Then, in 1950 I got a job with the Pittsburgh organization as a minor league manager in Mayfield, Kentucky, in the KITE League, Kentucky, Illinois, Tennessee. Best known as the KITTY League, it's one of the oldest leagues in the country. The teams were stationed in Mayfield and Jonesboro in Kentucky, Cairo in Illinois, and Jackson and Fulton in Tennessee. It was an established league at that time, Class D baseball. But it hasn't been in existence for quite awhile now because the towns weren't substantial enough to support it.

At that time they had two or three clothing manufacturing factories there, I think, and they had a couple or three places that made ceramic lamps and things of that nature. And there was lots of farming. Those little towns back then were all built around a little downtown area and people loved their baseball. As a matter of fact, when it rained and the field got wet, all the local businessmen would roll up their pant legs and get up there to help get the field ready to play. Those were the good old days of baseball for me as I look back.

From 1939 through 1942, the Arizona-Texas League was home. During those years we had four teams in that league. They were the Albuquerque Cardinals, the El Paso Texans, the Tucson Cowboys, and the Bisbee-Douglas Miners. Bisbee was a little copper mining town, and Douglas was a place on the Mexican border where they smelted this copper. It was owned by the Phelps Dodge Copper Company, but I think the mine is obsolete now. It was a below-ground mining situation, and when the war came along it became the biggest open pit mine in the world, copper mining. They moved one town completely for this, a little place called Lowell, which was alongside Bisbee.

We were in Albuquerque, which was the best town in the league. At that time it was only about 25,000 people and Tucson was a small place, too. Back in those days they didn't have lights in the Tucson park so we played games starting about 4 o'clock in the afternoon.

If you get on the bus at Bisbee, Arizona, and had to get to Albuquerque, New Mexico, after a ballgame, you never traveled in the daytime because it was too hot and there was no air conditioning. We drove up to the Benson Cutoff out of Tucson — it's a new highway now — which was a dirt and gravel road all the way to Albuquerque then. It was a pretty good drive. We used to shoot out all the lights with BB guns in these little towns along the way. They had these big lamps with a reflector in them in the middle of the road. There were no stop signs. We also shot rabbits. It was just a way to keep occupied and pass the time in the bus.

There were only a few places we could stop to get sodas and whatnot and we learned where they were so we didn't miss them. And there were a few service stations where we'd stop to get gas, maybe a soda and a candy bar. We had to take advantage of those places when we found them. Of course, now you can't go forty feet without finding all these places!

After the end of the war I broke my knee in '46 when I played with the Roosevelt Plumbers, which was a semi-pro team in Los Angeles. I had an old pair of shin guards, and a guy fouled the ball off his bat and it hit my kneecap and it happened. We had a little difficulty getting it back together and my leg was stiff for a long time after that. They didn't know all the things about it like they do now. So I had gone home and gotten a civil service job in a navy shipyard. I figured I'd better try to stay there rather than go try to play ball with a stiff knee. But I got so sick of that in a hurry that when '47 came I figured I'd go take a shot. I still couldn't bend it all the way. It took me about a year to get good flexibility, but it's never bothered me since.

I was always a catcher, but after the injury, the only thing that bothered the knee every now and then was a long plane flight or a long bus ride. And it really never bothered me playing. At the time I played I wasn't very big, about 155 pounds, so it wasn't much weight on my knee. The big guys are the ones who have problems.

The 1947 season was the year I managed the Anaheim club. I started there in '48 and wound up in Sacramento. Player-managers were typical in many minor leagues, especially for guys with a little age on them. You had to make enough money to be able to afford to play because most of us had families. I was 27 in '48.

In 1949 I was a bullpen catcher for San Diego in the Coast League. Gene Thompson, Jesse Flores, Luke Easter, Al Rosen, and Max West were some of the guys on that team. I never played regularly there. I was the third-string catcher. The only reason I went to Hollywood was because they had two catchers hurt. I only played there the last three weeks of the season.

Bill Werle was the last pitcher I hit against in professional baseball. I was playing

Player-manager Jerry Gardner, number 3, helps carry an injured player off the field during a Phoenix Stars pre-game workout in 1955, the team's first season as a Baltimore affiliate. The re-configured league, called the Arizona-Mexico League, lowered in rank to Class D, lasted 1955–1957. Gardner's team took a third-place finish with a record of 80–59 (Jill Mugford, daughter — Jerry Gardner collection).

for the Hollywood Stars when I came back from managing a club in the Arizona-Texas League. Later on, I think it was 1956, I'd been around managing minor leagues when I was told to come back to Hollywood in the Coast League because they needed two catchers. My season was about over so they brought me and another fella in there to catch. We were in the playoffs.

When I played for Hollywood, the team was independent and owned by a guy named Bill Star, and the old big league pitcher Bucky Walters was the manager. He managed a long time in the major leagues with the Washington Senators. He was a boy manager, about 24 years old, when he started managing them. He also managed the Yankees and several other clubs. Of course, when he was with us he was over sixty.

The last game I caught professionally, Bill Werle was pitching against us. How'd I do? Well, he struck me out, if you want to put it that way. We were playing in Portland that particular game and that was my last professional game. I went into full-time scouting after that.

Here's how I got into scouting. When I was working for Pittsburgh in the KITE League, I'd come home in the offseason to run the Saturday and Sunday rookie club they had during the wintertime. I did that up until '56, and that's how I got a lot of experience and learned about scouting. In the winter of '56, I went into full-time scouting.

The training was done on the road back then. It really was on-the-job training! And we had a good deal more territory than scouts have now. If we found a player, we called the office and told them we wanted to sign the guy to find out how much it would take because we thought he could play in the big leagues. They would then tell us, "We can't give him that much money. Go get him for this amount." And that's the way we did it.

We weren't restricted with junior college guys. We could go get them. But we couldn't sign high school players until after they graduated. We could sign them on the day they graduated, though. If we came across a player that we thought could play in the big leagues, well, we'd find out if he was a high school, junior college or college player, or if he wasn't in college, or wasn't planning on going to college after high school graduation. In American Legion baseball, they had rules that said if you didn't sign them by July first, you had to wait till his season was over to sign him.

It was more or less that we could sign these fellas when we came across them unless they were in school. So we just sent a report in on him, called the office on the phone to tell them what we thought of the guy and how much it would take. And he would give us a yes or no. And that was the way we operated in those days. For most of the fellas we scouted in our areas, well, we knew their families, their backgrounds and everything else.

It wasn't as risky as it is today because you have to give them a lot more money now and you don't get close to the family because of the way they work it. First of all, you can only tell them so much. You can't tell "the deal" with a family from the standpoint of "We're going to draft your boy." We can't tell them that because we're lying if we tell them that, because we just don't know how the draft will work out.

So the best we can do is get together with them and be on a talking basis to find out as much as we can about them. It's a little personal, but we're not allowed to make a sales pitch like we did in the pre-draft days because we wouldn't be telling them the truth. We don't know how it could end up because we don't even know our own organization's draft list until the last minute. And then we still have to work around the picks of the other organizations. It's just altogether different.

I think a lot of scouts feel the draft really took the fun out of it for them. There's no more challenge and all of that. It's more reporting now. Of course, now I don't do any more signing because I don't have a territory. I'm more or less a consultant now and just help them with big league free agents and cover the major leagues. And that's all done by reports.

I worked with free agent amateur players up until the draft in 1965. After the draft came in, I've worked strictly in the major leagues. I think in 1964 I signed eight players and four went to the big leagues, three more went to Triple-A, and one didn't do well. In 1964 I signed a kid by the name of Bill Rohr, Bobby Tolan, a kid out of San Diego named Lou Marone, and a kid out of Las Cruces, New Mexico, by the name of Henley, I think that's the correct spelling, and some others. In 1964, if I'm not mistaken, if you gave those players less than $4,000 and didn't protect them, they could be drafted by another organization for $8,000, but they had to keep them on their major league club.

I remember when we signed Bobby Tolan. We signed him in his house on Friday night and he was going to play an all-star game on Saturday. Somebody told him he couldn't play that game if he signed. Well, we signed him and simply held the contract so technically he was still an amateur for that game. When we started to leave, his mother said, "I want to see your contract."

I showed her the contract and she got kind of nasty about it. I got kind of perturbed about it and told her, "I doesn't bother me at all, Mrs. Tolan," and I tore up the contract. Bobby took a deep breath when I did that. But we signed him the next day after the game in the parking lot. In those days we did what we had to do. He was an easy sign because he wanted to play baseball. He was a very good player. We signed Dock Ellis about the same way.

Most of our signs in those days we signed for fairly reasonable money. That's partially because we had them on a kid club in the south-central area of Los Angeles. That's where our team was, primarily. Tolan played on it and Dock Ellis played on it and other players of that caliber. A lot of other good players played on it, but we couldn't come up with the money, either. Bobby Watson and two of Eddie Murray's brothers played there. Charlie Murray was the best one in the bunch ability-wise, but he never did anything with it.

I was with Pittsburgh 43 years. Then they had a big changeover there when the Galbraiths sold the club and Joe Brown and the others left. They got a new scouting director in there who wanted to this and that. Without even consulting me he just said, "This is the way we're going do it." Some of my friends had left that winter to go to Atlanta, so I went over to Atlanta, too, in 1994, I think.

In 1950 Pittsburgh was owned by a guy named McKinney, a big shot banker out of the Midwest, but then he sold it to John Galbraith in the winter of 1950-51. Galbraith then hired Branch Rickey to come over there. Well, Rickey was only there a short time and Galbraith fired him because he spent too much of his money. Galbraith was there almost all the time I was there except for a couple of years when he turned it over to his son, Dan. Then he got out because he couldn't get any cooperation with the city regarding improvements to the ballpark and so on. Since he wasn't having any fun anymore, he sold it.

So I went to Atlanta and the fellow (Chuck LaMar) who was in charge of the minor leagues and scouting there went to Tampa Bay and I went with him. That was in 1996.

Pittsburgh Pirates minor league scouting personnel, 1988. Front row, (left to right): Lenny Yochim, Larry Doughty, Jerry Gardner, Elmer Gray, Syd Thrift, Joe Lonnett, Chris Lein, Hal McRae. Second row: Bart Braun, Bill Bryk, Jay Ward, Jack Bowen, Dave Moharter, Jack Lind, Jim Bowden, Buzzy Keller. Third row: Julio Garcia, Bruce Kison, Angel Figueroa, Jim Thrift, Pete Gebrian, Fred Goodman, Woody Huyke, Rocky Bridges, Dave Trembley. Back row: Jackie Brown, Steve Demeter, Pablo Cruz, Bill Virdon, Gene Baker, Tom Dettore, Joe L. Brown, Larry D'Amato, Stan Cliburn (Jill Mugford, daughter — Jerry Gardner collection).

I've been with Tampa Bay since 1996. Al LaMacchia is one of the guys I work with here. He's a real good guy who loves baseball. I played against him years ago. He was with San Antonio when I was with Houston. He was a pretty good pitcher and went to the big leagues. He pitched to me, but I can't remember if I got a hit off him or not. I never played in the big leagues and I didn't even play regularly in the PCL.

I've seen things change in the game since I played and especially since I started scouting. Today there's several what we call "absentee owners" working the teams. They are businessmen with lots of money but no love for the game per se. They treat the personnel like workers, not that there's anything wrong with workers, but you've got to hire people with certain skills in this business if you want to get by. Sure, you can hire a kid with a fresh college degree, which is fine, but he probably won't know what the hell he's doing!

These type of owners usually have no interaction with personnel. They can read the rules and learn the rules, but they can't get a feel for a player unless they've played and went through it to find out what it takes to be a player, what kind of a makeup and mentality you have to have to be a good player. There are certain things you pick up over the years with experiences you have that the other guy wouldn't have. So they miss the boat on occasion by hiring people who have a pretty good resume, but they don't have the experience and skills it takes, the instinct and the intangible things that you have to have to "know" about baseball and the players. Sometimes it takes awhile to acquire that and sometimes you never acquire it.

Look at all the young scouting directors today. They have a good resume. Remember that although he'll be supervising some guys many years his senior, most of the scouts with age on them work in the professional ranks, and the scouting director primarily handles amateur free agent scouting. The GM usually works with the professional scouts or has somebody in charge of them. Today they're getting away from mixing the two. They're keeping the free agent scouts in the amateur work and using the pro scouts to cover the major leagues and the pro leagues, AAA and AA primarily. Today, the way it is with professional free agency and the money involved there, they scout much more rigidly than they did in the past.

When I first went into scouting there were three or four well-respected scouts down here. There was Johnny Moore, Hollis Thurston, and Bobby Mattick, and those fellas all played in the big leagues. But then when the money ballooned and the pension got so good, it wasn't necessary for them to work. So they did other things. Most of the scouts in my area were Double-A and Triple-A type players who loved the game and wanted to stay in it. Scouts love the game, sure, but many are not skilled in any other areas of business. I worked in oil field construction, mainly in the offseason during my playing-managing years, and didn't care for that. It's hard work and the money was better than I could make as a scout, but it was seasonal. We worked like a dog for a month then wouldn't have a job for two weeks. Of course, there are no guarantees about this, either, but if you can do the scouting job, you've always got a job.

The camaraderie among scouts is quite nice. We compete with each other for players but we're all basically friends. We don't like to take too much personal credit for anything.

Jerry Gardner, second from left, is honored as Coach of the Year in the Arizona-Texas League, 1954. As player-manager he led his team to a first-place finish with a 93–47 record. The young man to his left in the white jacket is Jimmy Bryan, described as a "hard driving" player. The man far right with carnation is comedian Phil Harris, part owner of the Pirates at that time. The others in the picture are unidentified (Jill Mugford, daughter — Jerry Gardner collection).

One of the biggest changes in this game in my lifetime was when Branch Rickey and Jackie Robinson crossed that so-called color line in 1947. I was still a minor league player and didn't feel any direct impact that year, but here's a little story to let you know how I feel about it.

I was scouting in Mexico one time, running a tryout camp in Mexicali. I was running a club there in 1954. I was in there with my club out of Phoenix. Somebody came in and told me in English that a Mexican reporter wanted to talk to me. We were fighting Mexicali for the pennant and we'd gotten into a fight the night before. This reporter was one of those negative guys, and he started out by asking, "You guys don't like the blacks, do you?"

Our third baseman had a fight with one of their pitchers. And I said, "What do you mean?"

And he said, "Well, you don't have any blacks on your major league club and you only have one black guy here."

So I told one of my players, "Go get the paper."

I put the newspaper down on the table and I told the interpreter, "Now you tell this guy about the black players on the Pittsburgh club."

There were nine blacks because we had a black man pitching that night. The whole club is black. So I finally threw this reporter out of the room because he was telling me that Pittsburgh is racist. I was telling him if you can find me a black player, a pink player or a green player that can play for this team better than the ones we already have here, I'll put him on it. I'd almost forgotten about that.

In addition to the quality of play improving with the addition of black players, we had one of the best Latin American scouting systems around. We had a fellow by the name of Howard Haak who used to sign thirty or forty people out of there a year. We heavily scouted and promoted scouting down there by giving baseballs and bats, having promotions, and getting people down there teaching.

Pittsburgh never had any money to run a complete baseball academy or anything like that. In 1969 when we won the pennant and World Series, we only drew between about 700,000–800,000 fans to the games. When the bigger market teams were drawing a million to a million five, well, that puts a damper on the budget.

Many organizations operate baseball academies in the Latin American countries so they can teach them without signing them and promote baseball. If you go to Caracas or the Dominican, if you go about a hundred yards outside the city limits, you're in the jungle. So there's no way to do some of that teaching there. But the kids there play baseball. I mean baseball is everything. They use broom sticks for bats and rocks for balls when that's all they can get.

So if you can take the big, strong kids who have speed and can throw the ball at age 14, 15, 16, you bring them in and teach them, well, in a year or two you might have something. I scouted in Mexico and Howie Haak scouted in South America.

The Dodgers started with baseball schools where they worked with kids without signing them, just trying to develop them. But when they started calling them academies, they had to sign them to get them in there. And then they had a league down there like a rookie league. And that's the way they did it then. They could sign quite a few good players, not the big standouts, and not put out the big money, and try to develop them into ballplayers. In those countries they don't play much basketball or football. They do play a little soccer, but, as I said, baseball is everything. South of Mexico you'll see a lot of soccer fields, but in the north you'll see a lot of baseball fields.

Astroturf was a new thing in the sixties and though I've never played on it, I have some thoughts about it from a scout's standpoint. I've been on it and it's just odd. As far as the infield is concerned, it's faster and easier to play on because it bounces truer. By that I mean it has more bounce to it and doesn't skip as much unless it's wet. If it's wet, then it'll skid on you. But if you hit a bouncer, then you're going to get a bouncer. Of course, if it's an old rug, then all bets are off. Baseball was meant to be played on grass. The Pirates had it for awhile but finally went to grass. Astroturf increases the temperature on the field by fifteen to twenty degrees and the players get such hot feet. The only place in all of baseball I've ever left the field and gone to the press box during a ballgame was in St. Louis because the heat at field level was so hot I just had to get out of there.

And it does affect the outcome of games and the big picture with stats. For instance, you get an outfielder who's been playing on turf who you think can really run, you might put him on grass in your ballpark and find out you haven't got so much. And you can also reduce his batting average because you can pitch him. But there's no way to pitch him on Astroturf.

The last time I was on it was in Pittsburgh and it was brand new when I was there. It had a fairly thick pad so guys weren't too worried about getting injured while sliding and doing baseball things. But at that time, if the fielder missed a pop fly, the ball would bounce so high a guy could run from first to third before it came down. Teams that went to it usually had good reason. In Pittsburgh there was a weather trough that went through there and they just lost so many games due to the field being wet, so they tried it. Well, the field still got wet, and people still didn't come, but they could play on it. Now I think they have a good drainage system.

Another thing I don't like is that one league has the designated hitter and the other doesn't. The strategies are altogether different. And you have to have more and better pitchers in the National League because you can leave a pitcher in the game longer in the American League. And also, you have to have a DH that's adequate and to do so means you'll add about $5 million to your payroll. Another side to it is that it adds a few years to the careers of the better hitters who don't run or play the game as well as they used to, which is fine.

But in my opinion that's not baseball. All baseball strategy is out the window with the DH. The only reason you change a pitcher in the other league is because he's being hit and he doesn't have any stuff. But in the National League you change pitchers because of baseball strategy. It's how the game is played with pinch-hitters or relief pitchers for the late innings and so forth. The National League will play more lower-scoring games because of the strategy and American League pitchers have higher ERAs.

The wild card is good for business, but I don't see where it's good for baseball. If I had my druthers, I would not have it. I'd have divisions play divisions and eliminate the wild-card team. The wild-card team could be a lousy team, or it could be a good team playing against a better team in the same division and not advance. I just don't like it when second place is playing, well, like when Florida won it. They finished second and yet they made it to the World Series and won it all.

I just don't believe in that. They think doing it this way creates more interest, sells more tickets and yields more TV money, just like football. And you've got three divisions in each league now, and I think they should have four and let the divisions play off. I would like to see 32 teams with four 8-team divisions and no National or American leagues. Have each group of eight be teams that are geographically close so the fans can really get into it and follow their teams to any away game they play in because it won't involve a cross-country trip like it can now. Then the winners of these four divisions would play off and the two that got in it would play off to see which team is the world champions. The rules would be the same for all four divisions. And if you win your division, you're in it.

It's so expensive to get into baseball these days that it's hard to get cities to put up the money to do it. I mean what's the difference to a baseball fan who really doesn't know if a player has great skills or not? You could add another team or two and if the caliber of play at the big level drops off for a couple of years, well, nobody cares. Fans endure it when the organizations go through what they call "rebuilding" and that would be something similar to that.

So if a guy has "San Francisco" or "Podunk" across his chest, he's a big league player and nobody notices if he's not great. The two new expansion teams will get the best players in the world, and if they're not developed quite to big league standards as we know them now, who cares? They'll play good caliber baseball and the hometown fans will love them.

And let me tell you, whether you believe it or not, it's pretty hard to play in the big leagues, whether it's watered down or whatever. You're a highly skilled individual if you can play in the big leagues. They say the pitching is just so-so now and they could be right, but you still have to be pretty damned good to hit them.

To me the thing that's made the greatest impact on the game was TV. I mean, instead of playing well, if he plays for the Cubs without TV, he plays in front of a 33,000 full-house crowd at Wrigley Field. But with TV he plays in front of 125 million people. That's where the money comes from, there's just no question about it. You can only make so much money by having a park that will accommodate, say, 50,000. You could figure out that if this park is full every day, you could figure out their income and how much it would buy. You could make your budget for the year right there. But with television you're playing in front of that many people, well that makes players a draw.

Television made the big difference because it's the reason so much money is generated. TV pays organizations so much a year for everything. You know what they said in Atlanta? They said that the year of the strike, Turner made $77 million off that club. I don't know if it's true or not, but just think about it.

Scouts are a great group of guys. I don't know the young ones as much as I did, and I like everyone I've ever met. The remuneration in this end of the game isn't too great, but it isn't what you make, it's what you do with your money, and I'm not hurting. I don't have to work. I work because I like to. I like being a scout and if I had it to do again, I'd do it. People think we don't work much, but they don't see all that we do. There's always something we can be doing in this job and the good scouts are always out there doing it. I'd definitely do it again.

Jethro "Jeth" McIntyre
(1944–)

McIntyre born and raised in northern California, has devoted the bulk of his life to baseball in one way or another. After playing for McClymonds High School, he was signed out of a San Francisco Giants sponsored tryout camp by Cincinnati Reds scout Loyd Christopher and pitched one rookie league season before developing career-ending arm problems. Following his stint in the military, he worked for the Rainbow Bakery and then General Motors and began a volunteer program teaching baseball to inner city kids, where he provided uniforms and equipment out of his own pocket. The program snowballed and evolved into the Greater East Bay Baseball Development Program, which is still operating today. He's still involved.

His twenty-seven-year scouting career was also unique. He began as a bird dog for Loyd Christopher after returning from the military in 1967. In 1979 he became a part-time scout with the San Diego Padres for one year before working as a full-time scout for the Oakland Athletics from 1980 to 1984 when his contract expired. He spent 1985 as a manager for the San Jose Bees baseball team in California. He was a full-time scout for the Montreal Expos from 1986 to 1990 with a year off in 1987 to manage their rookie team. At the end of the 1990 season, he joined the Major League Scouting Bureau and scouted for them until his "retirement" at the end of the 2007 season.

Jethro McIntyre knows baseball. His colorful stories about his experiences on and off the field, in and out of uniform, and his no-holds-barred approach to expressing his opinions about the current state of the game speak volumes about him.

I was born and raised in Oakland, California. I graduated from high school in 1962. I signed my first pro contract with Loyd Christopher when he scouted with the Cincinnati Reds. I was a left-handed pitcher and they sent me to the Cedar Rapids Red Raiders in the Midwest League, Class A ball. I pitched that year and came up with arm problems and was released.

One of the biggest baseball events in my life happened before I graduated. It was a normal school day at McClymonds High School and I was heading out to practice after my last class, just like I did every other day. But that particular day Jackie Robinson and his wife were visiting the school. Well, I saw the people coming toward me and I said to myself, "Aw, man, I don't wanna be running into these people because they got suits on and I got these raggedy-ass jeans on."

So I'm trying to get out of their way. They're coming up the hallway and I run back upstairs to get up to the second floor to where they just came from so I can get out the back door and go on to practice. Well, something must've caught their attention because they turned around and came back toward where they just left. And here I come flying down the stairs and run right into them. Geez.

So our principal says, "Jethro, come here son, I want to introduce you to somebody. Jethro McIntyre, this is Mr. Jackie Robinson and his wife, Rachel." And I'm standing there. He's got this blue pinstripe suit on; I mean, clean cut and very neat. He extended his hand. As he did that, he said, "They tell me you're a pretty good player. I'm going to have some of the Dodgers people come over and have a look at you. And how are you doing in school?"

"Good, sir." Rachel was just grinning, taking the whole thing in. I even remember what she wore. She had a little stole made of little heads of foxes. Now this was 1962 and I can remember all the details. That's the kind of impression it made on me.

But as I shook Jackie Robinson's hand, well, that was a moment I'll never forget. Never. It was actually stirring to me. Wow. Just thinking about it now makes me feel that excitement and awe all over again all these years later.

So when I went to practice, I didn't even put my glove on. Our coach, George Powles, came over and asked, "Jeth, you okay?"

"Yeah, coach. I'm fine. In fact, I'm doing ten thousand!"

And he says, "Then why aren't you out taking ground balls off the mound?"

And I told him, "Mr. Powles, I had a life changing experience."

And he says, "Oh-oh. What's the problem? Do you wanna talk?"

I says, "Coach, I just shook hands with Jackie Robinson."

He was impressed, well, until I said I wasn't going to put no glove on that hand today. So he smiled and told me to get my running in. I did and went home. Then we're all sitting at the dinner table and my father came in and I got my right hand sitting there with my elbow on the table. And he kept looking at me as if to say, "What in the hell's wrong with this boy?" He called my mother "Poncho." So he looked at her and said, "Poncho, what's wrong with that boy?"

And she told him to ask me. So he leaned over and asked, "What's wrong with you?"

My father was a Jackie Robinson fanatic. And I told him, "See this hand right here? This hand shook Jackie Robinson's hand today."

He jumped up and said, "What? You shook Jack's hand?" And my father was so excited. "Where? Where? Tell me about it."

So coming out of high school the Giants had a tryout camp over at Candlestick, and Dutch Anderson, who was their part-time guy, and Eddie Montague, their full-time scout, were there. Dutch told Eddie, "You got to see this kid at McClymonds because he can hit and he can pitch."

So they invited me to this tryout camp and we got a bunch of guys and went to Candlestick. And the first day I'm sitting there, and there were 500 guys there, I mean they were coming out of the woodwork! So time goes by and finally Dutch came over by me and I said, "Hey, Dutch, am I going to pitch today or what?"

He says, "Sure, Lefty, come with me."

They had a big kid catching named Bob Joyce who was going to USF at the time. He was squat down and was taller than most hitters. He must've been 6'6" at least. A real nice fellow. So I go out and strike out two guys and Dutch said, "Okay, that's enough. Come back tomorrow."

The next day they finished cutting everybody and got down to where they had two teams. They started this big kid from Walnut Creek named Bruce Bellandi, a big kid who threw hard. The first nine guys got base hits, so Dutch walked down there and points to me and says, "You're next, Lefty."

And I'm thinking, "Oh fine. The first nine guys get base hits and I'm next." I get up and start warming up. Now remember Horace Stoneham, Chub Feeney, Carl Hubbell, and the whole front office of the Giants plus the owner is sitting in the stands. So I strike out the three guys.

Hubbell says, "I don't believe that!" I was skinny then, weighed about 145 pounds. He said, "I don't believe that kid has an arm like that! Did you see the breaking ball he threw? Send him back out there, Dutch."

So the next inning I go back out there and strike out two guys and get two strikes on the next guy. I throw him a 0-2 changeup, and I'm walking off the mound because I knew he wasn't going to hit it. And the ump called him out. So I go down the sideline and start running sprints. Well, here comes Mr. Stoneham and Mr. Feeney and Ed Montague and all those guys. Hubbell called, "Hey, son, come here." And I got the standard question. He says, "Have you ever thought about playing professional baseball?"

And I'm saying to myself, "Duh," but to him I say, "Yes, sir. But I really don't have the equipment to play. I borrowed all this stuff from friends, you know."

So one of them said, "Eddie, take this guy down to the Wilson store and let him get whatever he wants and charge it to the San Francisco Giants. You're going to be playing for our rookie club."

My mother's boyfriend takes me over there and they have this baseball room. The first thing I was looking for was travel bags. I grabbed the biggest bag I could find and filled it with shoes in sizes eight, nine, ten and so on to give to guys in the neighborhood. See the guys in the neighborhood had pick-up games all the time. I mean all the time. But we didn't have any decent baseball gear. And I got a second bag with room for a lot of right-hand gloves and left-hand gloves. I got sweatshirts and all sorts of stuff. It amounted to $4,500 worth of equipment! They told me they knew about me and said it was okay. I mean, I just wobbled out there with these two bags!

I pitched that night in Pittsburg, California, at the City Park against a Chevrolet dealership's team. There must've been sixty scouts there for that. I struck out fourteen and we beat them, 7–6. Oh, yeah, and I picked off two runners at first base.

Remember there wasn't a draft at this time. After the game I get a call from Montague and he wanted to sign me. I knew they'd just signed another guy for $150,000. So I'm thinking, hmmmm, I know I'm going to get a piece of change out of this. They offered me like $5,000 and I told them that was insulting. We sat around there and they told me to think about it and said, "Well, don't sign till you hear from us."

That's when Loyd Christopher came into my life. I had every team in both leagues except the Washington Senators looking at me. So then Loyd enters the picture. He phoned and said, "This is Loyd Christopher. Get any offers?"

I said, "Yes, but none to my liking."

He said, "Mind if I come over? I'll be there at three o'clock."

At three o'clock on the money he was knocking on the door. He came right in and sat down and said, "Look, I'm authorized to offer you $7,500 and school and the incentive bonus. I told him I needed to talk with my mother and we went upstairs.

And she told me, "Let me tell you something. Sign the contract. If you don't sign it, I'm going to break your arm." I tried to tell her that if I waited I could probably get more money, but there was no fooling with her. She told me we needed the money and she wanted me to have the chance and if I was good the real money would come in its time.

I signed with Loyd and the Cincinnati Reds at about 4:20 in the afternoon and I was relieved. Then Loyd pulled out a thousand dollar bill from his pocket and he said, "This is from me to you and I'm proud to be the one to sign you because you're going to pitch in the big leagues." There was no strings attached to this.

He left and we were whooping and hollering. I went to G and L Market down the street and bought lots of meat to take home to my mother. In fact, I bought all the meat he had in the store. She smiled and was so proud. I was sent to play in Florida for the Tampa Tarpons, Cincinnati's Class A team, for the 1963 season. I had arm problems early and got released.

Then I got drafted and did my three years in the military. When I came home in 1967, I went to work at the Rainbow bakery until something came up. That's when I started working with kids. I ran into John Carter, who was running the Colonel Young Legion Post baseball program when I was younger. He said it was all shut down for a lack of money and he worried that the kids was getting into trouble with nothing to do.

So I said, "Let's try to save some of them."

"But the Legion Post doesn't have any money," he said.

I told him not to worry about that. I'd handle it. I went down to the bank and got $3,500 out to buy uniforms and so forth and I started calling people I knew in baseball to get bats and balls. I explained what I was going to be doing as a free instructional baseball program for the kids. They were gracious enough to accommodate me. So we got started, and let me tell you, I had some of the best athletes you'd ever want to see. They just didn't know how to play the game. They knew nothing about bunting or other strategic things hitters and fielders got to do. They knew about it but nobody ever taught it to

In addition to his professional baseball duties for the last eighteen years and counting, Jethro McIntyre has organized and operated free baseball clinics for youngsters in the East Bay Area in northern California. He and his staff of former pro ballplayers all work for free. He says the skills he teaches not only build baseball skills, but good character and life skills. The program, now called "Sunday Baseball" because there's a ballgame on Sundays during their "season," was a starting point for such major league players as Dontrelle Willis, Jimmy Rollins, and C.C. Sabathia (Jethro McIntyre collection).

them. I mean, some of them were boys like Roland Office, Jerry Royster, Dion James, Leron Lee, and quite a few more.

So, from 1967 to 1976, I just hung it up and was working with the kids. Well, I kept my day and thought that was how it would be. Loyd called me and asked if I could help him with his area. He was scouting northern California at that time for the Angels, or maybe Cleveland, one of the two clubs. I said, "Sure. When I see kids with some potential I'll call you, no problem." I learned how to scout doing that.

Things were going along fine, and then in 1972 I ran into a real good friend of mine, Jimmy Wynn. He's the guy who signed Rickey Henderson and Claudell Washington, and he was a sergeant on the Berkeley police force and a part-time scout with Oakland. But he retired and just did the scouting. So we're talking about a guy named Tom Pearse, who just got the job at Laney Junior College. He'd been the head baseball coach at Berkeley High. When I was introduced to him, we had a polite conversation; I mean, I didn't know him from a can of paint.

About three weeks later, I said, "Boy, Laney got a baseball team. Think I'll go down there and have a look-see." I go down there and I'm watching these kids play. Worst thing I'd ever seen in my life. I said, "Holy smoke! These kids can't play dead."

So here's a new coach at the junior college level and he's pulling his hair out. He saw me in the stands and after the game he came to me and said, "I know you know baseball and if you could help me out with these kids, I'll pay you." I told him he didn't need to pay me because I was working for General Motors. "I can't be here only when you start out because I got to be at work at 4:30."

So me and Tom start a relationship there and it all worked out great. I became part of his family. But the baseball team wasn't accomplishing a thing. I mean nothing.

I told him, "If we teach them and start winning, the kids will come because Laney will have a winning team." And it worked. Most of my kids from the Colonel Young Legion Post were coming to Laney and they knew my teaching and my way of playing the game.

In 1979, I had started doing part-time major league scouting with San Diego. And there was a meeting and the first words that come out of their mouths was that I can't be coaching any more because I'm a major league scout. It's a compromising position because we can't have professionals messing with amateurs. So that was it for my coaching the kids, at least for a short time. I only stayed with the Padres that one year. Then Oakland came into the picture with Dick Wiencek and Billy Martin and those guys. That's when the Haas family had bought the club and Dick asked me to come to work for Oakland. And I was there scouting for about four or five years in the early eighties, as a full-time scout from 1980 until my contract expired after the 1984 season. When Karl Kuehl first came to Oakland, I had the A's rookie team at the Peninsula League and we won that league. I had the kids working out and we were running bases and taking fungos and sliding and doing everything you can imagine these young kids had to work on. It was the summer of '84 and he told the kids they were lucky to have me working with them. And in August after the season ended, I got fired. I got fired!

So the winter of 1984 going into 1985, I didn't have a job. But in January I got a call from Harry Staveros. We all call him Harry Steve. He asked. "Whatcha doing? Not much? Why don'tcha take a little drive down to San Jose?"

And I said, "I don't know. Will it be worth my while?"

He said, "I think so." So not knowing what was going to happen, I walked into his office and all the press was there and he said, "I want to introduce you to the 1985 manager of the San Jose Bees."

And I said, "Calm down, Trigger. We got to talk. Let's talk money. How much you paying me?"

He said, "I can't pay you a lot, Jeth, but I'll take care of you." I was the lowest paid guy in that league. He paid me ten grand for the season. But he took care of me in other ways, and I thank him to this day for giving me that opportunity where organizations never gave me that opportunity. That year in San Jose was probably my favorite year in pro baseball. The GM was Harry Staveros. It was a Giants team in the Cal League. I was runner-up for manager of the year. That was my favorite year in my entire baseball career.

I moved to the Montreal Expos as a full-time scout in 1986 and stayed there until 1990. In 1987, I was back in managing because they asked me to take their rookie team. Finally, after the 1990 season I joined the Major League Scouting Bureau and stayed there until I retired in 2007. Will I go back? Who knows?

Things are so different now. The corporate owners today think that anybody can scout. They really believe that and it's evidenced by the guys they hire. They hire guys that they're comfortable with, but they don't know the game. They may know business, but they're not what we in the game call baseball men. The baseball guys like me and scouts we both know are willing to teach them what we know and pass along things we think'll help them. But they aren't interested. Their jobs are safe. They're unbelievable.

And some of the things they say! We were watching a game and some Atlanta scouts and others were there. This big kid was hitting the ball all over the field with power. And these guys were watching him swing and the guy made the mistake of asking me, "Mr. McIntyre, what do you think of that?"

And I said, "Well, before we get into this conversation, let me ask you just one question. Where did you play at?"

He said, "Well, I didn't play."

So I said, "Well, see, that's just it. Whatever I say, you won't understand it, and that's why I try not to get into those conversations. And even if you did, you wouldn't believe me anyway because what I say may disagree with what you're reading out of that book you're carrying."

It's the same when we attend the meetings we have. A young guy will get up and say, "Yeah, this guy has a good arm but his fastball is a foot short."

I said, "Excuse me, but what the hell is a fastball that's a foot short? What exactly does that mean? I pitched when I played, okay? What do you mean, the ball bounced before it reached the plate? What?"

He said, "Well, it doesn't have enough to challenge the guy to get him out."

And I said, "Oh really. Well, why don't you just say that." But he was just saying it that way because he thought it was a baseball term and he wanted to make us feel that he knew more than he did.

So I said, "Oh, and by the way, have you ever seen a ninety-mile-an-hour fastball with a bat in your hand as the pitcher pitches it to you? If you were ever standing in the box, let me tell you, it's an experience you'll never forget. Trust me. Or if you see a guy who throws a twelve-to-six breaking ball that falls off the table, that's another experience you will never forget. Those things are baseball experience my friend."

I told them all at that meeting, "If you want to listen to this guy who hasn't played, hasn't even taken a pitch, and you're going to listen to his opinion over a fella like me who played the game and also happened to be a pitcher, well, what's wrong here?" The pitcher he was talking about happened to be Roger Clemens.

These things happen more than fans want to know and we as baseball people don't want to see the industry going in that direction. There's no more time to work with kids and develop them. Ironically, there's more coaches in the minor leagues now but less who know about the game and are capable of realistic development. A lot of this is due to free agency.

In my day when a kid went to the big leagues, there was always a sense of pride, a sense of "we did it, we worked with him and helped him over the hump to his big league career." But these guys today do absolutely nothing. Absolutely nothing.

In today's game it's all about free agency and the money. Development isn't thought of like it used to be. You can go from ballclub to ballclub and see how many kids have come out of your system that you and your own group of people have helped develop. Not many clubs can say that.

Free agency almost killed the minor leagues. Why should they invest lots of money in a high school kid or junior college kid when they can say, "Ho hum, Spike Owens is available. So he costs four-point-five million, oh well," and it's a done deal? And you have a kid in Triple-A or Double-A that had a great year and he's looking to elevate himself to the next level and he just gets stagnated. And now they got a kid that's unhappy because they hired a free agent and gave him all this money and didn't recognize this kid's ability or give him the opportunity to play to see if he could cut it up there. Because of things like that, you got a lot of kids just walking away from baseball now where thirty or forty years ago kids were hungry to play.

And here's an example of what I'm talking about when I say development. When I was managing the San Jose Bees in 1985, there was a kid optioned to me named Gary Jones, a catcher. I called him "Sugar Britches." We worked with him in the preseason and I started him opening night. Our team was on the field. "Watch," I said to one of the coaches, "he's going to look over here where I usually stand wanting me to give the signals." But I didn't do it and he didn't get it, well, not at first. But we were all laughing because he was doing just what I had taught him. He didn't need me telling him what to do for most of the game, just in a couple of key situations where I taught him to check with the manager.

At one point in the game I said, "Now watch, he's going to call a time out because he wants me to call the pitch." Time was called and he came to the dugout and said, "Skip, are you telling me that I'm on my own out there and you're not going to call this game?"

I said, "Son, you know what to do and when to do it and tonight's your chance to show all of us. You put it down and if he don't want it, give him another one until he tells you what he wants. Then give him what he wants. You'll learn what pitches to call on what counts when you have to think it through yourself. I have confidence that you'll do just fine, so get back to the plate and do it." That's just development, and he did fine.

Today in baseball they would say, "Oh no, he can't do that. He's getting too close to his players." Word would get back to me that they were saying that Jethro's getting too close to his players. But it helps them learn and gain self-confidence in their ability.

And it makes those kids better for the organization because he then plays his heart out for you because you took the time to listen to him and show him respect.

Then in 1987 Montreal gave me an opportunity to manage their minor league club in the Gulf Coast League. Like I say, I was where I wanted to be, on the field working with kids and all. The next thing I know, the following season David Dombrowski's calling me and telling me that they'd let me go back to scouting because they had other people in mind to manage. David Dombrowski's one of the smartest men in the game and he's very nice, too. I was willing to remain a full-time scout if that's what he wanted me to do.

Jethro McIntyre was a full-time scout with the Montreal Expos, 1986–1990, when they asked him to take a year off in 1987 to manage their rookie league team in the short-season Gulf Coast League. This old Florida-based league gives organizations an opportunity to work more intensely with its newest and youngest players to give them a better foundation for their pro careers. McIntyre led his young charges to fourth place in their division against the Dodgers, Pirates, Yankees, and Braves (Jethro McIntyre collection).

Here's something about scouting. Basically it's a crapshoot, and I'll explain what I mean. When scouts look at a high school player, they want us to evaluate the kid at major league standards, and that's unfair to that kid. And it's especially unfair to the scout if he never played. The scouts have to think about all the levels of baseball between that kid and the big leagues, all the minor leagues and the things they learn and how the game speeds up as they get smarter and stronger and quicker with their skills. Scouts have to project what these kids can do, and I have to see if he can play in the big leagues. I'm not looking at a kid's batting average at that level. I don't care if he went 0-for-5 or 0-for-15, I'm looking at his mechanical ability at hitting.

I remember scouting Xavier Nady at Cal Berkeley. So when I'm scouting, I call him over. I say, "Hey, Clifford," because I call all of the unsigned kids Clifford. And I say to him, "I'm not looking at your stats here. I don't care if you go 0-for-ever. But I'm telling you, you have the basics in your mechanics to be able to hit big league pitching some day. You have a chance to play in the big leagues, but you have to listen to the professional teachers, the coaches, and learn to improve yourself with their guidance."

When I think of all the kids in my area, like Dontrelle Willis and Tyler Walker and Conor Jackson, C.C. Sabathia, and I can go on and on about kids like this from my area that I have reports on and just about to the word it came to. My report on Dontrelle was "must get out of present environment in order to improve." But I wasn't going to draft him as a pitcher. I was going to draft Dontrelle as a first baseman, because if he didn't hit, then you got a fresh arm for the mound. Same thing with C.C. Sabathia. And look what they're doing today.

I recall one time we played in a major-minor game and Billy Martin was managing the team. The guys in the area that played in the major leagues turned out to play in the game in Washington Park in Alameda to raise money for the March of Dimes. You could come to that particular game and see stars. Willie Stargell in right field, Willie Mays in center, Tommy Harper, Aaron Pointer, Vada Pinson. I mean the Bay Area was loaded with major league guys at that time and the people were hanging off the roof the place was so packed. We made lots of money for the March of Dimes.

So this one particular day, Billy Martin said Ernie Broglio would pitch the first eight and I was going to pitch the ninth. I said it was fine with me. My coach and Bill Wight — he was a pitcher and that day he was a scout with Houston — were sitting together in the stands. Broglio pitched the eighth and I go mop up in the ninth. The first guy up to the plate was Joe Morgan. So my high school coach told Wight, "Watch this. Mac's going to walk him."

With Joe you got to understand that he had to be smart to become the player that he became. I mean that, as far as second basemen are concerned, there's usually a lot of players in that position. Lots of competition.

Scouting jobs are meant for guys who played the game, guys who know how to play the game, and know what it takes to be in the game. Baseball needs guys who are connected with baseball and understand what it takes so they can see the kids in that kind of light because we are supposed to predict their potential down the road and all that.

Today the baseball hierarchy does not give the scouts proper respect that's due them, especially the Players' Union. They won't incorporate scouts in their pension program. Think about the message that gives. And they treat scouts as if anybody can do this particular job. They don't recognize our expertise or professionalism or our contributions to baseball.

Let's face it. If there were no scouts, they'd have no Players' Union because they'd never have the major leagues because they'd never have the quality players that scouts bring into this game. I say that not to be downing the hierarchy, but to mention that the treatment of scouts should be a whole lot better for the benefits and the recognition for their involvement. And nobody knows that kid and his family or sees that kid more than the area scouts do. The area scout who goes out beating the bushes to find that particular kid is the one who knows him best in the game.

Remember how Walt Jocketty thanked the scouts when he received the world championship trophy? He thanked scouts for finding the kids and so on. The next day, they fired five scouts! Why? Because they thought they were saving money. BS like that happens all the time.

Even though scouts don't seek recognition, we just want to be treated fairly and appreciated. Scouting is the only part of baseball where they don't have a union and the reason for that is they tried to start one and the clubs started firing them. They don't have four-year degrees, and a lot of them don't have skills to do other things. Put that together with no union, no pension, and really no job security except at someone's whim, well, it's not good. But we still do it because it's what we do.

I hope and pray that the hierarchy of baseball will come to understand and start giving more humane treatment to the scouts and to their plight in life even after they retire from baseball.

When I started with Montreal in '86, the baseball pension for players was $47,000 a year and they could draw it at age forty-five! Now it's way more than that and goes up every year. We as scouts have a non-uniformed contract that we signed and our employers pay into a pension fund for us but it's just not enough, not nearly enough. I mean the paperboy could cash the check. Without Social Security, which is also another pittance, if you don't go back to work, it's a hard go. There's no getting around that.

Baseball's a great game, but the people that's running it, that's where you come into problems. It's a thing where we who are baseball men love this game and we would play for nothing, okay? When I was a kid, I didn't realize these guys were getting paid. Vada Pinson, a kid from the neighborhood so to speak, came home after his first year in the big leagues. Well, he didn't even have a car in the family and Vada has a brand new 1959 Thunderbird. I was living in the projects and he drives up there, offers to take me for a drive in his new car that baseball bought for him. Imagine that.

I am humbly asking for Major League Baseball to take a better look at the situation and take better care of the scouts.

Ellis Clary

(1916–2000)

Clary said professional baseball was always his calling. He was born in the little town of Valdosta, Georgia, and lived there all his life. He was a country boy through and through who enjoyed that label and the pleasures of the lifestyle. He was popular among his peers for his honesty, frankness, knowledge of the game, and his sense of humor. He spent fifty-nine years in the game.

Records of his minor league playing days are sketchy. We know the infielder played in 1934 in the Washington Senators farm system with the Chattanooga Lookouts in the Southern Association. During the Depression, when minor league baseball floundered due to a lack of funds, the Lookouts, now considered one of baseball's historic teams, hung on, had good fan support, and won the pennant. He remained in the minors and was finally called up to the major league Washington Senators in 1942.

He spent the following four seasons in the American League. On August 18, 1943, he was traded to the St. Louis Browns with Ox Miller and cash for Harlond Clift and Johnny Niggeling. He played with St. Louis through the end of the 1945 season when his major league playing days ended. He compiled a career batting average of .263 in two hundred twenty-three games. He then returned to the minor leagues as a player and manager for the Charlotte Hornets and proceeded to serve as a major league coach and long-time professional scout for the Senators/Twins, White Sox, and Blue Jays.

Talking baseball with Ellis Clary was a unique experience. I feel privileged that he agreed to do the interview. He apologized for having health problems that made him weak and tired, and then said he didn't do interviews any more. Yet he was obviously energized as he told stories about his baseball adventures. He had a bag of personal anecdotes for all occasions, and when he began talking he was like a runaway train. What a ride!

He died a few months after the interview below. In one obituary, columnist Richard Goldstein [New York Times, June 6, 2000] described him as "...an archetype of the baseball lifer who wisecracked his way through more than a half a century in the game as a player, manager, coach, and one of its best known scouts."

Ellis would have liked that. He poked fun at himself and situations around him. He loved the game. And he expressed tremendous pride about being part of the world of professional baseball. But he didn't brag about his accomplishments. In fact, he never mentioned that he was inducted into the Valdosta-Lowndes County Sports Hall of Fame, the Georgia Sports Hall of Fame, and the Charlotte, North Carolina, Sports Hall of Fame.

Boy, I got to say first thing that when I started scouting things were sure different. Today everybody's looking for a nineteen-year-old boy with twenty years experience.

You get into scouting accidentally. Before that I played baseball all my life. Let's see now, I played in St. Louis, Washington, Baltimore, Boston, Toledo, Atlanta, Chattanooga, Charlotte, and everywhere. I'm telling you, I played everywhere! I was about 18 when I started. I was playing semipro ball and the scout came through and scared everybody to death.

At that time there wasn't but three or four scouts. The Yankees had a couple, the Red Sox had one, and that was about it. There was only three or four that were known throughout the country. This was back in 1934. Let's see, I think a few minor league teams had scouts, or at least people who saw players and turned in their names hoping to get some money if they were signed. Back then you didn't have to draft them. It was more fun. You'd just go find somebody and make a player out of him.

As I said, I played all my life. Then they made me a coach in Washington. And then they made me a manager, a minor league manager. And then after all that is over and you get too old to do anything else, they make a scout out of you. They think that you've got the knowledge to go out and find ballplayers. I stayed in baseball fifty-nine years. And I wish I could do it again. It was a lot of fun. Oh, yeah. I tried to make it all fun. And, of course, when you play, it ain't no fun to get beat!

The only trouble with baseball is somebody's got to get beat every time. It's the manager's fault when you get beat, not the coach's fault. The manager gets all the heat. I was a big league coach for many years with the Washington Senators, which is now the Minnesota Twins. I worked for 40 years for the Minnesota Twins as a player, manager, coach and scout.

Here's how I became a scout. One day they told me, "Ellis, you can't play anymore. And you don't want to manage anymore. And coaching, well, to be a big league coach is like having a license to steal. So I guess that leaves nothing for you to do but scouting." And that's when somebody decided I should be a scout. I don't know, maybe it was me.

As a scout I didn't sign any players with big names, but when I was a coach I started a bunch of them off. I started Harmon Killebrew off. I started Rod Carew off. I started Tony Oliva off. By starting them off, I mean I managed or coached them when they were coming up. I wish I could've started Kirby Puckett off, but I had already been there 40 years when he got there and they thought I was too old.

Now here's the way it is in scouting. It's no scientific thing. It's just a matter of people who know how to play the game looking at others who want to play the game and deciding whether or not they're good enough. It all comes down to one man's opinion.

When I got to the big leagues you had guys like Joe DiMaggio and Ted Williams and there were no black guys around. You had great players then, probably much greater than you have today. But it's all just somebody's opinion. Just like a writer wanted me to pick an all-star team from my time. I mean, I've seen everything that's happened up there since 1941.

Well, I picked, in the outfield, Ted Williams, Joe DiMaggio, and Willie Mays. First I picked Brooks Robinson then went back and picked Mike Schmidt at third base. Luis Aparicio was the best shortstop I ever saw. 'Course we got five of them up there in the American League today. What I'm saying is that nobody can say one way or the other whether the game of baseball itself got better with black players or not because it's all one man's opinion. So what's that matter? So what I'm telling you is my opinion, and it's as good as anyone else's. Right?

Anyway, after I got through picking the best all-time team, the best players I ever saw from 1941 up until today, let's see, I put Roberto Alomar at second base, and I put Biggs (Craig Biggio) catching. A friend of mine said, "What about Frank Robinson and Stan Musial and Hank Aaron and them guys?"

I said, "Well, they're on the second team."

And he says to me, "The second team might beat your first team." Well, that's it. It all boils down to one man's opinion.

I hit a snag at first base. I got there after Lou Gehrig was gone. I got there after Bill Terry was gone. So I wind up with Willie McCovey playing first base. And, of course, the best first baseman defensively might have been Keith Hernandez of the Mets, but that's one man's opinion, too. You can't prove anything. I don't live in the past. I think Greg Maddux of the Braves is as good a pitcher as ever lived. And someone will say, "Well, who's better than Sandy Koufax?"

And I'd say, "Steve Carlton." And who's better than Warren Spahn? There ain't no better! And that's my opinion. My opinion is as good as anybody's because I seen it all. But my opinion ain't worth a damn because I ain't writing in the paper. Frank Robinson might have been the best hitter that ever lived. But you can only put nine on the team. And Bob Lemon, a good friend of mine, was as good a pitcher as I ever saw. And Early Wynn, I roomed with him and was on three teams with him.

And what about those great Yankee teams back then? Yogi Berra and Bill Dickey, why, both those guys were as good as anybody. You know that great four-man pitching rotation they had in Cleveland in my time? There was Feller, Wynn, Lemon, and Garcia. Now Feller is the only one left.

So those are my opinions and I'm sure every person they asked gave him a different one. So what?

Speaking of Early Wynn, I was in Sanford, Florida, in the Florida State League when Early Wynn walked through the fence. Wait, he walked through the gate, not through the fence. He was seventeen years old. Barefooted. His feet were dirty. He wore some old blue jeans and a t-shirt and one of them old Coca-Cola caps they used to give out. How about that? He walked into left field for a workout and ended up in the Baseball Hall of Fame. I just happened to be standing there looking in that direction when he walked in that gate. There was a big cloud over his head and somebody shouted, "Look what the storm has blown in." So he went from walking barefoot in that black sand they have down there to the Hall of Fame. A walk-on. That wouldn't happen today.

He was really hot to trot. He lived in Hartford, Alabama, a little bitty old town of about 200 people. He had hitchhiked down to Sanford to try out because his aunt lived in Sanford and he could stay with her while he tried out.

You know what? Scouting is no fun anymore since that draft thing started. Back then, before the draft, you just went out there and tried to isolate some player out there that nobody knew anything about. We didn't tell anybody about him.

But now that kid is known by everybody from coast to coast. You got this guy who lives eight miles from here that got ten million dollars to sign with the Cardinals a few years ago. They had all that mess going on about him when the Phillies tried to draft him. J.D. Drew's his name. He was at Florida State. And they give up ten million dollars for a two-fifty hitter. Whew. Of course, they didn't know that when they signed him.

The fun's gone out of it today. Everybody on earth knows everything about every kid out there. You cannot isolate one anywhere. They're all well known. There's no secrets anymore. But back then before the draft came up, well, I don't care how small the towns are, you could go to a place in Louisiana or Arkansas, somewhere in a town that only has a hundred people. If there's a player there, they all know about him.

Reminds me of the time we were in Coldwater, Mississippi, around forty years ago. They had a player, a big strong looking white kid that could play. Anyway, this kid come up three times and he didn't get a hit. Pat Gillick had to go to the bathroom and he can't wait any longer. He's got to go! It's a hundred yards back to the high school where he can go to the men's room. And he had to jump up and go. While he was in there, this kid came up and hit a home run over a house in right field. It was at least a five hundred-foot home run! Gillick had come hundreds of miles to see this kid play and he missed that home run because he was in the men's room. Pat Gillick was my boss when he was with the Blue Jays, and that tickled me to death.

Another story. I went to sign a kid one time way out in the country. It was real hot and we were sitting on the porch with me and his mother and father and little brother. And the hogs were all out in the front of the house rooting the front yard. You could hear them grunting. And I asked this boy, I says, "You ready to go play ball?"

And he says, "Hell, yeah, I'm ready! I wanna get away from these stinking hogs!"

I said, "Lookie here. In a few years them hogs are going to start smelling like perfume."

And sure enough, he couldn't play good enough to get to the big leagues, so he went back and inherited them hogs again. I'm sure they started smelling a whole lot better when he needed them.

I remember the time we went to see Johnnie LeMaster play. You know, he couldn't hit but he was a great fielder. He's out of Paintsville, Kentucky. Did you know you can hardly get to Paintsville, Kentucky? You have to fly in over there to, well, I can't think of the name of that place. Let's see, Huntsville, that's it. Then you have to get one of them rental cars, then you have to get a boat and go across on a ferry and then you have to get a pack mule to get to Paintsville, Kentucky. And when I got there, there were 20 scouts there from all over!

We all met there the same day accidentally. Nobody knew anybody else was going to be there. I remember Eddie Lopat was there. He and Al LaMacchia rode with me. And let's see now, I'm trying to think of that left-handed hitter who was with Baltimore and the Yankees. We all gathered at this little park and went in through this gate out there in left field. We was all watching the LeMaster kid. He didn't get a hit that day but he sure could field. In those days a shortstop wasn't expected to hit. But he had great range, a great arm, great hands. He was just a heck of a shortstop. And everybody liked him.

Anyway, he didn't get a hit in three at-bats in the game, and he's going to be the fourth hitter in the ninth inning. And we wanted to see him again but knew somebody had to get on for him to bat. So we figured the pitcher would get the first three outs and we wouldn't get to see him again and we all started walking toward that gate in left field. We were by third base and the second guy up hit a double. And we said, "Oh man, we're going to get to see him again."

So this guy's on second base and there's one out. Dang, he's going to bat! There's one hitter ahead of him, and then we'll get to see him bat. None of the scouts moved. We just waited. The third guy up hit the ball to right field and the fielder caught it easy. Now we're ready to see LeMaster hit. But the guy at second tagged up on the fly and the right fielder threw him out at third base. Game over! All the scouts was cussing and raising heck. "Aw, let's get the hell out of here!" And that was very unusual. He ended up being the number one pick of the Giants after that. I covered the big leagues for twenty years and got to see him play a lot up there. He was quite a fielder.

Here's one to tell your grandyoungins that I told you about. Now, I don't know if anybody ever talked about how it was when Jackie Robinson first played with the Dodgers. But my remembrance is sort of like this. When I went to Cuba to play in the winter of 1941, I didn't even know that black guys was playing down there. And it was a very unusual feeling for me to walk into the clubhouse with all those black guys. I had never been on a team with them before. So I got an idea about it in 1941 when I went down there to play winter ball. But it was no different.

I remember when Jackie Robinson came in and it was no big deal. Well, he was always in the National League and I was in the American League and we just didn't pay much attention to it. It was no big rumor. There was no big furor like you read in the paper today. There just wasn't nothing to it. But with all you read about all this stuff, you'd think there was a revolution going on, shooting at people or trying to kill somebody or something. It wasn't no different than before he got there. But he broke the color line. Or Branch Rickey did with him. And the rest is history.

The only abuse he took was from Ben Chapman, the manager of the Philadelphia Phillies. He gave him a going over every time he walked up to the plate to bat. But other than that, there wasn't a whole lot to it. It was no big thing, at least not as far as I was concerned.

When I was managing the Charlotte, North Carolina, baseball club, the black players couldn't eat where white guys could, and they didn't stay at the same hotels as the rest of the team. Sometimes they slept on the bus or stayed with black families in the area, and things like that. That was in effect when I managed down there. When we went to Jacksonville to play, they had to stay at a different place. But it wasn't that big a deal. Wasn't nobody making a big thing out of it. They just accepted it and went and stayed where they were supposed to and ate where they were supposed to. And the bus would stop on the road, you know, for gasoline or to get something to eat, and the white fellas would go inside and get the food and bring it out there to them and they'd have it right there on the bus. They never made a big deal out of it. It was just something that happened. There was nothing unusual about it. If you'd been standing across the street, you wouldn't have paid any attention to it. You wouldn't have even noticed it. That's just the way things were back then. I'm glad that's all changed now.

I had a heart attack in 1970 and stayed in the hospital for six weeks. And I'm in Seattle one day covering the major leagues. I'm there with Jim Davenport, who used to play third base and then became a scout for the Giants, and another scout, Gordon Lakey, who had been with the Blue Jays for years. Anyway, we all got into that cab to go to the ballpark. It was thirteen years to the day since I had the heart attack, so while we're in that cab I says, "Boys, I'm thirteen years old today. I died thirteen years ago today."

Well, we laughed a little bit. Then about the third inning of the game, somebody poked me in the ribs and said, "Look at the scoreboard out there." And the scoreboard, the thing's at least as big as a house, said, "Happy thirteenth birthday to Ellis Clary." I laughed and said, "Now how in the hell do they know that?" One of these guys had told them and I didn't know it.

Seattle was playing the Angels that night and the next day Bobby Starr, the Angels' announcer, said, "Will you be on my pregame show?"

Well, I knew you get gifts for doing it, a wristwatch and a radio, so I said, "Yeah."

So we got on that pregame show, now this is when Reggie Jackson was playing with the Angels, and he said, "You know, Ellis, you had your name on that scoreboard last night bigger than Reggie Jackson."

And I said, "Well, hell, I'm having a better year than Reggie Jackson!"

My bossman was in Los Angeles and heard the show. He called me and said, "That's the biggest bunch of hogwash in the world, all that stuff you was giving to Bobby Starr on the radio yesterday." We just laughed about it. I told him that as long as they give those free gifts for it, I'll do all them shows. We laughed. But I did a lot of them after that.

Well, they always mail the gift to you. So they sent it to my house. And the next time I saw Bobby, I said, "Thank you for that great gift you sent me. I appreciate it." He sent me a man's hair dryer. And my hair was scarce even then! I gave it to my grandyoungin' and he really appreciated it. I told him I really wanted the radio and watch and he laughed and said, "It's on the way. We sent you the dryer just for a laugh." He got me on that one.

Another one. Joe Garagiola was a good friend of mine. We shot the bull a lot. We was in Tucson one year in spring training and Garagiola had a pocket recorder. I was telling him a bunch of crap and he was recording all of it. Somebody said to him, "What do you want to give him all those good stories for? Why don't you save that for your book?"

And I said, "I don't have no book."

Anyway, I'm in Denver and I'm in the hotel and got my little pocket radio sitting on the desk there and I got it on but I ain't paying no attention to it. I'm writing a letter. All of a sudden I said, "Wait a minute. That's me on there." And there I am listening to that tape I gave to Joe Garagiola at Tucson. I said, "Now ain't that a hell of a note. I'm listening to myself on the radio. On this little pocket radio and I don't even know what station it is." He was always playing pranks on me. We laughed together a lot.

Ellis Clary began his major league career with the Washington Senators in 1942 when he was twenty-five years old. During the 1943 season he was traded to the St. Louis Browns with Ox Miller and cash for Harlond Clift and Johnny Niggeling. He was on the Browns team that played the St. Louis Cardinals in the 1944 World Series. His loyalty to and admiration for Calvin Griffith remained the rest of his life (Ellen Clary, daughter — Ellis Clary collection).

I had to go just recently to deliver one of the eulogies for Calvin Griffith's funeral. He was the owner of the Senators when they moved to Minnesota. He was the owner of the Minnesota Twins. I had played for him when he was managing Charlotte, North Carolina, and I had known him for years. He was not much older than me. He died down in Florida. His boy, Clark, who is a lawyer in Minneapolis, called me and wanted me to come to the funeral and deliver a eulogy there. I was glad to do it and I went up there and we tried to make it fun and tell a few stories on him.

I said I'd give a eulogy before I remembered that I didn't know nothing about eulogies! So I called a friend of mine, a preacher in Macon, Georgia. I said, "Rev, I got to deliver a eulogy at eleven o'clock. So what do you do?"

He said, "Never you mind what I do. But whatever you do, don't make it too long. And whatever you do, don't make it too flowery. Because if you do, somebody from the audience may want to come up there and peek in the box to see if you ain't burying the wrong guy."

There were fifty or more baseball people there. Paul Beeston was one of them. When I was with the Toronto Blue Jays, he was president of that organization and now he works in the commissioner's office in New York City. He's a Canadian. A great guy. Anyway, I went up there and we had a very fine memorial for him.

Calvin Griffith was an interesting guy. Just before he died, he had written me a card from Seattle. He told me in the card that he had been to the ballgame in Seattle and some friends of mine asked him to say hello to me, but he couldn't remember who it was. So I called him and said, "Well, who in the hell was it?"

He said, "Well, I've forgotten who it was, but they said to tell you hello."

"Well thank you very much. That really helps me out," I told him.

Did I tell you my remembrances about the Scouting Bureau? Well, it also changed everything for us scouts in a way. Most of the clubs got in on it, and some didn't want nothing to do with it. But we got in on it and scouting became altogether different. You shared your reports on everybody. You sent in your reports on a guy you would've had hid out and the next day everybody knew about him. You get the player to fill out a card like before, but now if he fills out a card for one guy, then everybody winds up with that information. They want his age, birthday, height, address, phone number, family, and everything. And they wouldn't believe that if you give that information to one guy, everybody would have it.

I like the guys in the scouting bureau. They're fine fellas and love the game just like I do. But they have a different job than I do. They find players who maybe can play the game, and they put numbers on them kids that's much more than they really are. The numbers are just ridiculous, and I don't even pay attention to them.

I know when I first started scouting with the Twins, Atlee Donald for the Yankees had been scouting for years, and Spud Chandler for Cleveland had been out there for years, and Paul Florence had been scouting for years. We formed our own what you'd call "underground scouting combine." You were not supposed to do that, you know. You were supposed to keep your information for your club only. But we had a four-man underground scouting combine. Paul was the only National League guy, but that didn't make any difference. The main thing was it saved us a lot of mileage because you might ask them, "Have you seen that guy out in Montgomery?"

And they might say, "Don't waste your time. Don't go because he can't play." But if he could play, they wouldn't give their scouting rundown on the guy, but they'd say, "You'd better go see him." And that's how we did it. That saved us all a lot of trips.

Well, you know, them high school and college coaches don't know a player when they see one. They don't. Their best player is their sister's boy or their neighbor or something like that. So you get there to see the kid and he weighs a hundred ten pounds. So you learn fast to depend on your own judgment. Can he play? Or can he not play? It all boils down to that.

When I was with the Twins we got Rod Carew for five thousand dollars. Well, he's a Panamanian who was living in New York City. Our scout up there, Herb Stein, said Carew was glad to get it. Back then a guy could buy some things with five thousand dollars.

Tony Oliva was one of the best hitters who ever played baseball. When I was managing Charlotte, they got him out of Cuba the day before Castro took over. One day later they couldn't have got him out. When he came out he wasn't ready to play in nothing but the rookie league, and they had to put him somewhere. He was about seventeen, or maybe sixteen. Anyway, they had to put him somewhere until the rookie league started, which wasn't until June the first, a whole month away. So they sent him to me in Charlotte. Well, he couldn't play in that league because he was just a boy, but he had to stay somewhere so he stayed with me for a month. He was with me in Charlotte. I let him take batting practice and work out every day. He damned near froze to death. It was cold that spring and his coat hit halfway between the elbow and the hand and his pants were about a foot too short because he'd outgrown his clothes. Back then down in Cuba, they didn't have anything.

Anyway, we got all the Cuban players. Joe Cambria was our scout. He got them all for nothing. He finally says, "Well, Camilo Pascual cost me a five-dollar phone call. But I got the rest of them for nothing. Like Pedro Ramos."

Cambria got all those kind of guys and hundred of others you didn't hear about for nothing. He'd send a boatload of them over here and there might be one of them in there that could play good enough. Joe Cambria was from Baltimore but he moved to Havana and lived down there where he could get them all. And the whole Washington ballclub was filthy with Cuban ballplayers. Hundreds of them you never heard of, but they were good enough to play in the minor leagues.

Another story. I don't collect a lot of baseball stuff except things I get accidentally. Anyway, I wanted to get a ball for my grandyoungin' and I was in Milwaukee. And this is when Hank Aaron was with them. I gave the ball to the manager and said, "Take that ball in there and get Hank Aaron on it, and I'm going to mail it."

I just thought of one more. I asked Stan Musial one day at one of them old-timers games right after they put that Astroturf stuff in the ballpark at St. Louis. They started out with that turf, you know, but have since changed it to grass. We were sitting there on the bench, and something happened, and I said, "Stan, how much do you reckon you would have hit with this Astroturf?" You know, he's like a little boy. He's so afraid he'll say something that sounds like he's bragging.

He just shook his head and said, "Oh, I don't know, I don't know." He wouldn't say nothing about nothing because he was afraid it would sound bad, maybe. By the way, he's a great guy. A great guy.

Every year we have a St. Louis Browns get together in St. Louis and every year I get my picture made with him. I'm going to one in Washington and another in Atlanta. We have most of them in February before the spring training starts. I stay pretty busy going to reunions.

Anyway, scouting is a great career and most fans don't know nothing about us or what we do. Let me tell you, we put our jobs on the line every time we sign a guy. Either they make you look good or make you look bad. And we sign millions of players who can't get out of D league. But who knows? You can't look around a corner. You take a kid with a lot of determination and if he's got some ability, he'll get there. When that lazy guy that don't want to apply himself, he ain't going to get anywhere. You got to love this stuff because it's a game of coming back. You come back every day. Somebody gets beat every day. And if they get you out twice and you get a hit, you're a great hitter.

I got a young grandyoungin' that I go to all his games. They can't play but they have a lot of fun. And during his season, when they get started playing, I'm hauling him somewhere for a game once a week. There's a town here 59 miles away, and I made five trips there last year because they had a tournament there. And another one is thirty miles and I took him there five times. And there's about six towns around here and I have to take him somewhere to play. He has a lot of fun. He's a catcher. I was there one day when he had 47 passed balls. Somebody said," That must be a record."

I said, "No, he had 49 the day before!"

Another thing I remember is when I was scouting Ted Williams during his heyday at Fenway. I was there as a player when he started. Then when I came back as a coach, he was still there. I was talking to a guy yesterday about all them years he spent in the war in the Air Corps during his heyday. Why, he would've had records that would never be approached if he could have played for those years. He's the best hitter that ever played the game and everybody that played against him knows that. It's a shame. One of the things he did for this country was to land one of them multimillion dollar planes on fire and saved it when anybody else would've bailed out. It's a shame. He might of hit 800 home runs for all we know!

I remember when the Dodgers and Giants moved to California. I was a coach then with the Senators. We were all keeping an eye on it. Charlie Dressen was there as a manager. During the season before the Dodgers ever went out there, Charlie Dressen got a leave of absence from Mr. Griffith and flew to California for the purpose of moving the Washington Senators to Los Angeles. He tried to arrange it before the Dodgers ever went out there, but he couldn't swing the deal. He flew out there and talked with a bunch of them people out, but they didn't have the money, I think, is the main thing. The Dodgers went there the following year.

'Course the Dodgers, you know. It was an illusion. There really was no Dodgers; they were only a state of mind. Scouting-wise, the Dodgers had an attitude that your players are no good and theirs are great. Every player they ever signed should be in the Hall of Fame before he ever played a game. To hear them tell it, every pitcher they ever signed could throw over a hundred miles an hour, and every position player could run to first base in two and a half seconds and had a cannon for an arm. Everybody was great.

And you get out there and see these players and decide something's wrong, either his reputation or my eyesight because it don't add up. It was a lot of hooey! It's still that way over there.

Al Campanis was a friend of mine. One day at a ballgame I was sitting with him and he showed me a guy warming up. He said, "This guy throws a hundred miles an hour."

And I thought to myself, "Now I been knowing this guy all of my life. We even played against each other way back yore. And now he must think I came out of a blind academy or something. He don't know I'm sitting here looking at him." That's an example of what went on. And then you couldn't make a deal with them.

I got a picture of Tommy Lasorda on my wall. I had my picture made with him and he put on my picture, "You and the Dodgers are both great. Sincerely, your friend, Tommy Lasorda." Then down at the bottom it says, "P.S.: Please do not put this picture in a cheap frame." How 'bout that? So the next time I saw him I told him that I didn't put it in a cheap frame. I went to Wal-Mart and paid $2.97 for that frame.

He was a friend forever. You heard about the guy who went to him wanting to lose some weight, didn't you? Tommy told him to get himself a can of that Slim-Fast. So the guy got himself a can of Slim-Fast, mixed it with a pint of bourbon, stirred it up and drank it. He called Tommy a few days later and told him he'd lost fifteen pounds and his driver's license!

When they put me in the Georgia Sports Hall of Fame, he was the speaker. And I told him, "Tommy, I'll kill you if you get up there and embarrass me."

He got up there and he said, "Ellis made a very kind gesture lately. He gave a ten thousand dollar donation to the family of the unknown soldier."

It used to be that those of us in the game all knew each other for years and years because of our jobs in baseball. But now everything's changed. Some guy buys a club and makes his daughter's husband the general manager and hires all his cronies. The fact that they never played a game makes no difference. These new owners today are a new breed all right. Few of them ever played a game. Few of them ever went to a game, but they're kin to somebody in the front office. It used to be they hired ex-players and people with experience. That's not in effect anymore. I used to know everybody in baseball and now I hardly know anybody anymore. All the scouts I started with and worked with over the years have died, unfortunately. I used to love to go to San Francisco or Seattle. I knew everybody in the office, the manager, some of the coaches. But they're not that way anymore.

I remember when old Al Rosen was running the Giants out there. That was a good time. And I remember the Dodgers announcer, Vin Scully. What a nice man he is. I remember he had Don Drysdale with him as a color man on the air. Don Drysdale and I hated each other when he played. But once he quit, we got together when I was with the White Sox. He was doing the White Sox games over there. He turned out to be one of the best friends I ever had. He had me on the pregame show at Dodger Stadium once. Now, see, here in Valdosta, Georgia, where I lived my whole life, we got a football tradition that's the greatest in the whole United States. We won the state championship twenty-three times and the national championship six times! Don Drysdale's first wife was from Valdosta. He knew about the Valdosta Wildcats football team. So we get on his pregame show on the TV one day and talk baseball for awhile, then he said, "What about the Valdosta Wildcats?"

And I said, "We beat somebody every Friday night." See, every Tuesday they rate high school football teams across the nation. So, at that particular time we were rated number eight in the nation and a team in Realto, California, was rated number one. So

I was on there for awhile and run my mouth off and I say, "If Valdosta ever plays Realto, I'll give you seven."

He said, "Seven points?"

I say, "Hell no. Seven touchdowns!"

He finally got back to talking baseball. You know the Dodgers have always had trouble scoring. They win game with pitching. And I was with the Blue Jays at the time and we were leading and the Dodgers were losing. He says to me, "What do you think would happen if we played together in the World Series?"

And I say, "Well, I'll tell you. We got to where we can't score, and the Dodgers never could score. They remind me of that cross-eyed discus thrower from Waycross, Georgia. He can't score either but he keeps the fans loose!"

I scouted in the big leagues for 20 years. I was an advance scout for awhile, and that's the toughest job in baseball. You can't tell jokes and have fun at the ballgame if you're an advance scout. You got to watch every pitch because if a player hits a home run, you got to know what kind of pitch it was and the location of it. Knowing that helps your team when you face those guys yourself. The same thing for every batter who hits the ball. What was the count when he hit it? How did they field him? There's ten thousand things you got to do. You just got to pay attention. I didn't like it.

When you're not an advance scout, covering the big leagues is easy. It's nice. We're scouting players at the major league level. And it's easy to say, "We don't want this guy." Because there's a lot of them that's not that desirable in the big leagues. I mean, you wouldn't break your neck to get them.

I knew Branch Rickey but not very well. I mean he was always around and we always knew that. But we never spoke about anything but baseball and never went out to dinner or anything like that.

I knew Rogers Hornsby. He was managing the Seattle club and I was with him during spring training in Palm Springs. You know, a lot of people didn't like Hornsby and Hornsby didn't like many people. He was tough! When we'd go on a trip, like over to Riverside to play, he told me a lot about Branch Rickey. He didn't like him, but he worked for him. He tolerated him. He was a very brusque man. But I liked him. I thought he was great.

Rickey was ahead of his time, you know. He was smarter than anybody else about this farm system thing. You hated to play a Cardinals team or a Dodgers team in the minor leagues because they'd run you right out of the ballpark. They went for speed back then before anybody else did. They'd run you to death if you didn't watch out.

When Branch Rickey was general manager or manager, he wouldn't go to the games on Sunday. Rogers Hornsby always said, "He wouldn't go to the game, but he counted the money."

I thought Rickey was a smart guy, probably a lot smarter than the other people and he would hornswoggle you if you didn't watch out!

When I used to write on the paper here years ago a good friend of mine was Buck O'Neil. He was scouting for the Cubs. He was one of the icons of the Negro Leagues. I mean, he was one of the big, big people there. He was a player and a manager and everything else. I used to bump into him in Florida and all over the place when we were both scouting and going around. But they made me retire and he's not scouting any more either, so we don't see each other any more.

I saw Josh Gibson play, by the way. I saw him hit three home runs in a game one night in Washington in left field. And in left field you could land a plane it was so big. He hit three in one game. Bob Johnson was our left fielder and I said to him, "What kind of baseball you reckon they're using?"

And he said, "It's the same ball we use."

The future of the game is worrisome. So many things have changed just during my life in it, and most of them aren't making it better. I don't like the way the new owners are running things and them agents ain't nothing but leaches who should be run out of town. Scouts don't really get the chance to do scouting the way we used to.

Dick Wilson

(1920–2009)

Wilson was a serious baseball man. He impressed me from the get-go with his persistence and vast knowledge of the game. In all things he told it like it was, warts and all. He pulled no punches and left no doubts. His account of his minor league baseball playing experience provides an eye-opening look at how things used to be in the game. It clearly demonstrates the tenacity required to be successful in professional baseball as a player, manager, and scout.

He took the time to write his baseball history in longhand. During his sixty-plus years in the game as player, player-manager, and scout, he saw many changes which he described as follows: "Some were good, some not so good, and some just plain bad." As a player, a feisty catcher/third baseman, he was known as a good hitter who had a quick bat and a lot of power for a small man. When he became a scout, he evaluated players' hitting skills and was well respected by other scouts. In fact, they often solicited Dick's assistance in assessing one of their struggling hitters.

As a player and player-manager for thirteen years in the minor leagues, he progressed from the Ontario Orioles and Mexicali Aguilas (Eagles) in the Sunset League to the Visalia Cubs, Modesto Reds, and Bakersfield Bears in the California League to the Hollywood Stars in the Pacific Coast League, and he finished up with the Wenatchee Oaks in the Western International League in 1960. He was voted all-star catcher in Mexicali and Visalia, and the California League MVP at first base with Modesto, where he was an all-star at first base and missed winning the Triple Crown by two RBIs. He scouted from the end of the 1960 season through 2002 when he retired from the game due to poor health.

He discussed all the ups and downs of the game and his part in it, his opinions about how the game had changed during his tenure, and his concerns for the future.

At almost ninety years old, his body was frail and let him down but his mind was sharp. His recollections of his years in the game give a real inside look at the conditions in minor league baseball during the years most of the veteran scouts were players. He continued with a hard look at scouting.

Along the way he mentored many players and scouts. One of them, Wally Walker, longtime scout for the Cubs, Marlins, and Padres, said he was blessed at the beginning of his own scouting career because he was one of the beneficiaries of Dick Wilson's expertise and guidance.

My playing background started early. By that I mean my dad was a good semi-pro pitcher in Southern California. I was pitching and playing other positions in high school in Inglewood, California, when LAX was just a bunch of bean fields and duck ponds. My dad was always available after work and on weekends to hit me fly balls and ground balls and encourage me.

Looking back, I wish I would have listened to him more than I did, especially when I started scouting, because he had an instinct for it and I firmly believe right now that the instincts or "gut feelings" are the most important things to have ... more valuable than a ray gun and a stopwatch. I believe to a great extent that being an ex-player is necessary to have these instincts, though not always. But to a great extent it's a definite advantage.

Growing up in Southern California in the late '30s and '40s was great. You couldn't ask for better conditions to be a ballplayer. I played all the time, both softball and baseball. There was no slow pitch at that time.

I played on a state championship softball team and outstanding high school team. At one point we won 21 in a row. I was on a state champion junior college team, Compton J.C. Before that I played semi-pro with and against pros when I was 16. It was a real lesson because the pros and ex-pros let you know when you made a mistake and were out of line. You didn't argue with them.

Then Pearl Harbor happened and for a few years everything stopped. I spent two years in the service and was discharged due to an injury that left me deaf in one ear.

There were only a few scouts in those days before and after World War II. The way we players used to be seen was to go to a tryout camp. The Dodgers, Cardinals and White Sox always had tryout camps. At those tryout camps we played one long game and everybody played. At one Dodgers camp Duke Snider played and I can still remember the impression he made on me with his power and throwing arm. He was in a class by himself.

For years the Dodgers scout was Tom Downey, the Cardinals had Ken Penner, and later on Bill Delancey, who was Dizzy Dean's catcher with the Cardinals. His career was ended early because of an injury. Hollis Thurston was the White Sox scout. There were some others but these are the ones I remember the most.

The local PCL team, the Los Angeles Angels, always held tryout camps at Wrigley Field in Los Angeles. This was a time when there were 16 major league teams and all kinds of minor leagues, from Triple A to Class D. The classifications were AAA, AA, A, B, C, and D. Some clubs like the Cardinals and Giants had more than 20 minor league classifications operating. I think baseball was at its best period for talent in those days. It was hard to advance because there was so much tough competition.

I had two offers to sign. One was with the San Francisco Seals and the other was with the Hollywood Stars. The Seals saw me play in a semi-pro game one winter and I hit a home run off Erv Palcia, who had been a major league pitcher with the Dodgers. They offered me $350 a month.

I was going to sign, but first I went to where Hollywood was having spring training in Ontario, California, and asked for a tryout as a third baseman. After the workout they called me in and said they wanted to sign me. I told them the Seals wanted to sign me also.

They asked, "How much did they offer?" I told them $350 a month and they said that was no problem. They said they'd give me $350, so I took the Hollywood offer because it was close to home.

Catcher/third baseman Dick Wilson and some teammates from the 1944 Hollywood Stars team in the AAA Pacific Coast League. (Left to right) Third base coach Marty Krug (former ML infielder, AL Boston, 1912, and NL Chicago, 1922), second baseman Billy Knickerbocker, outfielder Brooks Holder, outfielder Otto Meyers, pitcher Earl Embree, Wilson, infielder Ray Olson, player-manager Charlie Root (former Chicago Cubs RHP with 201 wins). The team's 83–86 record earned the Stars a sixth-place finish. Wilson was twenty-one years old (Dick Wilson collection).

At Hollywood my manager was Charlie Root, the ex-Cubs pitcher who served up Babe Ruth's called home run shot in the World Series. Root was okay, a tough, hard-working guy. He didn't say much to me or any of the younger players, and it wasn't long after the season started that three of us were sent to Little Rock in the Southern Association. That was a tough league with a lot of established older, hard-drinking players.

I want to mention that Babe Herman was with Hollywood that year. He was 45 years old and, I think, one of the most underrated players in history. He should be in the Baseball Hall of Fame.

The first game I played in at Little Rock was my first pro game and I think we played against Atlanta. Their pitcher was Ellis Kinder and I had never seen anything close to what he served up to me. I broke my bat twice then blooped a single over the infield. I thought my career was going to be over in a hurry if that was the kind of stuff I was going to see.

Thinking back, I faced some pitchers who were really tough: Bill Hands, Larry Jackson, Jim Kaat, Steve Dalkowski, and some others. But Kinder was as tough as any, maybe tougher. He was a 20-game winner with the Red Sox later when they had their best ballclubs with Ted Williams, Vern Stephens, Johnny Pesky, and Bobby Doerr.

Billy Goodman was an outfielder on that Atlanta club with Ellis Kinder. Later Goodman led the American League in hitting. Also in the Southern Association that year was Pete Gray, a young one-armed outfielder who played for Memphis. In one game against us, Gray hit a home run just over the right field fence in Memphis.

My manager that first year at Little Rock was Bob Seeds, a former Yankees outfielder nicknamed "Suitcase" because he played for so many teams. The manager the second year was Willis Hudlin. He was also the owner of the club, and a former major league pitcher with Cleveland.

I was doing okay with Little Rock but the next thing I knew I was optioned to Portsmouth, Virginia, in the Piedmont League, a B league. When I got there I found the team was mostly composed of Cuban players.

The American manager was Bill Steiner. The Cubans resented me because I took the job from one of their fellow Cubans. I got a lot of "hard" looks and was never accepted. At this point I didn't feel like playing any more under those conditions. My mental state was down. I did not have a good attitude. So I quit and went home.

I got my release from Hollywood, called the San Francisco Seals, and they signed me to a Triple-A contract at the same $350 a month. I reported to the Seals in San Diego. The manager was the famous Lefty O'Doul, and he immediately put me in the lineup at third base.

In those days, the Pacific Coast League was the place to be. It was composed of older players, former major leaguers and veteran Triple-A players. In my case, I never thought beyond the PCL. It was the ultimate to me. My dad had been taking me to PCL games since I was eight and I thought they were all superstars. I pitched batting practice for the Hollywood Stars when I was sixteen.

Scared to death, I hit the first pitch I saw in the PCL for a triple in right-center. I hit the ball hard that entire week, close to .400. But I made some mistakes and when we went back to San Francisco, I wasn't in the lineup. Nobody told me why and I didn't question it. I didn't have the experience and that meant a lot in that league. The rest of the season I only pinch-hit and played a little. We won the playoffs and won the final four out of seven against the L.A. Angels.

The next year I reported at the same salary as a catcher. The Seals had two veteran catchers. Joe Sprinz, who got his face busted up when he attempted to catch a ball dropped out of a dirigible at Treasure Island, and the other was Bruce Ogrodowski, who had also been Dizzy Dean's catcher with the Cardinals. There was no opportunity for me to play and somewhere in midseason I was released.

I called Little Rock and they wired me to report immediately, same salary. I reported, played regularly at third base, and was improving and getting confidence. But it was a long way from California and I hadn't been married very long. So again I quit, made a lot of people mad at me, and went home.

The Seals contacted me and offered me an opportunity to play at Salt Lake City, the Seals' only affiliate. This was the Pioneer League, Class C. The owner was Eddie Mulligan and the manager was Joe Orengo, called "Cable Car Joe."

I told Eddie Mulligan I had a family, a wife and one child, and that I needed a higher salary than $300, which was the usual salary in that league. "Just sign the contract," he said, "and we'll fill in the amount later. I'll get you as much as I can depending on the salary levels they had in those leagues." This is illegal, but I didn't know it. Back then that extra fifty dollars a month paid some bills and I needed it.

They had salary caps in the minor leagues in those days. Each league's cap was determined by how high up the food chain it was, and all were expected to operate on tight budgets.

We trained at Seals Stadium, and the day we played our final spring training game, I told Joe I wasn't going to Salt Lake that night until my contract was finalized. Orengo hit the roof! Blew up! He didn't know anything about the contract business and he was counting on me to be his third baseman.

He went and got Mulligan and Mulligan hit the roof also. Denied he had me sign a blank contract. Said that $300 a month was what I had signed and that signing an untried contract was illegal!

Orengo was really mad. He told me, "Go ahead and go on home and drive that damn dirt truck or whatever."

And that was it! Once again I went home. I knew I could hit, but things weren't working out to where I could prove it. It was as much my fault as anybody else's.

I stayed out that entire year, got a job and played semipro ball in Southern California that winter. I learned more about catching and hit the ball hard all year.

The next spring Rosey Gilhousen, a scout for Hollywood, approached me and asked me to play for him in Idaho Falls, Class C. I was still very young and was playing better all the time, so I said okay to $250 a month and a $250 signing bonus.

I got off to a tremendous start. Hit over .400 with three home runs in the first three games. But then I woke up one Sunday morning and had this terrible headache and fever and was a little out of my head. My wife was with me. They finally got me to a doctor at the hospital. I don't remember too much about it. I was delirious.

What had happened was that I had a blister on my heel and had it treated in spring training. But it scabbed over and got infected. The doctor said if I hadn't gotten to the hospital that Sunday, I may have died. I was loaded with infection.

As a result I lost thirty days, a lot of it in bed. When I came back I was in poor condition and went into the worst slump of my life: 0-for-48. Funny thing was I never struck out in those 48 at-bats.

Meanwhile, Rosey Gilhousen was fired. A new manager was brought in who didn't know me. His name was George Oldenberg, a guy with an eastern background.

Before the 1944 season Dick Wilson works on his swing at spring training camp at Catalina Island off the coast of Southern California with the Hollywood Stars, Chicago Cubs AAA affiliate in the PCL. Though he spent the bulk of the season in the AA Southern League with the Little Rock, Arkansas, Travelers, he did have two cups of coffee in the PCL, first with Hollywood and then with San Francisco, but accumulated no stats with either team (Dick Wilson collection).

Anyway, I wasn't hitting. My right leg was still stiff and weak, so they released me. I couldn't blame him, but I knew he was wrong.

I took my family back home to Inglewood. Somebody heard about it and told me that the Ontario, California, club might want me. This was close to home, so I went over there and worked out with them. The manager was Danny Reagan, a catcher and a playing manager. He offered me $175 a month. Since it was close to home and I could go back and forth with Reagan, who lived close by, I took it. This was in the Sunset League, Class C. It's one of the oldest leagues in the country. So I spent the 1947 season with them trying to keep my hopes and ambitions alive

I didn't play much at first, in and out of the lineup, giving Reagan a rest. And then one night in Las Vegas something happened that turned things completely around.

We were playing in the Las Vegas park and I was on the bench. We had a big outfielder named George "Moose" Stassi who was supposed to be the hitting star of our club. In this game the Las Vegas pitcher was Rex Jones, supposedly one of the best prospects in the league. He had already been sold to the Yankees organization for $20,000, which was big money in those days. He was to report after the season ended.

Anyway, Jones was beating us, and in the fifth inning we got the bases full with two outs and Stassi was hitting. Jones threw two strikes right down past him. Stassi put up a big beef on the second strike and got himself thrown out of the game. He didn't want any part of Jones.

Reagan called me off the bench to hit with two strikes. The first pitch Jones threw me was a high fastball and it looked like a grapefruit to me. I hit it a mile over the left field fence. I honestly think that one at-bat turned me completely around.

Reagan and Stassi never got along anyway and after this game Reagan released him and I started playing regularly at several different positions. I just tore up the league the rest of the year and finished hitting .380.

Danny Reagan made quite a name for himself as a scout after that. The Ontario club was owned by Babe Dahlgren, famous for replacing Lou Gehrig at first base when Gehrig came down with the disease that killed him.

The Ontario franchise lost money. At the

Dick Wilson, 1948, all-star catcher and manager of the Mexicali Aguilas (Eagles) in the Class C Sunset League that lasted from 1947 to 1950 before it merged with the Arizona-Texas League. That season was a record-setting one for Wilson as well as minor league baseball. He hit .347, had 188 RBIs, and became the only 40–40 catcher in minor league history with 42 home runs and 40 stolen bases. Bobby Balcena was one of the future major league players he brought along on that team (Dick Wilson collection).

end of the season, Dahlgren sold it to a group in Mexico. Every single player was released except me. The Mexican group wanted me included with the franchise, and so I was Mexican property!

I was beginning to be better known and was invited to play in some charity-type games with current professional players, some of them major leaguers. At one of these games I had a good day. I hit one over the fence and stole a couple of bases. After the game a man came down and introduced himself. It was Mike Gazella, known for being Babe Ruth's roommate with the Yankees.

He said, "Listen, kid, I'm managing Denver in the Western League and I would like for you to play for me. I'll give you $500 a month."

This sounded great to me. I told him I was the property of Mexicali and he said, "If you can get out of that contract, I've got a job for you."

It was close to spring training at that time, so I drove to Mexicali where we were to train to try to get my release from the owners there. The three partners of the Mexicali group were Mario Hernandez, Tufie Hashem, and Carlos Moreno.

Hernandez was young and wanted to play first base. He was, I guess, very well off. He owned La Estrella Azul, the Blue Star, which was a clothing store, and he owned the ice franchise, supplying ice to everyone. Tufie Hashem was a World War II veteran who had been shot up, which left him with a lot of facial scars just short of being disfigured. Carlos Moreno owned the Buick dealership in Mexicali. He was a quiet, sinister looking guy with a big black moustache. He looked as tough as Pancho Villa.

I told them I wanted my release because I could get a better deal in Denver and I really didn't want to play in Mexico. Nobody said anything and then Moreno said, "Come on, Wilson, I want to take you for a little ride." We got into his big black Buick and they took me out to where they were building the ballpark.

"You see," he said, "all my money is tied up in this park." Then he looked directly at me and added, "Wilson, you are going to play here for me or you aren't going to play for anybody."

So, I signed for $250 a month with a clause in my contract that I was to receive 33 percent of my sale price if I were sold to another club. Our manager was Dominic Castro, a former minor league catcher with the White Sox. I liked him. He was supposed to be a playing manager, but he really didn't want to play anymore. And on top of that he had a serious gambling problem. Mexicali had a big bookie joint for off-track betting and a wire to all tracks in the United States. Dominic was there a lot.

I had a great spring despite the heat and was hitting better than I ever had, including a lot of long balls. Dominic predicted I was going to lead the league. The club started out mediocre and Dominic had a personal problem with some of the players, especially a Filipino outfielder named Bobby Balcena. He had a lot of talent and was a great guy on the club. I liked him. Dominic didn't and made no attempt to hide it.

I got off to a great start right away and kept it up all year. One night in Las Vegas we lost a game, and in the clubhouse in front of all the players, Dominic got into a long verbal argument with Tufie Hashem, who traveled with us.

At three A.M. Tufie came into my room and asked if I would manage the team "temporarily" because he had fired Castro. I told him I needed more money to do that and we agreed on an extra $7 a day until they could find a replacement. That brought my salary up to $460 a month.

I was the youngest manager in organized baseball that year. I even had a story in the *Sporting News*. We started winning. Balcena started hitting and we came from way back in the pack to win the pennant. Bobby Balcena hit .360 something and eventually played for the Cincinnati Reds in the National League. The best Filipino player I ever saw. He was tremendous that year.

I ended up catching all the games after Castro left, and 1948 turned out to be a great year for me. I had a .347 batting average with 42 home runs and 41 stolen bases. No other catcher in baseball at any level has had a 40–40 season! I can't find one that's had a 30–30 season.

They had a habit of passing the hat for a home run in Mexicali and I got as high as $72 for a home run. They also had a "night" for me at the end of the season. I got all kinds of presents, including an English pointer dog covered with ticks.

And to put the frosting on the cake, at the end of the season I was sold to the Los Angeles Angels in the Pacific Coast League for $6,000! They were the top farm club of the Cubs at that time. But I had a hard time collecting my 33 percent and finally had to appeal to George Trautmann, president of the minor leagues. Eventually I got a check for $800 from Mexicali. They had taken out $1,200 for various Mexican deductions, most of which were phony.

So that winter I signed with the Angels. They offered me $500 a month. I told them about the extra money from passing the hat, so they offered $600 and I took it. In spring training I realized one of my goals. For two years I had been trying to get a bat contract from Hillerich and Bradsby, who produced Louisville Slugger bats. Their western representative, Roscoe Hovatter, told me to "go out and lead the league or something," and that's what I did at Mexicali: 42 home runs and 188 RBIs.

True to his word, Hovatter signed me to a Louisville Slugger contract and they put my signature on Louisville Slugger bats. They offered me a choice of $100 cash or a set of H & B golf clubs for using my signature. I took the golf clubs and used them, but not often. I had a pull hitter's swing and that doesn't work with a golf club. I had as wicked a slice with a driver as you could find on a golf course.

I had a good spring with the Angels and started the 1949 season with them. I was on the bench, used only as a pinch-hitter at first. Then our first baseman, Butch Moran, sprained his ankle and the manager, an old-timer, Bill Kelly, put me at first. I didn't even own a first baseman's glove. But there was a man in L.A. who made baseball gloves out of elk hide. His name was Hemus. The leather was soft and you didn't need to break the glove in. He made one for me in one day.

I started at first base for quite a while and did okay. Butch Moran was a hard drinker and a slow healer. All the time I played for him I hit over .300. When he came back, the Angels wanted to send me out along with our third baseman, Ransom Jackson, who later played several years in the major leagues for the Cubs and made the All-Star team.

Jackson and I were both hitting over .300 but they told us we were too young to play in the PCL. One thing in those days, there were a lot of minor leagues. Many organizations had two Triple-A clubs and three Double-A clubs with as many as twenty or more affiliates at the lower levels. They wanted to send me to Springfield, Massachusetts, and I told them no. Then they said Nashville, and I said no. I told them I wasn't going east anymore, so they sent me to Visalia in the California State League. I went as a catcher. The California League was known as the best C league in baseball. It's called A ball today.

We had a poor club at Visalia. The manager, Red Treadway, was fired a short time after I got there. The Cubs asked me if I would temporarily manage the team for the remainder of the season. I asked for my extra seven dollars a day to do this, but they said no, and brought in Coast League legend Jigger Statz. My dad had taken me to see him play for the Angels when I was around ten years old. Statz stayed a short time. They replaced him with Claude Passeau, an outstanding major league pitcher with the Cubs who was forced to retire when he injured his back fielding a bunt on a wet field. Passeau was a French-Canadian. Tough. Fiery. Still a fierce competitor. A great guy to play for. He would come in and pitch an inning if we had a chance to win. The first time I caught him I walked to the mound to get the signs straight and he said that Clyde McCullough caught him without signs. I said I'd try it and I did. He threw hard with a short, quick slider and it wasn't any trouble.

I got really sick that year with a severe attack of gastritis and had to go to the hospital. I couldn't keep anything on my stomach and it weakened me, especially catching in the heat of the San Juaquin Valley. Despite that, I ended up hitting .300 with 26 home runs and made the all-star team.

That winter the Angels sold my contract to Modesto, a Pittsburgh Pirate affiliate in the California League. The GM at Modesto in 1951 was Charlie McGrew, a really shifty guy. Loud dresser, baby faced, and a big-time con man who did a lot of under-the-table illegal deals. There was a salary limit in that league and he got around that by paying certain players cash under the table. I was one of those players, and my salary was $900 a month. Our manager was Marc Carrola, a playing manager and a catcher. So I went back to first base again. This was a good move for me. I felt good, was strong all year, and hit .319. I led the league with 30 home runs and 154 RBIs. We won the playoffs in a very good league that year.

It was hard to advance in those days. There were so many teams. With the Pittsburgh Pirate organization, Branch Rickey was running things. His claim to fame was the St. Louis Cardinals and Brooklyn Dodgers farm systems. But he was noted for not paying a decent salary. I bring that up because of what happened at the start of the following season. The organization wanted me to go to New Orleans in the Southern Association in 1952 for $500 a month. I tried to tell them about the under-the-table money, but the GM at New Orleans was Joe Brown, later to be the GM at Pittsburgh, and he would not accept my point of view. I couldn't afford that much of a cut. My family was growing, two children now. So I held out and worked at home.

During this time things reached an impasse. Joe Brown would not accept the fact that I was getting $900 a month from Modesto. Of course, $400 a month of that $900 was illegal, under the table. And with a family to support I wasn't about to take a big cut in salary after I had just completed a very good year.

So I called Branch Rickey and asked if I could meet with him to tell my side of the story. He was very busy but said that he would be in Los Angeles the next week to see his big league team, the Pirates, play their first exhibition game against the USC Trojans. He said he would be staying at the Olympic Hotel in Los Angeles and if I would meet him there he would talk to me in his limousine during the time we drove from the hotel to USC and again driving back from the game to the hotel. So there wasn't any choice but to agree.

I drove to the hotel, met him in the lobby, and we got in his limousine. He didn't ever drive. He had a chauffer, a fellow named Kenny Blackburn, who drove and ran errands and what else I don't know. During the ride I tried to explain that I just couldn't afford the cut in salary and that I was certain I could get $900 or very close to it with someone else if he weren't willing to pay it. One thing I found out for sure was that he wasn't willing to let me go where I could get it. The point he made, and punctuated in a loud voice, was, "Free agency will be the ruination of baseball." I wonder what he would think if he could see what has happened with free agency today. His worst fears realized. I don't think he could operate in today's world of baseball.

It all ended for that season with me returning to Modesto where I got my under-the-table money. I really did want to go to New Orleans and play for Danny Murtaugh, but it was too expensive. I got there in time for opening night and had no spring training. Our manager was the legendary pitcher Tony Freitas, who had won 340 games in the minor leagues and a few more in the majors. He was a friend of mine along with being the manager. At the age of 43, he won 25 games for us that year and was a pleasure to play behind.

I had one of the best years of my life in many different ways. I led the league in hitting at .371. Closest to me was 30 points less. I set a new California League home run record with 40, and set a new record for two-base hits, 55. I broke several other records in number of base hits and total bases. Also, I set a new record with 97 extra-base hits. And, surprise, I set a new fielding percentage at first base. Some of those records still stand. But we didn't make the playoffs and it was a disappointing season in that respect. The ball club held a "night" for me at the end of the season and I got many gifts, including a deep freeze.

The next season with Modesto, the Pirates' farm team in the California League, Class C, was disappointing for the team because we didn't make the playoffs. My contract was sold to Hollywood, in the Pacific Coast League. They had a good club and I was looking forward to going to spring training with them. Fred Haney was the manager and he invited me into his home in Southern California. We talked and I signed my contract in his living room for $800 a month. Fred Haney was a smooth talker in public and had been a play-by-play announcer with Hollywood for a few years before he got back in the league in uniform again.

One of my idols was broadcasting the games — Tommy Harmon, the great running back at Michigan and a war hero in World War II. As an added attraction, Virginia Mayo attended a lot of games with her husband, Michael O'Shea. She sat in the front row behind our bat rack. She was a drop-dead knockout. Wow! Always smiling.

Fred Haney went on to manage Pittsburgh and Milwaukee in the National League and eventually won a world championship with Milwaukee, with a lot of help from Hank Aaron, Eddie Mathews, Warren Spahn, Lew Burdette, and others. He was the smartest manager I ever saw.

Before I went to spring training with Hollywood, I got a telegram from the Pirates asking me to report to San Bernardino for a special camp. The Pirates had a dismal club and Rickey wanted his best prospects in this camp so he could see us all at once. When I got there he called me in his office and told me that in his view I had just had the greatest season of anybody in baseball. I think he liked the 97 extra-base hits and that I never struck out much.

Then he told me he wanted me to return to catching. He said he had three catchers but none of them could hit enough to satisfy him. The three were Clyde McCullough, Eddie Fitzgerald, and Joe Garagiola. I hadn't caught in two years, was very happy at first base, and I knew I didn't have a strong enough throwing arm to be a major league catcher, but I wasn't about to argue with him.

The manager of the Pirates was Billy Meyer, who had been at Kansas City as manager. It was clear that Rickey ran the entire operation. He was in the field all the time in a baggy, wrinkled suit and a crumpled hat, no baseball uniform, and he would embarrass Billy Meyer by over-ruling him or correcting things in front of everyone. Billy Meyer was not well. Nice man but just a front man for Rickey.

At that time Rickey was introducing the batting helmet. He was the original designer and had a company or interest in a company to manufacture them. He insisted we all wear them and I hated them. They sat heavy and awkward on my head and I felt unbalanced. Many times I would go up to hit with only my baseball cap. But he caught me every time and made me get a helmet.

Every morning after breakfast we would meet in a big room for an hour and he would lecture. He was an outstanding speaker. I have always rated him and Billy Graham as the best I ever heard and I'm not religious.

I would get my first base glove when I wasn't catching and wander out to first base and field a few ground balls, hoping Rickey would take the hint. But it didn't work. He would chase me out of the infield. He favored a little guy, about 5'9" tops, named Tony Bartirome, kind of flashy but no power. Tony was a good guy and I liked him, but I knew I could run him off first base if I got the chance. But I never got the chance. Rickey had it in his mind that I was going to catch.

I went to a Pittsburgh-sponsored camp to be evaluated to see if I would go to the major league team for the '52 season. George Sisler, one of baseball's all-time greats, was at this camp as a hitting instructor. He was a Rickey man from way back. Sisler was not a well man at this time. He was there but not very active on the field. One of the instructors at this camp told me that it looked like I would be spending the summer in Pittsburgh, but it didn't happen. Rickey was desperate for a catcher who could hit, and it was at this camp that he experimented with making Dale Long a left-handed catcher. That didn't last very long. Everybody thinks a left-handed hitting catcher is the ideal. I don't know why there were so few of them.

One of the reasons I fell out of Rickey's favor may have been that during the camp we had a day off and the Santa Anita Handicap was being run that day. The track was nearby, so a few of us went to the track. One of the guys in our group was Danny Murtaugh, at that time a player-coach with the Pirates. Danny was a great guy and later became famous as the Pirate manager when they were world champions. Danny and I split a bet on the winner of the Handicap, a long shot, I think named Miche. It paid off at fifty-to-one.

Of course, this got out back at the camp and the next morning at breakfast, Rickey came in and sat down across from me and asked me a lot of questions about gambling. Did I play cards? Gamble a lot? And so on and so forth. I told him I liked to go to the race track. I liked the fresh air and the horses and the atmosphere. I didn't like a card game in a smoky room or anything like that. I didn't smoke and I didn't drink.

Well, that 1952 Pittsburgh club has gone down in history as one of the worst. Maybe it's better that I didn't get to play on it. Everyone said Rickey was such a genius, but I didn't think so. Maybe it's just sour grapes. But that was my only chance to try to get to the major leagues and it didn't happen for me. When I didn't make the Pirates' major league club, I had the chance to be a player-manager in minor league baseball, which I found challenging and satisfying. I was player-manager for the Modesto Reds, the Bakersfield Bears in the California League, and the Wenatchee, Washington, Oaks in the Western International League. I had some good players in those years and even put up more good numbers myself. My final year of playing was 1960 and then I went into scouting. It really wasn't much of a decision. I was finished playing and wanted to stay in the game.

I became a scout because of one man, Loyd Christopher. He was an outstanding scout. He loved the game and contributed to it with his persona. His work ethics were an example for others to follow. He was thorough and knew what he saw in young players. He understood them and was always willing to help other scouts and pass along his knowledge.

He was a scout who took an interest in me as a player. He was a player also, an outfielder with the Oakland Oaks in the Pacific Coast League. He put up big numbers and would have been a major league player except for injuries that slowed him down.

In my playing days in the late '40s and '50s there were not nearly as many scouts in the field as there are today. And back then most of them were older and experienced. If there were younger scouts, they were around forty and ex-players who had long playing careers. The exception might be a player who had his playing career cut short by an injury and went into scouting only because he couldn't play anymore.

The ones I remember as a young player in high school and junior college were older and we all knew them. It was more than just our job, it was a matter of personal pride to stay on top of things that were going on in the game. Now I see a lot of young scouts and I have no idea of who they are or who they work for. But they have the stopwatch and the radar gun, so they are easily identified as scouts. Back in the day we didn't flash neon signs or advertise that we were scouts. We just scouted. Anyway, the scouts all had pro coverage in those days before the draft. Loyd Christopher covered the Northwest League, among others, and spent quite a bit of time following my club at Wenatchee. He used to talk to me a lot, and since I liked to hold morning workouts, I would invite him to come out in the mornings and come down on the field. We found we had a lot in common, not only in baseball, but in our views on life. He told me that when I was finished playing to be sure and contact him if I wanted to stay in baseball.

When I finished my last season in 1960, I went home with no idea what the future held for me. I had four children at home, so I couldn't wait for a job in baseball to open up. I went right to work at Harrah's Club in Reno. Started out in Bill Harrah's Old Car Museum. All I did was walk around with a mop and clean up the oily spots where there was even a tiny leak. Then I was promoted to the main cashier's cage. That was a busy job and time went fast, especially if you worked the swing shift. New Year's Eve was a complete madhouse. I worked there all winter, and wrote to Loyd and told him I was open to listening to anything he had for me. He was working for the Kansas City Athletics at that time. His boss was Hank Peters, a solid and very capable baseball man. Loyd was in pretty good with Hank.

Loyd had a pretty large territory, a big part of central California and northern California, plus the northern United States and part of Canada. He wanted to split his territory and he wanted Kansas City to hire me for the Northwest.

Joe Gordon was the Kansas City manager and Al Zarilla was the West Coast supervisor out of Los Angeles. Gordon and Zarilla wanted to hire a friend of theirs, a former major leaguer named Harlond Clift. This was strictly a good-old-boy move. Clift was known to have problems with booze. He lived in Yakima, which was in his favor. But Loyd met him and interviewed him. He told me, "If they hire Clift, it'll have to be over my dead body."

His influence with Hank Peters paid off because I got the job. I moved my family to Portland, Oregon, and rented out my house in Nevada. I think deep down under I didn't trust anything in baseball too far. I have always felt that next to the U.S. Government, baseball was the worst run business in the world. And today, baseball may have taken over the top spot as the worst run business ever. I soon found out that despite all my years in the game, scouting was a whole new experience. It wasn't completely foreign because it was still baseball, but I didn't know half of what I thought I knew. I don't care how many years you have in as an active player, scouting is an entirely different world.

The Northwest was different. A lot of rain. A lot of miles to cover, and I just never really liked it up there. Just too many gloomy days and not enough sunshine. I floundered around that first year. Didn't sign anybody. Made a few friends, but I mainly got paid for nothing. And then Charlie Finley took over the Kansas City club. Charlie was a maverick who didn't think his organization needed scouts and he didn't really like them anyway. There was a lot of upheaval which ended when most of his scouts just up and quit, leaving him with a skeleton crew. His philosophy was, "If we hear about a player that everybody is going to try to sign in June, we'll just get in there and outbid the rest."

We had an organization meeting scheduled in September in Kansas City. There were rumors flying around about more scouts leaving the organization, but I really didn't know what happened until I got back to KC. My closest friends, Loyd Christopher and Art Lilly, had quit. Al Zarilla had also quit. They didn't like Finley's methods. I felt a little bit lost. I didn't have any credentials as a scout yet, and I wasn't in any position to quit. In fact, I was about as ignorant as I could be about the whole thing. It was something of a mutiny against the way Charlie Finley was running the ship.

Clyde Kluttz was the spokesman for what was left of us. Nobody consulted or even talked to me. I was just a dumb rookie in the scouting department. Clyde Kluttz got some concessions from Finley in certain areas, like expenses and such. Finley gave in to some extent, but only because he was in danger of losing everybody that counted. I didn't count and I found that out a few days later. We all had individual meetings scheduled with Bill Bergesch and his assistants to discuss our territories. I thought this was a chance to get out of the Northwest. Since all of the West Coast scouts had left except me, I thought I would let them know how I felt. When my meeting came I asked for consideration of a territory change to either northern California or southern California. It was a friendly meeting and I did not make any demands or give any ultimatums. I said, "If you don't think this is practical for you, then, okay, I'll stay put."

I thought this was reasonable, and when I went back home I felt good about it. Since the West Coast was cleaned out of KC scouts, I thought I had a great chance of being relocated. I had been home just a couple of days and we were having a birthday dinner, one of my sons was born on October 3 and my birthday is October 4. We were just getting ready to eat dinner when the phone rang. It was Western Union and they had a telegram for me. I asked them to read it and it said, "Since you find so much dissatisfaction with the way we run our business, you can look for employment elsewhere. You are hereby terminated from the Kansas City baseball club." This was not only a shock, it ruined the birthday. My scouting career was over after only one year.

I think Finley was in a rage over the mutiny and I was a handy target. Anyway, it was sell the Portland house and move back to Nevada again. I had to move out the renters and start again. But it was good to see the sun again. I took a job at the post office. Temporary job at first, but it was steady and I figured this might be it. Baseball and the U.S. Government, what a combination!

I had not been home a month when the phone rang and it was Bill Bergesch. He had quit at KC after the meetings and was with the newest expansion team at that time, the New York Mets. He wanted to hire me to scout for them with a territory back in the Northwest. So we picked up and went back to Portland, bought another house using my GI bill. On our trip back we were all in a 1959 station wagon pulling a two-wheel trailer when the right rear wheel collapsed and caught fire. This was on the freeway between Eugene and Salem, Oregon, only 40 miles from Portland.

I got everybody out of the station wagon and off in a field at a safe distance and went back to try to salvage something. A truck driver stopped and got out an axe and tried to break the hitch for the trailer. I had a rifle and shotgun in the trailer with some ammunition for both. He couldn't break the hitch and the fire got hotter and hotter. A sheet of flame singed my hair and eyebrows, and I looked in the field and saw my wife and four kids standing out there illuminated by the fire in the night and I realized how much trouble they would be in if something happened to me. So I gave up the fight and we watched the station wagon burn. The trailer wasn't damaged, except for some surface scorching.

I called a friend in Portland and he drove down and hauled us to our new home in Portland. We didn't have anything, but he loaned us some blankets and we got through the night. We then drove down and picked up the trailer and hauled it off to Portland and home. The station wagon was just a charred shell. This friend also loaned me his second car to use until I could get things squared away. But it wasn't over yet. To make matters worse, Allied Van Moving Company was moving all our furniture and they did not deliver on time. We waited eight days and I had to go down to their Portland office and raise a lot of hell to get it delivered. Our belongings had been sitting in Spokane. I told the Portland office that I was going to give them more bad publicity than they could possibly imagine if they didn't get our stuff delivered, and right away! We finally got settled. I made a down payment on a 1959 Pontiac, and although we had lost some valuable things in the fire, we were all in one piece. Realizing that and appreciating it helped all of us to look forward and keep going. I was looking forward to going to the Mets. I just wanted to get my feet on what I felt was solid ground again.

I did a little better with the Mets; signed a few quality players with potential. One was picked up by Pittsburgh in a first-year Major League Players Draft. There were some complicated rules at the time, which were all directed to keep signing bonuses down. I never bothered to try and get into that part of it. They had enough paper shufflers in the front office to take care of that. My job was to try and find and then to sign the best prospects in my territory.

I was not familiar with our front office people except Bill Bergesch. Bill was not a strong personality. I thought he was weak and that he was not really a factor in the decision making. He must have been okay with the paperwork. Johnny Murphy was one of the higher-up office people. He had been a reliever with the old New York Yankees, and was a big name in New York. He was eastern oriented and the West Coast scouts were Al Lyons in Southern California and Roy Partee in northern California, and myself in the Northwest. Danny Reagan in L.A. was our top guy.

Our immediate boss was Wid Matthews, who had been a long time Branch Rickey man with the Brooklyn Dodgers. Wid was a Southerner and favored the South for ballplayers. It seemed to me the West Coast was a poor third in their favorite preferences. Wid Matthews was a closet drinker. Drank in his hotel room, scotch whiskey. He poured me a glassful one time and I couldn't stand the stuff. Wid was also into the racial thing, black and white. With him being from the South, I suppose it was important to him but I did not have any feelings about it. To me, people were people and there's good and bad in all races. He once asked me about the NAACP and I didn't know what he was talking about. I could tell this irritated him. We didn't have much in common and I never did feel at ease around him. We had a serious disagreement about a couple of things. Our West Coast farm team was Santa Barbara and our manager was Gene Lillard, a long-time baseball man who once hit 56 home runs for the Los Angeles Angels in the Pacific Coast League.

Wid and Lillard had a personality conflict. I had known Gene Lillard for some time and had complete respect for him. One day toward the end of the season at Santa Barbara, Wid called all of us West Coast scouts into his room for a meeting. He told us he wanted us to turn in a negative report on Lillard as a manager so Wid could fire him.

I didn't know what the other scouts did, but I knew I couldn't and wouldn't do that. I told Wid later on in private that I wouldn't do it. He didn't like it but he couldn't do much about it. In fact, I turned in a good report on Gene. I knew I was not in Wid's corner and figured my days were numbered, but I had some pretty good players going for me in the organization, so that helped. Wid got his way and Lillard was let go after the season and the franchise was moved up to Salinas for the following year. Wid hand-picked his own manager, from the South, of course, an ex pitcher named Ken Deal.

The next spring all of us scouts were assigned to spend a month with Salinas in spring training to help Deal and to decide who to keep and who to let go. It was apparent from day one that Deal resented us being there. He had his own ideas about everything, even though he didn't know straight up about hitting, catching, infield play, running bases, all of it except pitching.

We were supposed to have a meeting at the end of spring training with Deal and us scouts to make the final decision on the Salinas club. Wid was to be on the phone from the East Coast and we would all say our piece. The correct way to do this would have been for Deal and us to get together before the conference call and sort it all out. But this didn't happen. When Wid got on the phone with Deal, Deal started right in with what he wanted to do. Partee and I couldn't believe it and we both raised a lot of hell. We made a little headway, but the meeting ended in confusion. I was so disgusted with Deal I wrote a letter to Wid and told him not to send me to spring training again. I told him they could hire some local coach from a high school or junior college to hit fungos. That was all Deal wanted. Ken Deal was in contention for the worst manager I had ever seen in professional baseball. He was a beer hound. Couldn't wait for the game to end. As soon as the last out was made, he would race to the concession stand for his beer. He would beat the paying customers and be first in line. But he was Wid's boy and Wid would not listen to any criticism about Ken Deal.

In Portland I lived near Madison High School, and my oldest son went to Madison. It had the reputation of having the best high school baseball team in the area. They had a pitcher who was attracting some attention. I used to see this pitcher sneaking off and lighting a cigarette. He was not really a popular guy on the team. Then he came down with mononucleosis. Since I was negative toward him anyway, that word scared the hell out of me. I really didn't know what it meant but it gave me a good excuse not to get involved with him. This was a big mistake on my part. It turned out to be a big bidding war with a few clubs involved. The pitcher was Rick Wise, who turned out to be a highly productive major league pitcher.

I spent three years with the Mets when Wid Matthews finally got around to firing me. Can't say as I blamed him. One of the memorable events with the Mets was the year the Yankees played the Giants in the World Series. The Mets invited Roy Partee and myself. We had seats way down the right field line, closer to the right field fence than to home plate. Partee had to use binoculars and he wasn't happy about our seats. We were invited for the first two games, but after the first one, I flew home and watched the rest of the Series on TV. The TV was better than where we were seated. I did get to meet George Weiss and Casey Stengel and Yogi Berra. Whitey Ford pitched for the Yankees and they beat the Giants in that opening game.

Most of the major league clubs did not consider the Northwest productive enough to keep a full-time scout there. Except for a few clubs, the full-time scouts from the San Francisco Bay Area had the Northwest added on to their primary areas of northern California. Most of these scouts had a part-time man who lived in the Northwest. The part-time man was supposed to screen out the area and have a select list for the scout to come in and pass judgment on.

Over the years there have been a substantial number of players signed out of the Northwest who have gone on to be outstanding major leaguers. Idaho has Walter Johnson, Harmon Killebrew, Larry Jackson. Washington has Earl Averill, Ryne Sandberg, Ron Santo, John Olerud, Ron Cey, Randy Myers, Larry Andersen. Oregon has contributed Dale Murphy, Mickey Lolich, Rick Wise.

Things changed when the Yankees hired Eddie Taylor as a full-time scout in the Northwest. Eddie had spent his life in baseball as a player, a coach, and a scout. Eddie covered the area like a blanket in his white Cadillac. He put the Northwest on the baseball map. Right away he signed Mel Stottlemyre for pocket change and Stottlemyre blazed his way to the major leagues in a hurry. Taylor's success actually created a lot of full-time jobs. He was making a clean sweep of the area, and so to keep up with the competition, almost all of the clubs went to full-time scouts in the Northwest. The only thing that really slowed Eddie Taylor down was when the free agent draft was installed in 1965. Then he had to wait his turn.

I got a job with the Giants. My supervisor the first year with the Giants was Eddie Montague, the father of current major league umpire Eddie Montague. Montague had been with the Giants a long time. He was an ex-player and a good scout. He didn't sign a lot of players but all the players he did sign could play. He sent me one or two a year when I was managing the rookie clubs. One he sent me was Ron Bryant as a seventeen-year-old. Another was Bob Knepper, also a high school kid. Both were left-handed pitchers.

Eddie also got credit for signing the great Willie Mays. I know different people like to claim credit for Mays, but Eddie Montague is the scout who is in the record books for signing him. Bryant later won more than twenty games one year for San Francisco and Knepper was a good major leaguer for several years. I finished up that summer for the Giants. My daughter graduated, and in September we packed up and went home to Nevada with no idea of what the next year would hold for us.

I packed up all my scouting equipment and supplies and sent them to Jack Schwarz in San Francisco. I told him I would be in Nevada to stay and I gave him my phone number and address if he wanted to reach me. I went back to work at Harrah's Club as a cashier again and worked through the winter. Jack Schwarz called me early the next year and gave me a choice of two jobs. Both were field manager jobs in the Midwest and South. I wasn't interested in going into that part of the country so I proposed to Jack that I could scout the San Juaquin Valley from Bakersfield to Stockton in the spring and then manage the short-season rookie club in Twin Falls.

Jack thought this was a great idea and a week later he sent me a contract. I was full time now with a dual job. He sent me back the box I sent him with all my supplies in it. He hadn't even opened it. I asked him about it and he said, "I knew you would be back with us. I just didn't know when." Jack Schwarz was the best scouting director I ever worked for. He didn't try to be a scout like so many of them do now. He liked scouts and he trusted them. He could give you a royal chewing out every so often, but he didn't hold a grudge or carry it over. He had his say and that was that. And he knew about players and what it takes to play the game of baseball. That's another thing so many of them don't get these days.

The Giants also had a bunch of veteran scouts who were some of the best in the business. Carl Hubbell and Hank Sauer were the crosscheckers, and Hubbell was the farm director. This was the great Carl Hubbell, one of the greatest pitchers who ever lived. He was a lean, hard-muscled man with a crooked left arm. The left arm was bent at an unnatural angle from throwing his famous screwball. Hank Sauer was a big, strong, aggressive, loud guy. You always knew when Hank was around, all you had to do was listen. Hank had a long major league career, was a home run hitter and former National League MVP. They were both good, very good baseball men, and we spoke the same language. It is a lot different nowadays with a lot of people in high places making decisions. In reality, they do not have the background and experience to be in those roles.

Some of the other Giant scouts were Gene Thompson, Buddy Kerr, Johnny Hudson, George Genovese, and George's brother, Chick Genovese. And we had the great Latin scout, Alex Pompez. The Giants had some great black players and some great Latin players: Mays, McCovey, Jim Ray Hart, the Alou brothers, Juan Marichal, Orlando Cepeda. Pompez had a lot to do with that part of it. Alex was a gentleman, a class guy, and it was an honor for me to be associated with him and with these people. Dave Garcia and Charlie Fox also had a lot to say as scouts and managers. It was quite a group and everyone always worked hard, and some of us got rewarded.

The Giants invited me to spring training in Casa Grande, Arizona, and I stayed two weeks. I was in uniform every day and I enjoyed all of it. Hubbell didn't have a lot of tolerance for the young pitchers who complained of sore arms. To show his own toughness and what he expected from his players, he never smiled on the field. He told me once, "I pitched with a sore arm all my life. You just pitch your way through it." The

May 26, 1970

Mr. Dick Wilson,
549 K St.,
Sparks, Nevada.

Dear Dick:

Your report on Dave Kingman arrived this morning. It is the best and most thorough report on an outstanding prospect I have ever received in this office. Many thanks.

Sincerely yours,

John S. Schwarz

Dick Wilson was one of many scouts who turned in reports on USC player Dave Kingman. The five-tool player, initially a pitcher, was converted to an outfielder after he was the first pick in the 1970 June draft by the San Francisco Giants. Although SABR credits George Genovese with signing Kingman, Dick Wilson received this letter of appreciation from the Giants' scouting department before the draft. Kingman went on to a sixteen-year major league career (Dick Wilson collection).

screwball is an unnatural pitch, a reverse strain on the arm. Hubbell really showed the effects of it. His left arm would flop like a chicken wing when he walked. Hubbell and Sauer hit the scotch whiskey pretty good, too, but it never interfered with their work on the field.

At that time I left spring training and rented a house in Fresno. We spent the summer there. I signed three players who all performed well in the minor leagues but never reached the top. In June I moved the family back to Nevada and took over the Twin Falls team. I had thirty-seven players but no coaches. Hubbell and Sauer were there for the training camp. Before the first workout Sauer said, "We'll work out from ten until noon and then Hub and I want to play golf."

I told Hank, "You go ahead and play golf, but there's no way I'm going to get off this field until 4 P.M."

Tom Lasorda was a rookie manager that year at Pocatello, Idaho, and we took turns playing practice games in each ballpark. One day in Twin Falls and the next day at

Pocatello. It didn't accomplish anything one way or the other but we felt it was fair to the players.

George Genovese signed a lot of players. He had signed 18 of the 37 I had on my roster. The major league draft was in by then, but that didn't slow George down. The trouble was that at times he was liable to sign three second basemen and then he'd have his own players competing against each other. George was very loyal to his players and he would stand up for them. But the thing with George was that the bonuses he gave them didn't always match their ability. One of his $5,000 players might be better than one of his $25,000 players. You could not get too hasty with one of his players because they all had something he liked.

George signed players in quantity, just like Eddie Taylor, and some rival scouts used to make sarcastic remarks about that. But nobody signed so many good major league players as George Genovese did. George belongs in the Scouts Hall of Fame. Some of his players were not good citizens, and in the years I managed I had to suspend a few and send some others to another of our farm clubs. He had a few bad apples along with his diamonds in the rough.

George Genovese was a particular favorite of Jack Schwarz, and for that reason Schwarz would draft a player for George over the rest of us. Schwarz had good reason for having such good faith in George, but in reality it cost the rest of us some players. One case I remember clearly was that of Lenn Sakata. Lenn Sakata was a Japanese infielder at Gonzaga University in Spokane, my territory, and I had followed him closely and made friends with him. He was the best Japanese player I ever saw and I put that into my report. The Giants wanted a Japanese player very badly because of the large Asian population in San Francisco. They had a Japanese left-hand pitcher named Masanori Murakami a few years before and they drew bigger crowds on days that he pitched.

Gonzaga made a big swing into Southern California that spring, playing against USC and a lot of top colleges. I alerted Genovese to this and told him to take a good look at Sakata. I was hoping for a good report from George, knowing this could help in the draft. I picked up Gonzaga at the tail end of their trip and I asked coach Larry Koentopp, "How did Sakata do down south?" He said he'd had a real good series and that Genovese had been at the games. So I felt the chances were good that I could get him in the draft.

However, it didn't happen. The Giants drafted a couple of high school infielders, Genovese's players from Santa Maria, California, by the names of Lee and Pride who never got very far. And Milwaukee got Sakata and he played for several years in the major leagues and is still active as a coach. That's the way things happen in the game and in other businesses, too, I guess. Sometimes all you can do is roll with the punches, if you know what I mean. Maybe it was all the better for Sakata.

These are types of situations that happen because of the draft. What it does is pit your scouts against each other. When a scouting director is putting his preferential list together, he has to decide who gets priority, and George Genovese got priority in that situation. Now don't get me wrong. I love George Genovese. He is a dedicated baseball man and I don't know of anybody who can match his record as a scout.

The Twin Falls club started slow but finished strong. We tied for second place with Lasorda's club. The next year I stayed in Nevada. The Giants hired a scout by the name of Bill Marshall to cover the Northwest and I still had the San Juaquin Valley. Bill Marshall at the time had been a top scout for the Milwaukee club when they had plenty of money and there was no draft. Milwaukee put out a lot of money in signing bonuses.

Marshall's style was always the same. He would go into a player's house and tell the family, "Go ahead and listen to the offers and then give me the last chance." He had the money to spend and he did it. He could get just about anybody he wanted because he had the money and could out-bid any other scout.

Bill had a serious drinking problem. It was serious enough that he was shunned as a bad risk. He was unemployed when the Giants signed him. Marshall was an old friend of Eddie Montague and Eddie was trying to straighten him out and get him back on his feet. It didn't take long for Marshall to fall off the wagon. Jack Schwarz called me one day and asked me to get into the Northwest again. He'd had no reports from Marshall and was unable to locate him. That was the end of Bill. He dropped out of sight and I had to pick up his territory. That happens every now and then and none of us likes it.

I got the Giants' number one pick in the draft that year — Bob Reynolds, a right-hand pitcher out of high school called "Bullet Bob." He was six-feet tall, close to 200 pounds. Strong. No student. Good fastball. He was easy to sign for $25,000 and went to our rookie league team. A lot of scouts thought he was dumb, but he wasn't dumb when he threw a fastball. He threw bullets and he threw strikes. Also, he knew how to find a shady spot on a hot day. He tore up the rookie league. He struck out more than twenty in two successive starts.

I saw those two games and I called Jack Schwarz and told him he could move up Reynolds at any time, all the way to Triple-A if he wanted. He was just overpowering the hitters in rookie league. They moved him to Fresno [California League, A ball] and he finished the season there and never looked back. The Giants lost him in the expansion draft. They received $225,000 for him and he went on to become one of the top relievers in the American League for the Baltimore Orioles.

I stayed with the Giants for 22 years. My primary job was as a free agent scout, but several times I filled in for different managers in the organization. Had pro coverage every year and major league coverage for one year, and went back and managed the rookie club again in 1970 and 1971. Along the way I picked up two part-time scouts. One was Jack Shafer, a fireman in Portland, and the other was Jim Lyke, the postmaster in Caldwell, Idaho. I couldn't have done any better. Jack Shafer was invaluable. He was all over and on top of everything. Knew the coaches. Knew the players. And had good judgment. In my mind he was better than a lot of the full-time scouts who worked up there. When you scout a big territory, or a small one for that matter, if you're smart, you learn quickly how valuable the part-time scouts are.

I had a system to beat the rain. I would drive my car into Portland and work until the rains drove me out, fly home and pick up my truck and go to work in the Sam Juaquin Valley until Jack would call me and tell me the weather was okay. I lost very few days with that system. Back and forth depending on the weather. Jim Lyke was also a valuable man. Southern Idaho was not a large area and Jim knew everybody that mattered and he knew the good citizens and the bad citizens. The weather was usually good in southern Idaho. I almost lost Jim when the Giants joined the scouting bureau. Jack Schwarz did not want the bureau but was forced into it by the Giants ownership. Schwarz said I'd have to sacrifice Jim Lyke. Now Jim was only making $500 total and I told Schwarz that he could cut my salary by the $500 to keep Jim. Schwarz agreed to that and told me, "This is the first time in my memory that I knew of a scout willingly taking a cut in salary." I asked Jack not to tell Jim and I never mentioned it. So Jim never knew. I considered it a bargain for me and the Giants.

I had a few periods of feeling burned out, but kept going and signed a few major leaguers. One was Dave Rader, a catcher from Bakersfield High School. Dave was considered too small by most scouts, but I fell in love with him. He was really quick and had great hands. He was a tough kid. A left-hand hitter who didn't strike out. One of my all-time favorites. I got Carl Hubbell to see him and Carl told me he never dropped a ball the entire game. We took him in the first round and I signed him for $22,000. Can you imagine an organization's number one draft signing for that money today? He advanced through the organization easily and in his first year in San Francisco he named the *Sporting News* Rookie of the Year.

I signed Steve Ontiveros, a third baseman out of Bakersfield High School. I knew Steve's dad, Frank, and I signed Steve for $12,000. He was a good-sized kid, thick, who could hit and he could throw. A switch-hitter, better from the left side. Strong physically. Good family. Mexican descent. Steve hit his way all the way to the major league level with the Giants and did a good job until he was traded to the Chicago Cubs. Steve eventually went to Japan and was a star over there. He came home a millionaire.

There's more to the Steve Ontiveros story. One year all our scouts had received a bulletin from Jack Schwarz to have our final draft list in by June 3. Chub Feeney would be going to the meeting on June 4. I think the meeting was to be held in Chicago that year. It had been a wet spring in the Northwest that year and I was hustling right up to the end to see a few players up there one more time. The state of Washington was holding its high school all-star game in Bellingham on the Memorial Day weekend. On the way to this I dropped the transmission in my car in Seattle. I had to have it towed to the Aamco Transmission shop to be rebuilt. I caught a ride with another scout to Bellingham.

While in Bellingham I got a call from Jack Schwarz and he jumped all over me. "Where in the hell is your draft list? Chub Feeney was just in here and he wants those lists now! He's leaving for Chicago three days early."

Jack was really upset and when he tried to explain to Feeney, Feeney told him, "I can't be responsible for your laggards!" My impression of Feeney all along was that he was arrogant and considered himself all-important. I never felt comfortable around him like I did with Hubbell. But Feeney was calling the shots. He was one of those guys who would listen to a fella's excuse, no matter what. There was no excuse he would listen to, even though the mix-up was because he decided to leave three days early. I was not the only scout who had not completed his list.

All this uncalled-for criticism really made me mad. I told Jack, "Goddamn it, Jack, I'm busting my tail up here to get you the best information I can and you get all over me for something I'm not to blame for. Nobody told me Feeney was leaving three days early."

Jack understood because he was caught in the same bind, but he never said anything. Feeney was the boss and he wanted what he wanted when he wanted it. So I told Jack, "My car is locked up in the Aamco shop for the holiday weekend and all my paperwork is in the car. But I can give you the tentative list off the top of my head." I don't think he really thought I could do it, but he calmed down when I let off steam, and there was a moment of silence, deadening silence.

I told him, "Get Ontiveros." And that's how we got Steve Ontiveros. The Giants took him in the sixth round, pick number 136 overall.

I signed Jim Willoughby, a right-hand high school pitcher out of Gustine High School near Stockton. Signed him the same year as Dave Rader. Jim was part Indian. No father at home. Lived in a ramshackle type farm house. Jim was an outstanding high school athlete. In this rundown house he had a room full of trophies. He was also a good student.

We drafted him around the eighth round. He stalled a little. He'd been given some bad information by some frustrated ex-players and he was uncertain. I offered him an $8,000 signing bonus and a college scholarship. His mother thought this was great and so did his girlfriend. But Jim wouldn't make a decision. Finally I told him, "I'm going to Bakersfield to sign a catcher and should be back in a couple of days. Now don't talk to your barber or anyone else who is full of free advice and doesn't have to back it up with money. I'll see you in a couple of days." When I got back after signing Dave Rader, Jim was all smiles and ready to sign. The whole thing took only a few minutes.

Jim advanced steadily in the organization and soon was in the big leagues. In and out of the big leagues. Some good games and some not so good. He was traded and wound up with the Boston Red Sox where he made a name for himself as a reliever. Jim pitched especially well in the World Series versus the Cincinnati Reds.

I signed several players for the Giants who appeared in a major league box score and several more who made the 40-man roster and were good Triple-A players. I signed Dave Heaverlo out of Central Washington University and Frank Williams out of Lewiston, Idaho. They both pitched several years in the big leagues. Dave Heaverlo, known as "Kojak" because of his shaved head, finished up with the Oakland A's.

Frank Williams was a side-arm right-hander who gave right-hand hitters a lot of trouble. He was especially tough on two of the National League's better right-hand hitters, Dale Murphy and Steve Garvey. Frank Williams was a full-blooded Indian and he was a twin. Williams was traded to Cincinnati and had some nerve damage to his pitching elbow, which forced him out of baseball in his early thirties.

The Giants were having some lean years and finally Horace Stoneham was forced to give up. For several months the Giants' employees were getting their paycheck from the National League. Finally Bob Lurie bought the club and things began to change. Carl Hubbell retired and Jack Schwarz was forced into retirement. Bob Fontaine, Sr., was named scouting director. Fontaine had been a long time Branch Rickey man with Pittsburgh and more recently had been with the San Diego Padres. Fontaine was the type of scouting director who didn't trust his scouts. And so he was always on the road doing his own scouting instead of being in the office the way Schwarz had been. Fontaine was not well liked by most of the older scouts and the younger ones were intimidated by him.

I had known Fontaine for a long time when he was a young scout for the Pirates and I was a player in the organization. He had a great personality at that time. Very friendly, and I thought he was on the edge of being brilliant. He never took notes; kept everything in his head. But when he took over, several old friends of his and mine also told me he had changed and they no longer trusted him. They told me, "Dick, don't turn your back on him." But I wasn't worried. I still remembered the way he used to be. It wasn't long before it was clear that they were right. He had changed!

Right about that time I started having a problem with my eyelids. I couldn't always control them and it got worse to the point where driving became a problem and I was afraid I would hit someone and do some serious damage. After going to several different doctors who didn't have a clue, I finally went to a neurologist who ran some tests. He called in another neurologist and they diagnosed the problem as blepharospasms, a rare disease that affects the eyelids. There was only one doctor on the West Coast who worked with it, and he was in Beverly Hills. Dr. Norman Shorr. I went to him and had my first operation. Eventually I had four.

He took out all the nerves he could find in my face and then in a later operation took out all the muscles that support the eyelids. I finally got to where I had enough control to where I could drive and I could get by. It got so bad before the surgery that I would pick up hitchhikers and let them drive. But some of them were worse than I was!

When the season ended I knew I would have to have a talk with Fontaine to see if we could work something out to where I wouldn't have to do so much traveling. I never got the chance to talk about it to anyone. Fontaine called me one day in September and stuttered and stammered around until I told him, "Go ahead, Bob, spit it out. I know what you want to say."

I then wished him and the Giants good luck. I did ask him for the reason why they fired me, but all I could get out of him was that my philosophy on the organization's players differed from theirs. I had only covered one of our organization's clubs, and that was Fresno. And then I more or less got what Fontaine's problem with me was. He had handpicked the Giants' number one draft pick in June. It was Steve Stanicek, an outfielder, college player from Nebraska. In my team report on Fresno that summer I had turned in a negative report on Stanicek. He didn't even want a scout to make an honest report if it disagreed with his, I guess. Apparently Fontaine took this personally and I was gone. Apparently I was right. Stanicek didn't make it.

George Genovese was really upset over this. He said, "Go to Lurie. Tell him who you've signed and tell him how long you have been here!" George had no use for Fontaine and this was a good way for me to sort of fight his battles for him. I know George was concerned about me but he also had his own personal axe to grind.

I told George, "Thanks anyway, George, but I can't think of anything worse than working for somebody who doesn't want me around. " They gave me plenty of notice, like three months, and paid me through the end of the year.

I received a call within a week from Gary Hughes, then with the Yankees. He offered me a job, smaller territory and more money. I didn't argue and gave my okay over the phone. Thirty minutes later Kansas City called and I had to tell them, "Sorry." But if I would have known I would have gone with Kansas City because their farm teams and main office were a lot closer than New York.

George Genovese told me he was going to outlast Fontaine and Fontaine's right-hand man, Bob Miller. They didn't show him any respect and he felt they would have gotten rid of him if they could. But his track record was too good, he was one of the best, and eventually he did outlast them both. Bob Miller was killed in an automobile accident and Fontaine died a short while later. The Giants front office was in new hands. Tom Haller was out and Al Rosen and Bob Kennedy were in.

I had worked for Charlie Finley and now I was working for George Steinbrenner. I found that the office in New York was in a state of confusion much of the time, especially when Steinbrenner showed up! We had some good people. Bill Livesay was a good, solid baseball man. Murray Cook was the GM when I joined them but soon after that Murray and George had a big falling out. Murray had neglected to do some paperwork or something and, if I am correct, I think it cost them pitcher Tim Belcher. Steinbrenner punished Murray by embarrassing him in front of a group of Yankees people and demoted him down from GM to scouting director. Murray Cook had been a scout for a long time with Pittsburgh. He was easy to work for.

During that one year with the Yankees I realized I had to change my status from full time to part time. The spring scouting was not a problem. Things move at a fast pace. Busy every day running down leads on players and compiling a draft list. Usually, after the draft, things slow down and usually you get some pro coverage. I signed three players for them. One made it to Triple-A and the two others played A ball a few years and then disappeared. I didn't get any pro coverage. Murray Cook told me, "Just go over to the Bay Area and cover American Legion baseball the rest of the summer."

To me that was the last thing I wanted to do. I had 25 years experience and in my mind I had progressed beyond that type of scouting. So I wrote Murray a letter and told him that I wouldn't be going to San Francisco that summer or any summer and that I wanted part-time work. Special assignments and so forth.

Murray Cook was a Canadian and he left the Yankees and so did Gary Hughes. They both went to Montreal. The man I was dealing with now was Doug Melvin. He didn't want to talk about part time for me. He was very vague. He seemed uncertain and I really didn't know if they had any plans at all for me. It was really a strange feeling, and I finally wrote to Melvin and told him I appreciated the opportunity I had been given to work for one of the great names in baseball history, the New York Yankees, but I was going to contact a few clubs to see if anyone had any use for me in the limited role I wanted.

I wrote one letter, to the Detroit Tigers, and I got immediate results. George Bradley was the scouting director and Bill Lajoie was the GM. Lajoie was on top of the entire operation. He had advanced within the system and still wanted to be active in the scouting and player development process. The only problem for Bill was that the agents were becoming more and more numerous and it took a lot of Bill's time just dealing with them and the big club Tigers players. Lajoie was a good baseball man and a successful GM, but I don't think he enjoyed dealing with these agents who were, for the most part, non-baseball people. And it wasn't too much longer until he quietly removed himself from that stressful situation and went over to the Atlanta Braves as special assistant to John Schuerholz.

I signed with the Tigers for a big cut and took an early out on Social Security, age 62, and started a new phase of my life in baseball. George Bradley was my immediate boss and was just great to work for. I enjoyed that year as much as any of all the years I'd scouted. At that time, Bradley would give me an assignment like this: "Dick, I want you to go over to Stanford and cover the Stanford-Arizona State series. Here is a list of players we have an interest in. Call me Monday morning and tell me about them."

And there was, "Dick, there are two catchers on the West Coast we are interested in. Todd Zeile at UCLA and John Ramos at Stanford. Go over there and let us know which one you prefer."

Or, "Dick, we have a pitcher under control at Cerritos Junior College in Southern California. Go down there and watch him pitch and let us know what he's worth."

I loved these assignments. It was perfect for me and George Bradley was perfect to work for. The trouble was that George resigned after that first year and the "perfect" situation was not there anymore. I stayed with the Tigers for eight years and we had a succession of changes in the scouting department. Roger Jongewaard, Tom Gamboa, Dick Wiencek, and Bill Schudlich were all my immediate supervisors at different times. Joe McDonald also came in as a vice president, and we had Bo Schembechler, the famous football coach at Michigan for a while. None of these people was a problem for me. It was a good working experience and I enjoyed my time with them.

The only problem I had was when Bill Schudlich took over. He was a good scout. A good baseball man. I still liked his judgment on players. But he was biased against West Coast players. He wasn't even subtle about it and everyone in the organization knew it. He definitely favored other parts of the country to draft players from. Things were smoothed out by Joe McDonald and my resignation was not accepted. I did not want to leave the Tigers but I couldn't keep quiet when this type of favoritism was going on.

Lajoie and Schudlich were close but I think Lajoie could see this situation wasn't healthy and so he promoted Jax Robertson to scouting director and Bill Schudlich went back to scouting where he was better suited, in my opinion. I say this because he was instrumental in signing John Smoltz, Travis Fryman and many others. He was more effective for the organization as an area scout. No doubt in my mind about that.

Jax Robertson was a young guy. Very intelligent and even tempered and just great to work for. He seemed easy going but he had some steel in him that would show up at our meetings. Jax had been with the Yankees and had signed Don Mattingly. He gave me the most responsibility I had with the Tigers since the year George Bradley was there. He sent me all over, even to Arkansas, Iowa, and Texas. And he relied on my opinion. I also had Joe McDonald in my corner. Joe was very conservative with money. I was kind of the same way, but not as extreme as Joe. He had been a GM with the Mets and Cardinals, and was with the Cardinals when they were the world champions. He was close to being burned out dealing with the modern players and the demands of their agents, and he didn't want to do it anymore. He had some bitterness from his GM experience, but he was a good man. Some of the scouts didn't like him because they couldn't pry the money from him and they wanted to sign their drafts. I liked Joe. I had his confidence in my judgment and I did not find it difficult to get Joe's okay on the few deals I handled.

I was really not involved in signing players anymore. Only a few that I knew personally that had been high on my draft list. Two of these were Rob Ritchie, an outfielder, and Kurt Knudsen, a right-hand pitcher. Both made it to the top. Ritchie was on the verge of major league stardom when the Jehovah's Witness religion got into his blood and he quit baseball just as he was reaching his prime. The church convinced him that "God and baseball don't mix." I tried to point out to him that athletes in all sports were proving him wrong every day, but he wouldn't listen. He disappointed his parents and entire family.

Kurt Knudsen was in and out of the big leagues with the Tigers for a few years. He had some good moments but Tiger Stadium was a hitter's ballpark, and Sparky Anderson is, in my opinion, hell on pitchers. It looked like his career was over prematurely due to a disc injury in his back that limited his flexibility. He had a major league arm and I thought he never reached his potential. He was the last major leaguer I signed: fifteen in all.

Jax Robertson was caught between Bill Lajoie and Joe McDonald. Friction had developed between them to where they actively did not speak to each other. It was a tough situation for Jax. I think he looked forward to getting out of the office and going on the road. I always looked forward to his West Coast trips. Enjoyed being around him, not only for business, but I liked him personally.

After Lajoie resigned, Joe McDonald took over the GM job temporarily. He didn't want the job but he had the experience and he held out until the Tigers hired Bo Schembechler. Bo was a football man and he immediately upgraded the Tigers' training facilities at the minor league levels. Joe McDonald was there as a consultant and advisor for Bo. Lajoie's presence was still there. He had come out to the West Coast to see our top draft preferences and Tony Clark and Marc Newfield were two of the better ones. I personally favored Newfield, but Lajoie made sure that Tony Clark was to be the number one pick. We had a high pick that year, number two or three in the country.

Jax Robertson told me later that this was the only time he was ever told whom to draft. Bill Lajoie wanted Tony Clark. Clark was an outstanding baseball player in high school and he and his father insisted that he be allowed to play big-time college baseball at the University of Arizona and he would only give baseball a few weeks in the summer. I was against it. Rob Wilfong, a recent National Leaguer and now one of our scouts, said he didn't think Clark could develop properly since he was giving very little of his time to baseball. But Bo Schembechler okayed the deal. Bo personally visited the Clark family and gave in to their demands. Bo admitted he didn't know much about baseball, but he prided himself as a recruiter and so he recruited Tony Clark.

After wasting three or four years playing basketball, Tony Clark made it to the Tigers' major league club and established himself at first base and hitting home runs. Newfield made it to the big leagues also. He was a first-round selection, but it looks like Lajoie was right. Newfield was plagued with injuries and Clark pulled ahead of him in career success.

All too soon Jax Robertson quit as our scouting director. It caught us all by surprise and caught the Tigers by surprise also. Jax went over to the Florida Marlins expansion team as a national crosschecker to help them with their important expansion draft that was coming up. Joe McDonald was in a bind to fill Jax's spot as scouting director and he didn't have a lot of time. Joe Klein had been with the Tigers as a national crosschecker, had been with the Texas Rangers, and had been with Kansas City. Joe had also held a lot of corporate jobs, front office positions. And he was an ex-player and spoke the players' language, which a lot of GMs and scouting directors do not speak these days.

I soon found out that while Klein was qualified, I didn't like the way he ran the scouting department. In some ways he was like Bob Fontaine, Sr., because if he didn't see players personally then a scout had a hard time getting his player drafted high. Joe ran our meetings like he was in a big hurry to go somewhere. Usually, in all of the meetings I had been in on in my career, we would go over each player and everybody who had seen the player would have his time to comment and we'd go back and forth.

But this wasn't the way Joe did it. He hardly gave anybody a chance to talk and it made me wonder what we had been running all over hell for. It seemed to me that all our reports and paperwork and attempts to get the best evaluation possible were just ignored by Joe. They were passed over by Joe Klein's careless approach to all our efforts. When the meeting broke up, I was pretty disgusted with the way Klein handled it and I made up my mind that I would not be back the next year. And then, to top it off, we had a workout scheduled for the next day for some players we wanted to see in action.

Ted Williams
P.O. Box 5127
Clearwater, FL 34618

FEBRUARY 10, 1992

MR. RICHARD WILSON
DETROIT BASEBALL CLUB
~~████████████████████~~
~~████████████████████~~

DEAR DICK:

    I READ YOUR LETTER WITH GREAT INTEREST. YOU HIT IT RIGHT ON THE HEAD WHEN YOU SAID THAT SOME OF THE NEW THEORIES ON HITTING ARE ABSOLUTELY BULL ----. THEY HAVE SET BACK THE RIGHT WAY OF HITTING A BASEBALL 35 YEARS.

    I HOPE SOMEDAY WE'LL GET A CHANCE TO SIT DOWN AND TALK ABOUT IT.

                                              SINCERELY,

                                              Ted Williams

                                              TED WILLIAMS

TW/g

Dick Wilson was well respected by minor league managers and his peers in the scouting community because he knew about hitting. He could analyze it, evaluate it, and assist players who were having problems with it. While he was scouting for the Detroit Tigers in 1991, he wrote a letter to Ted Williams expressing his theories. This letter was William's reply (Dick Wilson collection).

    One of these players was a catcher named Del Marine. He was a junior college player that we had control over but that control was right up against the deadline. We had to sign him by midnight the next day or lose that control over him. This was a decision for Joe Klein to make and I couldn't believe it when he said he was flying out of Los Angeles the next morning and wouldn't be staying for the workout. I don't know how anybody can explain that decision.

I left him a voice mail message after the workout and recommended we sign Marine. I felt that we scouts were only going through the motions without a leader. Maybe I wouldn't have been asked to come back for another year. I don't know. I did know that Joe Klein was no Jax Robertson and it was time for me to leave.

Atlanta had contacted me earlier and wanted me to come over with them. At the time they called I told them to call back in July after the draft and I would know more about how I felt. They did call and I told them I was ready to go. They wanted me to resign from Detroit right then, but I didn't want to do it that way. My contract was up October 1 and I told Atlanta I would work out that contract and then sign with them. Just before October 1 I called Klein and told him I was leaving. He did not seem to care much one way or the other. I don't think Joe was too interested in the scouting department. He had told me one time he liked the office work, the telephone action, and deals and so forth.

I got a raise in salary. So it was over with the Tigers. If Jax Robertson would have stayed, I never would have left as long as he wanted me. I was with the Tigers for eight years and each year they offered me a multi-year contract, but I didn't want that. Jax told me I contributed more to the Tigers than many of his full-time people. The conditions were more important to me than the salary.

I knew most of the West Coast scouts for Atlanta and had played against Bobby Cox. The Atlanta pitching coach, Leo Mazzone, had played for me in the Giants organization. But the man who recommended me was Bart Braun, the right-hand man for Chuck LaMar, who was the scouting director and also in charge of player development.

Bart and I were both helped by and started out as scouts because of Loyd Christopher. So we had a common bond. Bart advanced quickly as a scout. He was aggressive and not afraid to sign players. He did his homework and knew his business. He had scouted for Detroit and Pittsburgh. He and LaMar were in Pittsburgh at the same time, and when LaMar came over to Atlanta in a supervisory position, Bart came with him and was his national crosschecker. Bart was always an extremely hard worker, to the point of risking his health with constant travel, lack of sleep, and irregular eating habits.

Chuck LaMar was a dynamic guy and seemed to have endless energy. I never saw him appear tired and he could talk forever at our meetings and never run down. He wore me out just listening to him. I had told LaMar that I had wanted to include my son, Dan, who was twenty at the time, in my role with the Braves, and eventually maybe he could become a paid scout. LaMar said he wanted to meet us personally and after a few dates and cancellations — he was always too busy — we finally flew to San Francisco to meet with him. He was traveling with the Braves and they were playing the Giants in Candlestick Park. We had lunch with him. Laid it all out, and it was agreed that Dan and I would be responsible for a small territory in northern Nevada in addition to me crosschecking whenever LaMar wanted me to. I had confidence in Dan becoming a good scout. He had traveled with me and was serious and reliable and really wanted to get started as a scout. And, above all, he had good judgment and instincts about ballplayers.

Dave Wilder was the Atlanta scout in northern California and northern Nevada. LaMar said to us, "Well, you guys live in northern Nevada and it would be stupid of me not to give you that territory." Chuck loved to have meetings and it wasn't long before we had one scheduled in San Diego. I wanted Dan to attend and get a feel for the things that would be discussed and so forth. I was under the impression that Dan was going to be invited. This was the first time things happened differently than I thought, but it wasn't the last. Dan didn't get to go.

At that meeting LaMar called in each scout individually and had a private meeting with each one. When my turn came he told me he wasn't going to give Dan and me northern Nevada. Things were going to stay the same and Dave Wilder would keep that territory. So, where he had called it stupid before, now he himself was doing what he called stupid. I worked the next year for him and he used me a lot. Even had me in West Palm Beach in the fall to report on the Atlanta rookies.

In all my years in baseball, close to fifty at the time, I had never been in Florida. Always had trained in Arizona and Southern California. So I enjoyed that part of it. In my mind it kind of completed things. I took Dan on as many trips as I could, and in September the Braves sent me to Los Angeles and San Diego to follow the big club for a week and then send my final report on the Braves to John Schuerholz. This was good duty and Dan and I both enjoyed it. Dan helped me with handling the ray gun and giving me his impressions of the players. I said hello to Tom Lasorda and we reminisced about his beginning as a manager when he was at Pocatello and I was in Twin Falls.

I signed with Atlanta for my second year and we had another meeting in San Diego. This one dealt with computers. For this one they definitely should have brought Dan in because it just gave me a king-sized headache! I was really glad to get that meeting over with. I packed the computer home and gave it to Dan and he figured it out in minutes.

We set up our system whereby if he was traveling with me, we or he could do the reports on the computer and send them from our motel room. If I were on the road by myself, I would send my reports verbally to Dan on our voice mail and he would repeat them on the computer and send them in for me. I paid him for this work and it was well worth it. Some of the older scouts refused to use computers. They weren't being stubborn, so to speak, but they were intimidated by the whole thing and felt that after all the years they'd done it "the old way" and it worked fine, why should they be forced to change? I would have refused also but I had Dan to rely on. It was good for both of us.

The next spring I was sent to West Palm Beach again. More meetings in spring training games. LaMar would also fly the scouts in for the draft meetings in June. The second year we were hardly there for twenty minutes input. Jerry Gardner, a long-time scout, couldn't believe it. We could have done our little bit by telephone and saved a lot of money, not to mention our time. But Chuck LaMar and Gary Hughes have one thing in common. They are both good at spending other peoples' money!

I completed my second year with Atlanta. They have some quality people in that organization. I was impressed with the GM, John Schuerholz. Paul Snyder had everyone's respect, and in Bill Wight they have one on baseball's best scouts.

Then the strike happened. LaMar called me personally and told me things were uncertain and he didn't know what was going to happen. He said he had to give me a twenty-five percent cut in salary to keep me on. I told him that I understood and could see where baseball had gotten itself into a mess and I was willing to do my part and take the cut. A few weeks went by and then I received my contract in the mail. It wasn't the kind of contract I had been signing for over thirty years. It was more like an agreement and it called for a seventy-five percent pay cut, and there was no health coverage and so forth. I couldn't believe it! I had been told by more than one person in baseball that LaMar was a chronic liar but I just took all that as rumors until this proved it to me. I never accept rumors or gossip as fact. Well, now here it was in black and white. What he did was not what he said. I didn't bother to sign the contract or return it unsigned. I just didn't do anything about it. I called a good friend of mine, Dick Egan with the Florida Marlins. He came up with a suggestion that I thought was a great idea. He said, "This strike isn't going to last forever. Why don't you go ahead and sign the agreement with the provision that when the strike is settled, your contract will revert back to what it was before the strike."

This was a simple solution and made a lot of sense. I proposed it to LaMar the next time we were in contact and he said, "Oh, no. We can't do that. We don't know when the strike will end." I couldn't understand his reasoning. He wasn't risking anything, but he didn't even say, "Let me think about it," or anything. It was a flat rejection and all I could get from his reaction was that it was an invitation for me to quit. But before I relayed Egan's suggestion to LaMar, he had finally called me and asked why I had not responded to the contract he had sent me. I told him that I thought he had made a simple mistake because the document he sent me called for a seventy-five percent pay cut instead of the twenty-five we had discussed. He denied that he had said twenty-five percent. I didn't feel like getting into a phone argument, so I asked him to give me a month to think it over and he said that was okay. That meant my old contract with medical coverage included remained in effect for that time, the month of December.

My right hip was in bad shape, so I went to the hospital and had it replaced. I think it was a $30,000 operation and I certainly could not have afforded it without that medical insurance. The operation was done two weeks before Christmas. The coverage plus the bonus paid for most of it. I had a quick recovery, and on January 1 I passed word to a few friends that I was thinking about making a change. The California Angels soon called and I told them I would go with them but I wanted them to go through the proper channels and get permission from Chuck LaMar. It took some time to get this done because LaMar is hard to get hold of most of the time. But eventually he gave his permission and I signed with the Angels even though the strike was still on.

After two years with the Angels I decided I had had enough of the traveling, the motels, the night driving, and the Bay Area traffic, which seems to get more congested every year. So I told Tom Davis, my supervisor, that I would stay on only if they wanted me in northern Nevada. I took a token salary and expenses.

Over the past forty-five years I had scouted with Kansas City, the Mets, Yankees, Giants, Detroit, Oakland, Atlanta and the Angels. I was an area scout for most of those years and a special assignment scout for some of them. During my 22 years with the Giants, I signed thirteen players who played in the big leagues, including catcher Dave Rader out of high school, Bob Reynolds, who ended up with Baltimore, third baseman Steve Ontiveros, pitcher Dave Heaverlo, submarine pitcher Frank Williams, Jim Willoughby, Terry Cornutt, Rob Dressler, Ed Plank and Casey Parsons.

There's many things I remember along the way. There's always "events" in minor league baseball and I remember this particular one because it was so different. Cameron Mitchell was a well-known movie actor at the time. He would later have an ongoing role in the popular TV series *High Chaparral*. He also had a reputation as some kind of amateur player with a knuckleball that nobody could hit.

Well, with a lot of publicity he was signed by Vegas and scheduled to pitch against us in Ontario. Needless to say, that sold a lot of tickets. The game was a day game on

Sunday and the weather was hot, close to a hundred degrees. Mitchell had a short, thickset body, did not look like an athlete, especially a pitcher. Anyway, he went out to pitch in the last of the first inning. He started lobbing that knuckleball up to the plate and we just wore him out! Batted around twice, scored twelve runs and had the bases full before their manager finally took him out. That half-inning lasted close to an hour and he was soaking wet with sweat and completely exhausted when he was lifted. But the stands were full because of him, so they left him out there to suffer through it. I give the guy credit because he never quit trying, and you had to feel sorry for him. Fortunately for him, he was a lot better on the movie screen.

One of my favorite stories about a player happened when I was still playing and hadn't begun scouting yet. It was in 1951 with the Pirates' farm team in Modesto, the Cal League, Class C. The season was disappointing for the team because we didn't make the playoffs. I had a great year and at the end they even had a "night" for me. It wasn't a total surprise but the way people showed support for what I'd accomplished that year meant something to me. It also encouraged me for the next season. We had a rookie outfielder from the Bay Area. Eighteen years old. He was a tall kid, around 6'2", duck feet, slow footed, couldn't run much, not much of an arm, poor outfielder. But he had signs of tape measure power. His name was Dick Stuart and he later became famous as "Dr. Strangeglove," the first baseman for the Pittsburgh Pirates.

Stu was a likeable kid, but not ready to play in the California League at this point in his career. Tony Freitas, our manager, could not really stand him and only played him like once a week, mostly in left field. When a fly ball was hit his way, it was 50–50 whether or not he would catch it. He would paddle up to it and then stop and let it bounce when with one more step he could have caught it. He used to drive Freitas crazy and Tony was on him all the time.

Stu always referred to Tony as "coach" instead of "skip" or "skipper" like the rest of the players. It drove Tony nuts, but he understood Stu and let it pass. One day Stu came to me and said, "I don't know why coach doesn't let me play, after all, I'm leading the team in home runs in batting practice." And I guess he was. Most of us didn't keep track of batting practice home runs. But Stu did. He was always aware of his own stats and always tried hard to get better. He was pretty focused on his goals and always worked hard.

But he didn't use the good wood we got from Louisville. He would go to a local sporting goods store and buy his own bats, two at a time. He used to get a yellow one and a black one. They were poor quality wood and made a loud noise when he hit one. They also made a loud noise when they broke, and he broke quite a few. I used to get on him for using those "drugstore" bats. I think they cost a buck-twenty-five.

One night Freitas put him in the lineup and we were getting ready to take the field when Stu took off running toward a little convenience-type store about a block away. Freitas saw him and hollered, "Hey, get back here. The game's ready to start!"

Stu stopped and said, "I've got to get my Blackjack gum, coach. I can't play without Blackjack gum. I'll go 0-for-4 if I don't get it." And he took off running in the direction of the store. We never got upset at these antics because they were just part of who the guy was. And he was a good ballplayer. Another night Freitas put him in the lineup in San Jose, which was the Red Sox farm team. The Red Sox had a small organization. I mean, they had fewer farm teams than any other major league club. They went for quality instead of Branch Rickey's famous style of "from quantity comes quality." And the Red Sox gave out big bonuses like $100,000, which was about tops in those days. They always had a pitching staff of big guys who could throw hard. So in this game they used their hardest thrower, Al Curtis. It was twilight, and in the first few innings it was difficult to see the ball. Their pitcher started off just blowing us away. He struck out the first seven of us.

Stuart was hitting eighth. The first pitch to Stu was a low fastball and there were two loud cracks. One was the sound of Stu's drugstore bat and the second was when the ball hit the pitcher's kneecap. Stu hit an absolute rocket! The ball bounced off Curtis' knee into the third base dugout, and they carried the pitcher off the field on a stretcher. We all congratulated Stu because we didn't want to face Curtis again. That guy was just too much for us to face at the plate. That didn't end his career, but it didn't help much.

Just a few years later Stuart hit 66 home runs in a season in the Class A Western League and then became one of the premier power hitters in the National League. He also was the major league arm wrestling champion. He had a great set of hands and unloaded. I liked Stu. He was a simple, uncomplicated kid that year, with tape measure power.

Thinking back over other memories, I used to be in demand as a pepper hitter when I first started in pro ball. The hottest pepper games I remember were with Tony Freitas. And when I was with the Seals, I had some hot games with Elmer Orella, a left-hand pitcher, and Clark Pieretti. Pieretti was really something, just full of energy and life. These two would get me to hit to them and it was rapid fire. We would get to one hundred without a miss in a hurry. Tony Freitas, in the two years I played with him, never ran to keep in shape as other pitchers do. He would get a fast pepper game going, and then when batting practice began, he would go out to center field and play each pitch as if he were the center fielder in a live game. Tony Freitas, what a pleasure to play behind him. He was a master of his craft. I had a lot of respect for him and so did a lot of others who spent time around him.

When I was in Little Rock in 1944, the Cardinals sent Paul Dean, Dizzy's brother, to Little Rock to try to get his arm trouble straightened out. Paul had a sore shoulder. Probably a rotator cuff, but in those days it was called a sore arm. Paul would hunt me up every day as soon as we stepped on the field and get me to hit pepper to him. He was serious and a hard worker, and the pepper game left him soaked in sweat. Then he would go to the mound and throw for twenty or thirty minutes. He never wanted to talk about the pain back then, but it was no secret. Everybody watching him could see it. Later somebody told me that Paul had many nights where he actually slept standing up leaning against the corner of the wall. He said he did it for a long time after he stopped pitching because the pain was so great. He was some kind of a baseball player.

Gene "Junior" Thompson

(1917–2000)

Thompson, a right-handed pitcher, spent his life in professional baseball. He had a split major league career because of a 27-month stint in the navy during World War II. He was dubbed "Junior" by his teammates because his youth was somewhat of a joke to him, and he had the last laugh. His daughter recently told me that his mother wanted to name him Earl after his father, but his grandmother thought that would be too confusing and suggested his given name be Junior Eugene Thompson.

He was signed out of high school in 1934 by Charlie Dressen of the Cincinnati Reds when he was just seventeen years old. He successfully climbed the minor league ladder and played his first major league game in 1939. That season he compiled an impressive 13–5 record with a 2.55 ERA. In this rookie year he pitched in the Reds–Yankees World Series, Game Three, but lost as the Yankees swept the series.

In 1940 his record was 16–9 and he pitched in Game Five of the Reds–Tigers World Series, his only World Series start, and he received a no-decision. In his book, Memories of a Ballplayer, *teammate Billy Werber recalled some of the excitement of that day. He wrote,*

> Game Five was played in Detroit, and since the series was tied two games each, it was a pivotal contest. McKechnie decided to start Thompson, but he wanted to spare Junior as much pressure as possible and let him get a good rest. So he didn't tell Gene or announce his starting pitcher until just before game time. Junior had married a lovely young lady, Dorothy, in 1939 and she was seated in the box seats with the other wives. She had not imagined in her wildest dreams that Junior would be called upon to pitch in enemy territory or anywhere else on such a pressure-packed occasion. When the announcer bawled over the stadium amplifying system, "Pitching for the Reds, Junior Thompson," it was more than Dorothy could take. She gasped, "Oh my God," and passed out in her seat.

Thompson was often described as the ultimate competitor and a true quality pitcher of long standing. He pitched his final two seasons with the New York Giants in 1947–48, then hung it up. He appeared in a total of 185 major league games and posted a career record of 47–35 with a 3.26 ERA. When all was said and done, he recalled that his favorite thrill as a player happened back in 1937 when he pitched for Peoria in the minor leagues and retired twenty-seven consecutive batters. He then became a professional scout and contributed to the game in that capacity for more than fifty years. He was the recipient of the Scout of the Year Award, West Coast, 1989.

Gene "Junior" Thompson

In Chase Field, home of the Arizona Diamondbacks, a bronze plaque on the fans' side of the wall directly behind home plate facing a front row seat was dedicated in his honor on April 19, 2008, with more than twenty-five members of Gene Thompson's family from all over the country in attendance. In many ways, the plaque sums up his career to the game and the game's regard for him best. It reads:

> *This chair represents the personal seating location of Gene Thompson from the 1998–2006 seasons. From the first pitch of the Arizona Diamondbacks Inaugural season in 1998, Thompson used this seat while scouting for the San Diego Padres until he passed away in August of 2006. A member of the Cincinnati Reds from 1939–1942, Thompson pitched in the 1939 World Series against the New York Yankees and the 1940 World Series against the Detroit Tigers. Thompson served in the United States Navy during World War II from 1944–1945, and resumed his career with the New York Giants, pitching from 1946–1947. Upon his retirement as a player Thompson enjoyed a successful career as a scout from 1947–2006 as a member of the San Francisco Giants, Cleveland Indians, Chicago Cubs, and San Diego Padres. An inspiration to many, this plaque will serve to preserve his memory and continue to honor his legacy.*

He said he didn't have the energy to speak very long and asked if he could jot down some of his baseball memories and mail them to me. The following came a few weeks later.

I hear over and over as to how much baseball has changed. After giving it a lot of thought, I decided to give my version of what has and has not happened.

Charlie Dressen signed me in late October 1934 when I was seventeen years old. This year marks my sixty-seventh year in the game in many different capacities, but mostly as a player for seventeen years and fifty years scouting. I might add proudly that my time in the game represents eight decades.

Over that time I've seen a lot of things. I wonder if anyone just addressed the actual game and the way it used to be for the players. I'm reminded that the only change I can see is that the American League added the designated hitter and I hope I see the time that it is abolished. The game is still the same otherwise as when Abner Doubleday put the rules together. Three strikes and four balls, ninety feet between bases and sixty feet, six inches from the mound to the plate, and the plate is still the same size.

After seeing a lot of games like I do, I wonder if the strike zone doesn't change and a lot has to do with who is pitching. When I first started we had families that owned the clubs and for the most part baseball was their sole income. In those days those families were all very close and friendly toward one another.

But from what we hear and what we read, today there are a lot of these owners who are not real buddies. Not even close! I remember when I first went to the major leagues, there were owners that helped each other make payrolls in order to keep the game afloat. Can you imagine anything like that going on today? I repeat that these were baseball families who were not out to destroy each other. I think it's fair to say about today that it looks like the ones with the big bucks keep making it more difficult for some owners to compete.

I definitely see a world of difference in the role that the manager plays today. I played for some good managers, and as I look back I have the most respect for the jobs they did.

I spent most of my time in the major leagues under one of the greatest managers in the game, Bill McKechnie. He won four pennants with three different clubs, two pennants and one World Series at Cincinnati, and pennants with the Pirates and Cardinals. I think it's important to mention that Bill did it with only two coaches, where managers today have six or more.

In those days the qualifications to manage were many. Number one, the manager always coached at third base and not from the dugout. And, would you believe that one of us pitchers who wasn't pitching that day was smart enough to coach first base? In those days the two coaches had very little input in running the game, if any. The duty of one of the coaches was to take charge of the baseballs and pitch batting practice once in a while. The other coach was sort of an ambassador in that after the manager chewed you out for whatever, the ambassador would follow up and convince you that you had it coming and that all was well.

The manager was in complete charge of the pitching staff, who'd pitch what games and what relievers would be called when, and he had total control of the lineup every day. Nobody challenged his authority or his knowledge. Back then we had the same line-

The world champion Cincinnati Reds. Top row, (left to right): Jim Turner, Jimmy Ripple, Johnny Vander Meer, Mike McCormick, Milt Shoffner, Lefty Guise, Harry Craft, Lonny Frey, Joe Beggs. Middle row: Traveling Secretary Paul Moore, Eddie Joost, Ernie Lombardi, Bucky Walters, Frank McCormick, Paul Derringer, Johnny Hutchings, Bill Baker, General Manager Warren Giles. Front row: Lew Riggs, Ivan Goodman, Gene Thompson, Morrie Arnovich, Coach Hank Gowdy, Manager Bill McKechnie, Coach Jimmy Wilson, Billy Werber, Billy Myers, Elmer Riddle, Trainer Herman "Doc" Rohde (Pat DeMar, daughter — Gene Thompson collection).

ups every day regardless who the opposing pitcher was and the word "platoon" was seldom heard, if ever.

During my last year at spring training I recall Bill telling the pitchers that if your name had a "P" after it in the program, it meant you were expected to pitch nine innings.

We won the pennant in 1939 then lost to the Yankees in the World Series. We won the pennant in 1940 and beat Detroit in the World Series. In 1940 we won a hundred games in a one-hundred-fifty-four-game schedule. The four of us that did most of the starting pitched eighty-four complete games and won seventy-three games.

The four pitchers were Paul Derringer, Bucky Walters, Jim Turner, and me, Gene Thompson. I do not ever recall a meeting that was held for the purpose of telling you how to pitch to a certain hitter. We pitchers would often discuss this among ourselves and found that all pitchers don't get the same hitters out the same way.

For example, if you are a low ball type pitcher, possibly a sinker, and you are facing a low ball hitter, you are not about to change your style of pitching to compensate. You have to match strength with strength. From a pitching standpoint it was so much different in so many respects. We would have a short meeting in the clubhouse before each game and the manager would tell his starting pitcher to inform each of his players, especially his outfielders, how he would pitch to each hitter and how he would like for you to play him. We certainly did not have computers or all the sophisticated equipment that seems to run the game today.

Your pitchers and catchers were the ones that decided on what pitch to throw and it seemed to work out pretty good. I mentioned earlier that we had only two coaches and neither was a hitting or pitching coach. As a matter of fact, by trade they both had been catchers. And would you believe that we survived without a pitch count?

I'm told they have a pitch count to cut down on injuries to their arms. Keep in mind the pitch count of today and the fact that we rarely have a complete game pitched. Plus they use a five-man rotation instead of four and none of these pitchers today ever pitch batting practice. Even with all the protection pitchers

Young Gene Thompson, 22, watches a game from the dugout at Crosley Field during his rookie season in 1939. Originally slated as a reliever, he was quickly added to the starting rotation and posted a 13–5 record. In 1940 he contributed 16 wins to their 100–53 record, good enough to win the National League pennant (Pat DeMar, daughter — Gene Thompson collection).

get today, have you ever noticed how many pitchers are on the disabled list or are awaiting some kind of surgery? I mentioned earlier about our pitching the eighty-four complete games. We did this with the four-man rotation and we all pitched batting practice between starts without fail.

I was talking just recently with one of my teammates from the Cincinnati club, and we ended up talking briefly about changes in the game. He said what he noticed most is the lack of discipline amongst the players themselves and I thought that was quite a true statement.

I can remember many times when a player would chew another player out for not running a ball out or some other bit of just not hustling. The manager didn't need to get involved in this and we all respected each other even if we were the one getting chewed out. This action seems to be extinct today.

I think a good rule to consider changing with reference to the pitcher would be to require a pitcher to complete at least seven innings rather than five to gain a win. I never heard of long men, short men, set-up men or closers in my playing days. But I can readily see now that sometimes there are as many as four or five pitchers that are getting recognition for that one win and he and his agent thrive on this type of leverage when it's time to negotiate those contracts. If I was an owner, I would take a dim view of paying this many people for the same win.

Speaking of negotiating contracts, when was the last time you heard of a player taking a cut in salary?

Gene Thompson, next to the pitcher in the Wabash Freight uniform, attends a pitching clinic at Fans Field in his hometown Decatur, Illinois, in 1934 with other young pitchers from the region. Paul Derringer, on the mound, had a long major league pitching career with Cincinnati. Fans Field, built in 1924, was among the last of the old wooden baseball parks. It was later modernized and is now used as a softball venue (Pat DeMar, daughter — Gene Thompson collection).

I see and hear a lot of different styles of reporting in baseball. All the writers and radio and television people view it today. I can well remember that the writers of old were happy with their jobs and did a good job of reporting what happened on the field that day. They didn't push their way into our space in the locker room. We enjoyed their company and we were sort of a big happy family. They were always welcome and invited to our social get-togethers. There was a very mutual agreement of trust involved and the business of "off the record" wasn't necessary.

We had a lot of good radio men in those days and the two I remember best are Mel Allen and Red Barber. They could report that game and make me feel like I was seeing it from the best seat in the house.

Another thing we didn't have, something that almost escaped me here, is the high fives the players do today. I think they are really exciting and I wish we would have known of them. I am trying to think of what John McGraw or one of the old-time managers would have thought or done when someone got picked off at third with the score tied in the ninth and nobody out, and that player came in to a handful of high fives. Imagine!

And I can readily see how we missed out on bubble gum and the sunflower seeds. That all looks like fun to me. And besides that, they were all complimentary.

A short mention of the money then and now. I started the 1939 season at Cincinnati and had a salary of $350 a month thanks to the generosity of Warren C. Giles. I need to mention, though, that he raised my salary to $500 at cut-down time. And as for World Series money, well, our winners' share when we beat Detroit in 1949 was $5,800.

I signed a scouting contract with the Giants shortly after returning home from managing a team in Curaçao in the World League. Carl Hubbell, the Hall of Fame pitcher, was the scouting director of the Giants at that time. He called me and asked if I'd go into scouting for them. That was in 1952. I think I have worked in every state in this union and Canada and Mexico.

In my opinion the draft was a big mistake. It was supposed to be designed to level the playing field and to save money in signing. Neither of these proved to be correct. The draft had a lot to do with the approach of the scout. Prior to the draft we had maybe a half dozen or so players that we really wanted and we spent time with them and their families.

Now the big deal is to turn in all the names of players that you feel have any ability at all. Scouting was much more competitive before the draft and much more fun.

The expansion does put more pressure on the scout. We find ourselves reporting on more players now with less tools since there is such a demand for players just to fill the uniforms. Baseball could have survived better had the expansion never happened. The major leagues today represent a watered down version of what it had been with sixteen teams.

I think contraction will have to take place eventually and it will happen as soon as they find someone with enough money to gamble.

I have some serious thoughts about agents, and I think you can find them expressed best in an article I wrote to *The Baseball Scout* newsletter about Scott Boras. No matter how they impact the game, I'm afraid agents are here to stay.

[Boras was interviewed for the November 1997 edition of The Baseball Scout *newsletter regarding the signing of Jason Varitek, one of his clients, and his thoughts*

on elements of the draft. His views are presented by Thompson as he addressed them point by point in his letter of response in the February 1998 edition of The Baseball Scout.*]*

Please accept this letter as a response to the interview you had with Scott Boras, which appeared in the November issue of *The Baseball Scout* newsletter. You asked for his background in baseball, and I feel I should submit mine. 1998 will represent the 64th year since I signed my first contract. With the exception of 27 months in the navy, I have had 17 years in uniform, during which time I was in the National League with Cincinnati and the New York Giants (from 1939 to 1948), followed by 47 years of scouting.

Scott Boras speaks many times about fair market price for his clients, and I find that very amusing. In his interview he mentioned the figure of $750,000 in the case of Jason Varitek, who had been drafted by the Mariners, as being a fair market figure. Just because some club gave a player that amount of money doesn't set a precedent that everybody needs to follow.

To begin with, we have a person who is likely to be 22 or near that age [at signing] and has no eligibility left, and there is very little room for projection about his ability as compared to the player who is just 18 and out of high school. When a player signs a contract for whatever figure the contract calls for, that doesn't mean the player has to meet any standard of play. He is entitled to the entire amount agreed upon just for signing the contract.

Does anyone know of any other job that a person could pursue where he could demand this kind of money without even proving himself? No player has any particular value until he has proven that he can compete at the major league level.

Scott claims that he keeps extensive records of the amateur draft and also has conducted studies looking at bonus amounts paid, who has made it to the big leagues, and who hasn't. I don't know for sure just what point he was making, but what I read into it was that baseball has paid out a hell of a lot of money on non-prospects. Keep in mind that a good portion of these people that were signed had people representing them, just like Scott Boras does.

Scott Boras also said that baseball has failed to attract the quality athlete, and from that I am led to believe that at least some of those players are in this category that Scott Boras and other agents represent.

Scott speaks about coaches from colleges or universities that offer these athletes an education and a career. That, my friends, is a broad statement. In the first place, there are very few so-called "free rides" available each year that include tuition, books, and room and board. This means that many mothers and fathers are saddled with a good portion of that cost. In his extensive studies, perhaps he should include a study pertaining to the lack of graduating football and basketball players. A good portion of those so-called seniors that we draft tell us that they have at least one full year left to graduate.

Scott's statement that baseball won't offer an education is simply untrue. We do offer a scholarship plan, and I would like to inform you as to how it is implemented. We are furnished with a publication called *College Scope*. This tells us about the costs for everything included in a scholarship plan. This includes books, tuition, and room and board. The player is allowed to pick his own school and the club agrees to have him attend that school at the club's expense for four years. Scott might be surprised at some of the schools they elect to attend and he might be enlightened about this subject by contacting the Commissioner's Office to ask just how much baseball puts into scholarship funds each year.

One other point: this scholarship is made part of the player's contract. Mr. Boras made the statement that baseball won't offer an education, and yet he said, and I quote, "The game of baseball has been a very important part of my life. It has given me an education, an opportunity to play professionally, and the chance to meet people who have become valued friends and co-workers." End of quote.

Scott mentioned doing away with drafting high school players, with the exception of selected superstars. He would then proceed to draft only five rounds from the college ranks. I cannot believe that a person who claims to have gone to law school could make such a suggestion. This whole plan has discrimination written all over it.

He's suggesting that only those players drafted in these five rounds should receive signing bonuses. This just adds insult to injury. I think this kind of rule that you recommend would thrill a lot of high school boys, and also all others that were not included in the five rounds.

For example, suppose I was drafted in one of the five rounds and you weren't drafted at all. I could negotiate only with the club that drafted me, but you, in turn, could open up shop and entertain offers from any and all of the major league teams. With all of the players that were available, except for your five rounds, it might make it real difficult for you to get the fair market value for your clients. Maybe you could get them all a job in the Northern League [reference to Boras' client J.D. Drew, who was a holdout when Boras didn't feel the Phillies offered him fair market value to sign. [Drew played in the independent league and signed for the following season.] And then maybe baseball could go about determining a fair market value of its own.

For many years baseball preferred to sign high school players over college players for several reasons. When we take a college player, usually at least 21 and often 22, he has very little if any projection. He has already spent 3 to 4 years at the college level and has played with and against the same class of players. The class of play at the college level never changes due to the fact that each year you have a class of lower classmates coming in, and the juniors and seniors are leaving the program. The caliber remains the same.

The proof is in the pudding: the very highest percentage of all the college signs go to either our rookie leagues and/or to another A class [baseball]. When we sign the high school player, in the 3 to 4 years he might have spent in college, he could have been exposed to Rookie, A, high A, and even possibly AA or AAA competition.

I have a suggestion. Let us return to square one, as in before 1965 and do away with the draft entirely. The draft was put into effect for two reasons: one was to save money, and the other was to level the playing field and give the bottom clubs the higher choices. Both of these reason failed miserably.

Prior to the draft, it was calculated that there were probably 350 athletes out there that had a chance to play. Would you believe we draft 1,200 to 1,300 each year now, as compared to the 350 or so that we considered possibilities? That means that we're telling all of those that are drafted that they are worth some kind of bonus.

Since baseball spends the millions that it does in scouting, I would urge scouts to be more secretive about their reports and keep them from publications that thrive on printing the top high school and college choices in the country. We exploit all the possible prospects far too much.

Why should baseball spend all the money and then turn around and give recruiters and agents all our information? It would be interesting to find out how the agents would react if there was no draft and they had to go out and find their own players to represent in the first five rounds.

Scott Boras spoke about how he has studied the drafts, and especially the money that has been paid out. Perhaps a lot of people would like to know how much he has extracted from the players' bonus money, and from endorsement moneys earned during the players' careers.

Sincerely, Gene Thompson.

I don't know if you can use this or not, but I'm sending a letter Jack Schwarz wrote to my daughter in 1994 when he was the scouting director of the San Francisco Giants.

Dear Pat,

The first time I met your father was in spring training in Florida. I had heard of him before that as a very promising young pitcher with a major league team, I believe in the middle west. I believe his team got into a fight in Ebbets Field with the Brooklyn Dodgers and your father was an active participant. His major league pitching career was shortened when one of the Dodgers snuck up behind him and drove his spikes into Gene's ankle. This was a long time ago and I would like not to be held accountable for inaccuracies in my recollections.

The next spring your dad showed up in our spring training camp in Florida and shared a room with Bob Trocolor. They were the two biggest and strongest athletes in camp that year.

Your dad managed our first rookie league club in Hastings, Nebraska, that summer. After a year or two of that he became our top scout in the middle west for many years. He discovered and signed many players and passed judgment on whether or not to sign players discovered by the scouts working under him.

One player he recommended to me was a player with a Negro League club, the Indianapolis Clowns. I found out who the owner was of the Clowns was from Alex Pompez, who had scouted the New York Cubans — a black team that played their home games in the Polo Grounds in New York City.

Usually Alex would offer to call the Negro League owner for me to introduce me, as he did when we bought Willie Mays from the black undertaker in Memphis, Tennessee, who owned the Birmingham Black Barons. He told me the owner was a white man and did not offer to call him.

I called the white owner of the Indianapolis Clowns and he agreed to sell the player to us for $2,500. I asked him to confirm the deal by telegram and he agreed to do so.

The telegram did not show up so I spent the next day trying to reach the Clowns' owner. I finally caught up with him in Chicago and asked him why he had not sent me the wire confirming the deal. "I sold him to the Braves!" he shouted. He then hung up on me.

About thirty years later I asked John Mullen, then with the Braves, why that owner double-crossed us.

It turned out that the Braves had obtained a sixty-day option to buy the player. The scouting department forgot about it until John Quinn, the Milwaukee manager at the time, asked his assistants whether they had exercised it right away or a few hours after the player was orally sold to us. The player was Hank Aaron.

I remember the one we didn't get more than most of the ones we did get. Your dad was one hundred percent right about his description of Hank Aaron and deserved to get credit for him.

Your father was an excellent scout with very good judgment. If the melee hadn't occurred in Ebbets Field, he might very well be in Cooperstown with the other great players in the game.

Some day the rulers of baseball may wake up to the fact that scouts who had great careers should be enshrined in Cooperstown, too. I would have a few nominees and Gene is one of them.

With all good wishes, I remain,
Sincerely,
Jack Schwarz.

Bobby Mattick

(1915–2004)

Mattick was destined to become a baseball man from the day he was born in Sioux City, Iowa, the son of major league outfielder Wally Mattick.

After hanging around ballparks and baseball people with his dad from the time he was a toddler, his own career began when he played shortstop for the Los Angeles Angels in the Pacific Coast League in 1934. In 1936, he was struck in the face by a line drive foul ball that fractured his skull and left him with seriously impaired vision. Although he struggled with that and actually played in the major leagues briefly with the Cubs and Reds, he retired when he realized multiple operations had worsened rather than improved his sight.

He then coached the Birmingham Barons for a season and managed the Ogden Reds the following year before he changed directions again and began a fifty-year journey in scouting and player development. During those years he worked for the New York Yankees, Cincinnati Reds, Chicago White Sox, Houston Colt .45s, Cleveland Indians, Baltimore Orioles, Seattle Pilots, Milwaukee Brewers, Montreal Expos, and Toronto Blue Jays.

He found his baseball home in 1976 when he was hired as scouting supervisor and joined Al LaMacchia as the first two employees of the new expansion Toronto Blue Jays with the duties of staffing the new teams at every level. He was later named director of player development of the Blue Jays in 1978, and assumed field manager duties for the 1980–81 seasons. The oldest rookie manager, at age sixty-four, compiled a 104–164 record before Bobby Cox took over. He remained with Toronto and was honored with the title vice president of baseball operations until he died of a stroke at age eighty-nine.

The SABR list of players he signed is prestigious and long: John Oldham, Jim Landis, Frank Robinson, Jesse Gonder, Curt Flood, Joe Gaines, Bobby Henrich, Vada Pinson, Ken Hunt, Jim Maloney, John Flavin, Tommy Harper, Mel Queen, Wally Wolf, Ernie Fazio, Brock Davis, Leon McFadden, Don Baylor, Bobby Grich, Sixto Lezcano, Darrell Porter, Tony Bernazard, Warren Cromartie, Danny Ainge, and Glenallen Hill.

Bobby Mattick was inducted into the Canadian Hall of Fame in 1990. In 1996 the Toronto organization established the Bobby Mattick Award, given annually for excellence in scouting and player development. He was a recipient of the Scout of the Year Award, West Coast, 2000.

In 1934 I broke in with the Los Angeles Angels in the Pacific Coast League. I was seventeen and had not yet finished high school when I went out there, but they kept me. They had a farm club in the Western Association at the time where they sent most of the younger guys. But the manager kept me in the PCL and said he'd get me in enough games. I was pretty thin, only weighed 150 pounds, and he worried that the heat there might wear me down. So I played shortstop and hit .278 that first year. The next year I broke my wrist the second day of the season. The third year I was hitting three-sixty-something in July and was considered one of the better prospects at the time when I got hit in the head by a line drive foul ball that gave me a skull fracture. It caused double vision, which stuck with me for the remainder of my playing career. I finally got a full season in 1937. I played a hundred-sixty-five games at shortstop and hit .280.

I was with LA in the Coast League for 1934, '35, '36, and '37 and part of '38, when I went to the Cubs but sat out games a lot because of my eyes. In '39 I started with Milwaukee in the American Association. The Cubs recalled me in June. In '41 they traded me to Cincinnati and I was there '41 and '42. I played in the big leagues with the Cubs and Cincinnati but I had to fight the double vision all the time. Finally, by '42 I'd had three or four operations trying to repair that, but it actually threw off the vision more and things really got bad. So 1942 was my last year of playing.

I waited out of baseball, working on the eyes and so forth, and was a kind of coach and traveling secretary for the Birmingham Barons in the Southern Association. I knew the owner real well and he set that up for me. I was there three or four years, I think.

In 1945 I returned to the game as a scout for the Yankees. I got the job because the Yankee scout in San Francisco knew my father and knew me when I played. My father was an outfielder with the Chicago White Sox in 1912 and 1913 before I was born. So this scout, Joe Devine, felt bad because of my eyes and gave me the job.

I was living in the LA area and working under Bill Essick, quite a Yankee scout, in the winter time, then back to the Midwest in the Chicago area for the rest of the year. Essick is the one who got Joe DiMaggio when other scouts gave up on the guy because of his leg injuries. So I was a full-time scout for the Yankees and scouted year-round.

In those days there was no specific training to become a scout. It was more intuitive. Remember I was raised in baseball with my father and everything. Ever since I was a little kid, I hung out at ball fields and clubhouses. When I began to scout they more or less threw us out there and it was up to us to use our heads. The only thing I remember anybody telling me about scouting was Bill Essick. He said it's like being an insurance salesman. If you go see enough games you'll finally see somebody you like. He was right. He was with the Yankees a very long time and was very well thought of in baseball.

I was on my own from the very first day. It was up to me to spot baseball tools and talent. I was pretty lucky, actually, during the year in the American Association because some of the old-timers knew my father. Mike Kelly, the owner of the Minneapolis club, called me a few times and he said, "Let me tell you something, Bobby. Baseball's a game of mistakes. Keep them to a minimum." I always remember that because it was such great advice. And it's true. And I always remembered that when I made mistakes, and I made them, but I didn't let that get me down because I knew everybody makes them and you just have to keep forging ahead.

I was only with the Yankees for one year and then went to Cincinnati. I'll give you my so-called career. In a career there's some politics played, and it happened to me in this respect. The Cincinnati scout named Pat Patterson, who signed Ewell Blackwell, liked me and he got me over there. I stayed a few years. When Gabe Paul came in, he and Gabe got sideways and he had me leave one year to the White Sox in 1952. Then I went back to Cincinnati for about twelve or thirteen years with Gabe. Then he went to Houston and he took me along.

Then politics happened at Houston and Gabe left and went to Cleveland. Paul Richards came in and wanted me to stay there and be his assistant, but I'd already promised Gabe I'd go with him to Cleveland. So after that I went to Cleveland for three years.

Then on to Baltimore for one year. That was 1967. Then on to the Seattle expansion club for one year as scouting and farm director. Then I went to Milwaukee and Mr. Bud Selig as scouting and farm director, just as I was in Seattle. Quite frankly, we didn't see eye to eye on many things. Then Frank Lane came in as general manager.

In 1972 I went to Montreal for five years, and in 1976 I was with the Toronto Blue Jays when they first started. Pat Gillick got me over there.

Scouting is basically the same from organization to organization because everybody likes to look at the tools. And you can't knock that, but I think the good scout looks beyond that. What I found is that makeup is very, very important. Sometimes it's the real difference between being a good ballplayer and being a real good ballplayer and reaching the big leagues.

The most natural thing, for example, is to look at Pete Rose. He didn't have those kind of tools but he turned out to be a great player because it was in his makeup. He had so much tenacity that he made himself into a major league quality player.

What makes a great player in any sport is consistency. Consistency means executing day in and day out. Baseball is quite a grind. Players get tired and so forth and it's hard for them to give peak performance day in and day out, so the guy who can grind it out consistently is a real good player. If you have that makeup and you have the tools, then you're a star. But there's a lot of guys who have great tools who are just so-so ballplayers because they're not consistent.

Frank Robinson had the best makeup and best tools of them all. He was a competitor right from the start in anything he went into. He had the stomach, and most of all, and most who didn't play with or against him didn't know, he had a great head on him. He was very instinctive and he by far had the best makeup of anybody I signed.

Now I wasn't around him when he managed, but it's so typical of great players to expect their players to perform every day and grind it out consistently as they did. Frank has mellowed over the years, I think, and I think he's the way managers should be. Jim Landis also had good makeup.

I was instrumental in signing a lot of guys. But scouting has changed. When I first started, scouting a guy would scout a ballplayer in high school or college and then try to sign him. He'd negotiate a figure with him. The front office usually said the scout could go up to "X" amount of dollars. You would negotiate with the kid and his parents, then you could physically sign him. The clubs started having players like Ted Williams or Hank Aaron or Frank Robinson call a prospect they were interested in and tell him how good the organization is, hoping that would influence the kid to sign with them.

Then after that they started sending the GM out on negotiations for the top couple of prospects. That meant the area scout who found the kid would just sit in on this.

Luckily, with Cincinnati I never had that problem. Gabe just let me go ahead. For instance, with Jim Maloney, I saw him pitch in a junior college and about the sixth inning I called Gabe from the park to tell him. He asked, "Well, what would it take?"

I said, "Gabe, I just don't know." But I think we gave him sixty thousand and gave his mother something, I think a thousand.

After that the draft came in. It was really something I thought really hurt the aggressive scout. In my own experience, I might like Joe Jones, a kid from Pepperdine University. Without the draft I might get to know him and get in good with him and his family and sell the organization and be able to sign him. With the draft I can like Joe Jones but Montreal came along and drafted him before I ever had the chance to do that.

Then they said you have to get scouts who put in a lot of names and see the good guys and rank them, of course. Maybe the guys you really like, say there's five players, well, you might not even get a chance at four of them. If you're fortunate, you got one.

The draft forced organizations to get into the twenty-third or forty-third or forty-fourth rounds making decisions on kids that you'd normally pass by. I think the theory behind the draft was parity. And I've argued with Paul Beeston and Pat Gillick and all of them on this. Whitey Herzog believes the same as I do because we've talked about it and I've read what he said in the papers.

Before they used to think the Yankees, Red Sox, and Dodgers would get all the better players because they were so rich. There's a certain amount of truth to that. But it's way over exaggerated. And that's what they say now. Beeston and the others still say that the Yankees and the others can get any player they want because they can afford to go out there and get them.

There's no scout I know of, well, maybe some of the younger ones, who would say let's get a high school player and give him two million dollars to sign. That way you're really putting yourself on the spot. When a scout offers that kind of money and it's a mistake, he may be forgiven but he'd better not do that a second time.

But now they're giving that kind of money to a lot of kids right out of high school. It keeps going up. And here's the thing about it. With the draft each team has one choice in thirty, so we have our list of players and if that kid's our number one choice, we can't let him go by. And we have to sign the kid or we've wasted that pick. So the agent and the parents really have that club over a barrel. And I always try to preach that sometimes when the asking price is too high, it's got to be like poker. You have to turn over the winning hand.

If the draft was eliminated the clubs could save a lot of money. I don't think any scout would give any untried high school kid two million dollars without the rules of the draft. I think baseball would be much better off without it.

Also, the rules of the draft are a sort of double standard between the U.S. and the Latin countries. No high school education is required in the Latin countries. And because of the poverty there, baseball is the thing. Playing baseball is everything there.

I got to be a doublechecker, or crosschecker, so the office would send me out to double-check a kid an area scout recommended and determine if he really is a good prospect or not. If the area scout liked the kid but the checker turned him down, then it would be up to the GM to decide. Well, the area scout has seen the kid more than the checker, so I'm going along with him. We have great confidence in area scouts and I'm going with his judgment.

Or this happens when two scouts from different areas have recommendations for a certain position. They may send the checker to see both players to determine which is the better prospect because the area scouts haven't seen the players in the other guy's area so they can't compare them.

I was fortunate in that the clubs I worked for didn't require a lot of paperwork from me, probably because I was terrible at it. They just took my recommendations and my word on players. But it seems like that other organizations load down scouts with paperwork, and as the years go by, it gets worse and worse. Essentially, after all the paperwork is done and turned in, it all turns out the same. Do you want the guy or not? I used to get into it with Gabe Paul on that. For a long time he kept wanting me to send in reports and I'd say, "Well, I'll tell you about the guy and you can put down this and that," and he finally went along with me on that.

The draft seemed to have the result that they're trying to make it all too scientific. I still think scouting is like a good third base coach, intuitive, with experience. A bad one might get a little bit better but he'll never be that good, whereas with some guys you just put them right out there and they're good. I think that's the way a good scout is. If he's got any wisdom at all, he's going to learn and get better. But a lot of it is intuitive. And there's certain things you can't put down on paper, things you see in a guy. The thing you have to be careful of, and this has always been a pet peeve of mine, the more prolific a writer is in writing reports, the better the player looks. Then you see a good baseball man who didn't have the education or vocabulary who will just tell it like it is. "The guy's a good player so let's get him." I think the scouting directors really have to know their scouts and the way they think about the game and the way they work.

When we got the Major League Scouting Bureau I was one of the advocates of it, provided it was used right. Branch Rickey started that thinking many years ago. But so many scouts were against it. I certainly don't mean any disrespect, but we could use these guys as bird dogs to flush out players. But then they started turning in lots of names, and scouts would go over to see a guy and say, "I went over to see this guy and he wasn't worth a darned thing, or that guy wasn't worth a darn." They just ran scouts to death.

So I asked them, "You have your own bird dog who's your friend, right? Well, how many times has he run you all over the place looking at players you turned down?"

So I told my scouts that the bureau is something we can use as a tool, a supplement, but not something you rely on all the time. My scouts somehow thought they should be right if a bureau scout recommended a guy they didn't like. But I didn't think that. I told them to look at it this way: the bureau scouts uncover kids for you to look at and make your own decision on.

I think most clubs will take the best player available until they get way down in the draft and they'll say, "Well, we need someone to fill in at shortstop in Double-A," or whatever. The bureau scout has a tough job. They can't be too critical, whereas a checker can be more critical. They have to throw a player into the same mix and let the individual club scouts make their own decisions on each player they may consider.

I was involved with expansion with Montreal and it opened a lot of jobs for scouts, I'll say that. It's had a pretty big impact on the game, bigger than most people believe, and I don't know if it's for good or bad. I think scouts had to lower their sights a little. After expansion you water down the caliber of players that are taken because they need more talent these days. It's hard for most scouts to lower their sights, but it's necessary.

More clubs mean more scouting jobs, just like there's more players out there. The cream of the crop is still out on the field, but there's also players in the big leagues who wouldn't be there in the days when there were only sixteen big league clubs.

Scouting pitchers was one of the hardest things to evaluate. It used to be that scouts thought guys with bad deliveries were more likely to come up with bad arms. So do you take them or pass them by? Many people feel expansion causes players to be brought along too soon, but that has to be seen on an individual basis with players and organizational needs. The scouts look at players and cannot predict if a guy will get hurt or develop a bad arm or not.

Today's scouts usually have things to back up their judgment. For instance, the guns tell them how fast a guy's fastball, curve, or whatever is and so on, whereas in the past he just used his intuition. They could predict with some amount of certainty if a guy's fastball would get faster and so on. And there have been cases where guys would get faster.

One of the pitchers who did that was Don Drysdale out of high school. The manager in Bakersfield where he reported told me he could stick his thumb in his fastball. And the story I got from Lefty Phillips, the guy who signed him, was that Joe Becker took Drysdale in the spring, and instead of him being an overhand pitcher, taught him to drop his arm and he got faster. And they get faster as they get older and their bodies

Bobby Mattick (right), wearing his favorite "Team Mattick" golf hat, and Freddie McAlister, longtime scouting friends, got together to talk about the good old days at a minor league game in 2000. Mattick, son of former major league player Wally Mattick, grew up in baseball parks. He scouted and signed many successful players during his fifty-plus years in the business (Fred and Patty McAlister collection).

mature. This does not apply to everybody, but for guys who do, they get more consistently faster. But that's a piece that could start an argument in the barn.

It's just like years ago they said guys can run the fastest at ages fifteen, sixteen and seventeen years old and wouldn't get any faster. Well, if that's the case, then all the track records would be held by high school kids, not college and Olympic guys.

Oh, here's something I forgot to say about all the draft rules. You have to realize this: rules are made to be broken. Nowadays you can't talk about money with a kid prior to drafting him. But there's different ways of getting around to finding out an idea of what they want. It's not a big problem but you just have to be more careful under the current rules. Fortunately for me, I don't do that anymore because I'm now a consultant.

When Joe Devine gave me my first job, he used to say to the kid and his parents, "Get your best offer and I'll top it." So I'd say, "What does that mean?" Well, that means he wants the last shot. So if the kid comes back and says an organization offered him fifty thousand, Joe could either say, "I'll top it with sixty," or tell the kid that it's too much and he should go ahead and take the fifty. But it gave him the last bid, so to speak. It's just a signing maneuver.

And I remember people and events from long ago. One of the people I remember who really influenced the game was Branch Rickey. When I was sixteen years old I worked out with him and he wanted to sign me, but my dad wouldn't let me sign with him. He said that I'd never amount to anything in the game and I'd never make a good salary as long as Rickey was in charge.

Dad knew Charlie Grimm very well. In fact, he was the manager of the Cubs when they signed me and he found me because I'd worked out with the Cubs before a game when they came to St. Louis. They were there three days. So because he knew my dad and everything, he signed me and sent me to Los Angeles to start my career in the Coast League, Triple-A baseball.

The Coast League in those years was really great. The week-long series with Mondays off were great, although I remember some of those train rides. We used to go from LA to Seattle and they didn't have air conditioning at that time and we'd ride with the windows down and guys took off their shirts and played poker and so on. Those were good times. They had a six o'clock curfew in LA, so we'd go over to Glendale to catch the train, and we'd get to Seattle about five-thirty to six on Tuesday evening. We'd have to hustle around for cabs and go right from the train to the ballpark to play a game that night.

In those days, even when I got into the big leagues in the early forties, we had to pay our own cab fare and everything. The club didn't have to reimburse us for it. In the big leagues we got good meal money and ate real well then. And the hotels were great, the Warrick in Philadelphia, the Copley Plaza in Boston. Nice. The clubs didn't give us meal money. We just signed the checks and the team paid the bills.

Back to the present. Another change was the agents. I haven't been in on that area of operating for a long time, except for a couple of deals when Toronto was in on it. At first I thought agents would be a good thing for the players because players years ago didn't have the education or the smoothness of negotiations. I thought the agents would take up that slack, and they did. My opinion is only hearsay because I don't know this from my own personal experience. The agents have gotten way out of line in this respect. They ask for so much money. But apparently they're given the money so it must be there, and the only way they'll get it is by asking for it, so it's no bad deal. And you talk to players in the lower minors and they'll say, "Well, I have to see my agent." What do they need an agent for?

I don't know if agents impact the work of the scouts because I don't scout anymore. I talked to a guy who said some agents got to a kid and told him that he ought to get a million dollars to sign. I'd call that quite an impact. Well, if I'm working in a factory and I'm told I should get a million dollars, it would go in one ear and out the other. But if an agent says it, and they're not supposed to but those things happen, kids take it seriously just because the guy says he's an agent.

I just thought of something from out of the blue, out of the long ago past, that may interest you. You've heard of Carl Hubbell, the great screwball pitcher, right? When I was with the Cubs, we were playing the Giants and Gus Mancuso was our catcher. He'd caught Carl Hubbell in New York. He said, "You won't have any trouble with this guy because you hit to right field all the time."

Well, I struck out three times and then hit a little quibbler back to the mound for an out. I asked him one time, "How'd you come up with that screwball?"

And he said, "I was with Oklahoma one year when they was independently owned and I was about to get released. I wasn't doing any good." He told me about this old guy, a right-handed pitcher but I forgot his name, and he was winning. "So I went to him and asked him to show me how to throw that and he did."

And that was that. And it reminds me that years ago when I broke in they never had all these hitting coaches and pitching coaches and fielding instructors and all that. The veteran players would tell you something and then it was up to you to help yourself. Now Bill McKechnie, who I played for in Cincinnati, told me one time, "Bob, if a ballplayer can't help himself, he's in bad shakes." That was true then and it's still true.

With all the money on the table nowadays, there's a lot of kids who feel, "Our hitting instructor's coming or the fielding instructor's coming, and when he tells me what to do it's just a matter of doing it and I'll be a big leaguer." They don't try to work something out themselves. They're afraid to try and fail because of the money.

When I was head of player development, I'd always say, "Well, try this. It may not help, but if it doesn't help, what does that mean?" The kid would say he didn't know and I'd tell him to try and figure things out for himself. Try to do this. Look at somebody and try to copy him. Try different things until you find something that works for you. If you're not achieving results, then don't keep doing the same things day after day after day. Try to change. All kids have to make adjustments to get to the big leagues, but many of them were intimidated by their lack of success at something and were afraid to change, to adjust.

I don't know how this thing's going to end up in all sports. There's salary caps in football and basketball to help them with that. But in baseball the Players' Union is pretty strong and will fight that pretty hard I would guess. The only way the issue could be forced in baseball will be if a club goes belly-up. Then maybe they'll see that, heck, we cannot continue like this.

I don't know, but I would think the Players' Union would take the lead. Gabe Paul predicted this years and years ago when he said that the costs of the game will result in nobody but major corporations owning clubs. And at the time I thought he didn't know what he was talking about, you know, but it's happening now.

Individuals like Calvin Griffith and the Wrigleys and those guys owned the clubs then. But Gabe said just wait and you'll see companies like GE and Westinghouse getting in there. And now they're buying clubs and paying money to the clubs for naming ballparks for corporations and all that.

Having said all that, I think the most significant change I've seen in the game in my years in it is the change in the kids now coming into baseball. They have a lack of instinct and that's from not playing the game that much. Years ago they had semi-pro clubs sponsored by local businesses and they played all the time. Amateur kids played alongside former minor league players and they picked up things from the older players.

The kids today don't have the baseball instincts and they rely too much on the instructors. Back to Frank Robinson on that one. He was great because he had the sixth tool, if you want to call it that. He had creativity on the field. Vada Pinson was a great player too, but he didn't have the creativity and instinct that Frank had. I think the greatest tool guy I ever saw, and he was a great player but I never did think he got polished like Joe DiMaggio or Willie Mays, was Mickey Mantle. Mantle was the best natural athlete who ever played the game as far as I'm concerned. But he wasn't polished. He just had more raw ability than anybody I've ever seen. He was the most instinctive player I ever saw. Imagine if he'd been healthy.

And the money has changed. When a guy gets four million or five million dollars on a contract and has a bad year, it doesn't seem to bother most of them because they've got the money. But somewhere pride has to take over. Sadly, today human nature gets in there and they get an attitude of "I don't have to work hard anymore because I've got the money." So a lot of them don't take chances and don't work hard because of the money. I'm saying that we need to remember that not everybody makes big money, then pride kicks in and they work harder to get the money.

Looking back, I signed some pretty good players. After a while I got to be a cross-checker and I didn't physically sign players at that level, but I recommended them. When I was with Houston there was Rusty Staub. Well, at that time Houston had ten or eleven scouts and most of them said he was a good ballplayer. But Tal Smith came to me and said the judge wasn't going to give big money to Rusty unless I okayed it. So I went over there and saw that he was good and okayed it. Then Richards went over and physically signed him.

Sometimes it goes another way. I was following an American Legion team and everybody was talking about a player named J.W. Porter. Frank Robinson was the right fielder on that club. He was only a junior in high school then, but boy, could he drive a ball and run! I got to know him and his mother. She's a fine person. She's the only mother of a ballplayer that I ever signed who gave my wife a present. She was really nice. I used to go over to their house and talk with her and Frank and tried to talk him out of playing football in his senior year. But he wouldn't do it. And she couldn't get him to do it either. He finally got hurt and quit on his own because he wanted a career in baseball.

Another thing about Frank that people don't know is that they had a bonus rule and they had classifications of leagues from D, C, B, A, Double-A, and Triple-A. If you gave the kid over three thousand dollars, he had to go to a B or A league. So I told Frank, "Look, we're offering you three thousand dollars but it's best if you start in the Pioneer League, which is a C league. But if you force us, we'll give you four thousand and you can go up there to the B league. We want you."

I think Frank could have used the extra thousand dollars at that time, like I could have and everybody else, too. He told me, "I'll do whatever you think is best for me." And he took the three thousand dollars. There's not very many kids who would do that. All he wanted to do was play baseball. I could have offered him fifty cents and he may have taken it just for the chance to play.

When I joined Baltimore Walter Shannon was a friend of mine. When Gabe let me go I worked with Walter for one year. I got Bobby Grich for him. Then he sent me down in Texas to check a bunch of guys. I called Walter up one night and said, "I saw a kid who I think is going to be a heck of a ballplayer. He can run and swings the bat real good. His arm isn't real good, but I think we can help him with that."

He said, "Well, who's that?"

I said, "Don Baylor." He said that we already got him for the middle A draft.

"I don't care what you've got him in for, this guy's a big league prospect," I said.

So, to make a long story short, Shannon said, "Well, how we going to do this?"

I said, "Well, look, Grich might be taken but I think other clubs might shy away from Baylor because of his arm. So let's take Grich first and Baylor second." They discussed it and we finally went that way. We were fortunate to get them both. I understand that Atlanta and Al LaMacchia liked him very much, and he tried to get Grich, too. Baylor went on to quite a major league career and then managed the Cubs. He's a good baseball man. He wanted Frank to be his bench coach but for some reason that didn't work out.

I signed Grich in 1967. He wasn't very fast but he had bat power and a great arm and was very consistent in the field. He was a shortstop when I signed him for Baltimore. But they had Mark Belanger, so somewhere along the line they changed Grich into a second baseman and he became a good second baseman for Baltimore and later for the Angels, too. He's a great kid and a great guy. I saw him playing in a high school game and he caught my eye. He worked hard. He spent time in the minors in the days when Baltimore had such good clubs and they didn't rush those guys. When I was in player development, I offered him a job as manager at Knoxville, Double-A, after he'd retired but he wouldn't stay in the game.

I had the whole outfield at Cincinnati at one time. I had Tommy Harper, Vada Pinson, and Robinson. At Seattle I had Gorman Thomas and Darrell Porter and Sixto Lezcano. He was a real good kid, too. Jim Maloney was probably the best pitcher I signed. Al and I signed Dave Stieb, and I signed Jesse Barfield. When I was with Montreal Didier had me crosschecking. Bob Zuk was an area scout and he brought big names like Gary Carter, Ellis Valentine, and Gary Roenicke. Bob actually signed them but I approved them as the crosschecker.

There is a story about Jesse Barfield. Pat sent me out to Joliet, Illinois, to look at a pitcher named Gullickson, who ended up being a number one choice. Barfield was a lanky kid with a good arm and in the game he hit two line drives off Gullickson. So we talked about it and apparently nobody had seen him. I was told the coach of his team was a bird dog for San Diego, but I don't know if it's true or not. But anyway, he said we didn't have any reports on Barfield. I said I didn't care what other scouts saw because I saw something in him.

So the draft came and we went to the ninth round and I say, "Pat, when are we going to take Barfield?"

So Pat said, "All right, let's take him."

But Jesse struggled like the dickens for years. You look at his records and he only hit around .190 his first year out. He didn't do very well until he got to the big leagues. When I was manager at Toronto, I brought him up and put him right into the lineup. He began playing better, and when Bobby Cox took over, he had some good years. He had good power and was a good outfielder with a good arm. Accurate, too.

Over my career I've worked with five different organizations. The first one was the Yankees, when Larry McPhail divided up the territories. Anything west of the Mississippi was headed by Frank Lane. Anything east of the Mississippi was headed by, let's see, I can't remember the guy's name. Maybe it was George Weiss. The second year I was with Cincinnati when Frank Lane was the farm director and he'd come down there. Later he was the GM with the White Sox and I went over there and scouted for him. Then he was in Baltimore when I went there. And the last team was in Milwaukee and seems to me he was the general manager there. Well, Frank and I never did get along too well. We both had tempers. He had some phony ideas and he thought I had some phony ideas. It sometimes happens that way. It's just one of those things.

I've been with five different organizations with him and I'll tell you one thing. He was very aggressive and he wasn't afraid of making a mistake. One year I think he and Paul Richards tried to get together and trade team for team. They called him Trader Frank. I mean, I don't think a day went by that he didn't try to make one trade or another. He was a good ballman.

Curt Flood was one of my signs, too. He was playing American Legion ball after he graduated high school. At that time we couldn't sign players out of legion ball. So I signed him that fall and he went out there next year to the Carolina League and led the league in hitting. And they had guys in that league at that time like Willie McCovey, Wes Covington, and Willie Kirkland. So next year we sent him to Columbus where Birdie Tebbetts was the manager. He thought Flood was too small to be an outfielder and tried to make him into a third baseman. So at the winter meetings in Colorado Springs, St. Louis inquired about him and they had a couple of pitchers that one of our scouts back east had recommended highly. So Birdie traded him to St. Louis after two years.

Freddie Hutchinson was managing the Cardinals at that time and put him in center field. He was a real good center fielder and a good hitter there. He hit .300. He was a real good kid and he worked hard. He was a sensitive kid, so I can well imagine that when he was traded, he was deeply hurt and wasn't sure of the details of why it happened. I think that brought on the later problem when he was traded to Philadelphia and refused to report there.

Curt Flood did a great thing for the ballplayers. He forced the free agency thing when he took that stand, but that was the end of his own playing career. I guess his efforts weren't much appreciated at the time, but the players do appreciate what he did for them now.

Oh, I just thought of something else about Pat Gillick. His dad was pitching in the Coast League when I broke in and I used to tell him that I hit against his old man. He was quite a pitcher. So the story on that is that when he was serving as sheriff in Chico, California, he used to get the bad guys by throwing rocks at them.

Fellow scout Dick Wilson sent the following letter about Bobby Mattick:

I first heard of Bobby Mattick when I was living in Inglewood in the 1940s. Bobby was playing shortstop for the Los Angeles Angels, the Chicago Cubs farm club in the Triple-A Pacific Coast League and Bobby was considered to be the next shortstop for the Cubs.

The batting cages in those days were enclosed on both sides and the rear and the top. Later on they had a gate at the back. The only way you could enter to get your turn to hit was to run in from the front. The last few minutes of batting practice was accelerated by a little game called "base hits." The hitter got one pitch and if he got what was judged a base hit, he got another pitch. The judges were the other hitters hoping for their turn. But he could hit until he made an out. One night in one of these games, Bobby was due to be the next hitter and he was anxious to get in his turn. Carl Ditmar, a veteran player, hit one that was questionable. Bobby started in but Ditmar said, "Base hit," and swung at the next pitch. He hit a line drive that nailed Bobby in the head and this accident ended his career as a player.

A couple of years later I signed my first contract with the Hollywood Stars, also in the Pacific Coast League, and was optioned to Little Rock, Arkansas, along with Al Triechel, a right-hand pitcher. We traveled by train and Bobby was on the same train on his way to work for the Cincinnati Reds. His destination was Birmingham to learn the front office business under Paul Florence, the general manager at Birmingham. He learned a lot in a hurry and it wasn't long before he made a big reputation for himself by signing Frank Robinson and Vada Pinson out of high school in Oakland, California. He went on to be successful at every job he took in baseball.

Al LaMacchia

(1921–)

LaMacchia is an animated and colorful man who has been in professional baseball since he was eighteen years old. He had a promising minor league pitching career that was interrupted by military service and injury. He came back to make the major leagues and appeared in sixteen major league games with the St. Louis Browns and Washington Senators from 1943 to 1946. He compiled a career record of 2–2 with one save. But he had a perfect batting average, .000! He then began as a scout.

For more than fifty years he has scouted for the Philadelphia Phillies, Atlanta Braves, New York Yankees, St. Louis Cardinals, and Toronto Blue Jays. He was with the Blue Jays from their inception, and was one of the first two scouts hired by the organization, along with Bobby Mattick, to put together the expansion team. Some of the many players he signed include Jamie Easterly, Mickey Mahler, Rick Mahler, Larry McWilliams, Dale Murphy, Larry Whisenton, Bruce Benedict, and others during two stints in Atlanta; Willie Upshaw for the Yankees; Jim Gott for St. Louis; George Bell for Philadelphia; and Lloyd Moseby, Dave Stieb, Andre Robertson, and Jim Acker for Toronto.

Before he resigned from Toronto in August 1996 to help with the expansion Tampa Bay Devil Rays, Toronto established the Al LaMacchia Award for excellence in player development and scouting; the first recipient of the annual award was Duane Larson. He was a recipient of the Scout of the Year Award, Midwest, 2001.

In the 2009 season, at age eighty-eight, he is an advance scout for the Dodgers.

I signed my first professional contract in 1939 with the Pittsburgh Pirates. I was a right-handed pitcher. I was sent to Fremont, Ohio, in the Ohio State League and I was released there in early June and went back to my hometown of St. Louis and played in what was the Municipal Baseball League, the amateur league in East St. Louis. Later that year I was signed by the St. Louis Browns. In 1940 I went to Paragould, Arkansas, in the Northeast Arkansas League for the Browns. It was Class D at that time. I won about seventeen games there. In the following year, 1941, I played in the Michigan State League in St. Joseph, which was the farm club of the Browns, and I also won about seventeen games that year. The following year I went to San Antonio in the Texas League. At that time it was Class A, not Double-A like it is today. I pitched a whole year there, and at the end of the season, I won some fifteen games, and my contract was purchased by the St. Louis Browns.

The following January of 1943 I was inducted into the army at the Fort Leavenworth, the Kansas Induction Center. I was going through my physical and one thing and another when the master sergeant there asked me what my profession was. When I said, "Baseball," he picked up the phone and called a Captain O'Sullivan, who was in charge of recreation there. I realized then that they had a baseball team. I was asked if I'd care to play on the baseball team and I told them I was hoping I'd get to play some. So they kept me there on what they call "detached service." I played for them all that summer, up until the latter part of August. Then a directive came out of Washington saying they were going to eliminate anybody there on limited service. I was on limited service because of a back injury — I had a degenerated vertebrae — while pitching. It was something that nagged me and gave me trouble throughout my career. They gave me special exercises to do and I slept with boards under my mattress. The harder the mattress, the better I slept.

Anyway, I pitched for the Fort Leavenworth team and the Fort Riley team and I established a strikeout record at the Wichita National Baseball Congress there that still stands to this day. I struck out twenty men in eight innings. Then they called the game because of a "mercy rule," which is when one team is four runs or more ahead of the other after the seventh inning. Right after that I went through my examination to determine whether I was going to go to discharge or be okay for regular duty. Because of my back problem, they decided to discharge me.

So I joined the St. Louis Browns in the month of September of 1943 in the major leagues. It was my first time up. And then in '44 I went to spring training, which was up north that year because they were trying to reduce travel. They tried to keep teams training near their cities. We trained at Cape Girardeau, Missouri, which was very windy and cold. But we went through spring training. I hurt my shoulder there, just one of those things, but it took me a long time to come around. By June of that year I was optioned to Toledo in the American Association. Then I was recalled after September 1 because my arm condition wasn't a hundred percent prior to that date. Because I didn't get recalled before September 1, it made me ineligible for the 1944 World Series between the Cardinals and the Browns.

Al LaMacchia with the St. Louis Browns circa 1942. He accepted his status as a "wartime pitcher" and never overestimated his prowess on the mound. He began scouting in 1947, and earned a reputation as a feisty supporter of players he believed in. The most recent example was when the Dodgers considered and then resisted a trade for Oakland outfielder Andre Ethier in 2006. LaMacchia stood his ground, fought for Ethier's star power, and Oakland sent him to the Dodgers for Milton Bradley and Antonio Perez (Al LaMacchia collection).

I did play the month of September, but I wasn't considered part of the major league roster because I was brought up too late. It was a real disappointment. But during the World Series I was in uniform sitting on the bench and got to pitch batting practice. I helped by being a kind of cheerleader, I guess. It was quite a thrill to sit on that bench and watch us play the Cardinals for the world championship. We come close, but the Cardinals won.

So the following year, '45, was basically the same thing. I never regained the potential I had prior to the arm injury. But I did stay two months in '45 and went to Toledo again and was called up in September. I think my record in the major leagues is two wins and three losses.

A fellow once told me, a very dear friend named Ed Lippitore, a great scout who is now retired, said, "Well, not everybody can say they were on a major league roster and played in the major leagues, so that's quite a thrill."

And I said, "Yeah. I wasn't there long, but I was there and was one of the fortunate ones who got to play."

I started with the Browns in '46 and was traded in June to the Washington Senators, which are now the Minnesota Twins. The St. Louis Browns later became the Baltimore Orioles. I stayed with the Senators about a month and a half, then they optioned me out because I wasn't throwing all that well. My last stint in the major leagues was in the latter part of July. But like a lot of ballplayers in those days, I hung on. We never wanted to leave the game because we went into baseball right after high school and never went to college. I chose baseball because I love the game. My parents would like to have seen me continue schooling, but they knew my love of the game.

It was a different time back then. College wasn't emphasized like it is now, and there was no money to be made in baseball either. Let me give you an idea. My first big league contract was for five hundred dollars a month. And I made that money as long as I stayed on the major league roster. It was pretty good money in those days. Then, if I were sent out, my salary jumped back to about three hundred dollars a month.

At that time, baseball was ALL ownership, and it was inevitable as time went on that the players would try to do something to try to change that. The sad thing is the way it has changed. It went from ownership to players because ownership is not willing to give in to certain things. Because I began in the game as a player, I saw firsthand where owners controlled everything and if players didn't go along or put up any resistance, owners simply opted them out and no other club would touch them. Players had no say, and if owners didn't want to deal for you, they didn't deal for you. And they had the control over salaries. It was ridiculous back in those days.

The best example of that was when Babe Ruth first made $75,000 and everyone thought baseball was crazy to let him make that kind of money. He was the only one making anywhere near that much money! He was making more than the president of the United States at that time!

In 1945, had baseball listened to Happy Chandler, the second commissioner after Landis, it probably wouldn't be in the condition it's in today. Happy Chandler at that time, if I recall, and I may be a little off in some of the things, but he tried to get the owners to go along with the deal where the player could be a free agent after eight years or so, and let him re-sign. And he said once a player, after eight years, how many times can he be eligible to re-sign? If he plays sixteen years in the major leagues, he can only be a free agent one time to sign. But if you're making an effort to get the player something, I think you have a chance that the players will stay basically in line. But the owners didn't go along with Happy Chandler. They chose to keep the status quo relationship with players.

In '46 the players began to realize that they needed to do something and some of the players that were in the major leagues for ten, twelve, fifteen years decided to form a union. So the Players' Union was first started in 1947. One of the things it said was that a player had to stay in the majors for five years to be qualified for a pension. They later lowered it to four, and now they've got it down to where if you spend one day you're entitled to a pension. All a guy has to do is get there and play one day. Of course, the amount of the pension depends on how much time you play, so the guy who plays one day ... well ... I don't know what he'd be entitled to, but I'm sure he'd get something. I imagine, let's say, you take a player who only played fifteen days in the major leagues and never gets back, well, he's going to get maybe a hundred dollars a month. I don't know what the lowest pay is for one day up there because I never was in the majors after 1946, so it didn't apply to my situation.

But now it's exactly the opposite. Take, for instance, all the controversy over the designated hitter rule. The players are and forever will fight for it tooth and nail because it extends their careers and those huge paychecks for a couple more years. I don't mind voicing my opinion about it this way. In one breath the organizations will say, "We're doing this for the young players." But how can they be thinking of the young player when they won't let the DH rule go out? You keep the DH in and it's just for the old hitters who can't do anything but swing the bat. The American League wasn't drawing as well as the National so they put the DH in. And now, today it's almost breaking the owners because of the money they demand and get. And without his salary of five to six to who knows how many millions of dollars per year, they could get players who can play the entire game.

I've worked for AL clubs for the past twenty-five years plus and I don't like the DH. I go to the National League to scout for a couple of weeks then return to the AL and it's completely different. Like twelve noon and twelve midnight. Period. If you're a manager in the AL and you have a tremendous DH, you can just put the lineup on the wall and sit back and relax. In the NL managers actually "manage" games and use baseball strategy.

So baseball decided a couple of years ago to reach back and help some people who played prior to '47 that were still alive, but the criterion was that they had to have been in the major leagues for four years. Anybody who played four years in the major leagues prior to the pension in 1947 was given an "X" amount of dollars. So I said, "What about the player who only had three years in or two years prior to '47? There can't be more than 30–35 people who are alive today. And if they are, they're in their late seventies and eighties or better and they ain't going to cost you a lot."

And I understand they're giving them ten thousand dollars a year, those with four years. But they won't do better than that and include those guys who played less. But at least baseball's making those guys happy because this money tells them that baseball remembers them. I only had two and a half years credit to myself, so I'm not entitled to anything. But that's just the way it goes.

I wrote a letter to the commissioner, Bud Selig, asking him why not take in all living players who played prior to '47 but have less than four years in. But I have not gotten a good response from him.

For my own career, well, you know how baseball is. You go on. I stayed in the minor leagues. In 1946 I ended up in San Antonio, again in the Texas League. In '47 I started again in San Antonio in the Texas League, but went to Birmingham in the Southern Association, and I was in the minor leagues till 1954.

It was a different era than now. Back then we all played as long as we could. I mean, I only had a high school education. I loved the game. I didn't want to give it up. I always had that little spark, thinking maybe I had a chance. At one time in '49 I was almost going back to the major leagues, but for some reason the deal never went through, and I thought that was my last hurrah.

But I continued playing. I managed in 1954 for about half a year and didn't like it because of my temperament. I managed in Texas in the Class B Big State League. It was an independent club. I didn't have a good club and discovered that I was an impatient individual and somewhat of a perfectionist and didn't realize that you can't manage being that way. And I didn't like it. So it was a mutual agreement where I left and they were happy to see me go because we were in last place. It was a two-way deal.

So I stayed out of baseball in '55. Then in '56 a fella said to me, "You know, you got a pretty good feel for the game; I think you'd make a pretty good scout. Did you ever think about scouting?"

"Well," I said, "I never gave it a thought. Basically I know there's a lot of traveling involved. And if I were successful, then I'd reap the benefits. And I chose to give it a try. So I started scouting in '56 prior to the baseball draft that went in 1965. And that was the years that was, to me, what scouting was all about.

I scouted one year for Cincinnati, then went on to the Phillies, and from there I went to the Atlanta Braves and stayed with them for about 16 years. Then I left them and Bobby Mattick and I went to Toronto and I scouted for Toronto for twenty years before I left them. I was in on their heyday like Bobby was. We started on October 1, 1976, he and I together. We were the first two scouts that the Toronto Blue Jays hired. Bobby is a good person and a good, solid baseball man.

Bobby Mattick and I were the only two scouts in the history of baseball that were made vice presidents of a ballclub. We were both made vice presidents of the Toronto Blue Jays. In 1983. Peter Harding was the CEO of the ballclub, he said, "We want you two to become vice presidents of the ballclub because we know what you two contributed to the Toronto Blue Jays. But you did the legwork and made the player recommendations and we want you to know that you have contributed to the success of the organization." We were the only just plain scouts to receive that honor. There's been scouting directors and farm directors and so on, but we were just plain area scouts at that time. It was a proud time for us.

We were in on the ground floor of recommending players, making and suggesting trades, signing players, development and things of that sort with an expansion team that entered the American League in 1977. We started working for them a year prior to that. I can recall back in '78, and I can remember this like it was yesterday. I'm in Chicago scouting the Cubs, and the Seattle Mariners went into the league the same year we did. And they had finished like fourth in their division out of seven teams. And we never did get out of last place. And Harry Caray once said to me, "How can you let the Seattle people get ahead of you guys with you and Gillick and Mattick over there?"

I said, "Well, we have put in a plan and we're not going to deviate from it. I want you to come ask me this question again in three or four years."

Oddly enough, in about '83 he came up to me and he said, "Well, I see now what you people had in mind to do."

From about '83 on we won more games in baseball than any teams during that stretch. It was unbelievable. We had back-to-back World Series. We developed a lot of players. We got strong in the Rule 5 draft. We did a lot of things. We were very successful and Bobby Mattick and I played a big part of that and we were tremendously proud of that. Mattick and I have reached a point where we've been in the game for so many years that we've also scouted the sons of players we've signed.

Bobby is a guy who doesn't say much about what he does. He lets his work speak for him. I, on the other hand, felt so great about it. But most of the time we never toot our own horns because, well, back in the old days, if people realize what you've done, they would never compliment you for fear they'd have to give you a raise. In the late fifties and early sixties, they never told you that you were doing a good job for that reason. At that time teams had to have scouts, but there were some people who thought they were just a necessary evil.

I signed Cito Gaston when I was with Atlanta. He was about nineteen years old. He's a boy who never played much baseball when he was younger. He'd played a lot of softball. And then somebody told him that he had a lot of ability and asked him why he didn't play some baseball. So he decided to try it that one year, and I think he was just turning nineteen. Of all things, he's from San Antonio, Texas, right here where I'm from. He went to Holy Cross High School here.

What had happened is, well, one drizzly Sunday I didn't want to stay home. I said, "I've got to see some kind of ballgame." There was a league, what they called the Spanish-American League, playing in a park very close to my home. I sat in my car and watched the game when I saw this big tall boy about 6'4", skinny as a rail, playing center field on this day. He made some terrific plays and made some terrific throws. He could hit the ball and run well. Then he hit one out in the street, and I decided that since the rain had let up a little bit, I got out of the car and walked over to the field.

And when I got there a scout from the Houston Astros had gone out on the field and began talking to the manager and Cito Gaston. Well, that left me a day late and a dollar short. After their talk this scout left and never saw me because I stayed around out of the way. So I went out to him. As it so happened, the manager was a young man who had watched me play in the Texas League some twenty years before. He said, "I know you. You're Al LaMacchia. I used to watch you pitch for the Missions."

I said, "Yes I am." I suddenly realized that this was my "in." So I took both of them to my home. I lived on the north side and at that time it was unheard of to have a young black boy inside my home.

So we got out of the car. My neighbors across the street looked at me kind of strange. We went into the house. My wife and children were away from home. I sat down at the table with the manager and Cito and we signed him. This was in 1964, the year before the draft came in, and I was with the Atlanta Braves.

His first couple of years it was kind of tough for him. But finally he went to Utica, New York, and played in the New York-Penn League and almost led the league in hitting. From there his career took off.

Years later when we hired Bobby Cox as manager at Toronto, Bobby says, "There's a guy that's a hitting coach for the Braves that I think is tremendous. His name is Cito." So I told him I'd signed Cito, and went to talk to Pat. I told him Cito is a very, very bright young man, well mannered, well brought up, speaks well, and he'd make a good addition to our ballclub. I said I would definitely recommend us hiring him as a hitting coach. They interviewed him and hired him. So he came in '85 and I think it was '88 or '89 when he took over the ballclub as manager. He managed the club for several years.

I scouted Pat Gillick and a lot of people who are general managers now. Pat Gillick had a good arm, left-hand pitcher. He was then a little on the hyper side, as he still is today. He was a little on the wild side. I mean, he threw hard but his control was off. He was eventually signed by Baltimore, got up as high as Triple-A, but never could master the control. They finally at a rather early age decided he wasn't going to get to the major leagues, so they cut him.

Pat has a brilliant mind; I mean, he has one of the brightest minds I've ever been around. I've been around two people who could hold that job of general manager and he and Chuck LaMar are two of the brightest. They're two of the hardest working GMs you'll find in this game of baseball. He and Chuck LaMar are like two peas in a pod as far as work ethic goes.

Anyway, Pat's career was short in baseball. Never did get to the majors, but he played about four or five years and then he was released and went home. But how he got back into baseball was Eddie Robinson, the scouting director of the Houston Astros, remembered Pat when Robinson was the farm director of the Orioles. He remembered Pat's bright mind. They used to call Pat "Yellow Pages." He'd be in his room with nothing to read, so he'd get the yellow pages and he could memorize them like you wouldn't believe.

The night Toronto beat the Phillies in the 1993 World Series, I was there at the game and remember it very well. It was one of those baseball moments people always talk about. The thing about the night Joe Carter got the hit that won the Series for Toronto, well, we'd gotten into the seventh inning and they were beating us. Phillies manager Jim Fregosi made a change and brought in Anderson in the eighth and we got a run, and we were still a couple of runs behind. And then we go into the ninth inning. And you know what I mean when I say a player has a good at-bat, that he works the pitcher instead of the other way around. And that was Paul Molitor, who was hitting ahead of Joe Carter. And Paul Molitor fouled off several pitches. He had such a tremendous at-bat that he ended up getting a single. And that at-bat, to me, was one of the better at-bats in the whole ballgame. And then Joe came behind him, and I say to Mr. Beeston and Bobby Mattick, we were all sitting there in the booth, "I just hope that Williams hangs one inside." He did. And Joe Carter hit it and we kept hollering, "Stay fair, stay fair!" It stayed fair and that was when we won the '93 World Series.

And had he not gotten that home run and we hadn't won, I'm not too sure the Phillies wouldn't have been world champions in 1993. Because the very next day we would have had to face Curt Schilling, and Schilling was really big. But Joe came through for us like he did all the years he played for us. Joe was a tremendous help to our ballclub. He was a live wire in the clubhouse and kept everyone loose and went out and played hard every day. He always had fun with it

We had a tremendous ballclub and everybody contributed in their own ways, but Carter and Molitor solidified the whole thing. These two guys gave us the chemistry that we needed to win. Joe Carter was a big thing on our club. He was like the leader of the African American players. He never had to say much, just went out and played and led by example. He could talk to people, and when he talked, they listened.

Cito Gaston knew the players he had on the club. So he basically gave them a bat and ball, put the lineup card on the board, and let them go out and do their thing. And they loved playing for Cito because he was a ballplayer's manager. The best thing he had about him was that he could handle twenty-five men. Nobody on the club ever had anything against Cito Gaston.

But, getting back to scouting, to me, you have to think positive in scouting. If you think a little bit negative, it's tough to become a productive scout. You have to be positive in this regard: when you go to see a ballplayer play, you have to look to see what that player does best. If you start off looking for negatives and saying, "He can't run that well, he doesn't have any power," well, that's two negative thoughts you've got already on that player. Now you have to overcome that. I'm talking about high school and college players. You're seeing them in the raw and you can't think negatively about them at that stage. I always start with the idea that every ballplayer can do everything.

For example, let's say that he had a strong arm and has some power. Well, there's two things he can do. Then you look at the other three tools and say, "Well, how bad are they? Not enough to make this guy a non-prospect." After that, you have to have enough faith in our player development program to think they can help the kid improve the tools that he's weak in right now. I never sat near negative thinking scouts. I just got up and moved when they started that. They can influence your thinking about a player to the point where they can talk themselves out of a good player and talk you out of one, too.

Look at Nolan Ryan. There were always scouts around him in his senior year in high school. There was a lot of talk about him. But the New York Mets didn't draft him till the thirteenth round. And the scout who got all the credit for him, well, if they really thought he was that great, why did they wait until the thirteenth round? They took twelve other players ahead of him, and I'll guarantee you, eight of those players or ten never made it to the major leagues.

I was at that game when all the scouts turned out to see him pitch. And what happened was that particular night Ryan didn't do anything. And I says, "If I get the opportunity, I'm going to come back and see him in April." But I never got back. Not many liked him that night.

I later went up to Nolan Ryan when he was pitching for the Texas Rangers and Bobby Valentine, who is a very, very good friend of mine, was managing them. He's very knowledgeable, a very bright man. So anyway, I went up to Bobby and I says, "Bobby, I've got a shirt here and my son would like to have Nolan Ryan sign it."

So he says, "Oh, all right. Come on into my office." I sat there and he called Nolan Ryan in. I introduced myself to Nolan and he signed the shirt. And I says, "Nolan, I'm from Texas."

And he says, "Your name's kind of familiar to me. I've heard the name LaMacchia."

So I says, "Well, I was scouting you when you were pitching at Alvin High School in 1965. I was at a game and I can even tell you exactly when it was. It was February twenty-eighth, the first night of a three-day tournament in Alvin."

He smiled and said he remembered that tournament, too. Ryan struck out only six men in seven innings. He did not throw hard. He had a pretty good curveball. He had narrow shoulders, very skinny. I made a note to myself that I'd come back and see him if I get a chance. Well, needless to say, I never got back because I had a tremendous territory at that time. I worked New Mexico, Oklahoma, and the state of Texas, which always has lots of baseball games to see. I used to put on 45,000 miles a year. Well, anyway, I asked him a question. I says, "Nolan," and he interrupted me and says, "I remember that night. You're talking about that night we had that tournament down there."

I says, "Absolutely."

Nolan says, "Sure, I remember that. But what you scouts didn't know that night was that I had a blister on my finger." He said that nobody talked to him, so he didn't get a chance to tell us about the blister. If I would have gone up and said something to him, he probably would have showed me that finger and I could have kept the information to myself and possibly even recommended him for our own draft. But it didn't happen and that's why he went in the thirteenth round.

And there's more to it. A particular scout didn't like him and just wasn't impressed. So now he was signed and he was down in the Western Carolina League to pitch his first game there. One of the scouts that worked with this other scout was there that night. He calls the scout up and asked him what he thought of Nolan Ryan. And he said, "Well, he just didn't throw hard for me."

So he says, "Nolan must've gotten faster on the train coming down here, because he just struck out nineteen men tonight."

One of the toughest things to do in scouting is to know about the makeup of an individual. You can ask him about his background, or stay close to him and observe. Or if you talk to his coaches, they usually protect their players, especially in high school. "Oh, he's a great young man, he's this, he's that." And you're never going to get a true answer.

What I used to do just to help myself is I'd talk to other players on the team. If I was looking at a pitcher, I would take the catcher aside and talk maybe to a substitute on the bench and ask, "Say, what about so-and-so?" The young players at that age will give you exactly honest answers. They don't realize what you're looking for from them, and they'll tell you exactly what they feel about a particular individual. For instance, if I'm trying to find out about the youngster's intestinal fortitude, I may say to his teammate, "Say, I heard some guys said things to him and he turned around and walked away."

And they may say, "Oh, no, no, no, there's no way he'd walk away. He's not scared of nothing!"

Well, that tells me a lot about the player's makeup. It tells me that he's not afraid. If he got in a tight spot in a game and he begins to sweat and his rhythm is interrupted because he's in a tight spot, well, do you change spots on a leopard? Sometimes you can. Sometimes success will do a lot for an individual. But you've got to be cautious with that because you're dealing with a young man seventeen or eighteen years old and he really hasn't learned all that's involved with real self-confidence yet. But that attitude shows me that he's going to dig in and try to work his way out of the jam. He's not going to be scared to pitch with the bases loaded and three balls on the hitter.

A story that goes along as an example of this is the time Kirk Gibson came in to pinch-hit for the Dodgers in the first game of the 1988 World Series. The pitcher was working on Davis and should've gotten him out and the game's over. But he walks Davis. So Lasorda reached down and he had Gibson, who was hitting in the cage because he couldn't play because of his bad knee. And Lasorda told him, "I might need you just for one at-bat." It was rumored that he was told to hit the ball hard but he didn't have to run. Then the first or second pitch to him was a hanging slider and you know where Gibson hit it. What a moment! That was the first game of the Series, but the Oakland A's never had a chance after that. That homer won the Series for the Dodgers!

Now I'm going to backtrack and start my scouting career from the beginning. I started scouting in 1956 and there are little things that stand out and you always remember them. When I started out I saw a lot of high school games, high school tournaments, college games, college tournaments, and other amateur baseball games. You wonder how many games we really do see a year. It's unbelievable the amount of games you see a year as a scout of the free agents.

To me the best part of scouting was scouting the free agent field. That's what I call the grass roots scout, the guy who's a digger. He goes out and digs for baseball players. What I mean by free agents are players who are amateurs and have never been signed to a pro contract. That's the part of scouting that I've always loved, and I found was the most gratifying. You can't imagine the feeling you get when you see a young man, you sign him, and the next thing you see him in the major leagues where he's a tremendous ballplayer. The satisfaction is tremendous, but nobody knows it. You could be at a ballgame with two or three players out on that field playing their game and they wouldn't know that you had something to do with them. But you get the satisfaction when you hear people around you talk about what a good player each one is, or when they jump on one of them because he's made an error. You live the game with that individual. It's almost like he becomes part of your family, that young man that you signed.

And even if I didn't sign the boys — I mean there's no one scout that can sign everybody, it's impossible — but I get a tremendous kick seeing young men get to the major leagues that I scouted. Even guys I turned down and didn't recommend, like Nolan Ryan. Well, I got a tremendous satisfaction seeing him play in the major leagues all those years. I had a scout come to me one time and said, "Al, why do you pull for this guy or that guy? You didn't sign him."

I said, "I know I didn't sign him, but I'm so glad to see him doing so well. I didn't like him as much as the guy who signed him, but I liked something about him and I'm happy that he's been able to develop and play in the major leagues and make something of his baseball career." I get a tremendous satisfaction out of that also. I love to see them get to the major leagues because I can say they came from my area. And there's so many players from my area. I mean, some I liked and couldn't get them. Some I liked and got and they couldn't play. Some I liked and got that played. It's all part of being a scout.

To me the key of scouting is not looking back when you've made a mistake. Go to the next one. I've seen a lot of young men give up scouting because they've signed a young player who didn't do well and it affected them such that their scouting, well, they just couldn't scout anymore after that. They were always fearful of making mistakes. Everyone's going to make mistakes in scouting, but the key is to keep it to a minimum. If you take the approach that you're not going to fail, that's going to help you. But when you do fail, you can't let it bother you as you go on to the next one.

I quote Paul Richards a lot. I thought he was one of the brightest men in baseball. A lot of people say, "Well, what's he ever done?" When you manage the Baltimore Orioles and you're playing against the Yankees, he was one of those guys who could beat the

Yankees. Most people don't stop to realize there's not many teams that can beat the Yankees. Richards had some good clubs. And some say, "Yeah, but he was always second or third to the Yankees." What he had was a tremendous mind. There were things he would say that have just stuck with me.

Just to give you an idea. I'd say, "Paul, I like this player, the shortstop, but he doesn't have a strong arm and he doesn't throw well from the hole."

And he says, "Well, how many times is the ball hit in the hole that costs you a ballgame? But if he makes all the routine plays and is very consistent, I'll take that type of ballplayer." He says, "Most of the balls in a ballgame are hit up the middle anyway. So if the one thing is going in the hole he doesn't have a real strong arm, I'd take him anyway."

Ozzie Smith never had a strong arm, you know. He couldn't throw from in the hole. He had what I call a "Nanny-O arm." It was like a rainbow. It went up and down.

Richards always said, "Give me a pitcher who's not afraid to pitch inside." He'd say, "You live outside, but you pitch inside." That means you get them out with the pitch away, but you pitch inside to keep them honest. These are all little things that helped me throughout my scouting career.

Without bragging, I've signed some pretty good players in my day. I signed Bruce Benedict, who must've played a dozen years for the Braves; Rick Mahler, a pitcher, and his brother Mickey Mahler; Larry McWilliams and several more.

I had a lot to do with the signing of Dale Murphy for Atlanta in 1974. We were at the draft that year and our GM was wanting to take another player. I stayed with it for four days, insisting that Murphy was our player. I'll never forget the young secretary said, "Al, I'd back off if I were you. You don't want to lose your job because of this."

I said, "To me I'd rather lose my job than for us to pass up Dale Murphy if he's still there." Sure enough, up until the morning of the draft I kept saying that we need to take Dale Murphy. And he was wanting to take this other player.

And he says, "Well, what makes you think Dale Murphy will be there?"

So I went down to the lobby. The San Diego Padres were picking first. And I knew they were going to take a shortstop by the name of Bill Almon. So I says to Fontaine, "Bob, are you still going to take Almon?" And he said yes.

So I called the Texas Rangers, Hal Keller was the scouting director at that time, and he told me they were going to take Tommy Boggs. We were picking fifth that year. And the Phillies were going to take Lonnie Smith, which they did. And each one of these gentlemen took the players they told me. San Diego picked first and they took Bill Almon. Texas Rangers picked second. They picked Tommy Boggs, a high school pitcher out of Austin, Texas. Philadelphia Phillies picked third. They picked Lonnie Smith out of Compton, California, I think he was from. He was a tremendous athlete. The Cleveland Indians were picking fourth and I called young Bob Quinn, their scouting director, and he was hesitant to tell me. I says, "Bob, it doesn't make any difference. We're not picking ahead of you. We're picking behind you and we can't pick whoever you pick because you're going to pick your guy and we're coming in behind you." I says, "But it does give us a chance to know if the guy we want is still sitting there."

And he says, "Well, who you guys got in mind?" And I says, "I can't tell you because we pick behind you. But you can tell me who you got in mind if the draft goes like I'm telling you."

And he says, "And how do you know how it's going to go?"

So I says, "Look, I've talked to all the people like I'm talking to you."

He says, "Well, I know the Padres are going to take Bill Almon. But who's the Texas Rangers taking?"

I says, "Well, they're going to take Tommy Boggs. But this is just between you and I."

Well, sure enough, there was a pause on the line. And in my mind it made me think he wanted Tommy Boggs, too. But he was picking fourth. So I says, "Bob, are you still there?" And when he responded, I says, "The Phillies are taking Lonnie Smith and you're the next pick."

He says, "Well, if it falls that way, and don't tell anybody, we're going to take Tommy Brennan, a pitcher out of Louis College in Chicago." Actually Brennan was taken in the fourth round by the Cleveland Indians and pitched in the major leagues briefly, for the Dodgers, I think, but he never became the pitcher that some people thought he would be.

Anyway, that left us with the fifth pick, and I went back up and told them, "We got Murphy."

And he sat there and he says, "Well, I'm going to stick with this player, Mike Miley." Unfortunately he later got killed in a car accident. At that time he was a shortstop with the Angels. He went up the wrong ramp on the freeway and got killed in California. He was from LSU. Anyway, our scouting director said, "You should like Miley, he's from your territory."

I said, "I like Mike Miley, but if I had my druthers, I'd take Dale Murphy." I reminded him that he wanted me to find out if Murphy would still be on the table by our pick and that if all went as I was told, he would be available. And then I told him, "Mike Miley might not leave LSU. Don't forget he's the quarterback on that football team." I says, "I called him to see if he's made up his mind about playing and he never called me back."

"But anyway," I said, "What are you going to tell the press if you take Miley and you can't sign him because he chooses to stay in college?"

And he said, "Well, then, I guess we'd better take Murphy." And that's how we got him.

I also signed Cito Gaston. Bobby Mattick and I were both responsible for Dave Stieb. It was a funny thing about that. We were working together with the Blue Jays and we were told to go see three players. Eastern Illinois was playing a game with Southern Illinois. On that team was Gosset, a shortstop; Stieb, a center fielder for Southern Illinois; and two pitchers, Simons and Keaton. That's the four people we were sent there to see. We were hoping to see Simons and Keaton and their coach, Richy Jones, said, "Fellas, you're not going to see them now but you're going to have to come back later to see them pitch."

So we sat in the stands figuring we would see Gosset and Stieb. We saw Stieb in center and he was a pretty good fielder, plus he could hit and run, had a pretty good arm. He had a long swing so it didn't look like he was going to hit all that well. So we sat there, and about the fifth inning of the first game of the doubleheader the pitcher was getting in trouble. So I thought maybe Jones would bring in Simons or Keaton. But there wasn't anybody warming up in the bullpen. And all of a sudden he called time out and brought in Stieb, a right-handed pitcher, from center field to pitch. So Bobby and I were sitting there and all of a sudden he started pitching and we both kind of looked at each other kind of wide-eyed. There were about seven other scouts there.

After the game was over, Bobby said, "Let's go over there and get a Coke before the second game starts."

I said, "Go ahead. I'm going to walk around here a little bit."

And the other scouts at the game were all over getting a Coke, too. I went the other way behind the refreshment stand and I caught Stieb changing sweatshirts because he broke a sweat while pitching. He threw the ball just unbelievably. He must've thrown about 95–96 miles an hour.

So I went up to him, introduced myself, and said, "Young man, did you ever pitch before?"

And he said, "Naw, I just help them out, fill in here and there. I'm going to be the NCAA All-American center fielder in college. I didn't hit well the first game for you, but I'll show you how I can hit in the second one, I'm sure."

I said, "Well, let me ask you something. If you didn't hit, would you pitch?"

He said, "Oh, I'm going to hit. You don't have to worry about that."

And I said, "Well, now, look, I'm going to ask you a question. And don't answer me until you give it some thought." I said, "If we drafted you and signed you, if you're given the opportunity to play center field but you failed to hit, would you go to the mound as a pitcher?"

Bobby and I knew he couldn't hit. And I said, "Now don't answer me until you think about it."

And he said, "Well, I have to be the one to say that I can hit or can't hit. If I feel that I can't hit, then I'll give my maximum effort as a pitcher."

And I said, "Good enough for me. Now I'm going to test you." I says, "If any scout or your coach comes up to you and asks you if any scout talked to you about pitching, then I'd rather you would keep that between you and I, and mention this to nobody."

As soon as he finished school that year he went to Alaska to pitch, either with the Goldpanners or Anchorage, I can't remember. So Pat Gillick called me up and said, "You have to go up there." But I told Pat, "We don't have to go up there. Let's just give him the money he wants and sign him."

To make a long story short, we talked him into coming back for a workout with the Toronto Blue Jays when they were playing in Oakland. That gave him a chance to come back and see his mother in San Jose, and he worked out for us. During the three days we were in Oakland, he pitched batting practice and so on and Pat said he wants this and he wants that. I told him to give him whatever it takes and Mattie [Mattick] told him the same thing.

So we did and we drafted him in the fourth or fifth round and signed him. He pitched about twelve years in the major leagues. But before we drafted him, I told Bobby that we had to give him an opportunity to play center field. So we sent him down to play for Dennis Menke, our manager at Dunedin in the Florida State League. So they played him in center field for two days, then he DHed, then they pitched him, then they DHed him again, then he played center field again. And after a month and a half he was hitting about .198. So he said, "Well, I guess LaMacchia knew what he was talking about." And the rest was history.

I talked to the kids about different organizations that showed interest in them to help them make a wise decision about signing. I told them that if they knew about the different organizations, it could make a difference. For example, let's say, if you knew that the San Francisco Giants and the LA Dodgers were interested in a player, and they had several players like Pee Wee Reese and different players at his position. "Well," I'd say, "you don't want to get into that organization because you'll have all those players ahead of you." And we knew their organizations and we would quote the names of the players ahead of him, the one in Double-A, Triple-A and major league status. I'd say, "Well, if you sign with them, you'll be left way in the background." And then I'd tell them what our organization could offer. And then the money would come in. But you didn't run all over your territory trying to sign everybody. You'd put your first two or three players in order and then go after the one you thought you needed to sign first.

If the one you didn't have competition on, you were basically alone on, well, that individual, you'd then go and sign him. And if you had competition on another one, you'd say to that family, "Well, I'm tied up for four or five days, but I'll be there at that time, and I'd appreciate it if you wouldn't do anything until I got there." And then you go get the others first.

And that's how we did it. But then, along came the draft in 1965, and those things changed. When we got the draft, well, that all changed. The draft changed a lot about how we could conduct our business. Then we had to wait until after the draft and if a guy wasn't drafted, then we could try to sign him.

I always felt the draft shouldn't be more than twenty rounds. I just don't know what the thinking is to have so many rounds in it now, but I do know that they can draft more players and control them. A scout'll say, "I got a guy who's not ready to be a prospect for me but he's got some tools and I'd like to draft him in the fiftieth or sixtieth round and follow him and see if he develops this summer. And then all of a sudden, if he doesn't develop, you don't sign him. It's called draft and follow. But if he does develop, then he's totally your individual. For example, Mike Piazza was a sixty-second round pick of the Dodgers, so he was a guy to follow to see if he was going to develop. Everybody knows the answer to that.

We often discuss among ourselves what dictates a first-round pick. My way of looking at it was that he was scouted the most. Everybody saw him and knew who he was and how he played. But then there were guys taken, let's say in the fifth round, who were only seen by eight or ten clubs, and some didn't like him that well. Guys picked in the first three rounds or so are the ones seen and liked by the most clubs.

Take Todd Worrell, for instance. Fred McAlister and Marty Keough loved the guy, kept him as much a secret as they could, and got him as their number one when their first pick didn't come until twenty-third or something. I scouted Todd Worrell. He was in a school in the southern LA area. It was some kind of religious school and he was a divinity student if I remember right. I asked our scout to check him out more, but we decided he would be a tough sign for what we wanted to give him. Then the Cardinals got him. He went out as a starter but Jimmy Fregosi managed him in Triple-A and made a reliever out of him, which hastened his progress to the major leagues. Fregosi saw something in him as a reliever. Little things like that can make all the difference in a guy's entire career. People become different pitchers because of the roles they're put into.

This is the complete opposite of the Nolan Ryan story. He went in the thirteenth round and if anybody even thought he'd turn out to be the pitcher he was, he certainly would have gone sooner. He certainly wouldn't wait until the thirteenth round. But he didn't pitch well when McAlister was there or when I was there or when lots of others were there. He had blisters on his fingers but nobody knew about it. Now the scout who signed him could say he knew about it, but I doubt it. As I already said, so many scouts saw him and didn't think he was anything too special, at least not while he was pitching with blisters in that tournament anyway.

Red Murff gets credit for signing Ryan, he was a scout in that area. But you know who first saw him was the Mets part-time scout, Red Gaskill. He lived in Texas, about forty-five miles from Alvin, and he had a small territory in that area. He and Murff saw Ryan as a high school junior and word got out. Those two worked together and they both got credit for Nolan Ryan.

I can remember a story about the Blue Jays and Bobby Bonds when he was playing in Columbus, New York, for the Yankees, which was his last year in professional baseball, and Barry was playing in high school in San Mateo, California. I was a crosschecker and went all over the country looking at players. I had an off-day in San Francisco and had planned to stay in my hotel, but I said to our area scout, "There's no games on for today and no players I need to see, and gee, I hate to just sit in the motel."

And he nodded. So I said, "I wish there were someplace I could go."

So he says that San Mateo had a game and they have Bobby Bonds' kid on the team, but he's a guy who is an individual, an egotistical kid.

So I said, "Well, can he play? I want to go see him." The scout said he'd take me and we saw him play. Got there early and watched batting practice and I said to myself, "Oh my God, this kid has tremendous tools."

After the game was over, I asked the scout, "You're walking away from Barry Bonds because of his makeup? You can't do that." I says, "Is there anything else?"

And he says, "Well, you know, there's talk that he was on marijuana."

I says, "Well, that's a young kid experimenting with it, is that what you mean? That could be the end of it. But the way he plays, we got to consider drafting this guy."

So we went and worked him out and I told Pat Gillick. I says, "Pat, this guy has tremendous ability. He's a first-round pick in my opinion."

Anyway, Bobby Bonds was playing at Columbus. Bobby Mattick went to have lunch with him to see what it would take to sign his boy. He said it would take "X" amount to sign him. So we decided to draft him in the second round. We went into the second round and we were ready to take Barry Bonds and they switched and went to David Wells.

I said, "Oh my God, Pat!" Gillick says, "Well, you liked David Wells a lot."

I says, "Yes, that's right. But I don't like him more than the Bonds kid."

Well, we didn't take him and a few drafts behind us the Giants took him. But they offered him less than what they were prepared to give him, expecting him to negotiate, but they weren't comfortable negotiating with Bobby Bonds' kid. They went back and forth a few times and finally offered him about sixty thousand and that's when Barry said he was going to play at Arizona State. He told them he was humiliated with their offer. That was how they elected to do it and they made a mistake. Then when he was at Arizona State, the Dodgers and a few clubs passed on him in the same way we did and Pittsburgh got him.

It's one thing to look at a player's makeup and another when he's got Bonds tools. He's egotistical, he's got an air about him, but then you look at the guy's stats and that pretty well decided the issue flat out.

Another change besides the draft that happened during my career was the major league expansion. Bobby Mattick and I had the good fortune to be the first scouts hired by the Toronto Blue Jays the year before the team took the field, and it was an exciting time for us. A really wonderful opportunity for a scout.

Expansion has affected the game and the way scouts work, of course. We all had to adjust to it at the time and there are lots of opinions on it. One example of how it helped the game happened in Pittsburgh. The Pirates had been floundering for some years until Syd Thrift got over there. And when he got there he called us at Toronto. And I was with Pat Gillick one day when he called and said he so admired the way Gillick did it at Toronto, and he wanted to use the same concept there. And he went and made trades. He got Andy Van Slyke for little or nothing from the Cardinals, and Barry Bonds was moved quickly up to the big leagues, and they signed Bobby Bonilla and moved him quick, too. And all of a sudden they began to gel as a ballclub in 1990, '91, and '92.

Astroturf created a lot of three hundred hitters. I mean the balls move faster on that stuff and get what players call a "truer hop" so the defense is easier for them. But if the balls got through, well, you see what I mean. This stuff made clubs change and give more attention to speed. They're going for speed to offset the turf meant scouts had to look for speed, too. It's already one of the five tools, as they say, but the turf suddenly made that tool a lot more important. The turf began in Houston, then St. Louis, Cincy, the Pirates and several others all went that way. Then they began building bigger parks to accommodate the hitter's advantage with the turf.

Of course, the reason for all that ball action is because it's so hard. Under that turf is concrete, very hard on the players' bodies, but it saved the game lots of rainouts because they could get the Zamboni out there and literally vacuum off the water after rain and play the game.

But now, most clubs are getting away from it and going back to grass, so that stress for the scouts is not a factor anymore. Probably the only team that will have it in the future is Minnesota. But the turf makes the infielders seem like better players. They look a lot quicker.

Today it's sad to see how many clubs are owned by conglomerates. Most clubs have to do this in order to survive the financial operating costs. Problem with it is that these businessmen may not be baseball men, just businessmen concerned with bottom lines. Nobody knows what the long-term results of this will be, but there's certainly cause for concern. But there's one constant in baseball and that is how the game always seems to land on its feet, so to speak, no matter what things it has to cope with.

George Genovese

(1922–)

Genovese contributed much to baseball as we know it today. In addition to a long career as a minor league player and player-manager, which was typical in his day, he "made it" to the major leagues before he began a forty-four-year and counting scouting career with the Giants and Dodgers. He was among the first handful of scouts personally asked by Branch Rickey to begin the search for talent in Mexico and the Latin American countries. Genovese was not yet an official scout, but he knew the language, knew the area, and knew the players there. His efforts along with those of others like Howie Haak, Clyde Sukeforth, and the first to scout and sign hundreds from Cuba, Joe Cambria, led to the opening of Latin America for Major League Baseball. They were among the vanguards who opened the flood gates for the influx of the Latin players we enjoy in the major leagues today. Everyone who has spent time in professional baseball or knows anything about scouting knows the name George Genovese.

The Society of American Baseball Research (SABR) lists the players Genovese signed for the San Francisco Giants between 1961 and 1990 who played in the major leagues. The list is long and impressive: Frank Johnson, Ollie Brown, Bobby Bonds, Chris Arnold, Gary Ryerson, Don Carrithers, Greg Garrett, George Foster, Garry Maddox, Gary Matthews, Horace Speed, Gary Thomasson, John D'Acquisto, Dave Kingman, Randy Moffitt, Gary Alexander, Jack Clark, Guy Sularz, Alan Wirth, Rich Murray, Dennis Littlejohn, DeWayne Bice, Chili Davis, Rob Deer, John Rabb, Chris Brown, Randy Kutcher, Alan Fowlkes, Eric King, Ken Henderson, Jim Pena, Matt Williams, Royce Clayton, and Joe Rosselli.

Today, at the other side of age eighty-five, he is still a part-time scout for the Dodgers and happily keeps his hand in the game he loves.

George Genovese was the recipient of the Scout of the Year Award, West Coast, 1988. And the George Genovese Lifetime Achievement Award was created in his honor.

I began liking baseball because I had older brothers who played and I went along. We lived in Staten Island, New York. This was back in the early 1930s. My oldest brother had a team called the West Brighton Cardinals. He was probably eighteen or nineteen then. The bunch of them got together to play once a week, and they had uniforms, which was quite the deal at the time. I can remember my mother had a little concession stand there and I was the kid going around selling soda pop. I was maybe seven or eight years old. Then later I got moved up to batboy. I still have photos of that.

When I became of age they had various leagues, but, of course, not like they have today with Little League and all that. We just went down to the field and chose up sides. They threw the bat up and the first one to catch it put a hand at the bottom and they'd work their hand up and the person who got all his fingers on the knob was the winner and he got to choose first for his players and for home team advantage. It's like they show it in the old baseball movies.

Of course, I was always watching games. My first recollection of the World Series was the St. Louis Cardinals and the Philadelphia Athletics, but I don't recall exactly what year that was, maybe '30 or '31, but that was when Connie Mack had all the great teams with Lefty Grove, Jimmy Foxx, and numerous other players. I can remember listening to the games on the radio. Gabby Street was the manager of the Cardinals and he died soon after that.

I remember one famous name, the first baseman by the name of Jim Bottomley. Oddly enough, the next year, 1932, I think, the Cardinals played an exhibition night game in my hometown and I went along with my brothers and that's when they had Dizzy Dean and Gus Mancuso. Frankie Frisch was the manager and I can remember seeing them playing against our strong semipro team, which had good ballplayers. I guess now, as I look back, St. Louis probably had an off-day in New York when they were playing either the Dodgers or the Giants and scheduled this exhibition game to pick up a little extra money.

They had a sellout crowd and I can remember getting Jim Bottomley's autograph. I don't remember what I did with it, but I can remember running to get to him because I remembered him from that World Series. Let's see, I remember Dizzy Dean pitched a couple of innings and after he did his stint and went to the showers, he sat on the sidelines and chatted with the fans. And I remember the peanut vendor came around selling little brown paper bags of peanuts and Dizzy Dean gave me a bag of peanuts. He teased the vendor for a little while and made believe he didn't know he had to pay for them, just having fun, and he took all the bags of nuts and passed them around to all the kids there. But the kid vendor was waiting to get paid and, of course, he paid him. We all had fun with that even though the poor vendor wasn't too sure about it in the beginning. I remember the other guy standing beside him was the catcher, Gus Mancuso. These were my beginning recollections of professional ballplayers.

Ironically enough, in 1941, when I was in spring training down in Columbus, Georgia, Double-A baseball then. We were all assembled. Clay Hopper was our manager. I was just assigned over there in spring training. I guess Branch Rickey had scheduled a game with the major league Cardinals. This was going to be my second year in pro baseball. I had signed in 1940 out of a tryout camp. I was picked as shortstop on this team. I had played Class B the year before in the summertime. Anyway, I could see this was a big jump from where I'd played the year before and here we are playing the St. Louis Cardinals. They had Johnny Mize on first. I mean, they had a great ballclub. Ernie White was the pitcher.

One of the kids on our club had played a couple of years as a pitcher and part-time outfielder but he hurt his arm and couldn't throw the ball across the diamond. I always thought he could hit and I always said to him, "Gee, if I could hit a ball like you, they'd have to find someplace to play me."

At that time there weren't many people looking at that individual and he was pretty close to being gone, being released. But he could hit. So the manager took him to Springfield, Missouri, in the Western Association when that season started. I think he was there for two months and put up some fabulous numbers; I think he hit over twenty home runs. They moved him to Rochester and then he finished up in the major leagues. This was all in the 1941 season.

What was that kid's name? Stan Musial!

I mean, things were tough. We were all battling for jobs and we looked at Musial's rise from obscurity and near release to major league player and it inspired us. I remember we went to town to get breakfast. In those days we had to eat in a cafeteria using the meal tickets they gave us, a dollar and twenty-five cents a day. We got our meal tickets each day. There was no check for the entire week or anything like that, just in case we didn't survive beyond that day. So we had to line up every day and the business manager handed out meal tickets for that day.

It's still pre–Pearl Harbor in 1941 spring training and my brother had just been drafted into the army. He had been stationed in Fort McClellan, Alabama, and he came over on a weekend pass unbeknownst to me. The GIs in those days were paid $21 a month. So he was in the ballpark looking for me and they said I was with my friends in the cafeteria. I just happened to be with Musial that day and my brother came in. We'd had the breakfast and stuck him with the check. Of course, we had no idea how much money he was being paid, but figured it had to be more than we were. He always remembered that and always remembered me telling him how Musial could hit.

I eventually went back to Hamilton, Ontario, for a second year, which I had pretty much selected for myself because I thought I could be happy there. I could have stayed with the Columbus ballclub because Clay Hopper was impressed with me. But I felt I wanted to play with the player-manager in Ontario, who was a second baseman and felt he could help me. I went back to play for him and that was my first experience in pro ball. The player-manager's name was Roy Pfleger. He was a good hitter who had played in the American Association for a number of years and I think he had some time in the big leagues. But he had broken his leg and it slowed him down. He was a fine manager and a fine man. He gave me tremendous help. The grades in those days were Class D, C, B, A, AA, and AAA. So I stayed with that team and we played good baseball, let me tell you. We played the Brooklyn Dodgers, the Philadelphia Phillies.

How well I remembered Musial. He was a skinny kid who played as a pitcher and then outfielder and got a shot because of his bat. He was sent down to the Columbus camp because of a bad arm. He wasn't injured; he just didn't have a strong throwing arm. He could barely throw the ball from first base, I mean, his arm was that bad. But there was nothing wrong with the way he could swing the bat. He could hit and he could run. A manager named Ollie Van Eck was really responsible for his career. I later played for him.

I played in Asheville for that 1942 season and they'd lowered the army draft age from twenty-one to eighteen and we all had to register there. We weren't even registered one month and we all got our draft notices! I went into the service in October because they let me finish the last couple of weeks of the season and then report from my hometown in New York. But I remember Dick Sisler, Roland LeBlanc, and Frank Zera, a big strapping catcher and a wonderful kid, all left the club shortly after getting their notices so they could enlist in other services. These were the guys from my team I chummed with in those days. So later on in the war I wound up on Iwo Jima and Okinawa. Frank Zera got killed. I came across his grave on Okinawa. He was a fine kid, a really wonderful kid.

I was discharged from the military in March 1946, so I didn't have much time to get myself together before spring training, and I wound up going back to a Class B team at Lynchburg, Virginia. The franchise had been moved from Asheville to Lynchburg by then. It was called the Piedmont League, a very good league, good baseball. It was a strong league. Tony Lazzeri was the player-manager and he was a good ballplayer even then. As I look back, he was 33–34 years old. Just imagine at that age today, these guys are signing multi–year contracts. And Lazzeri was a Hall of Fame player.

There was another player-manager at Richmond in the league, Ben Chapman, a tremendous athlete. He played third base, managed, and occasionally pitched. And he went back to the big leagues in 1946. He had played nine or ten years for the Yankees and I think he was thirty-two years old. He was a great football player in college and signed out of college and I think he played eight or nine years with the Yankees. That was an outstanding ballclub then. In those days for those guys to make any money they had to be a player-manager. And Lazzeri and Chapman could both still play. It was just a strong league, classified as Class B. I can remember the Yankee farm in Norfolk in that league had Vic Raschi, who became a great pitcher for the Yankees for a number of years, pitcher Karl Drews, and Bill Wight, a left-handed pitcher who had one of the best moves I ever saw in baseball.

I had a chance to play in the major leagues. I was playing with Hollywood in the PCL in 1949. The year before I had played at Denver and had a pretty good year there. Hollywood had a working agreement with the Denver Bears in the Western League and they selected me as the player they wanted as part of their working agreement. I reported to Hollywood at the end of the '48 season, and I remember playing a couple of weeks after we were eliminated in the playoffs at Denver.

Then in 1949 I was with them all year and we won the pennant. Right after that I was drafted by Bucky Harris, who was the manager of San Diego and going back to manage Washington. He had previously managed the Yankees and was called "the Boy Wonder" in his early days. He was the player-manager for the Washington Senators in the World Series. He was also a Hall of Famer. But anyway, I guess I impressed him enough and he selected my contract in the fall-winter draft they used to have in the major leagues. It was before the draft as we know it today. I was so impressed with the Pacific Coast League, and all my life I wanted to be a major leaguer, and here I was getting my turn. We all had to wait our turns in those days. Nobody just crashed in. But I was sent to the Washington Senators to play in the major leagues.

I left the championship club at Hollywood, which I thought was a very good ballclub. In fact, I thought it could have competed with four or five clubs in the American League. My observations from watching games from the bench, you know. The top clubs in the American League at that time were the Boston Red Sox, New York Yankees, the Cleveland Indians and Detroit. The bottom four, well, with another pitcher or two, the Hollywood club would have been able to compete with them. And the conditions in the Pacific Coast League were so good that I was spoiled. In fact, I later found myself longing to get back to the Pacific Coast League. At that time, well, I had a home out in California, and I thought I was getting $5,000 to sit the bench in Washington and I'd be getting the same amount of money being home in the Coast League and be playing!

I know now it wasn't the right move, but we got beat one day in Fenway Park. I think Boston beat us by a score of 18–1. Well, I should have known that was not the time to approach Bucky Harris, the manager. It was my mistake. I said, "You know, Bucky, I'm not too happy here." Can you believe that? I was in my first game in the major leagues and I did something like that. As I look back I think "What an error!" But I was young and had thought about it and knew I wanted to go back to the Coast League but it probably wasn't in the cards.

So I found a note in my locker in the clubhouse the next day to report to Clark Griffith at Chattanooga in their farm system. It was in the Southern League. It was below the big leagues and the Coast League, too. I wasn't too pleased with that but I had to go or not get paid. That's the way it was then. Fred Haney bought my contract back and brought me back to Hollywood. I played there again in 1951.

George Genovese, shortstop, was twenty-eight when he made his major league debut with the Washington Senators in 1950. He had the proverbial cup of coffee at his own request after only three games and one hitless at-bat. He chose to ask team manager Bucky Harris if he could be returned to the Pacific Coast League. That was the day the Senators lost an 18–1 blowout game to the Red Sox in Fenway Park. He laughingly recalled that it wasn't the best career move he ever made but it turned out well (George Genovese collection).

Then Branch Rickey came to me and offered me a player-manager job. He said, "George, I don't think you're going to go back to the big leagues and I know you'd like to stay in baseball and I have an opening for a player-manager, which would give you an opportunity to stay in the game." So I took it. This was for the 1952 season, and I went to Batavia, New York, in the same league where I broke in. The team was with the Pirates at the time when Rickey was trying to rebuild the Pirates into a winner. He did accomplish that did, but he was gone before the fruition of his efforts were recognized. Just about the time the club was ready to win, his contract had expired and was not renewed. That was 1960, the year the Pirates beat the Yankees and practically all the Pirates players were from Branch Rickey's development system.

Branch Rickey was a very interesting man. The first time I ever met Mr. Branch Rickey, as everyone called him, was when I was with the Cardinals organization. He always made a trip to every farm club he ever had. He came into the clubhouse, shook hands with the ballplayers, and chatted briefly with them as a group. He was an amazing man. He stayed on the field all day long watching plays at spring training. He was tireless. He saw every player.

For baseball to exist in the old days, they had salary limits in each league. They could spend so much money on salaries. I know this from experience. A guy could say, "I want a $50 increase in my pay," and the general manager of that club would say, "Well, I can't do it because then I'd be exceeding the salary limit of the league." Each league was expected to get by on a certain specified amount of money and the higher the league the higher the salary limits were. Of course, within that certain ballplayers earned more than others for various reasons. Sometimes they would get a player on option from a higher club or the major league. Well, the major league would pay so much of his salary and the minor league club would be obligated for a lesser amount. If the higher club was contributing to his pay, then that amount of money would not count toward their particular salary limit. That was my understanding of it.

You can see why they had that because the clubs did depend on gate receipts in order to operate. Most of these clubs were not owned by the major league clubs, but just had working agreements with them and were getting so much money from that club for operating expenses. Now that club had to hustle, and for the league to survive, they had to have certain restrictions. See, minor league clubs could control their salary limits. They could increase them by getting lots of players on options from the major leagues where the major league club would absorb a good part of their salaries so they could stay within the salary limits. But that meant that they would be fiscally solvent to keep the leagues together and continue good player development.

I'm sure sometime in the future they'll have to have some restraints like that because I don't see how baseball can continue with the enormous salaries of today. So much today is so different, and I'm not into the politics of it.

In the old days I think there were fifty-seven minor leagues and only sixteen major league clubs. To make the big leagues and wear the uniform even for a day was quite an achievement back then. It was a tall ladder to climb. There was no such thing as learning on the job at the big league level like today. If you couldn't play, you didn't get there. And if you got there and couldn't play, you didn't stay. Period. They weren't developing you in the big leagues.

In our time if you wanted to stay in the game and were still able to play, and with the salary limits and all that, teams wanted managers who could help the team by playing and not just being a bench manager. So you had to be able to do a good job or you'd get run out of town. I started as a player-manager in 1952 and continued through '53, '54 and '55. In 1956, Mr. Rickey came through and talked to me. I'll never forget it. He said, "You know, George, the hardest thing for ballplayers to recognize is when they've slowed up. You have to forget about playing now and get on to different things."

At the end of the '55 season, the year we won the pennant, I was doing all right but noticed I had an infielder who was coming down by the name of Jim Baumer. He did a terrific job. So I knew he could play and his primary position was second base, but I already had a very good second baseman and an excellent third baseman by the name of Leo Rodriguez. I mean he was as good as Brooks Robinson. I found myself in a kind of a quandary. I wanted to get Baumer in the lineup, so I remembered what Mr. Rickey had told me about slowing up. Then in a game after a particular play, I remember saying to myself, "I should've had that ball."

I remember what Mr. Rickey said about a player-manager reaching a point where he's not able to contribute as well as some of the younger players on the team. So it was time for me to step out and just manage. I decided to put Baumer in there and I'd become the utility player. That's the way I operated until 1958. In 1959 I was the third base coach for the Pirates team in Salt Lake, which was in the Pacific Coast League. That's when they had Sacramento, Vancouver, Portland, Seattle, Spokane — Maury Wills was their shortstop then — San Diego and Phoenix.

Being a player-manager in those days you had to love it and you also had to be able to pull your own weight on the field. In the lower minors you were everything, including the bus driver. One year we had three station wagons and I had to drive one and I chose two responsible players to drive the other two. You also had to be the trainer and everything else.

Anyway, during that same period, Branch Rickey was interested in developing players in the Mexican areas and this was more or less the beginning of going into the Latin countries to look for talent. Howie Haak and Clyde Sukeforth went on scouting trips together to South America. I had played in Mexico, in Mazatlan, and other places there. So they requested I go with them because I was involved in playing down there and also I had been a player-manager for the organization and they thought I could really help them in the scouting end of it. I knew the countryside and all that plus I could speak Spanish pretty well, too. We ran some tryout camps, I think it was around 1954 or something like that.

Anyway, we went on that trip and I think we signed one ballplayer who got to play at the Triple-A level out of our camp. No, we signed two. One played in Triple-A and the other in the lower minors. But that was the beginning of trying to get a foothold in Mexico. It really paid off because Mexico has made a lot of contributions to the major leagues now. I loved scouting down there. I remember one outstanding hitter that every club wanted. He was an outstanding hitter who played shortstop named Besserio Fernandez. Outstanding talent, but he just would not leave Mexico. I remember Al Campanis was a scout for the Dodgers then and he said, "The Dodgers will give sixty thousand dollars for that ballplayer."

And I said, "Al, I don't care if it's a hundred thousand dollars. The boy doesn't want to leave Mexico." In fact, we even tried to keep him back at the end of spring training, hoping he'd change his mind. But as my bus was pulling out, he came running after it with his bags in his hand and tears in his eyes shouting, "Don't leave me here!" This is true.

There was another player a few years later whom I played briefly against when my playing career was finishing up, and this kid could hit. But it was the same thing again. This was a boy by the name of Hector Espino. There was no doubt in my mind that he had superstar talent if he desired to play, but he just wouldn't leave Mexico. He played his whole career, I believe, with Hermosillo and another ballclub in Mexico.

When I went to the Giants my first job was managing Artesia, New Mexico. It was a full-season league but called a sophomore league in those days. It was strictly a development league and you couldn't play there more than two years, and if you'd already played two years of pro ball you were no longer eligible to play there. It was a very small town and the facilities left things to be desired. In those days, if we had 150 people in the stands, it was really something. And by the end of night games, all the places to eat were closed. It was hard for the kids to find something to eat.

But, as I look back, we got some pretty good players off of that ballclub. I had a young Jesus Alou, and Gil Garrido, who we shifted from a pitcher to an outfielder and he hit well over .300 that year. We traveled in station wagons because we didn't have a team bus and went to places like Alpine, Texas, and Carlsbad, New Mexico. Lots of long drives. As I look back at the whole thing, I must say you have to love baseball because the parks weren't very good, either. One bright spot was to watch these kids develop. It was a very productive league.

In 1964, I was managing in the Giants organization when everything changed for me. I was managing in Caracas, Venezuela, that winter and was scheduled to go back to El Paso, where I'd managed the year before and won the pennant. While I was still down there I got a phone call from Jack Schwarz, the scouting director, who said he wanted me to leave managing and start scouting Southern California for the organization. He said I was good with players and knew about talent and potential and since I already lived in Southern California anyway, it would be a good fit for me, too. Well, it was quite a shock because I felt I was getting pretty good as a manager and had set my hopes on managing my way up the minor league ladder and maybe managing the major league club one day. I tried to explain that to him, but he said it was a done deal and he wasn't going to make AT&T rich by discussing it on the phone.

He asked me to come to San Francisco when my season in Caracas was completed to talk about it. I did that and we talked at Candlestick Park. He said they weren't getting any production out of Southern California and wanted to make some changes. To make a long story short, I said I'd agree to scout for one year, but with one condition. I wanted to start a team for young amateur players in the LA area. Schwarz agreed, and I finally agreed to scout for a year. That was over forty years ago.

Dave Garcia, one of the scouts there, and I traded jobs. Dave wound up managing the Angels and the Cleveland Indians. We're great friends, and Dave had a good career and I did, too. It turned out that scouting was my niche, too. It worked out well for both of us and we both did well.

That's the way my scouting career started. I like to think that along the way I helped some kids have a career. I know George Foster, well, I don't know if anybody else would've taken a chance on him but I saw some things in him. Jack Clark was a pitcher in a small high school with not much attention paid to him. Chili Davis was another one. He was seventeen years old out of Dorsey High School and I think he had a 20-year major league career when he hung it up in 1990. In fact, I'm looking right now at a World Series trophy Chili gave me when he was with Minnesota. It's right on my mantle there. It's got his name on it and all the flags. He sent his brother over to bring it to me.

Back to the story of the team I had with the Giants. Quick note, I still have the team, but it's called the Dodgers because I'm with them now. When I first began to scout, I wanted to have a team because there are a lot of kids who don't get seen. Your time is limited from the time school baseball starts until the draft and you can't be every place. So way back in 1964, since I was going to scout, I talked to my boss, Jack Schwarz, and I said I'd like to have some uniforms and I could get some people help me run a team because I believe Southern California has a lot to offer. There's an awful lot of kids who perhaps don't get seen in school. Maybe they don't have the grades to be eligible, or they get sick during a season, or they just move into the area and they're not playing on a team yet. So how do you see them?

A meeting of executives at the San Francisco Giants during spring training at Casa Grande, Arizona, 1960. Row 1 (left to right from wall): Horatio Martinez, Dominican scout; George Genovese, area scout, Southern California; Sal Taormina, Giants minor league manager; Buddy Kerr, area scout, West Coast. Row 2: Carl Hubbell, Giants farm director and Hall of Fame pitcher; Dave Garcia, area scout, later manager of California Angels and Cleveland Indians; Frank "Chick" Genovese, scout, Latin America, Florida; Alex Pompez, scout, Latin America with Chick Genovese. Row 3: Jack Schwarz, Giants scouting director for 30+ years; Ray Murray, Giants minor league manager; Hugh Poland, area scout, Southeastern states; Richard Klaus, Giants minor league manager. Row 4: Andy Gilbert, minor league manager; Doyle Alexander, East Coast scout; Red Davis, minor league manager; Frank Burke, clubhouse attendant in spring training; Hank Sauer, Giants hitting coach (George Genovese collection).

The Giants gave old uniforms for the kids to wear and some bats and other equipment for them to use. We had workouts and regular practice during the week and played games on Sunday. Down the line many people referred to that team and the ones we played against as the Sunday League. I could work with them individually as time permitted and watch them improve their skills. I really feel good about the successes they all achieved and like to think I made a little contribution to it. But that's baseball. It's a great game.

So how'd we find the kids? Now, if a kid wants to play ball, he will find you. Many times people come up to me and ask how to get on the team. "How do you get on my team? Come on out and we'll take a look at you," is what I tell them. Over the years it's proved very fruitful. Some of the best ballplayers I've ever signed were on that team, like George Foster, Garry Maddox, and Gary Matthews.

Bobby Bonds was another kid off that team. Evo Pusich brought him out to our ballclub. Evo was scouting the east side of California at that time. So what happened was, that year, 1964, I liked Ken Henderson down in San Diego and wanted to sign him. I told Evo to sign Bonds and I don't know what happened, but when I got back from my trip to San Diego to sign another boy, I asked him, "How'd you come out with Bonds?"

And he said, "Well, I brought him out with the team and had Tom Sheehan come down and look at him. Tom Sheehan was Mr. Stoneham's right-hand man. In fact, he managed the San Francisco Giants when they fired Rigney. Nice man, a pitcher, I think, in his day. Anyway, he caught Bobby Bonds on a bad day and wasn't impressed. So when I came back, I heard what happened and said, "Evo, I can't believe that. Bring that kid out again."

Evo brings him out and I talked to Bobby and said, "Bobby, what happened?"

And Bobby said, "Well, I didn't do too well." At that time Bobby just got out of high school, but he was married and his wife was expecting a baby, whom they named Barry.

So I called up Jack Schwarz and said, "You know, I would really lose sleep over not getting this boy. I think he's a good athlete and he definitely wants to play ball. He did have an athletic scholarship."

Well, Bobby wanted to play and skip college and the rest is history. He didn't exactly light up everybody in spring training. But I stayed in his corner and convinced Max Lanier, the manager of the Giants farm team in Lexington, North Carolina, that the kid was for real. "Stick with him awhile, Max," I said, "because he's going to do something for you." So even though he struggled in spring training, Max took him and he had a tremendous year. I think he hit more than thirty home runs. He was on his way.

This was a time when a scout could stand behind a player he believed in and try to get a spot for him so he could get his shot. Bobby was the type of kid, if he gets on base he can show speed, and if he hits the ball he hits it nine miles. But he can also look terrible striking out. Sometimes scouts have to follow their instincts and I believed that Bobby would put it all together. And he proved me right. I always feel good about that.

That was a time when the scouts did the job differently. At the end of our conversation, Jack Schwarz said, "Don't worry about it, George. I'll take your word on it and I'll call up Evo and tell him to go sign him." It's not that way today, but I'll always remember that. Today the supervisor, which is what Tom Sheehan would be called today, but in those days he was Mr. Stoneham's right-hand man, would have looked at Bobby Bonds and rejected him and that would have been the end of it, at least as far as the Giants were concerned.

This was before the draft that began in 1965, so at least we didn't have to worry about losing him in the draft. But that's what scouts did and still do. We look at kids who have potential and will be able to pull it together as they go through the development process in the minor leagues. When you're a scout, you're trying to project what you see. You're not always right, but you've got to feel that the goods were there.

Going back now to when I was a player-manager in Latin America. Winter of 1954-1955 was the beginning. When I went down to accept a job as player-manager, it was for Branch Rickey in the Pittsburgh Pirates organization. I had been playing winter baseball. He wanted to put a team in Poza Rica, a little place about 150 miles from Mexico City. I had been playing in Mazatlan, where Pittsburgh had developed a working agreement in the winter league in one of the coast leagues there. And so there was another league on the other side called the Vera Cruz Winter League, which included Mexico City and Pueblo and others on the east coast.

He wanted me to be the player-manager in Poza Rica for the Pittsburgh players. They have summer and winter leagues there and play all year round because of the weather. Anyway, as things turned out, Mazatlan won its league championship and my club won the Vera Cruz League championship. So we had what they call the Mexican World Series with the Pittsburgh farmhands. It turned out to be very successful because future major leaguers and future Pirates came out of that. Let's see, there was Ronnie Klein, a pitcher who pitched well up there for Pittsburgh, Dick Hall, and others.

It was the beginning of minor league development plans in Mexico for the Pirates players. Before that there would be players haphazardly contacted from all over the country to play there but not as a unit or part of an organization.

So then, in 1955, Mexico entered the realm of organized baseball for the first time due to the influence of Branch Rickey. He wanted Mexico City, our farm club; there were two teams in Mexico City, but one club was more or less independent. They were called the Reds. There was a natural rivalry. We were called the Tigers. Mexico City is a tremendously large city and supported this rivalry very well. That two-club rivalry existed there previous to having any farm systems or working agreements. There were always two clubs that thrived there, the Reds and the Blues.

Then there were six cities in the beginning and they went through expansion just as we did here, and now there are teams all over the place. They have about twenty clubs now, or maybe even more than that. And so my club proceeded to win the pennant there in 1955 with a fantastic finish. We finished in a tie for first place on the last day of the season and had to have a playoff with the Nuevo Laredo team in a best two-out-of-three series. Their club was managed by Adolfo Luque. His full name was Adolfo Domingo Luque Guzman, a fiery Cuban pitcher who was called "the Pride of Havana." Many agree he was the first Latin American player to have a star status career in the major leagues for close to twenty years, I think. He was a very good pitcher in his day, and very proud. "Hell, I could strike out Babe Ruth any time," he'd laugh. "He couldn't hit my curveball." He pitched against Babe Ruth many times and really could handle him.

And there were other players from the Negro Leagues there, players not allowed in the majors at that time, Cubans and Puerto Ricans, who were versatile and talented players in their time. That was the beginning of organized baseball in Mexico, and they still play under the National Association rules. They used to have affiliations with different major league clubs, but I'm not sure how it is now. Reggie Otero was managing there when I was and I think he had Cincinnati players. Anyway, lots of players from our major leagues were sent down there on option or on loan.

Branch Rickey was a genius. He was a pioneer. I got to know him well, having worked for him and sitting in on meetings and all. He was a very progressive thinker. He knew these markets were going to be opened. At that particular time there weren't too many ballplayers. I mean Santo Domingo wasn't very productive, and Cuba had been the only place where ballplayers were coming out of. Of course, this changed after Castro came in. Most of the players arriving at the major league level were from Cuba. But then Mr. Rickey could see that Puerto Rico, Santo Domingo, and Mexico liked baseball. Well, he saw a market there to be explored. He felt Mexico could be the next area and he wanted to get an inroad there right away.

I think other organizations and scouts saw what he was doing and just followed suit. Other scouts sent down there saw what the Pirates were doing. The scouts are more or less the ones who get things started. I mean, I think I was really instrumental in getting Mr. Rickey interested because he knew I was playing ball down there and getting good looks at other teams and players there. When he asked me about it, I told him how I felt about things there. Bull fights used to be a big thing there and so was soccer, but baseball was taking over.

When I was back for spring training meetings and all that, he asked me questions about the cities and people's reception to baseball. Back then Mazatlan was a wonderful little village on the coast with about 35,000 people. Now it's a huge tourist center for the area. We had to be careful all through Mexico because of the sanitary conditions and so forth in some areas, but in many areas it was okay. It depended on where you wanted to go.

Some players didn't like it. And I felt the players who didn't like it should leave. There's no sense in being unhappy. We only wanted players who really wanted to play. That first year I developed a wonderful team. Kids like Paul Pettit and Joe Bauman, and a wonderful pitcher who was outstanding named Fred Waters. He was a big favorite with the fans. We had a great third baseman, Leo Rodriguez, probably as good as anybody I've ever seen, including Brooks Robinson. I think he was just kind of overlooked. I think he ended up in the Mexican Hall of Fame. I had the pleasure of playing against him and that's where I recognized his ability. Then I got him for our team.

There was Felipe Monimehor, an excellent player from Monterrey, Mexico, but he was never quite good enough to make it with the Pirates at the time. The Dodgers drafted him from us and somewhere along the line he fell short. He was an amazing athlete. I had a first baseman, an old-timer by the name of Angel Castro, probably the best left-handed hitter I ever saw in Mexico. He was an old man when he was playing for me, probably 35 or more. I enjoyed playing with him at Mazatlan. In those days none of them ever went to the big leagues, but he definitely had a big league bat. He was a legend there.

I managed there through 1958, then went as a coach in Salt Lake in '59. At that time Rickey had been replaced by Joe Brown, and that year the Pirates won the World Series. Not to take anything away from Joe Brown, but the foundation was Rickey's. Joe Brown made a couple of good deals. One was a trade with Frank Lane. He traded Bobby Del Greco and Dick Littlefield to the Cardinals for Bill Virdon. But that made it for the Pirates. Of course, we had Clemente, and Wright, and they had the pitching in place. All of that was previously done by Mr. Rickey.

I became fairly close to Mr. Rickey and always called him Mr. Rickey. We all did. But we called Branch Rickey's son Branch. He was a good baseball man in his own right. He really was. He lived under the shadow of his dad. He died fairly young with diabetes, around the age of 45. He was a sound baseball man and made good judgments about ballplayers. But his dad, Mr. Rickey, made tremendous contributions to the development of baseball into what it is today. In the beginning the facilities were crude compared to what we see up here. But now practically every city has had a modern stadium built. In our time, there were the old ballparks. Some were kept up pretty good, other not.

When I got to Salt Lake City for 1959, I was strictly coaching. Larry Shepard was the manager. That was my final season with the Pirates. I went over to the Giants after that.

In 1981, I had been scouting for the Giants quite a while by then, but was asked as a special request to go down there and manage Mexicali. So Jack Schwarz gave his permission to go manage that club, and I brought the Giants ballplayers down with us — Dan Gladden, Randy Kutcher, and a few others — and we had a pretty good season. We got beat by Hermosillo in the final game to see who went to the Caribbean series. That's the last time I managed.

One interesting story I remember about managing in Caracas, Venezuela, which wasn't affiliated with a major league team. I had players from the Angels, the Giants and other teams. That was the winter of 1963-64. Things were not very good down there at that particular time. The political situation was bad, and they had a lot of terrorist activities going on, so it was rather unpleasant that year. The baseball situation was fine, but it was overshadowed by the political conditions that were so bad.

For instance, I always held morning workouts because it was cooler. I remember I held a morning workout one morning and all of a sudden I'd get a few calls from the local players who lived in various parts of the city, not the imports — the American players — because we all more or less stayed together. But the local players called and they'd say in their best Spanish, which I understand and speak well, saying, "I can't make the practice."

And I'd say, "Why?"

And they'd answer, "Muchas valas volando!" That means "A lot of lead flying!" So they were stuck at home.

Now I want to get back to scouting, and I have a few things to say that may seem like I'm jumping around, so I hope you can make sense out of it. My first territory, my only territory, has always been where I am now in Southern California and southern Nevada and Arizona. It's quite big. I used to go from Fresno clear to San Diego and all over.

You had to space your time out and organize your priorities of where you wanted to be. Every stop a scout makes, the first stop is always the newspaper rack. And we had plenty of bird dogs keeping an eye on the local talent. To me, the more people you know and cultivate as friends in this business, you can call them bird dogs or associates or whatever, but the more of them you know who like baseball, the better off you are. In fact, I've gotten several of them started in full-time jobs in baseball as a result of being with me. Pay attention to what they tell you because they're usually people who are hanging around locally in the area and they are well appraised of what's going on there. If they tell you they like a certain kid, you got to take the time to go out and see him. I always did. Their observations are usually based on seeing the kid several times in game situations. When they ask me to have my own look at the kid, I say, "Yeah, I'll go see him. Let's both go," and we drive up and have a look at him.

Sometimes it wasn't so, but it's up to the scout to sort it out and decide what to do next. He has to be able to sift out the good ones. And while I'm there looking at the one kid, it also gives me a chance to see all the others on both teams that day. And you never know what you may find. I think the people I associated with were just friends, not bird dogs, but they had something to tell me. It was then up to me to use my professional judgment. That's one of the things that makes scouting a great job. I just know that some of the best players that I came up with were not highly touted, but through my associates and all, they led me to these players and I saw things in them that could be developed.

How do scouts get the ability to spot talent and potential in players? I really think the fact that I played helped tremendously. But more than that, becoming a manager gave me more of an insight because when you're just a player, you're so focused on what you yourself are doing out there that you don't have time to notice things in other players around. You don't have time to be looking around in a judgmental way. You're only judging yourself.

So in that capacity you think of yourself as a ballplayer and you think you know baseball, which you do, and the average guy will know a certain amount of baseball. But I don't think you really become a person who is able to start judging until you're in a managerial capacity where you have decisions to make and you have to take a deeper look. And scouts send you ballplayers and you try to read into that ballplayer what that scout has seen in him to sign him. And this is where I think a good scout should have at least managed. There are exceptions, of course, and even if you're a player or not, it doesn't make any difference. Some people, by associating themselves with the game for many years, have developed a good skill for recognizing talent and potential for development even if they didn't play or manage. But I think by and large, the fact that a person has played and then became a manager for a few years, and then got into scouting, he has a better sense of what he's trying. I know in my case that has been a great help to me.

Today I don't know how many scouts or what percent of them are former players or managers. The game is changing so much that it's difficult to even guess.

When Jackie Robinson broke that color line thanks to Branch Rickey, it changed things for scouts because it opened up an entire new population of players we could scout and sign. But don't forget that they already had the Negro Leagues for many years and we'd seen them play there, too. I was a player-manager when he came in. I went through all the preliminaries of eating in the kitchen with the colored ballplayers because they couldn't eat with the others when we were traveling and picking them up in different parts of town because they couldn't stay in the motels. But all that's gone and past now, thankfully.

I found that in those days there was never a problem per se. I can remember when I was a younger player playing down South before the war, like in Asheville, and the blacks had a certain section where they could sit and watch the game.

Let me tell you a story. I always remember I used to go along with my older brother when they were playing in New York in the 1930s. At that time he was playing semi-pro, for the House of David team. They played a triple-header every Sunday. I want to tell you something. My brother's team would play a double-header in Dexter Park. I think he was 20, 21 back then, and the Red Sox signed him off that team. He had the beard, and the hair. He drove one of the Pierce Arrows they had so he could make an extra fifty bucks a month. They traveled in Pierce Arrows just like we traveled in station wagons.

So they'd played a double-header in Dexter Park, and then drive over to Union City, New Jersey, for a night game. They always booked triple-headers. I was lucky to go along as a batboy if they needed one. I saw the Black Yankees play, the Pittsburgh Crawfords play, and they were good Negro clubs. Their stars, of course, probably made as much or more than players in the minor leagues.

The players in the games were whites and blacks. It was a game and afterwards they all went their own ways. My brother hit off Satchel Paige several times. The Negro players and the white players respected each others' abilities. As I look back, those clubs were very popular in New York. The Cuban Stars team, one of whom was Alex Pompez, who was later a Giants scout, owned that team. The Giants were so dominating with the Latin players was because of Pompez. He had all the Cuban connections.

My brother, Chick, and Alex Pompez toured the Latin countries together. Chick would be the judgment scout and Pompez would have all the connections. That's how they came up with Juan Marichal, the Alou brothers, Orlando Cepeda, Jose Pagan, and

George Genovese (seated, right) talking with Willie Mays, a guest at the Professional Scouts Foundation Dinner in 2004. Standing (left to right) Bob Harrison, Mariners scout; unidentified man with back turned; Phil Pote, Athletics scout. The Professional Scouts Foundation, founded by agent Dennis Gilbert, former White Sox executive Roland Hemond and scouts David Yoakum and Harry Minor, offers support to baseball scouts who suffer financial setbacks due to illness, retirement, or job loss (George Genovese collection).

others. The Latin places were beginning to be tapped at the same time Jackie Robinson broke the color barrier for the Negro players.

If you could insert this, it tells you something about what can happen to scouts as things in the game change. I scouted with the Giants until 1994, the last strike we had, and I left the Giants and went to the Dodgers because I was very disappointed with what the Giants had done to me. It was during the summer of that strike when the Giants had new ownership. This would never have happened to me under Horace Stoneham or Bob Lurie. They were all good people. It's the present group that owns them that's different. I get a phone call from Bob Hartsfield, the new coordinator of scouting, telling me, "I just want you to know we're not going to renew your contract for next year."

That was the end of my 34 years with the Giants, a phone call. That has left a bitterness in me. I gave my life to the Giants. I still haven't had an explanation and I still can't believe it. I gave the Giants many outstanding players. But it was during the strike and they panicked, I guess, because they didn't know how long the strike was going to go on, I guess. They were figuring they would have to pay salaries for people not doing anything. As if there's ever a time when scouts aren't doing anything. Luckily, I still see the scouts I worked with back then at ballgames and functions here and there.

This is one of the things that have been happening in baseball since the 1990s. And it's not the way you do people who have given to the game and helped make it what it is. I mean, the game is run by corporate people who are more concerned with the bottom line than they are about baseball. They know business to a point, but they know little or nothing about baseball.

The way it used to be in baseball was that scouts proved themselves and then spent their careers with that team. They were appreciated for the knowledge they imparted and the players they found and signed. But without baseball people running things, it's just different.

Baseball is its own family. Even though you're on opposing teams, you're still members of the family, and we always looked out for each other and supported and appreciated each other. That's the way people who have been in the game for a long time think.

But nobody's bigger than the game and it will survive in spite of these developments. It may take time, but it will eventually turn in a different direction. It's a great game. It really is.

Julian Mock

(1929–)

Mock described himself as "nuts about baseball" since he became a Yankee fan at age six. Unlike his peers, his path to scouting wasn't as a minor league baseball player. Instead, he played in high school and college, played while in the military, and completed his education at Auburn College. He then taught and coached at the high school level and later became a principal. In 1960 he began as a part-time scout on weekends with the Pittsburgh Pirates. By 1968 he was a full-time scout with the Cincinnati Reds, and from there he was on his way to a longtime scouting career that saw him progress from area scout to crosschecker to scouting director. SABR credits him with signing Mike Smith, Chris Hammond, Jeff Richardson, Jeff Branson, and Mo Sanford.

During his tenure he tutored and mentored numerous up-and-coming scouts and ran multiple tryout camps. At eighty he continues to do that, and runs the Southeastern Baseball Camp for boys thirteen and up to hone their baseball skills. He ran the camp for the eighteenth consecutive year in 2008. His interview is a unique scouting tutorial.

I was born in 1929 and I saw my first professional baseball game, a Class B game, in 1937 in Selma, Alabama. And I saw my first major league game when two teams came through town, Boston and the Cincinnati Reds, I think, in 1938. It was a spring training game coming through. They used to work their way up. I started keeping up with baseball when I was six years old and was pulling for the Yankees.

I'll just carry you down a trail through my baseball experiences. I was born in Selma and went through high school there and played high school baseball and some basketball there. Then I went to Auburn College and played baseball as a regular in my three years there, '49 through '51. Back then freshmen were not eligible to make the teams, so you could only play three years and I did that. At that time I was playing in the outfield, but my normal position was second base, except they had a second baseman who was there on a basketball scholarship and they kind of guaranteed him the job. I could hit, and the coach asked me if I could play in the outfield, and I said, "Coach, I can play any place you got, except pitch and catch."

After that I went into the service and played there. See, I knew in college that I wasn't any kind of a pro prospect. But at that time they had a different minor league structure that went from Class D to C to B to AA to AAA. I made up my mind when I went into service that if I came out single at the end of my two years, I would go and play a couple of years of minor league ball.

Well, I came out married, so I said, "Well, I'll just try to help somebody else try to get to the big leagues." And that's what I did. I started coaching and teaching at Atlanta, Georgia, in the fall of 1953. I did that for eleven years. Coached all sports, but particularly coached the varsity baseball team.

During the time I was coaching I signed on as a part-time scout with Pittsburgh in 1960 and did that on weekends and different times during the year. Then I left coaching in the fall of 1964 and became a high school principal and continued my part-time scouting job. I moved over to Cincinnati in 1968 when Bob Howsam came over from St. Louis. He brought Rex Bowen over from Pittsburgh as a scouting director and Rex brought all of us that wanted to go. That included me. Howsam was a superstar. He was a great, great general manager, probably one of the best of all time. He had a sensitivity for the people who worked for him.

I'll detour for just a minute. At one point he left and the franchise went down so far they brought Mr. Howsam back in the mid '80s. He brought in Dave Parker and Pete Rose to manage and play and when he did that I was out on the road in Nashville, Tennessee, and I got a message from his secretary saying Mr. Howsam wanted to talk to me. I called him and the secretary said, "He's in a meeting and can't talk now."

I said, "Well, I got to drive to Memphis and I should be there in about three hours and fifteen minutes. Would it be all right if I call him then because I got to be over there where I can see a game and I can't wait around?" She said that would be fine. I called him right away, as soon as I got over there. And all he wanted to know was that he was thinking about me and wanted to know how I was doing. It wasn't because I was anything special, but he'd do that with the scouts from time to time.

Getting back, I went to Cincinnati in 1968 and Rex Bowen was the scouting director. Later Joe Bowen, his brother, became scouting director. He always told me, "When you finish teaching school, I'll have a job for you."

So I totally retired from the school business in March of 1981, but I had taken over a territory in 1980 and worked it during the summer and all the time I could get off during the spring. I worked an area in the Southeast — Alabama, Mississippi, Louisiana, the panhandle of Florida and western Tennessee. I went on with them and retired from Cincinnati in 1997. From 1990 through 1997 I was the scouting director.

Geographically that's a big territory, but you have to consider population and the length of the baseball season and so forth. By population I mean the number of teams there, production, and all of that. We had one guy who had the Midwest, the Dakotas and all, and it came to nine states. There just wasn't much talent coming out of there. You look at the draft and there were maybe three guys out of South Dakota.

Areas are set up by what comes out of them. So Texas, California and Florida, where the biggest numbers come out of, usually have the most scouts. The seasons are longer in those areas and there's just so many kids to see in high school, junior colleges, four-year colleges, American Legion baseball and all that.

Well, you know scouting departments. If you recall, and I can't remember exactly when it was now, but they started the Major League Scouting Bureau. In the beginning, Mr. Howsam wouldn't be a member of it until the commissioner made everybody join. So I told my scouts, "Don't depend on the bureau for anything." I'd rather my guys would do the signability because I had a chance to kind of train them. But the bureau guys would just ask players, "What do you want to sign?" They'd write down whatever that player said and that pretty well planted that figure in the kid's head. So to avoid all that bickering back and forth, we got them to drop that signability part of it.

When the bureau first started, some clubs went down to about six scouts. Now it has all built back up because they realized it takes about eighteen or so to do the job right. Like in Cincinnati, the Bowens, Rex and Joe, kind of set the pattern for Cincinnati scouting for modern times. Rex worked under Mr. Rickey. So he used Mr. Rickey's theories, that you ought to have to run and throw. And that relates directly to the world championship that we won in 1990. If two of the outfielders wouldn't have been able to throw, we wouldn't even have gotten into the World Series. Eric Davis and Paul O'Neill threw batters out at key times. Without that we would have lost to Pittsburgh. We wanted guys who could run and throw and who were athletes.

But baseball tools of different players are still kind of relative. For example, Ted Williams. He couldn't run but he could flat hit. So for him, running was a relative tool and his hitting made up the slack in that department. They talked about Barry Bonds here a few years back and said that he was probably the best player. And yet Sid Bream scored from second on a grounder hit straight to Bonds in left to win the game. He just can't throw well. But when you think about it, how many great outfielders played left field? Probably none. The great ones were in center because he could run and throw.

The biggest thing you have to guard against with your scouts is you don't want to get them defensive. Most scouts don't want to make a mistake. That's the reason for all the crosscheckers and everything. It used to be in the olden times before the draft you didn't have crosscheckers unless you needed to make up your mind between two players, and then the scouting director came in. And that was when it was a matter of big money. Nowadays scouts are out there with no training at all. And, in fact, a lot of them have never even played. They go out there and scout.

In the Cincinnati organization, we held a tryout camp in Florida in January. George Zuraw and I used to hold it. It began in the latter part of the '80s and we'd bring young scouts down there and we'd kind of have a seminar for about three days, teaching them what to look for and how to do this and how to do that and how to hold tryout camps and how to work a territory. So, for about twenty-five years, that's the way we trained scouts.

When I learned how to be a scout, it was a little different for me. Let's just put it this way. I didn't weigh a hundred pounds in the eleventh grade, and being small like that you got to be an over-achiever to accomplish anything. I was a baseball nut! I couldn't run or throw but I could hit. I tell you all that because I had to really study and work to learn how to be a scout. And I did it because I not only wanted to be a scout, I wanted to be a very good one!

How'd I do that? Well, in 1960, and I'm going to ramble now, I took a legion team in 1959 to a tournament in Augusta [Georgia] and I ran in on a coaching friend who was sitting there with a little black book. So I said, "What on earth are you doing?"

He said, "I'm scouting. I work for the Pirates in the summer."

I'd coached against this guy for the state all-stars. So he said, "Are you interested in doing this?"

And I said, "Lordy, yes. I need something for my wife to think I'm working and I want to go and see a ballgame every night," I kidded. So I signed a contract with a guy by the name of Fred Herring, who was with Pittsburgh. Well, Rex let him go from Pittsburgh that winter and hired a guy, a newspaper man that was helping him around Pittsburgh in the valley up there by the name of George Zuraw. So we kind of started together and learned together by doing tryout camps. See, I was coaching and I'd go with him all summer and we'd take our families. He had two kids and I had two kids all about the same age and the wives sat around the pool while we'd run the tryout camps.

We held about twenty camps around Alabama, Florida, and Georgia. We started this in 1960. Well, you know, George knew more than I did, so he taught me what he knew and then we trial-and-errored the rest. And Rex had kind of taught him out of the office, so we kind of knew what we were trying to look for and we learned from there. You know, the little things like, for example, you don't ever make a final decision on a guy from a workout. Because in a workout, you can't measure instincts.

In workouts we learned other things. Like when a guy led off first base, you know that arc is thirteen feet, so if his right foot is at the very end of that arc, he's got seventy-seven feet to go to get to the bag at second. And you can tell his body control and quickness by letting him run and timing him on that seventy-seven foot run. See, Rickey had you time him on sixty yards. We did that, too, but you can tell body control, quickness, and especially instincts on the seventy-seven-yard run to the bag. So things like that we learned as we went along and other things developed, too.

Cincinnati always held tryout camps as did Pittsburgh. For example, in tryout camps, George and I developed a numbering system, you know, rather than just saying, "Okay, you're number one, what's your position?"

"I'm first base."

"All right, you're number two. What's your position?"

"I'm a right-hand pitcher."

Well, I really started this. I came up with it according to the position numbers in the scorebook, for example, catchers were 20s ... 2 in other words ... 20, 21, 22 through 29. And if you had more than ten, you had 120 through 129 and so forth. So the outfielders were 7, 8, 9 and the shortstops were 60s and the pitchers were 1 through 19. It made good sense to us to do it that way, so we did. See, we could field a whole team of zeros, 10, 20, 30, 40, at each position, or a team of ones, like 1–1, 2–1, 3–1 and so forth for each position.

We developed that because we had a tryout camp at Birmingham, Alabama, and we had 150 kids in that one. It was a hot-hot-hot day. The field had high walls so no air could get in there and we were about to panic. So I told George I had some 3x5 cards and I made up teams using those numbers. I made the catcher the captain of the team. And what we did was always try our best to get each player in the game to get a look at him in a game situation.

So what we did was play the zero and the one team one inning. Then they'd rotate out and we'd go with the two and three for one inning. That way the guys didn't have to sit around for three hours waiting to play. And then we'd come back around and we got everybody in the game and finished by about four o'clock in the afternoon. It was efficient for us. George loves to talk about that.

We were trained on how to conduct those camps and we were out on the field working the whole time. I remember one we held in Mississippi and a well-known team jumped in front of us and held one there the week before. I heard two kids there talking in the dugout and one of them said these people know what they're doing and those other guys were crazy. They didn't know what they were doing. Naturally that made us feel pretty good because we put a lot of thought into the way we ran the camps.

Eventually I was the man training the young scouts and I liked that. Being a teacher, I had a little advantage for this. See, for example, if you're standing by the fence watching infield practice, well, I always wanted to know what this guy was thinking about when a play happened. Like the right fielder throwing. What's he thinking about? Well, number one, you got to rate his accuracy. Then there's the way he throws the ball to the cut-off man and that. You can tell by that. And you can tell whether he's four-seaming the ball by the way it spins. Today there's a lot of outfielders who just can't throw and they give on that one now. But the thing is, if you can't throw, you can't get anybody out.

On an infielder, what do you see on this guy? What's locking in for him? First thing you want to know is whether the guy can throw decently to each position. These days they're giving on that one because you don't see that many guys who can throw. So I always wanted to know what my veteran scout was thinking, so whenever I started teaching, I'd take the guy over there with me and tell him what I was thinking. "Look, this guy's got slow feet and with slow feet he's going to have trouble throwing accurately because he's not going to get his feet into position under him." Another thing I always noticed is when you see a guy who's hyper and can't stand still. You very seldom see a good infielder who's hyper. If he's hyper, he keeps his legs stiff and he's going to make a lot of errors. Furcal was a lot that way for Atlanta.

We always talk about athletic instincts in our scouts. Without that, I doubt that you can ever scout. Guys who haven't played the game do become scouts and some are good at it because they have the athletic instincts. Like I used to teach guys, "What's instincts? Instincts is reacting to the first stimuli, such as bat hitting ball." So a guy with less than good instincts, I call it weak instincts, reacts to the results of the first stimuli. Like, for example, Bo Jackson, who is probably the best athlete I ever saw, he didn't have good baseball instincts. But if he'd have just played baseball, he would've developed them. Bo, when he was in college, would react to the ball in center field when it got over second base and he could outrun it.

When you're watching instincts, you scout kind of in triangles. I want to be in a position with the wide-angle lens of my eyes through the hitter straight into left field, taking in the shortstop and the left fielder. That's one triangle. Another triangle is the shortstop, second baseman and center fielder. And then I got a right triangle. The pitcher is never part of the triangles.

So when I watch the play, this way I can look for what kind of reaction I get out of these guys. You know, when I'm looking at this real close, you find out which players you really want to look at. Say I want to watch the shortstop and the right fielder, and the rest of them are just part of the background at that point. When you pick out the ones you're interested in, I want to see him every time he does something on the field and in the dugout, too, if I can.

He'll also want to see the thing that's so important, his makeup. His eyes. I always judge the eyes. For example, you watch a guy go into the dugout and he isn't even paying any attention to the game. Shakespeare said in MacBeth that you can see the structure of the man in the face.

Whenever you're going to put big money into a guy, you want to know everything about him. Whether he's got the courage and all to play and to learn. Whenever I used to interview a guy who wants to be a scout, knowing he's played some baseball and has some makeup matters to me.

I used to tell the scouts, I'd say, "You know, I have five questions to ask you. First of all, do you love baseball? Do you have a passion for baseball? Number two. Are you willing to work? And I'm talking about working twenty-four hours a day, seven days a week, because you're dreaming about it while you're sleeping. Number three, are you willing to learn? Are you going to pay attention to whatever we're trying to teach you? Number four. Are you willing to have some fun every day? You got to have some laughs, some fun, every day. That's just got to be part of it. And number five is that you'll never forget where you came from. The values your mommy and daddy taught you, don't ever forget them."

For example, look at the story of a guy who may or may not go into the Hall of Fame, Pete Rose. He forgot where he came from. There's a guy that nobody wanted, and Tommy Thompson is the one who signed him and Tommy had to beg the Reds and they turned him down. So he took Rose to another camp and another but nobody signed him. So finally it came down to "Aw heck, sign him." And that snotty-nosed kid just wanted a chance and he got it. Then he forgot where he came from. I saw Pete Rose in Double-A when he played in the minor leagues and he was a joy to watch. It's just a shame to see what happened.

Julian Mock never turns down an opportunity to speak about baseball, especially to aspiring youngsters. He's known for his knowledge and his patience. At the same time, his "tell it like it is" manner is well respected by all who know him and work with him (Julian Mock collection).

One of the biggest things, well, there's two or three detriments to scout development. One of them is, well, I told you about being defensive, scared they're going to make a mistake. Well, hey, you never will be able to scout if making a mistake is going to kill you. We've all made them. Another is to depend on the bureau. That's a loser, nothing against the bureau, but good scouts must do their own work and their own thinking. And another thing is that scouts become measuring scouts. And by that I mean they use a stop watch and a radar gun and make up their minds based on those. So we have to break them from becoming measuring scouts.

You can't just go on measurements. There's so many other important things. And many good scouts don't even use a stop watch or gun. You can look at a guy and tell if he can run. And a gun is one of the worst things because some guys sit there for the whole game and gun every pitch.

I remember the guy with the Panama hat who sat behind the plate at all the Dodgers games gunning every single pitch. Well, they say he's wasted more money for the Dodgers. But he signed Valenzuela and they got to thinking he knew what he was looking at. But he used the gun, wrote down the number each time, but had no idea what it meant. But see that's another measuring guy. See what I mean?

For example, a bunch of scouts are watching a pitcher and they ask, "What does he throw?"

"He throws ninety." Then everybody's blood pressure goes up. But he's so wild he couldn't throw it in the ocean.

If you want to see how fast the ball moves from the pitcher, go halfway down the first base line, off the side from the front row in the stands, and watch the ball as it gets to the plate. And you can tell how hard it is to that hitter. You can see how it looks to the hitter.

I always sat in that spot on the first base side when scouting a pitcher while all the other guys were climbing on top of each other behind the plate to look at pitches and use the gun and so forth. "Whatcha get? Whatcha get?" they'd be asking each other.

I remember one time I was out in Billings, and I don't want to be "braggadocios," so don't take it that way. Anyway, I didn't have a gun out there but the other team had a gun. I was sitting off the first base side and he'd come around and ask me, "What's this guy throwing?"

And I'd say, "He's probably got up to 91."

And he'd say, "Well, here's what I'm getting, " and I'd be right with him, never off more than two miles per hour the whole time in that park. I was reacting to what the hitter did with it, too. And most scouts just look at the pitcher or that darned gun.

As you look at players, you have to make a decision on them. They're all different. Some players will show you they'll never make a play unless he has to. I remember George Zuraw and I were working together on a guy named Andy Johnson. He was a quarterback at the University of Georgia and probably one of best baseball players to ever come out of Georgia. He turned down a hundred thousand dollars to go play football, and that was a lot of money then. Anyway, I told George, I said, "George, when you come in here to see him, you got to see him three straight games because if he doesn't have to go into the hole, he'll never show you he can make the play." After the second game, he said, "I know what you're talking about now and that makes sense."

But you know another thing, you try to judge another person and you want the guy with that good makeup. You shake the right hand and usually put your left hand on his wrist and you want to see whether it's stiff. You can tell a thick wrist is usually stiff and those guys usually don't throw a good curveball and could end up being a slider pitcher. There are exceptions to that.

I am an old school scout, and one of the things about an old school scout is that he made up his own mind. See a lot of these guys out there now want to know what everybody else thinks. They even call up scouts on other clubs and ask, "What do you think about this guy or that guy?" And they even travel in packs to do their scouting.

I remember I was one time in Mississippi coming out of a restaurant and one of the guys who left the rest of the pack said to me, "Let's go to the room and make out our draft list." Well, when I made up my draft list, I told my wife I wouldn't even tell her what's on it. That's the way it was. And I used to laugh and say, "Honey, if I die before I can turn this thing in, just put it in the box with me." That's how private it was.

I really don't care what everybody else thinks. So when I get fired, I want to get fired for my own mistake and not somebody else's.

Now, if you look at this in reference to when the draft came in, well, you know before the draft scouts had to be a lot more private. The old-timer guys didn't want others to know what they thought of a player or if they were even interested in the guy. They call that "deking him." Like decoying the other scout. In old-timer days, you'd have an appointment with a guy and his family at seven o'clock and I had one at 7:30 and another guy would be out there waiting because he had one at eight. And you'd come out of there and already signed him. It was that kind of deal.

Blue Moon Odom was down in Macon, Georgia. Boy, he was a hot number. And a black scout worked from Boston and he was down there and he even lived with Blue Moon and his family when he was down there. Charlie Finley went down there and brought them groceries and everything else. And that was kind of a dog-eat-dog. And none of it was illegal according to the rules at that time.

But then when the draft came in, that changed things around because if you knew a guy was going to be a high pick, say he was going to go in the top twenty, and maybe for some reason you didn't pick till the third round, well you wouldn't even go to see a Chipper Jones or whoever because we knew he'd be gone before we got our first pick. Blue Moon Odom would be gone. So you wouldn't waste time on those guys and you'd go try to pick one out that might still be available when it was your turn to make a draft pick.

And then, as it went on, and this is bad, guys got to sharing interest in players. I never believed in that. The Bowens would fire you on the spot for that or if you even rode with a scout from another organization. Later on they all started traveling in packs and share guys they liked. Not me. I wasn't going to share my work with them. I wanted to find somebody and get him in the draft. Why share my work with somebody who wasn't willing to do anything?

I remember one year Travis Fryman, the third baseman for Cleveland, was coming up and there was another boy out of Mississippi, another high school boy. Whenever they started playing that year, I think I was probably the only scout who knew who that other boy was. Everybody knew Fryman. Anyway, a guy who'd never scouted before came in for Detroit and got both players. He's a friend of mine now, but at the time he was a rookie scout who really didn't know much about what he was doing.

When we worked with the families, it was to find out the signability for the guy. And we used to spend time at our organizational meetings talking about signability of the players we may draft. We really need to know that. It's the nitty-gritty of the thing. We don't want to waste a draft pick on a player we can't sign. Say we're willing to offer him the going rate, which is a hundred thousand dollars, but he wants a million dollars. We're not going to sign him because we don't have that kind of money. So that's one of the things the draft has done. It limits a lot of teams that don't have a lot of money and gives players to teams on the upper end of the financial scale.

But, say it's a high school boy. You want to sit in with him and his mommy and daddy and find out, number one, who's going to call the shots? Will he sign for the money that goes with the round in which he's drafted? Everybody pretty well knows what the money is for each draft round. I went in and talked to Travis Fryman and he made it clear and his daddy did, too, that it was going to be his own decision, but that he was going to sign. Chipper Jones was the same way. He made it clear in front of mommy and daddy that he wanted to sign out of high school, and they agreed with him.

You got to try to figure out who's going to make the decision because if you're sitting there talking with that high school boy in their living room and his daddy is in there with him and the dad is big-dealing it while the mama is down the hall shucking peas, who do you think is going to make the decision? The mama, because Dad's got to go clear it all with her. She wouldn't be listening if she wasn't going to make the decision. Mama is going to look out for her boy. Daddy's thinking that his son's going to be something he always wanted to be but wasn't good enough.

One of the things about it is that scouts have to be able to read what they see there in that setting and decide what to put on the draft report. On that report they ask you what round would you take him in. What is he worth? What would I give him? Or how much should the organization give him? I prefer to ask what round would you take him in because that also tells me what he's worth based on the money that goes with that round.

When I get that, then I'd ask, "What do you think it will take to sign him?" When you consider what round you'd take him in and what it would take to sign him, what percent of the players that fit into that with those variables would sign? I don't want a scout to fill out the boxes that say "Good, fair, poor" on this one. No-siree. I want that scout to tell me the percent involved. Let me know what kind of chance I'd be taking to use one of our draft picks on this kid. If I lose this kid, there's 29 other teams each picking a player before I get another draft pick and that's a lot of other good players that could be gone because of a misjudgment on this kid and you really can't make that up.

In the eight years I was the head of the thing as scouting director, we signed our first-round pick player every year. Eight of them. By that I mean there were some stars, but just about all of them got at least 50 games or something at the big league level. Danny Wilson, a catcher for Seattle, was the first one I picked. The second year it was Pokey Reese. Pitcher Brett Tomko was another one. Just about all of them except two got to the big leagues. See, I always figured whenever I was scouting that if I signed a guy and he played for three years, and he wasn't a big money guy, then he was a good sign whether he played in the big leagues or not. I would worry if I signed a guy and he never got out of the rookie league and only got to play one year. Then I'd figure I'd made a mistake.

Another thing we did is we gave a guy eye tests. In fact, one of the last guys I signed had bad eyes and we found out first and then signed him anyway. But he struggled. A lot of organizations give players what they call the ISAM tests before they sign them to determine mental makeup and so forth. But we didn't. I feel we trained our scouts to find out answers to that stuff by using their own expertise. I don't like store-bought tests. They're just another tool for the measuring scouts.

The one thing that they've finally remedied is that the draft goes too long. I could be talking to a guy on the street corner and before I walked up to him, he had no value as a player because nobody had ever talked to him. But as soon as I walk up and talk to him, he thinks he's got value. Now he thinks he should get $15,000 or whatever. So by having a draft so long, guys are drafted that you should be able to talk to on the street and sign, but by being drafted in the 40th round, they got value.

See, we'd still sign those guys with a shorter draft, but they just wouldn't go through the draft. But all kids who are out of high school and not going to college are considered eligible for the draft and must go through that amateur draft one time before they can sign as free agent amateurs if they're not picked in the draft. The reason for that is it keeps guys with deep pockets like Steinbrenner from just going around and picking all the best amateurs. If that happened, the draft wouldn't mean anything.

What people not in the game may not get because they don't see how things work is that having a draft changes how we can work. Because of the way we're allowed to pick players in the draft, we need the involvement of crosscheckers now and unfortunately there's more measuring scouts and all. And there's times when organizations will have eight or nine guys at one game. I was taught by the Bowens that they don't want more than one or sometimes two guys at a ballgame. I could see the player one day and he'd have a bad day. Then a couple of days later another scout from my organization could see him and he'd have a good day. Well, if a bunch of scouts all saw him on that bad day, we'd get off the guy. But all players have bad days, and by not all going on the same day in a big group, we get a better look at a kid that other organizations may pass up because they were all there on his bad day and didn't go back.

Besides the draft, another thing that's changed baseball dramatically is the movement from the family-owned teams to corporate organizations. The families like the O'Malleys, and in my opinion O'Malley controlled baseball in the late '40s and '50s, the old man not the son who sold the club. But the O'Malleys, the Griffiths, the Yawkeys, the Wrigleys and so on owned clubs. They eventually sold out to what amounts to corporate groups.

One result of that is that rather than have the veteran general manager like Bob Howsam, they got that corporate thing in and if you'll notice, for the most part they want young general managers so they can just kind of be puppets. They're not necessarily baseball people. They're either business people or the son-in-law or something like that. Some folks may get mad that I said that, but if you'll notice, look at the guys who are the young pups around. Corporate people put their own staff in there so they can dictate to them.

And this is a kind of example. I worked a couple of years for them. Look at Arizona. See, there's a guy that was the general manager there who never had worked in baseball, but they spent money like it was going out of style there. In fact, they had to go back to the sharcholders and borrowed something like twenty million dollars just to meet budget. And there's been rumors that some of the big money players took their salaries on a deferred payment basis to help the club meet budget. They even had to borrow money from the commissioner's office. Milwaukee had to borrow money from Montreal for the same thing.

However you look at it, baseball is in a bad situation because they don't really have a commissioner. They got a milk toast used car salesman. For example, how in the world could you put two teams in Florida, one in the Miami area, which is mostly Latin, and one in St. Pete, which is a place where probably only twenty percent of the people are under 80? And in Orlando and Jacksonville, the two best sites, don't have anything! Orlando with Disneyworld and all would be a huge draw for baseball. It's just ridiculous the way those clubs were located.

There's been some talk around about contraction. Looking at the idea of contraction from a realistic standpoint, well, there's no way the union's going to approve of that! There's no way that union's going to approve of giving up fifty to seventy-five major league jobs. No way they're going to approve of that. I don't think contraction will happen because who's going to get those players to vote for it? They ain't going to vote for it because union leaders won't let them because that's doing away with jobs!

Then there's been talk that some folks, including some scouts as I hear it, want thirty-two teams and no American or National leagues, just four divisions organized according to their location. Well, here's what I think about it. You know the one thing that will put a blight on that is that they've gone to that uneven schedule. For example, the Yankees have played Tampa Bay umpteen times, whereas Seattle will only come into New York for three games. I don't think the fans will buy that idea because they get tired of seeing the same handful of teams all the time. They get tired of what I call "the have-nothings" rather than the teams with all the big names and big money players. The only thing you could interest people in that kind of division-making is a matchup like the Yankees and Boston.

I don't like the idea of playing each other all the time like that. I think they got to spread the schedule so fans can see all the players. I don't know what the answer is to the thing because it's so uneven.

The Yankees were at one time getting something like sixty million dollars in television revenue a season, and a team like Cincinnati was getting only four million. I don't know what it is now, but I would say that if you came in with your team to play me in Cincinnati, then you got to pay me so much of that revenue for the right to televise games in my ballpark. Revenue sharing is something they talk about all the time, and I think visiting teams ought to be charged for what they take out of my park, especially when one club makes sixty million and the other only makes four million.

And then they've started this DH business. See, the worst thing going is the DH and the only way they can get rid of that is to change the rule and allow twenty-six players on each roster instead of twenty-five. See, you got to buy it from the players because they're not going to give up that position. I despise the fact that they have records made by the DH. Managers have to be able to manage without the DH and anybody can wear the title of manager with the DH. It's that simple. The impact of the DH changes the strategy and possibly the record books, changes made by guys who can't even play the game anymore. All they can do is hit and collect big dollars for doing it.

Branch Rickey could easily be called the father of scouting. He devised the 60-yard dash to run the guys. I didn't have a personal relationship with him, but a lot of guys who were scouting directors like Rex Bowen were Rickey men. They said when he was trying to teach a pitcher to throw a change-up, he'd lay his hat on the ground just short of the plate and he'd tell the pitcher to hit his hat because you pull down kind of like pulling a shade down to do it, and they were throwing up too high. So that's the way Mr. Rickey used to teach that.

Fred McAlister

(1927–2008)

McAlister, known as "Freddie" to his many friends, had been in professional baseball since 1944. This lifelong St. Louis Cardinal served his organization in many capacities throughout his long career. His love of the game and understanding of it came through loud and clear as he remembered baseball stories and baseball history that he witnessed.

Most scouts from his era began as minor league players and he was no exception. He signed out of high school in 1944 and played fourteen years in the minors before he hung it up. At that time the Cardinals asked him to manage their Class D team in the Alabama–Florida League in 1960. After one season he decided that wasn't his cup of tea, and he became a scout in 1961.

By 1981 he had become the scouting director, a position he held for twelve years. Under his direction the entire department experienced tremendous success and many of their number one picks made it to the major leagues. During his tenure he was a mentor to many scouts who are still with the club. When he chose to step down after the 1993 season, he requested and got the job of special assignment scout.

In 2008, after sixty-four years in the organization, the only thing that kept him away from baseball was a stint in the military during World War II. At age eighty-one he was still a special assignment scout who attended as many games as possible until his death in November 2008.

Fred McAlister was a recipient of the Scout of the Year Award, Midwest, 1997.

I signed right out of high school in 1944, and I've been with the St. Louis Cardinal organization ever since. First I played shortstop for 14 years in the minor leagues at the Double-A and Triple-A level, with two years away in the military in 1946–47, but I never played in the majors. In those days the leagues went D, C, B, AA, AAA before the majors.

Let's see, I started in Johnson City, Tennessee, at age seventeen, spent the next two years in the navy, and returned to Johnson City in January of 1948. I then played for the Duluth Dukes in the Northern League and the Omaha Cardinals in the Western League. In 1950 I played shortstop on the all-star team. I began the following year with the Houston Buffaloes in the Texas League, and then the Triple-A Columbus Red Birds in the American Association. After that I was sent to New York to the Cardinals' other Triple-A team, the Rochester Red Wings, in the International League. When I stopped playing they asked me to manage their Class D team in the Alabama-Florida League in Dothan,

Alabama, for the 1960 season. Well, I guess managing wasn't my strong suit because our team finished last.

So, in 1961 they made me a scout and put me in the territory of Texas, Louisiana, and Mexico. It was a huge area. There was a lot to do and a lot to learn, and I enjoyed all of it. I did that through 1966. The next year they moved me to St. Louis to be their assistant farm and scouting director under George Silvey. That was through 1969. Then in 1970 they brought in Bob Kennedy as farm director and he really didn't need an assistant, so they gave me the Midwest territory and I worked as scouting supervisor there through most of 1976.

During those years I signed some good players: Marc Hill, Bake McBride, Jim Dwyer, Glenn Brummer, Ken Oberkfell, Al Olmstead, and Mike Ramsey.

The first year I had the territory, 1970, I signed Marc Hill. Here's how that happened. Joe Cunningham, who worked in the office, had a friend who ran a dairy in Elsberry, Missouri, which is about sixty miles outside of St. Louis. His friend, Edward Hill, had been a minor league pitcher in the St. Louis Browns system and his wife had been a pretty good softball pitcher. Joe's was telling me that his kid is a good athlete. He plays basketball, and is a catcher for his school baseball team. So I asked him to send me the schedule and he did. By the time I got it, there were only like twelve games left. Every time I went to see him play, three times, the games got rained out and I never got to see him play in high school. So I called him and told him this fella had given me his schedule and I told him about the times I'd been up there and that I'd called his coach to get permission for him to come to St. Louis to work out.

We usually have a workout the Saturday before the draft and just invite the kids we want to look at, maybe fifteen kids. It's not a tryout camp. We don't play a game. But we have them throw and hit and stuff like that.

So when Marc Hill came in, I met him at the door and shook his hand and he about tore my hand off! He was a big, strong kid, six-two, a hundred ninety-five pounds. I said, "Well, damn, you're big enough to play and you look good enough." He was a good looking kid. So that day in the workout he showed a good arm and good hands and he hit the warning track a few times I think. So we drafted him in about the twelfth or thirteenth round. But I know there were a couple of other clubs that showed some interest in him, but not a lot or he would have gone sooner.

After the draft we take him back to St. Louis, George Silvey was my boss, and I said, "George, I want to see him play in a game situation before we offer him any money because I've never seen him play." Vern Benson, who was some kind of an advance scout at that time, went with me. And when I got up there they were playing in Hannibal, Missouri. When we got there his daddy met me at the gate and said, "Well, when are you going to sign him?"

And I said, "Wait till I see him play. I've never seen him play."

So that night, well, let me put it this way. If I wouldn't have seen him play and signed him as a number one, that would've been fine with me. Hill got three hits, a home run, single, double, and threw a runner out, caught a pop fly, and did everything you could imagine. So I told his daddy after the game that I'd get back in touch with him. And I told my boss the next day, "That boy really looked good last night."

And he said, "Well, why didn't you sign him?"

And I said, " Well, I want to go back and see him a couple more times."

And he answered, "Freddie, if you like him the first time you see him, just sign him and don't worry about it. Why don't we offer him $2,500?"

And I said, "George, the kid is going to sign for any amount we offer him, so let's give him $5,000."

And he said, "If you offer him five, he'll want eight."

And I said, "No, he won't. He wants to sign, his daddy wants him to sign, and he doesn't want to go to school. So let me give him $5,000."

George gave in and said that would be okay. So I called the kid and said I wanted to sign him and asked if he wanted me to go up there or if he wanted to come to St. Louis. And they came down in a pickup truck, his mother, daddy, and the boy. They came in the office and I did most of the talking. I offered the $5,000, and didn't even offer the incentive bonus, which you give just about everybody, and he signed for the $5,000.

Later on he asked me, "Why didn't you give me that incentive bonus?"

I said, "Well, if you would've batted an eye I would have given it to you, and maybe even a little bit more signing bonus."

Marc played with the Cardinals, Giants, and White Sox and had about twelve years in the big leagues. After that he became a minor league coach. He's like my son and I'm still very close with him.

Another player I signed that year was Bake McBride. He played at Westminster College, somewhere in Missouri. We had an old scout there, Roy Smith, who liked him. He called me one day and said, "Freddie, this guy looks like Willie Davis."

And I said, "Well, send me a schedule so I can get up there and see him play." But I never did get up there for some reason. But, anyway, we got him in the ballpark and worked him out before the draft like we did Marc Hill. McBride had that type of swing that he hit down on the ball, so the ball had a backspin on it, you know, and then he ran. He ran like a deer! His arm was all right, not great, but it was okay. So we drafted him somewhere, but not very high, probably down low.

But I wanted to see more of his play, especially in a game situation, and as I recall, we invited him to come to a tryout camp after we drafted him. We didn't do the workout like we did with Marc Hill because I'd already seen him perform in a game situation. We played ballgames in the tryout camps and I wanted him evaluated in that setting. Later that day, after his game and workout, I took him into George Silvey's office and we gave him $2,500. Looking back, if we would've known what he was going to do, we would've probably drafted him at number one or two real quick! He played in the bigs ten years and was still going strong when he had some kind of problem with his eyes that cut his career short.

A little later, 1973 or '74, I think, I signed another catcher, Glenn Brummer. What a good kid he was! I remember I'd seen him play in junior college with our scout Jim Belz, in Mattoon, Illinois, or somewhere in that area. Anyway, we got him into St. Louis and worked him out. Bing Divine happened to see the workout. A little while later that day he asked if I'd signed him. So I explained that he had one more game in his college season and he's not eligible to be signed until that season's over.

I said, "He's going to play his last game Monday and his coach is going to invite all the scouts to look at him and whoever makes him the best deal with him, well, he'll sign with that scout." That particular game was a reschedule of an earlier game in the season that had been rained out, so technically we could've signed him that night in St. Louis because the schedule was over. But the kid wouldn't sign with me and kind of got upset. We offered him $8,000, and Bing got upset.

But I said, "Bing, we'll sign him. The coach told me that if nobody beats the price, he'd sign with us." So Monday when the game was over and not one scout turned up there to sign him, we gave him the $8,000 and signed him.

I called Bing and said, "We signed Brummer for the $8,000 you said I could give him and in my opinion he'll be better than Marc Hill." At that time Marc Hill was coming along pretty good. Looking back I don't know who had the better career, but Hill stayed in the big leagues longer.

In 1976 the GM, Bing Divine, offered me the scouting director job, but I turned it down because Bing always wanted to make a lot of trades, make a deal every day, and I just didn't feel comfortable with that position knowing how he was. Rather than take the job, I just told him I didn't feel I was ready for it yet. I knew he was going to be on my ass a lot because he wanted to make a deal every day. He got that from Frank Lane, and when he made a deal he was very happy and when he didn't, he wasn't. Of course, any time we lost he wasn't very happy either, and when Bing wasn't happy, nobody else was happy either.

Scouting director Fred McAlister was "wheeling and dealing" as he watched a St. Louis Cardinals game from the private box of general manager Dal Maxvill in 1990. That was a tough year for the Redbirds as they finished in sixth place (Fred and Patty McAlister collection).

I was just a little bit afraid of Bing, and I really don't know why. I talked it over with Joe Baines, the guy who took the scouting director job when I turned it down. I told Jim I didn't want to go back to Texas because I'd had a lot of success in the St. Louis area with Kenny Oberkfell, Marc Hill, Glenn Brummer, and Bake McBride, and I'd signed Jim Dwyer.

Then I said to Bing, "Bing, if you want me to go back to Texas, I'll go back tomorrow because I work for the St. Louis Cardinals and I'll do whatever they want me to do. So he said he'd like for me to go back down there, and I did. While I was down there he used to go to Mexico to check all the players. He'd come down to Arlington, Texas, or Houston and I would pick him up. That's when I really got close to the man, and wasn't afraid anymore. One day he said that I should be doing more than I'm doing and asked if there were any other jobs in the organization I wanted to do. I told him that if a special assignment scout job came up, I'd be interested in that. He nodded and it looked like he made a mental note. Anyway, we got along great and I can honestly say I loved the man.

In 1976 the scout in Texas went to be a coach in Milwaukee and Bing was wanting me to go back to Texas because the Rangers had a team then and Houston was also there. Bing wanted me to scout the big league clubs down there. I went as a scouting supervisor because I knew the territory so well. I stayed there doing that till 1979. John Claiborne was the GM then and he wanted me to be an advance scout under Kenny Boyer, which I did until the middle of 1980, when Whitey Herzog came over.

Whitey asked me to go around the circuit one more time for him, and then explained he wouldn't need an advance scout for the rest of the season because he did all his own charting. But he wanted me to do something in the organization. He said I was a good Cardinal man and wanted to use me. And when he brought Joe McDonald over from the Mets, Joe wanted me to be scouting director, but Whitey told him, "He won't take the job because he turned it down when Bing Divine was GM." So Joe called me and asked if I'd like to become the director for the Cardinals and live in my home in Katy, Texas. I said I'd do whatever they wanted me to do.

I began as scouting director in 1981. In that job I traveled all over the country. I was in St. Louis for the preparation of the draft list and the draft itself, but the rest of the year I was out there. Here's how that worked for me. When the free agent draft was getting ready to come up in June, I went to California for about three weeks in February, and then I spent time in Florida. Throughout the year I went all over the country to work with our sixteen scouting supervisors. I stayed with each one in his territory for a week, and if they had ten or fifteen players they liked, I went to see the top four or five. I couldn't possibly see all of them on every scout's list. I didn't want to see the guys they were going to offer eight or ten thousand. I wanted to see the guys they liked for the number one, two, three, four and five top draft choices.

The reason I did that, why all scouting directors do similar things, is because somebody has to be in charge and put all those names in some sort of order on our final draft list. The California scout has a list of his top choices, and so does the guy in Florida or any of the other scouting supervisors. But they have no way of comparing the players they like with the names on the other guys' lists. So it was my job to work all that out.

One of the things that makes scouting so interesting and so challenging is that when we see players we like, there's still no cinch that he's going to play in the big leagues. For example, in 1991, we signed fifty-five guys and hoped to get four of them to the big club. That year we spent an all-time high to date on Cardinal bonuses, $1,500,000.

I'm pretty proud of my record on that. From 1981 through 1987 every one of my number one picks played in the big leagues. Let's see now, 1981 was Bobby Meacham. I think we traded him in the Willie McGee deal and he had some good years with the Yankees. In 1982 we signed Todd Worrell, and later I'll tell you a little story about that. In 1983 it was infielder Jim Lindeman, who played five or six years with us before we traded him to Detroit. We signed pitcher Mike Dunne in 1984 and he played briefly for us before we traded him to the Pirates for Andy Van Slyke and Tony Pena. We all did well in that deal, and Dunne went on to nearly ten years in the big leagues.

We selected a real good pitcher, Joe Magrane, in 1985. We got Luis Alicea, a good little infielder, in 1986. In '87 we got Cris Carpenter, a good looking right-handed pitcher out of the University of Georgia. In 1988 things didn't go as well for us. We had two number ones that year and drafted two pitchers, Brad DuVall and John Ericks. Unfortunately both of them hurt their arms early on and we had to let them go. The following year we selected outfielder Paul Coleman out of Frankston, Texas, but he didn't make the majors. I'll tell you more about him later. We drafted pitcher Donovan Osborne number one in 1990 and he made it to the big leagues the very next year and stayed there for a dozen or so seasons. In 1991 we signed outfielder Dmitri Young. He was a husky kid who could really hit the baseball. He had some good years in the majors.

Another thing I did as director was to hire scouts for the Cardinal organization. It was always an individual process, and by that I mean we didn't give a scouting test and hire the guy with the best score. I talked with the guy to find out how much he knows about baseball. I liked to talk to them a lot about baseball and how to look at players to reinforce the fact that they shouldn't be afraid of making a mistake. I mean all scouts, rookies and the best in the business, make mistakes. It's all part of it.

I liked to ride to the games with the new scouts and talk about the players we were going to see on the way. I'd ask, "Well, what do you think of this player? Tell me what you see in him."

After seeing the game with him, I'd either like the player more or less. And if I liked him less, we would discuss it and I would say, "He doesn't run as good as you said he could. I didn't see him run that good."

And the scout would say, "Well, he ran good last time. Maybe he's hurt."

So we'd take it from there. And, of course, there's no set way to take it from there. Each player is different and each situation is different. But I think the scouts have to respect the director and trust his judgment because usually he's the one with the most experience. Or at least it used to be that way. And I don't think any one of my scouts thought he knew more about scouting than me. I really don't. But I think in some cases with some clubs today the scouts think they know more about it than the director. And that's not a good situation. I never had a problem like that. When I was hiring scouts, I had already been with the Cardinals fifty years and I knew most of them as players before they became scouts.

And another thing while we're on that subject. Nobody who wants to scout expects to get rich. Of course, we don't make the money the big league players do, but I never felt I was underpaid. And I think ninety percent of the scouts feel like I do. That's their job and they like it. I mean, you're your own boss. And you're out there by yourself. And

I honestly don't think I've ever heard a scout say that he ought to be making more money or things like that. Scouting is something you have to like to do and you have to want to do it because you like being around baseball. Money's not everything.

It's funny how many people would like to be a scout. Most of them think you just go out there and eat popcorn and watch a game. They don't consider that we may have to drive from here to El Paso to see that game. The kids are spread out and you never know where a ballplayer's going to pop up. One day we could be in Abilene, Texas, and the next in Oklahoma City. And we had to go directly from the first game and drive all night to get there in time to find the park and see the next one. When they pop up, we've got to go there and see them. The only way to know about a player is to see him, the way he runs, his coordination, and all his baseball skills.

When I first started scouting a lot of scouts told me they like to look the kid in the face and see whether he's got a strong face or not. And I guess there's something to that, just like knowing what body type the kid has. You know, they don't talk about that anymore, and, of course, it doesn't mean he's not a big league player material if he doesn't look at you or whatever.

I remember a story about a kid I drafted who didn't make it to the big leagues, Paul Coleman. I was in Savannah one time looking at him and another kid on his club. After the game I got permission from the manager to talk to them. They were both hitting about .190. I talked with them about fifteen minutes and Coleman never looked at me. Not one time, even when I saw him after he was signed. But it didn't mean anything because that was just his nature. He had all the tools in the world but something was missing. I don't know what it was. Maybe it was because he was from such a little town that he didn't have any confidence or didn't think he should've gotten all the money he got. I don't really know. You never really know what a ballplayer is thinking about. You know he can run and field and hit or pitch or whatever, but when he goes into spring training, things you don't expect can happen. For some it's their first time away from home, away from mama's home cooking, some are just mama's boys and can't break away from her, and some just can't make it on their own. Or it could be something else altogether. And a lot of kids fail because of that.

Until I stepped down as director in 1997, I was an amateur scout looking at amateur players we could sign for the St. Louis Cardinals. When I became an advance scout and then special assignment scout like I am now, I'm a professional scout because I only see the professional players. We have a different work schedule and a different life than the free agent scouts, where you jump around so much. We scout the major leagues primarily. I often take my wife, Patty, and we go to whatever towns and stay there for four or five days and see the games. We look at players on big league clubs that we may want to deal for at some point in time later. Or we may need a third baseman in a hurry and want to make a trade. It all depends. But all players are scouted every time they take the field, from their first day in the pros until the day they hang it up. It's the nature of the game.

Here's an example of my schedule, which is pretty typical for a professional scout. I'll be home in Texas in January and most of February because I might see a few high school and college kids before I leave for Florida. I'm down there the whole month of March for spring training. After March I come back to Texas and do four clubs in the Texas League and then I'll do four clubs in the Southern League in May. Then back to the Texas League in June and the Southern League in July. August is usually varied depending on what needs to be done then because the minor league seasons are wrapping up.

During my career with the Cardinals I've seen changes in the game and the way things are done. Probably the event that impacted scouts most was when the draft came about in 1965 because it changed the rules concerning things scouts could and couldn't do when following players.

For the older veterans like me who scouted before 1965, the adjustment wasn't too popular in the beginning. Remember that in those days we were all former players, competitive individuals, and the friendly competition among us was all part of the attraction of finding players and getting them signed.

When I started scouting there was no draft and we did things very differently. In those days we not only gave the players a good look, but we had to court the parents. I'll tell you a story about Dalton Jones, the first player I ever scouted, in 1961, before there was a draft.

I really liked Dalton Jones, a kid from Baton Rouge, Louisiana. That was the year Rusty Staub came along, too. They were both good and I liked them both. But I leaned toward Jones. I was just a rookie scout and didn't know what I was doing yet.

Then one day George Kissell, the minor league coordinator who looked at every kid we were trying to sign, went with me to see Staub, and he got five hits that day. I remember George saying he was concerned because he couldn't run. I told him that the way he hit, I didn't care if he could run or not.

Walter Shannon and the people who hired me told me to get to know the player and to court his family, too. So, for starters, between games at a double-header one day, I took a Coke to Mrs. Jones, Dalton's mother, and we talked awhile. The other scouts around that day kidded me good and told me that wasn't going to do it. I guess you could say I learned the hard way, but I soon learned. It seems laughable now, doesn't it?

Walter Shannon was a great man. When I first signed here in 1945, he was like a farm director of the D, C, and B clubs, and Joe Mathes, another great man in the organization, worked under Branch Rickey.

I'm sure the Cardinals were the first organization to ever have a tryout camp. They started the whole thing of tryout camps. Joe Mathes was a part-time scout under me when he was eighty years old and he told me he was riding with Rickey one day and he was dozing off when he woke up and said, "Joe, I just got a wonderful idea! Why don't we, instead of working out one or two guys, why not bring in a whole bunch of guys and have a whole workout? A tryout camp." He said that's where it started. They gave every kid there a number. The shortstops, say you had ten of them there, would be numbered 601–610 because six is the shortstop position on the scorecard. So that's where it started. He went on to work for several organizations. He had a great baseball mind.

But I got off course there. Back to the topic. So what happened with the two players is that Staub signed with Houston for around a hundred thousand dollars, a lot of money back then. And Dalton Jones, well, Ted Williams wasn't playing then but he was working for the Red Sox organization, so he went down to Baton Rouge himself to see Jones.

As it so happened, Williams and Stan Musial were Jones' two favorite players, so he signed with the Red Sox for something like forty thousand. George Digby was the scout who signed him. Back then kids had favorite teams or favorite players and having that contact to influence kids to sign was all part of the process.

Of course, all that changed after the draft. We could still talk with the parents, of course, especially if the player was a minor and needed their permission to sign. But we weren't allowed to discuss money at all with the families. We couldn't promise to draft the player because we never knew if we would get him or not in the draft process. It had become a matter of numbers.

I remember the first draft was kind of confusing. When it first started, everybody went to New York and stayed in one of the big hotels up there. Each club would take three or four people and that's where we did the drafting from. They'd call a club's name and the scouting director would get up and say, "I draft Joe Doakes," or whatever. I think that lasted three or four years. Then they decided it was too expensive, so it went to conference calls.

I remember being told to just put the names of the guys I liked on a piece of paper and hand them in. I picked fifteen or twenty guys, I can't remember now. I do remember that Johnny Bench went in the first or second round, which surprised us because several scouts liked him number one but they didn't get him. Nobody knows how that happened. I'd bet it was probably more confusing in the front office not knowing how to get the lists together and all that stuff. I wasn't there. I did go up there in '67 and was involved in the draft from '67 through '97, when I stepped down as scouting director.

I liked being involved in the draft. It was an exciting time, what the scouts worked for all the rest of the year. The first day was especially exciting because the number ones, twos, and threes would be taken, and that's the cream of the crop. Once in a while you get lucky down below and pick up a Vince Coleman or whatever.

Speaking about Coleman, here's a little story about him. With the Cardinals, anybody who can run when we sign him, George Kissell tries to make him a switch-hitter. Most kids can't do it, but for those who can, that could be their ticket to play in the big leagues. You've got to keep working with them and it takes a while. With Coleman, it took three or four years before he got to the big leagues. Anybody with great speed like that can get a lot of bunt hits, so we teach them to bunt for hits. We also teach them not to try to pull the ball for home runs, but to hit the ball down to the opposite field. If he hits the ball to the right of shortstop, you can't throw Vince Coleman out. We want the left-handed hitter to hit the ball to left field. Coleman got a lot of hits that way.

Although it created excitement and stuff, it really didn't impact the game so much. When I was director we had a lot of fun going back there and going over the preferential list and getting the names all in order and getting them up on the board the way we wanted them and hoping we'd get the players we liked. It was a lot of fun.

Anyway, I like the draft and think it's good for baseball, but I just think they should put a bonus rule in it or something because we're giving these kids too much money. I think each organization should give so much for its number one, so much for a number two and three and on down. Of course, the top five in the country should have similar limits, too, but those would no doubt be much higher.

Let me tell you, one of the best things about being a scout is running into the other scouts. We talk about baseball, sometimes as a way of feeling each other out without getting into too much detail. For example, if I go into a ballpark someplace and run into a scout I haven't seen in two months, say Milt Bolling because we've been good friends for a long time. Well, we'd get together to get a bite to eat or something. We never discuss specific players we're scouting but we always talk baseball. And why not? It's the only thing we know anything about anyway!

There's always stories about certain players, especially some of those who "got away" that I remember quite well. The first name that comes to mind is Paul Molitor. In 1974 he was a high school player in St. Paul, Minnesota, which was part of my area then when I was working in the Midwest. And I had a guy named Sasser, who was a part-time scout. At that time Molitor had mono, and he said, "Don't come up and see him now, Fred. He's weak. He's better than what you would see. But I'll put him on my list to keep watching for the summer."

I said, "Okay." So we drafted Molitor that summer. One of my scouts, Brian Humphries, saw him play in an American Legion game in Omaha. Molitor said he wanted ten thousand dollars to sign and Humphries offered him five. We could've signed Paul Molitor for ten thousand dollars. Imagine that!

And there's others. We drafted Greg Vaughn out of college. He didn't sign. We had all the rights to Jeff Blauser. Didn't sign. In 1969 we had the rights to Bill Madlock. In 1978 we drafted Mike Moore out of high school. Didn't sign. He later went back into the draft and was taken number one overall by Seattle. In 1980 we drafted Dan Plesac. He didn't sign. Every organization has its list of players who didn't sign. But there's some pretty good names there. I wasn't scouting director until 1981. But these things happen no matter who's in charge. It's just the way the game is.

Here's a story for you. In 1971 I was scouting in Charleston, West Virginia, in the International League, and I had a friend there I'd played with in Columbus, Ohio, back in 1951 named Cot Deal. He was our pitching coach then. Cot was a pitcher who played in the big leagues in the late forties until he was sidelined with arm problems. He was a great guy.

Anyway, I was in West Virginia scouting and Cot called me over and said, "Freddie, there's a boy named Joe Niekro here, brother of Phil Niekro, and he's going to be a good pitcher. He's working on a knuckleball. Why don't you recommend him to the Cardinals because he's going to be a good pitcher?"

I said, "Well, Cot, I can't recommend him to the Cardinals if he's just working on it." I said, "If he already had it and was pitching well with it, well, that would be different. But I can't recommend him without knowing if he's going to come with a knuckleball or not." So I didn't recommend him.

Later when I was living in Florida, a scout down there wanted me to take a look at a boy named Kenny Kelly, a football player around Tampa. He was playing baseball at Lakeland High School in Lakeland, Florida. So my wife Patty went with me to go over there and have a look. We got there early and were sitting there watching batting practice before the game and this kid was hitting balls over the fence. I told Patty, "I'm going over there to find out about this boy." I thought he might be Kelly, but didn't know. I didn't even know which team was out there because nobody was wearing a uniform, just sweatshirts and shorts.

So I got the coach and asked, "Hey, Coach, who's the kid hitting all the balls out of the ballpark?"

He said, "That's my son."

I asked, "What's his name?"

He said, "Niekro."

I said, "You mean Joe Niekro?"

He said, "Yeah." So I had to tell him the story about how Cot Deal recommended him and everything. But anyway, he did come up with the knuckleball and went on to pitch for Houston and a few other major league teams, and had a great career. It wasn't as good as Phil's, but it was a good one.

But, back to the story about the Kelly kid. When the other team shows up, the Kelly boy plays center field. He seemed like a good player but we didn't pursue him. He eventually signed a four-year deal with the Devil Rays. I don't know why it was such a long contract for such a young player, except that he also plays football and maybe they wanted to keep him away from that. I don't really know.

Oh, and here's a story that I'm sure is one of Kenny Boyer's favorites. I played with him at Houston, and he's one of the best players I ever played with. He went on to be a big league star and a manager. One year, 1962, Kenny managed in the Gulf Coast League in Sarasota, Florida, and I was scouting supervisor in the Midwest. I called Kenny and told him, "I just signed this kid out of Chicago. Joe Martin is his name, and he's going to be your best hitter. Put him in hitting fourth as soon as he gets down there." So it happened when I went down to see a tournament in Lincoln, Illinois, when I was on my way to Northwestern. The first day I ever saw him, I only saw him bat once and he hit a home run. I got his schedule from his coach, and the next time I saw him he was playing a morning game. He hit another home run. Well, he showed me something out there and I decided I'd better grab him.

So we signed him and sent him down to Sarasota where Boyer's the manager. And in about ten days Kenny called me and said, "You know that Martin kid you signed?" And I said, "Yeah. How's he doing? Bet he's leading the league in home runs, isn't he?" I was expecting a simple "Yes" to that.

But Boyer said, "He's mostly getting hit with the pitch a lot, so we took him to this eye doctor and found out that he's blind in one eye."

Well, we had to release him because we were afraid he'd get hurt. That was many years ago now. After that, every time Kenny Boyer ever saw me, he always tells me in front of all the people standing there that I signed a blind player! It happened so long ago yet the people he told about it still tease me every now and then.

The player who gave me the biggest satisfaction probably in my whole scouting career was Todd Worrell. Our scout, Steve Flores, asked me to check a shortstop named Tony Woods in a game between Whittier College and Viola University. There must have been twenty-five scouts there, all looking at that kid. About the seventh inning I asked, "Who's the big guy pitching for Viola?" He was six-foot-five, 200 pounds, strong. There was no gun on him but I know he was throwing 89 or 90. No one was paying any attention to him because they were making runs off him. Flores tells me he's Todd Worrell, a senior.

I said, "Was he drafted last year?"

He said, "No."

When I asked why not, he said he didn't know. So I told him to see Worrell every time he pitched and I'd see him at our workout in May. We always have an invitational workout the Saturday before the draft to get a last look at some of the top players. Area scouts, the crosschecker and I, when I was scouting director, did it, too. It's done by a lot of organizations. In our case it paid off in many instances.

When we had him throw, he was throwing 89, 90, 91. Then we let him throw batting practice and he asked to hit. He looked like Kingman hitting. He hit all the balls over the fence into someone's yard. No one was home and there was a dog in the yard. We were scared to go after the balls because we were scared the dog might bite us. So the workout was over because we ran out of balls! I remember walking off that field saying to Marty Keough, our crosschecker on this one, "Can you imagine that? Wouldn't you love to get this guy number one?"

"Oh my God," Keough said, "there's no way he can get that far in the draft." We were 23rd or 24th to select that year. But he did, and we got him! All those other clubs passed right over him and we drafted him.

Brian Jordan was probably one of three of my favorite players I signed, with Todd Worrell and Dmitri Young being the other two. He went to the University of Richmond, where he also played football. I sent a scout out there to have a look at him and he had a great day for me. I mean he was really outstanding that day. The University of Richmond played the Richmond Braves, Atlanta's Triple-A farm team in the International League. It was an exhibition game before the university's season opened in a couple of days. Jim Beauchamp, who coached for Atlanta for a long time, was managing Richmond that day. Jordan did everything you could do in that ballgame. He hit a home run, stole a base, and played great defense. I just fell in love with him.

And then we get him into the supplemental pick and I got him number one. Dal Maxvill made the deal. He told me, "Freddie, you go down there and offer him $32,500 and tell him we'll let him go back and play football his senior year, but just go out and play in the rookie league this year. And in the end if he doesn't decide to play professional football, we'll give him another $64,000."

So, I signed him and he agreed to do that, and we gave him the $32,500, and he agreed that if he didn't play professional football we'd give him $64,000. As it turned out he was drafted by Buffalo to play football, and he went to their camp, but he got cut and came back to us. We never gave him another dime and he signed with us for that $32,500. That was some of the best money we ever spent! He was just "one of those players," you know what I mean? Yes, that was a honey of an investment for us.

I saw Nolan Ryan pitch twice in his senior year of high school. There were 15–20 scouts there the day I was. I wasn't that high on him because I didn't see nothing. I saw a skinny little kid with a loose arm and good delivery, but I never dreamed he'd ever be able to throw 95! He was drafted like 400 or 500, and if any organization thought he was going to be as good as he turned out, throwing bullets for over twenty years, he'd have been taken number one.

Let me go back a little bit. There's a shortage of good baseball players in the United States and I don't think any scouts will argue with that. There's especially a shortage of pitchers. When we were kids we had sandlot teams and played all day long every day of the summers. When kids use baseball skills and do baseball things, they develop whatever tools they may have. Kids that can run do that running out hits or chasing balls and throwing at defense. But now kids are into soccer and arcades and their computer games and don't get passionate about baseball like we did. So we see more players from other countries, where baseball is everything, playing great baseball at the major league level.

The Cardinal philosophy is that if a kid can run and throw, he can learn to field and hit. A player that comes to mind with that is Vince Coleman. He could run when I saw him with our scout, and his arm was decent. His arm got better once we got him here and he learned to stretch his arm out. George Kissell did that. And he made a switch-hitter out of him. He was taught to hit left-handed and he's probably a better hitter from the left side.

And then there are stories of the self-made players. I remember Solly Hemus, an old-time player, hard-hitting shortstop. When I was playing for Columbus back in 1951, he had played there the year before, and I said, "Who's the old guy fooling around out there?"

They told me, "That's Solly Hemus, shortstop for the Cardinals."

I said, "You got to be kidding me!"

Even then I could see he was a below-average runner and he had a below-average arm. But he was a hustler, an Eddie Stanky type player. He made the routine plays, and made himself a hitter. He later managed the Cardinals and the Phillies, I think, too. But he was one of those guys who worked hard and made himself into a major league ballplayer. That was way back in the days when you could get there by being what I call a self-made player.

Pete Rose was one of those, too. He had that old ingredient they call "heart" that caught the eye of scouts. He didn't have outstanding tools to speak of, but he wanted to play. He worked hard and made himself into a great player. I know a lot of clubs didn't like him when he was looking for his chance, but being in Cincinnati, they got him into the ballpark and worked him out and signed him. This one scout, Carl Ackerman, told me he signed him but I've heard other stories. Gabe Paul was the GM at that time.

I can tell you more stories and probably will, but I don't want to forget to mention some other changes in the game. One is the change in who the scouts are anymore, another is expansion, and another is the Major League Baseball Scouting Bureau.

Today there's a lot of scouts who never played the game and they really don't understand. In fact, probably half the scouts and half the scouting directors never played. It's a part of their education they've missed and there's no way to make it up. When I started everybody had played themselves and a lot of them had even seen me play. You felt they were more qualified to be a scout than some guy who's never played. And some general managers never played, either, I guess. I mean, somebody has to hire all these people.

The other thing is expansion. Now there's thirty big league teams instead of sixteen like when I started playing. Common sense says that makes more jobs for scouts. And that's good for scouts. But it's not necessarily good for the players, because the talent pool was dry already and expansion, as gradual as it was, caused them to be moved up before they're ready.

It's especially hard on the young pitchers when they're moved up too fast and they're not ready when they get there. That's why the pitching seemed so bad. But I guess there's such a lot of money involved in expansion that the organizations are willing to rush these kids and let them complete their development in front of the big league fans.

People can guess about whether rushing these young pitchers can cause them problems that could eventually shorten a career or even cheat them out of a complete career. Of course it's a possibility. But on the other hand, if you've got a good pitcher in Triple-A and one of your starters gets hurt, he's going to get called up early, too, because you don't have anyone else. Personally, I think a college pitcher develops best if he spends a year at each level: A, AA, AAA, and maybe by the fourth year he's ready for the major leagues. But when pitchers are put into the big league situation in the second year, I think it's kind of jumping the gun and it's a tough thing for the kid to do.

A high school kid, even a good pitcher like Kerry Wood, should stay in the minor leagues three or four years. They need to be allowed to have success at every level and that allows them to feel good about themselves and gain professional confidence. They say success breeds success and that's true. In Wood's case, he only pitched a little more than a year in the minor leagues and ended up with serious arm problems after a little more than a year in the major leagues. On the other hand, he could have hurt his arm in the minor leagues, too. It's one of those things we'll never know. And, of course, my theory can sometimes jump up and bite you, too. Look at Rick Ankiel. He came up through all levels and then discovered some sort of a mental block pitching in the big league level.

The other thing that's changed was when the Major League Baseball Scouting Bureau began in 1974. Originally when the bureau came in, it was intended to save the teams money and joining it was optional. We didn't join because we felt we have our own scouts and we'd just keep doing the job like we'd always done. But then they forced all teams to join, and I wasn't happy about it. However, later when they started putting out video on the players, well, I think that's the best thing they do.

The bureau sees lots and lots of players and projects a lot of things on them. For example, like a high school player. They might give him a five arm now and a seven future. Well, it's fine if he comes to that, but the chance is he won't. And they project running, like a 4.5 below-average runner to an average 4.6 or an above-average runner. Most people don't get faster after they're seventeen years old. You can either run or you can't. Scouts for the bureau put those inflated numbers on the kids and they don't have to pay them the money based on their reports. And if we take them, we got to give them the money. So they can just go look at them and put any number on them they want to. So what we do, and what most organizations do, is take a look at their reports and if something interests us, we have to send our own scout out to see them anyway!

The bureau scouts are fine. I like them. And the bureau's fine. It has a job to do, and the additional scouts it puts out there increases a kid's chances of being seen. No question about that. They see a lot of players and put in reports on them. And every good report they put in on a player, well, then we send that report to our scout. Anything with a total score of forty or above on it, our scout will go see the player. Our list may have three hundred players on it from all the scouts, but the bureau might have as many as eight hundred players on theirs. One fault, maybe, is that once they see a player and put a number one or a number two draft pick on him, they keep going back to see him again and again. I don't think they should do that. But it's not my job to tell them that. To me, once they put in a report on a player, they should just move on down the road and let the clubs make the decisions on them. But I guess they think it's being careful or thorough or whatever. I didn't have my scouts do it that way.

Here's another story that goes way back to 1966, the first year after the draft started. I was refereeing basketball during the winter in Houston. I was working for the city and the black players and the white players were just starting to play. There was an old guy there who was a coach for the black team. One day I was up at Prairie View College for a baseball game and this guy was umpiring at first base. He called me over to him and said, "Hello, Freddie. Did you ever hear of a kid named Joe Atilee, right-hand pitcher?"

I said, "No. Where does he live?"

He said, "Somewhere in Houston. He throws bullets."

I asked, "What's the name of his school?"

"D. C. Elmore," he said.

I said, "So, do know his coach's name?" He gave it to me and I called the coach.

I found out he was going to be playing down around Texas City or somewhere in that area, and I went there to see him. Well, there's only one scout in the ballpark. There were no guns then, but he had to be throwing at least 93 or 94. "So," I thought, "nobody knows about him." I hadn't heard anybody talk about this kid at all. So I was over at Grambling College a couple of weeks later. There were several scouts around there and some asked me, "Fred, have you ever heard anything about a kid named Atilee around Houston?" I don't remember what I told them, but I'm sure it wasn't much. I don't even know why they asked me because they knew I wouldn't tell them anything much. I never did that. So nobody's seen him and we draft him, and I go over to his house to sign him. Well, most of the players then were getting around $8,000. His mother wants me to go downtown and see his lawyer, which was kind of strange in those days. We go down there to see his lawyer in one of those big buildings in Houston, and the guy said, "Well, I wouldn't let him sign if he was my boy."

I said, "So, did you have a boy playing baseball?"

And he said, "No. My boy's a musician."

And I said, "You can't compare your son with this guy. This kid's got a great arm and could play major league baseball some day. There's a young pitcher on the Houston Astros named Larry Dierker and he's going to make a lot of money in this game. And this kid can do the same thing."

And he said, "Well, I wouldn't let him sign."

So, I took him back home and called him about a week later and he told me he was pitching in some kind of game. School was out so I went over there and watched him. He pitched three innings and he came behind the screen where I was standing and laid down in the grass. And I sat down with him and said, "Joe, if I was a ballplayer and you were a scout, what would you think of me if I was laying down on the grass while you were trying to talk to me?"

And he said, "Well, I would think you were tired." I just sat there and stopped talking to him. Later I called my boss in St. Louis and said, "George, I don't want to sign the guy. I'm not sure about his makeup.

And he said, "Freddie, does he have a good arm?"

And I said, "He has a great arm." But there was just something in me that kind of put me at arm's length on the guy.

He said, "Then let me tell you a story. We saw Willie McCovey in Mobile, Alabama. He laid in the grass. We didn't sign him but the Giants did, and he went on to hit over five hundred home runs. I'll tell you what. The Cardinals are coming to Houston next week. I'll set it up and take you and the kid out there and let the big boys have a look at him." So I took the kid to the Astrodome and had Bill Gagliano talk to him about what it means to have his talent and get the chance to possibly play in the big leagues one day. The kid never looked at him. Not one time. So when the kid went down to warm up, there was an old coach there, Joe somebody, who caught him. The kid threw so hard it knocked the mitt off his hand. And he said, "That kid throws so hard I'd put him in the game tonight, that is, if he could only put the ball over."

The next day he did sign for eight thousand and he went down to the rookie league. I wasn't about to call about it. I was just glad to get him out of my sight. So I get a letter from the scout, a guy who played in the Texas League when I was playing there. The letter said that he was the best pitcher in the Gulf Coast League. Now the last month of that season Sparky Anderson is managing in St. Pete in Florida, and Atilee goes over there and pitches for Sparky. We had a meeting in October in St. Louis and he raved about this boy. Said he was another Gibson. Then, when I was assistant farm and scouting director in 1967, the kid hurt his arm and never pitched again.

Now things like that can happen for many reasons and sometimes it's the kid himself that causes it. Sure, he does everything the team asks of him and it's tempting for him to blame them. But if you look at it more closely, sometimes young players feel pain or are somehow injured and they're afraid to tell anybody. That can result in costing the kid his entire baseball career.

Fred McAlister, left, and two unidentified friends before a game at Enron Field (now Minute Maid Park). Notice the official identification badge on the ribbon around his neck. These entitle scouts admittance to the park and seating directly behind home plate (Fred and Patty McAlister collection).

Gib Bodet

(1932–)

Bodet took the long way around to get to his forty-plus years in scouting. After high school baseball, semipro ball, and being scouted heavily by the New York Giants, his hopes of a pro career as a shortstop were interrupted just as he was about to sign a contract because he was drafted into the army during the Korean War and served almost four years. His lifetime in scouting was the result of years as a volunteer coach for teams on which his two sons played, starting with pee-wee league. He also ran an American Legion team for a few seasons. It was during the latter years that he was approached by the Montreal Expos about a possible career in scouting.

By 1968 he was ready to scout and wrote letters to various organizations hoping they could use his services in his home area of Southern California. Neil T. Mahoney of the Boston Red Sox hired him as a part-time area scout under the mentorship of longtime super-scout Joe Stephenson. One of his responsibilities was running the Scout League team for high school players who would soon become draft eligible. But when the Red Sox and several other organizations cut back scouting departments in lieu of using the services of the brand new Major League Scouting Bureau in 1974, Bodet was let go. He then scouted for four more organizations, the Detroit Tigers, the Montreal Expos, the Los Angeles Angels during the Gene Autry era, and the Kansas City Royals until he found his niche with the Los Angeles Dodgers nearly thirty-five years ago. With them he moved up the ladder, from area scout to regional crosschecker to his current position as national crosschecker/special advisor to the amateur scouting director.

He is described as a tireless worker who is respected throughout the baseball community for his astute ability to evaluate talent, his good humor, and his old-fashioned common sense. SABR credits him with signing Brad Wellman, Dave Hansen, Mike Munoz, Eric Karros and Mike Piazza. He was also closely involved in the pre-signing careers of many others who dazzled the diamond over the years, including Jack Clark and Jason Thompson.

I was a high school player at Fair Lawn High School in East Jersey and played some semi-pro baseball. I played first base, shortstop and left field in high school and was scouted pretty heavily by the Giants. The scout's name was Bob Trocolor. And just when I was about to sign a pro baseball contract, the United States Army drafted me. So I served close to four years in Europe, where I played a little ball.

When I got out of the service we moved out to Southern California. I still could have played professionally. I was still young enough and a pretty good shortstop, but we had children and I couldn't afford to go to work for a hundred-twenty bucks a month in the minor leagues.

I really didn't get interested in scouting at first. My connection to it was sort of a roundabout thing. When I was playing in Europe and they had a group of people, players, umpires, and so on, and a guy that was with the Red Sox, Neil Mahoney, who eventually became their director of scouting. Anyway, I was noticed and he talked to me about signing with them when I got out of the service. At that point he gave me a card and all that stuff, which I kept.

Actually, it's kind of unusual the way it happened. I went to watch the Little League tryouts, and my kids were too young for Little League. Anyway, they had a guy hitting fungos there that was, let's say, not very proficient or patient with the kids. So I said, "Why don't you give me that fungo stick?" because I didn't want to see one of those little kids get hurt. So I started doing that and a guy came up and asked me if I'd like to coach the little seven-year-old kids in pee-wee league, or maybe it was called tee-wee. So I did that and after a year or two my older boy was old enough to play, and then my second son. So that involved a few years.

Then I ran an American Legion team and a Scout League team. There were scout teams around Southern California back then. Let's see, the team the Red Sox had was called the Red Sox Juniors, and Montreal, the Angels, the Cardinals and the Reds all had teams. These kids were all high school kids to the best of my knowledge. So they'd play some in the fall and in the summer after the draft. A lot of them, of course, weren't yet draft age.

After I did that with the younger kids and the Legion stuff, I think the first club that talked to me about doing some scouting was Montreal. That's when I began giving scouting some serious thought. Simultaneous to that, I wrote about a dozen letters to different clubs expressing my interest, and I actually got four responses. One of the clubs was the Red Sox because I had originally talked about signing as a player with Neil Mahoney many years earlier and I still had his card, so I sent him a letter.

In Mahoney's case I put in the letter something like, "You probably don't remember me, but blah-blah-blah," and he wrote back a nice letter and said that he did remember me. He said he could use a scout as a part-time guy and their scout who runs Southern California, Joe Stephenson, would contact me. He did and that was my first connection with professional baseball, as a part-time area scout with the Red Sox.

I worked with Joe a couple of years in Southern California and I always remember finding out what my territory would be. I asked him, "Where do you want me to go?"

And he told me, "Just go wherever you don't think I'd go." So that was the start of a great association with him. In fact, I think if I'd started with somebody, else maybe I wouldn't have liked it as much. But I had such a good association with him that I got very enthusiastic about doing it.

I did that a couple of years and then a lot of the clubs cut way back on the number of scouts they used because the Major League Scouting Bureau was coming in. Not all the major league clubs belonged to the bureau, so not all of them cut back on their scouting personnel, but the Red Sox did. So I went through the letter-writing process again to see if another team could use me to scout in Southern California. The progression of clubs I worked for was Montreal, Detroit, the Angels, and Kansas City before I joined the Dodgers thirty years ago.

And as it turned out, running the Scouts League team gave me sort of a line on some of the kids who were going to be draftable down the road. Let me tell you a story that shows what a small world baseball really is and how the choice of one certain player can change a lot of things.

I think it was the last year I worked for Boston that I had Jack Clark on the Scout League team. He went to a fairly small school in the San Gabriel Valley, Gladstone High School in Azusa. I forget what year Jack was drafted, possibly '73 or '74, but I do remember just prior to the draft Joe and I used to meet maybe once every couple of weeks. On one particular occasion I met him near his home in Fullerton, and he said, "You keep yaking away about this kid, Clark, so tell me something about him."

So I did. He said he'd like to see him play. As I recall, the high school season was over but the draft hadn't happened yet. So Joe came over and saw Jack Clark and he really liked him. When you get to know the scout, you get a pretty good idea if he really likes a player or he just says, "Well, he's okay, I'll put him on my list, but I'm not nuts about him." But he really did like Clark, and he knew talent, believe me. He had signed so many good players, like Fred Lynn, Rick Burleson, Dwight Evans, Bill Lee, and a string of others. I mean he signed a ton of good players.

At any rate, I was encouraged because he was encouraged and what happened was that the draft came along and we didn't get him. The Giants got him. They drafted Jack in like the tenth round and they drafted him as a pitcher! You get all kinds of versions on that. But the kid could pitch. That sort of gets lost because of the way his career turned out.

There were two scouts who used to call me about Clark. One was Evo Pusich, an old Giants scout, a terrific guy. He always wanted to know about players on the Scout League team I had. He always wanted to know when Clark was going to play the outfield and not pitch. He was interested in him as an outfielder. Subsequent to that, Evo worked with George Genovese, and what happened was they selected him as a pitcher. He was a prospect as a pitcher. But he was too good a hitter to keep out of the lineup. For a guy with power, he didn't get himself out a lot.

Boy, was he a confident kid. I remember this real well. I had a guy helping me with that team named Paul Bueler. I think Paul had been a DI in the Marine Corps. So we split the squad up a lot of times before playing games. And those kids we had were from Gladstone High School, North View High School in Covina, and I forget the third school, might have been Covina High School. That particular Scout League team produced three kids who got to the big leagues: Jack Clark, Mark Clear, and Kevin Bell.

Anyway, we had enough kids we could get four teams and play two games. The coach at Citrus Junior College let us use his two diamonds once his season was over. This particular year it was sometime near the end of May and Clark calls me up one night, and he usually never said much, and he says, "Gib, Jack Clark here."

And I said, "Yeah, Jack, what's happening?"

In a very quiet and matter-of-fact way he goes, "Gib, I got to quit the team."

"Why?" I asked him.

He says, "Coach Bueler says we can't have guys that don't show up for practice and so on." Now you got to remember this is a kid whose dad worked in the local hardware store and he probably had an after-school job, plus he didn't have a car and had to depend on another player to get there, and so on. And a lot of these kids worked. So I figured he was going to tell me practice interfered with a job or something like that. I mean, it would have been a perfectly believable excuse and nobody would have questioned it.

But he says, "I can't come to practice on such-and-such a day or on Memorial Day."

So again I said, "Why?"

He said, "I'm going fishing."

I said, "So what's the deal? Do you wanna be a fisherman or a ballplayer, Jack?"

He said he wanted to be a ballplayer and explained he had to go fishing because he'd promised a friend who had gone in the army but was coming home for a leave to take him fishing when he got home. He said they go with their dads and have been doing this ever since they were eight years old. Then he said he wanted to play but he couldn't disappoint this guy. So I told him to go ahead and go fishing and we'd worry about the other stuff later.

Think about Clark's character. He could have lied, but he told the straight out truth. Anyway, Jack hitched rides to practice with his catcher, Worth Valentine. Well, about a week or two later, Worth shows up to practice without Jack.

"Where's Jack?" So he tells me Jack had to go to LA, and that Jack would tell me about it when he got back. So in a day or so Jack was back and I asked him about LA, and he said, "I wanted to see the CIF Game in Dodger Stadium."

So I said, "That's great, Jack. We're working out here and you're at a ballgame in LA. What's with that?"

He said, "I wanted to see [Gary] Roenicke play." He had gone to a high school a couple of miles from Jack's school as the crow flies, and he was supposed to be one of the best prospects in the country that year. I don't think he was thought of as the top prospect at that point, but he was certainly one of the top three as far as I was concerned. Jack acted like he wanted to talk to me about it and I deliberately stood there for a minute without saying anything.

Then I asked him, "So, what did you think about Roenicke?"

And he said, "Well, you know, I've been told that some club's going to draft him first."

And I said, "Well, I don't know, that may be."

He came right back and said, "Well, you work in pro baseball, do you think somebody might take him in the first round?"

I said, "They might. What did you think of him?"

He calmly looked me straight in the eye and said, "Well, if he's a first round pick, I am, because I'm a better hitter, I have a better arm, I'm a better runner, and I can also pitch." Now he wasn't bragging or putting Roenicke down, not at all, he was just giving me honest answers to my questions.

The crazy part of it was that I don't think there was a soul in the world who thought he was a better prospect than Roenicke, and he was taken in the thirteenth round and Roenicke actually was taken in the first round. There was probably a difference of a hundred thousand dollars in what they got, or close to it, which was a pot of money at the time. I remember that conversation very well to this day. He was so confident in his own ability. He wasn't cocky or arrogant about it, but he felt he was the better player. As it turned out he was. He was a better big leaguer, but they both had good careers.

I'm going on about this because scouts look at more than just the playing ability of the kids. We look at their makeup, too. And everything Jack was went into his playing.

He was always honest, a fierce but clean competitor, and he strived to get better than he was the day before. That's who he was. But when he didn't hit well, he'd pout. And he got to the big leagues so young, only nineteen years old, so he didn't have time to mature as a man. But he came into his own when he played for Whitey Herzog. Jack loved him. And Herzog liked a lot of the same things Jack did. But he wouldn't put up with any foolishness. He traded Garry Templeton for Ozzie Smith because, as the story goes, Templeton was too hard to get along with or something like that. The story I got was that he told Jack, "Look, over there with the Giants they say you're a moody guy and you don't always play a hundred percent." But Jack stood his ground and said he did.

My understanding is that Whitey said, "It's real simple. I like the way you play, that's why we got you. If you do that over here, we're going to go to the World Series and we're going to make a lot of money." Those two hit it off and he did just great. He ended up having a great career, and later became the hitting coach for the Dodgers for a few years.

I remember about five or six years ago during batting practice, I told him what he said to me about Roenicke and asked him, "Do you remember that?"

He said, "Did I really say that?" and he shook his head.

And I smiled and said, "Yeah, you did." And I smiled.

We both went over to the cage to watch them hit and he came back to me and said, "You know what, though, Gib? I was right." And we both laughed.

Getting back to scouting, let me mention something that we all think about. When you get paid to scout, you get to find good players. Say in 2008 you find a kid you think could be the next Jack Clark. Then when the 2009 draft comes around, you're expected to find somebody better. There's a sense in the organizations that they always have to improve.

And then there's the concept of money. In today's game the money is big, real big. But the players didn't cause that. It's just part of the environment where they work. And the public thinks nothing of it when Robert Redford or Clint Eastwood make millions for one picture they do. But there's resentment when players get it, without regard for the short amount of years they can play at their peak and make that money. Entrepreneurs and others have careers they can successfully pursue until they're in their sixties, seventies or even eighties in some cases.

Here's another thing I'd like to mention because there's always confusion about this issue. It's about money and the way scouts are allowed to interact with the players and their parents. We are allowed to go to the kid's house as many times as it's convenient for them and us. And we are allowed to talk with the parents. But the catch there, and it's a big one, is that we're allowed to inquire about what kind of money they are looking for him to sign. We're allowed to inquire about the signing bonus, but we have to be very careful how we word that. Let's say, for example, just for the sake of argument, the dad says, "Well, we want $100,000."

We are not allowed to say, "Gee, whiz, that seems awfully high, or that's acceptable." I'll tell you what the catch there is, and it's a damn shame, but it's true. Major League Baseball is explicit about not doing that because it means you tamper. Let's say the kid says the hundred thousand and we say it seems fair. On the face of it that doesn't seem out of line. You're in the kid's house and you went there for a reason. You want to know what it would take for him to sign if drafted, but you're not allowed to say it because there are twenty nine other clubs, and somebody may draft that player before you can.

So let's say I'm working for the Dodgers, and the Angels come in and select him and go in to negotiate with him and tell him, "Well, son, for the order in which you were drafted, we feel we can offer you $50,000."

And the kid and his parents get upset and say, "You can't do that. The Dodgers promised him a hundred."

Well, we really didn't make any promise or even say we would consider the hundred. We just wanted to know what kind of money they were considering. But any comment that says, "that doesn't seem out of line," or "that's fair," or "that seems reasonable," can be easily misconstrued. The line on how to talk to them without giving the wrong impression is a very difficult line to walk because parents, even when they're trying to be as open as they can, will quite often say things like, "Does that seem out of line to you because he has a scholarship to go here or there?"

The big problem here and the tough part of it is that baseball is very sloppy how they handle that. The bottom line is this. If you're an area scout and you work for any one of those thirty clubs, and you have a good prospect and you've had him crosschecked and maybe even the director has seen him and everybody likes him, they want to know what you think it will take to get him. So part of our job is to find out. Generally scouts do their darndest not to violate the rule, but it all comes down to the exact words we use when talking to them. Perhaps the worst thing is when scouts ask, "Would you take 'X' amount of money or 'Y' amount of money?" And that gets misconstrued as a kind of offer.

And here's the Catch-22 of the whole thing. Naturally the clubs need to have some kind of ballpark knowledge because they don't want to waste a draft pick on a kid who won't sign for the money the club has to offer. The organization pressures the scout and tells him, "Look, we don't want to waste a high pick on this kid."

So the area scout is caught in the middle, and the tough part of it is nobody at this point in time gets nailed for tampering, so it exists. I can honestly say that when I was an area scout out there signing players, I did not violate the concept that was set down by Major League Baseball, and it took a lot of skills to have those talks with players and families without being misunderstood. I'd ask them what they were looking for and try to be very open and say, "Look, obviously I like him, that's why I'm in your house. But I can't promise you where he's going to be selected because I work for others who make those decisions. And he may not be as high on the board as I would want him. But if in fact he's selected in a particular round, how do you feel about him being selected? Do you have your heart set on him being a number one or picked in the first four or five rounds?"

And that's how I tried to get around it. You could work at a disadvantage because there could be ten other scouts walk in there and tell them, "All we have available is a hundred thousand dollars if you're selected after round three or four."

So they've thrown a number out there and the chances are not very great they'll get the player. There's twenty-nine other clubs out there. So whoever gets the player, the word "untrammeled" comes into play, which means the club who does select the player has the right to negotiate with him without somebody having been there before the draft throwing around monetary figures that may or may not be realistic.

And I have another thing to say about the money in the game. I've said this over the years and I mean it. There's a lot of lip service given to scouts, calling us the backbone of this and the foundation of that. I've been around the game over forty years now, and let me tell you, they say it, but do they really mean it? Because the trash collector is probably making more money than the area scout is. And when you think about it, what happens quite often is that when a guy gets some seniority and maybe has a measure of success, the first time the organizations decide to economize, they let the guy go. And then they turn around and hire somebody who is forty years old and a former junior varsity coach or something who then has to learn how to scout, like on-the-job training. But he says, "Hell, I'll do it for half of that."

When I worked for Kansas City, I worked with Art Lilly, Rosey Gilhousen, and Al Kubski. Between those three guys, they probably signed over a hundred guys in the big leagues. Rosey was very upset because [of] Don Lindeberg, who had been a teacher for a number of years but always a part-time scout. Anyway, Lindy had been around forever, what a great guy, had finally ended his teaching job and was now going to work with the Yankees full time. Rosey was really upset because Lindy was going to make $20,000 a year. Well, that's what he was making and that's what Art Lilly was making. Of course, I was low guy on that totem pole and I was making under $10,000. Now that's over thirty years ago, but still, there were three guys that were experienced and had so many major signs, really successful guys, well respected in the business, and they were only making $20,000 after many years in scouting.

In the entire realm of the payroll structure of professional baseball, scouts are not well-paid guys at all. But scouts do what we do for the love of it. If we were in it for the money, we wouldn't be in it for long because we wouldn't be good at it. Tommy Lasorda always says we can't call it work when we have so much fun doing it and go home exhilarated at the end of the day. And there's truth in that, too.

The public doesn't get it. Everybody wants to be a scout, because what could be better than going to ballgames every day? We get to see the best kids who may get drafted. But what they don't know is that in order to see some of those kids, we may have to fly across the country and sit in a ballpark that's down to 40 degrees that night. The public doesn't really understand all the facets of scouting.

Another thing that baseball is sloppy about is giving credit to scouts for players they've signed. When I scouted for Detroit, I signed Jason Thompson in 1976. Years later I had a friend look up Jason Thompson online to see what the records say about who signed him, and it said Dick Wiencek. Well, that's a prime example of this. I handled everything on the Thompson deal, even the signing bonus. And what happened is when Jason came back from Hawaii where he had played in an all-star game, I called him and said, "We drafted you, Jason." So he and his dad came back to California to sign.

Jason had a nice career. He wasn't a star in the big leagues, but he was a pretty good player for the Tigers where he had a couple of good years and then they traded him to Pittsburgh and that's where he found a home. He liked playing there and so on and spent about ten or eleven years in the big leagues.

He was a fourth-round pick as I remember and, to show you how times have changes, the agreed signing bonus was $15,000. I scouted the kid, wrote the reports, and handled all of this, and Wiencek saw him one time. He did like him, but the problem we had with it was that he didn't see him until very late in the season and I had been on the kid all year. The bottom line was this. Because he had access to the front office, when the kid came back to California and went home, Dick tried to sign him for less money than was agreed on with me. I got the money from Bill Lajoie, who was running the Tigers at the time.

So the bottom line to that whole thing was that they wouldn't sign for the money Dick offered and they walked out. I later learned that they said they wanted the $15,000 I offered them, and Wiencek said that Bodet wasn't running the Tigers, or something like that. Finally we ended up giving him the money and it all worked out.

I mention this to show that sometimes people don't pay attention to details and years later it turns out some of the records turn out to be inaccurate. Here's another example. When the Dodgers got Eric Karros, I signed him. That's true. But the guy who scouted him and did all the leg work and preliminaries was Bob Bishop. I tried to get that record changed, but it didn't do much good. Funny thing was, I wouldn't even have known about the mistake except for one year when Eric made the Rookie All-Star team or something, I got a silver plate that said, "Eric Karros signed by scout Gib Bodet, 1988." I called to correct that, but I don't think anything was actually changed. [SABR credits both Gib Bodet and Bob Bishop.]

I can't mention any names here because I don't want to embarrass anyone, but I remember a time when my scouting director was going through a pile of scouting reports on a particular player and he asked for my opinion. Well, when I asked where the reports were, he pointed to his desk and said, "Those two piles over there. One pile is from scout A, a kind of Joe Friday guy who writes down 'just the facts, ma'am.' The other is from scout B and there's 'a lot of yeast in his reports.' So we waded through all of that and tried to make a fair decision about the kid's baseball future."

Here's another thing about scouts. Every now and then we'll get a phone call about a player asking us to take a look at him. Well, my belief is that we should always check the records to see if we'd already made reports on him, and if not, try to get to see him in a game someplace. Send a scout from his area to check him out. Who knows what you may find?

So one day a few years ago we got a letter about a player that was passed to us from his father, who said he had a son on a collegiate team or whatever and wondered if we would take a look at him. He said, "I wonder if you could come by and work him out." So the scout passed the letter along and we asked him to take a look at the kid and let us know what he thought of him and then we can respond to the dad. The scout said he was too busy and didn't have time for that.

I always felt a kind of kinship to that because, when I was looking for my first job in baseball, my first contact was Neil Mahoney. I had a seven- or eight-year-old card from him that I'd kept all that time and eight or ten addresses I'd accumulated. And after the Red Sox, when I was out there again, Dallas Green, even though I didn't know him from a bar of soap, gave me a lot of encouragement. And I never forgot that. So in our business, why would any scout be too busy just to go see a kid play a game? Besides, that's our business.

Another kid I signed was Brad Wellman. He was the last guy I signed when I worked for Kansas City before I went to the Dodgers. He was from northern California and as I recall he was attending Chabot Junior College at that time. I saw him play in a tournament during the summer. I liked him a lot. Agile infielder who had potential with the bat. I worked with Rosey Gilhousen and Art Lilly and Al Kubiski. They were all three veteran scouts. Kubski was a great guy, a real competitive scout who knew how to spot things in players almost right off the bat, and sure enough, what he said was right on. His son, Gil, is now a scout with Baltimore. But anyway, I called Rosey about Wellman and he said to me, "Do they have any more games left down there?"

I said, "Yeah, they're playing a couple more games."

And he said, "Well, are you sure about him?"

And I told him that I really liked the guy, and Rosey told me to go back and see him again. So I went back and saw him again and called Rosey. He said, "How much money would you give him?" I said I'd give him around ten thousand bucks. Now that was a lot of money back then for an undrafted player.

So, anyway, the whole process took a few days. I called John Schuerholz, who at that time was the scouting director for Kansas City. And we went through the same process again. And I said, "All I can tell you from what I've gathered is that the kid would've been selected by some club in the draft except Stanford was chasing him and the organizations who thought he was a prospect didn't think he was the kind of a prospect that you would try to buy out of Stanford. That's a lot of money, plus it's a terrific academic school that always had good baseball teams."

At any rate, what happened was, I think that Brad couldn't get into Stanford. That was the thing. He had good grades but I think his SAT scores are what kept him out. So he was undrafted. So when I got back to Johnny Schuerholz about this, he said, "Well, go back up there and see if you can sign him." When I asked how much money I could give him, he said something like eight to ten thousand, somewhere in there. With the incentive program and so on, it was a nice deal. So I went up there and Brad's dad picked me up and we visited and so on and so forth, and it took the better part of a day.

The kid wanted to play, and I think his dad was somewhat reluctant but he gave in. I think Brad played seven or eight years in the big leagues. And I was always very proud of that fact because he was an undrafted player. Occasionally undrafted players do play in the big leagues, but it is unusual.

He didn't start his career with Kansas City. In fact, he went through there pretty quick. As I recall, he was one of four players traded for Vida Blue, in 1982 I think, when Vida was at the tail end of his career with the Giants. Anyway, he ended up back with Kansas City for the final two years of his career.

I have to tell you about Dave Hansen. He was just a great kid, a good looking left-hand hitter. I think David played fifteen years in the big leagues, almost entirely as a pinch-hitter, and he was not a home run hitter. But he had eight pinch-hit home runs one year, which is terrific. He was the kind of player that fans gravitate to. He was like that even when he was in high school. He was a real hustler. He ran everywhere. He was almost hyperactive. Later in his career he played in Japan for one season, 1998 I think, and he still played another five or six years in the big leagues.

When I signed David, Al Campanis was the GM and at that point the scouting director was Ben Wade. They liked what I liked about him. The thing I always admired about him was that as a young player they gave him a chance to be a regular player and he struggled with his hitting. He really did struggle. And then, well, the irony of it was, they didn't just cast him aside, but I think they decided very early in his career that he wasn't going to be an everyday player. I think that was the determination. But that doesn't really follow. If you're saying that, why would you want to keep him as a pinch-hitter when he struggled hitting? The point was, I guess, when you look back on it, is that he was such a good kid and a good competitive guy. He used to take a hundred ground balls before every game even when he rarely played and he knew he was going to pinch-hit.

He told me, "I think I can play every day, but since they got me as a pinch-hitter, I'm going to do my best to be the best pinch-hitter they could have." And that's unusual. I been in this game a long time, and when a young player feels that he isn't appreciated, they pout and grumble, "Why don't they trade me? I know I could go play for this team or that, blah-blah-blah." It was unusual that he wasn't like that. His attitude was always, "You know what, I know I can play and I'll make the best out of whatever slot they put me in." He was always that way every place he played. He wanted to play and contribute to the team in any way they thought he could do it best. What a great kid.

Mike Munoz is another real good kid. Mike was a skinny kid, about 150 pounds, left-handed pitcher with a pretty good delivery and he went from a Catholic school in Covina, I can't recall the name right now, and went to Cal Poly Pomona. He got bigger, filled out, and really became a good prospect as a college guy. I think he played about ten years in the major leagues. He was the guy, the left-handed pitcher with a pretty good delivery. We took him the same year we took David. David was drafted second and Mike was drafted third. He struggled early and we traded him away, but I don't remember the first club we traded him to, maybe Texas. But he spent a long time in the big leagues. He had been in a great program at Cal Poly Pomona. He was a very good kid and I liked him a lot.

I signed Alan Wiggins, and his story was very different from theirs. I think it was. He was out of high school in Pasadena, and was one of the kids out there when I had a Scout League team. There were a lot of kids on those teams who were eligible for the following year's draft. I worked for the Expos then and we had a team, the Dodgers and the Reds had a team, the Red Sox Juniors were out there, and I think the Mets had a team. So I had seen Al Wiggins play in high school and, boy, could he run. He ran like the wind! That's the best thing he did. He didn't have any power or any of that stuff. He was one of those kids that you hoped you could make a player out of so you could use his running. The thing that he did, which is unusual, a lot of times you see players who can run but they don't have instincts to steal bases. He had instincts and great speed, and so anyway, I put him on that team. He had played first base in high school, if you can feature that. They had him at first base and he had no power. But that team, well, that must have been the fastest group of players I've ever seen on one team. They had four or five guys that we call "eighty runners." An eighty runner is as fast as you can get. I think Johnny Lind from that team went to UCLA and then played football as a defensive back for a long time.

Anyway, I put Wiggins on the Scout League team that winter and that's how I became acquainted with him. Then, what happened was, I went to work for the Angels, so I knew a little bit about him and I convinced them to draft him in the winter. They were not particularly interested in him because he didn't have any strengths in him except for his speed. He was just a wiry young kid. I worked with him, trying to teach him to switch-hit because I was taught that at a young age. The guy that spent the most time with him was Bob Clear. He spent a lot of time with Al, teaching him to switch-hit, which he didn't particularly take to because he didn't have a feel for it. But Clear taught him to bunt for hits and that's what got him to the big leagues.

Todd Hollandsworth was another good find. I didn't sign him. I always call players like Todd "blue collar players" because he was a hard-nosed, hard-working kid. He was Hank Jones' player. Hank's our scout in the Northwest and one of the best scouts in the country in my opinion. He followed him and wanted me to see him when the kid was a senior, so I went up and saw him.

It rains a lot up there, and those kids are used to playing in the rain. I saw him at one of Todd's away games. A lot of times up there kids take batting practice, but kids do not take batting practice in Southern California. It has to do with their scheduling, and they're not allowed to come out early and hit. But up there in Washington they are. But since it was an away game and it was raining, all that was available was the batting cage and that could only be used by the home team and not the visitor. It was a league rule.

Hank was talking to the coach, trying to get him to let Todd take a few pitches in the cage because I was there and wanted to see him, but the guy said he couldn't allow it because it was a rule. So Todd was standing off to the side there and leaning on his bat and Hank said he didn't know what else he could do. I said, "Well, we'll get a chance to see his swings."

Hank moved further down the line to watch, and I'm standing in between home plate and first base. Todd came over there with one of his buddies with a batting tee. He planted the batting tee right in front of me, right where I'm standing. I'm standing about two feet in front of a chain link fence. And he says to the guy, "Okay, start feeding me." He must've swung the bat at least fifty times, saying, "If you want to see me swing, I'm going to let you see me swing."

Later when he had been in the big leagues awhile, I reminded him of that day and he said, "Honestly, Gib, did I really do that?" He was embarrassed. But he had grown up and matured. Things like that go on with lots of guys.

Hank and I talked about him when we were driving back after the game. I never did see him get a base hit, but I did see enough good swings out of him to see the potential. Todd was such a strong kid. He was one of those kids that didn't leave anything to the organization's imagination in terms of effort. There's a common thread in kids like that. Pete Rose was that way. Steve Sax had that. And when you see that, it jumps out at you. David Wright with the Mets today is another one of those players.

In connection to this, let me mention another player, Mike Piazza. By the time of the draft, the world of baseball scouts knew about him, but for a lot of reasons nobody knew for sure whether or not he'd even get drafted. He was recommended by probably the most well-known manager in baseball, Tommy Lasorda, his godfather. But everybody knew that if he wasn't picked by round 63, he'd go undrafted. And I remember all through the process, about every thirty minutes, Tommy popped his head in and asked, "Anybody take him yet?" At that point in time if he'd gone undrafted, his career probably would have been in the automobile business.

I have to tell you a story on Tommy Lasorda. For several years I've been interested in the Black Sox Scandal and have been doing some reading and other research on it. A guy who's a researcher out here named Bob Hoie tracked down the possible connection between Peaches Graham and Jack Maharg because "Maharg" is "Graham" spelled backwards and some legend has sprung up about those two being the same person. To make a long story short, Hoie sent me a tape about Graham and Maharg and all of it where he had people playing each one of them. And there was another tape done the same way that seemed like an interview with Buck Weaver as an old man in the 1950s. So I played that one for Lasorda, and since it's on tape, Tommy said to me, "Hey, Gib, I'd love to meet this guy."

I said, "Tommy, how can you meet this guy? He'd be over a hundred eighteen years old, or whatever, if he were still alive."

So Tommy says, "Then how'd you get him on tape?" We still laugh about that.

Another one of my favorite Dodgers stories concerns a guy who was a pitching coach with us for many years named Red Adams. He's one of the greatest guys. He knew so much about pitching mechanics and worked wonders with pitchers at all levels for the Dodgers. Well, I wouldn't tell him this, but he retired too young because he's got such a good baseball rating. I mean, he retired about thirty years ago and it was baseball's loss. He's about 85 now. He still keeps an eye on the game and is always ready to talk baseball. He probably has more friends in the game who remember him well than most retired guys out there.

When I was back in New England several years ago, I ran into Lenny Merullo. He was a shortstop for the Cubs the last time they were in the World Series. He knew Red and I asked him, "Lenny, would you sign a ball for me? I was a Cubs fan when I was a kid. I remember the whole team, Peanuts Lowrey, Cavaretta, Don Johnson, and all of them."

And he said, "Sure," and took the ball.

And I added, "And besides, Red Adams is a good friend of mine."

He just had a big smile as he signed the ball. He then said, "Oh, what a great guy. Do you have his number? I just want to call him up because every time I talked to Red, I feel good afterward." Ask anybody involved with the Dodgers or any of his teammates and they'll all say he's a smart baseball man and one of the nicest people connected to the game.

So, as I said, he was a great mechanic. He knew what made pitchers tick, and he could watch their movements and help them get better. And he has such a sharp baseball mind. I mean that doesn't ever leave a guy. I remember one time I was visiting him at his home and we were watching the Braves in the playoffs. And Steve Avery was having a lot of trouble. That's when his trouble started. The kid had great stuff and then all of a sudden he hit a brick wall. Anyway, the kid ran into trouble in that game and all of a sudden Red said, "Hot damn! I could fix him in five minutes!"

Phil Rizzo

(1929–)

Rizzo was nineteen when he completed high school in 1951 and started his life-long baseball journey. Although his professional progress was interrupted after three seasons when he was drafted into the military during the Korean War, he was asked to play baseball during that time, and returned to the game upon his release in 1954. For the next five years he played in six minor leagues: the Midwest League, Big State League, West Texas–New Mexico League, Florida State League, Evangeline League, and the Longhorn League.

Then he hung up his glove and scouted for the next forty-plus years. He was an amateur scout for the Washington Senators, California Angels, Chicago White Sox and Milwaukee Brewers. As a major league scout he's worked for the New York Yankees, Seattle Mariners, and Los Angeles Dodgers. He also worked for the Arizona Diamondbacks when his son, Mike, was scouting director there. He jokingly says that if he keeps up the pace, maybe he'll be able to work for all thirty clubs.

He's proud of the players he's signed, including the Angels' number ones he and Nick Kamzic signed four years in a row, plus several others who made it to the major leagues. But the thing he seemed especially proud of happened in the summer of 2008. The Goldklang Group, owners of six minor league clubs, joined forces with the Topps Baseball Card Company to establish the Professional Baseball Scouts Hall of Fame. Phil Rizzo was among the first twelve inductees. It was an emotional experience for this old scout who sincerely believes that professional baseball neglects and underappreciates the efforts and contributions of the scouts.

I signed in 1951 at nineteen years old out of high school. Signed by Frank Piet. My first year I played for Danville, Illinois, in the Midwest League, the Danville Dans. It was Class D back then, but they changed all that and it's a Class A league today. My position was infield: short, second, third. Played there for two months and I was drafted into the Korean War. I went to my hometown to be inducted and they saw on my papers that my profession was baseball player, so they pulled me out of line and asked me to play ball. But I had to go through boot training first, and then they shipped me to Camp Chaffee in Fort Smith, Arkansas. There were a lot of major and minor league ballplayers and we played all the teams from the other camps. It was entertainment for the soldiers, you know. I was away for three years. At the time the team manager was Carl Sawatski, a former big league catcher, and he was the president of the Southern League for a lot of years.

When I got out in 1954, I went right back into playing. But while I was in the service, I was traded to the Temple Eagles in the Big State League in Texas and that was a Class C league. I did pretty good there. I was still considered a rookie. I played there for the year, sort of on loan like they did it in those days. After the season they sent me back to Danville because they still owned me. From there I just bounced around in the minor leagues until about 1958. I played in six minor leagues in those years: the Midwest League, Big State League, West Texas-New Mexico League, Florida State League, Evangeline League, and the Longhorn League. Then I decided to go in a different direction. So I retired as a player but stayed in the game and worked for the Washington Senators for one season as a scout. I scouted one year for them. But I had to get another job because baseball scouting doesn't pay nothing. I was very fortunate because I got a job with the City of Chicago. I was a civil service foreman, streets and sanitation. I had to do that because baseball never paid much and never did take care of its old-time scouts. Now, let me rephrase that. We made a little money after they started paying a little better. But at the time when guys my age were young, they didn't pay much, there was no insurance, no pensions, no anything. That's all come into play lately. The scouts today are making a decent dollar, but they're still not making what they should be making. They keep saying things like "the scouts are the backbone of baseball" and things like that. But they have yet to prove it to me. They haven't shown me that they believe that.

I don't have nothing against the young scouts today, but let me tell you, if they were out there in our day, I don't they would have lasted. They don't know enough about the game and I don't think they're strong enough to deal with the things we did. In our day, us old vets weren't selfish. We loved the game and we stayed in it in spite of the short money because we loved it. But to support my family, I had to have at least one other job all the time. Some of the scouts had two or three jobs just to get by. Not these kids today.

After the Senators I worked with a scout from around here named Nick Kamzic. Chuck Cottier and I played together and became very close. So when my son, Mike, who has a hell of a job now as assistant general manager and vice president of baseball operations of the Nationals, anyway, back then he was a kid and anytime Chuck was around, I took Mike to the ball field to work out. Chuck told Nick he was looking for a guy in the Chicago to work as a part-time scout and go out on weekends and look at high school and college kids. He said, "I don't know if he'll do it, but I think I have the perfect guy for you." And he gave Nick my phone number. He called and we talked and I put him off for about a year because my son was still in high school. But I told him, "I can't do it yet because I promised myself and my wife that I'd stay with Mike and work with him because he had a good chance to sign a professional contract." The way it worked out, I introduced him to Nick and Nick ended up signing him for the California Angels. And then I started working for Nick as a part-time scout for the Angels.

Later Nick wrote a tremendous letter about me to the ballclub, telling them what my duties were and what I actually did and what a tremendous help I was to him. I worked for Nick ever since, until he passed away. When I started, they didn't even give us a contract. And in the beginning they gave us an employee's information sheet to fill out. At least they asked for baseball experience, professional and amateur. Then every year after that they sent out a letter, saying I'd work for them for the next year at whatever amount of dollars, and I signed them. And the scouts had to kind of get rehired every year like that.

I signed a lot of good players in my career. I started with the Angels and was with them around seventeen years or so. For four years in a row, Nick and I signed the Angels' number one draft pick. Dick Schofield in '81, Bob Kipper in '82, Mark Doran in '83, and Erik Pappas in '84. That's something I'm pretty proud of. I also signed Glen Carter, but he got caught up in the drug thing and is out of baseball. It's too bad because he was a pitcher with a good chance to make it, but he had a million dollar arm and a ten-cent head. Bruce Hines and Paul Robinson and I signed Mark Holzemer.

Dick Schofield was the first of those four, and it was in 1981. When we scout, we go out there and we see what we see. I look at the tools they show me and if they have the tools that I like, then I keep tabs on them. At the time I first saw Schofield, he was playing for a semipro team out of St. Louis. He was like the youngest kid on the team. He couldn't have been more than sixteen years old, but he was holding his own with the older players out there. That's how he stood out so easy. He was a big kid, a nice kid, a quiet kid. His dad was a major league infielder and I knew it and knew he had the genes.

I got to know his mom and dad pretty well. The dad wasn't the easiest guy to get along with, but Dick was a real nice kid. A gentleman, and that always impresses me. I'm the type of scout, I don't go ask questions about players. If I like them, I like them. I watch them and go where I can see them play and I make my own decisions based on what I see on the field. I don't ask anybody anything. What I thought of a kid maybe another scout didn't think of him, and I don't worry about what other people think about the players I like. I had a gut feeling about him. He had all the tools to make the plays and the makeup to take the pressures of going up the ladder to the major leagues.

So when I first saw him he was, I think, a junior in high school, and I told our cross-checker, Nick Kamzic, and the club kept an eye on the kid and when he got out of high school, we drafted him. See, the more you like the kid, the more people like the cross-checker and the scouting director and sometimes even the general manager. If they all like him, he's given a number on the draft list and we go from there. Once he's drafted and signed, the guy who gets the least credit is the guy who saw him first, me! And that's how it goes.

Bobby Kipper was a left-handed pitcher who went to Aurora Catholic High School and I just accidentally went and saw them play. I liked what I saw with Kipper. Tall, healthy and strong looking. He was a nice kid, well mannered. He threw pretty good. Pretty smart. Good curveball. But then again, I look at the tools. Frankly, I was a little bit down on Bobby because I didn't know if he had the guts to throw the ball and knock somebody on their ass. Know what I mean? Pitchers have to have a little mean streak in them and I wasn't sure if he had that. I found out that he was kind of meek, and I think he just needed a little better makeup, the meanness, and by that I mean if you got to drill them, you drill them. I'd say that was really the only weakness I saw and they can teach kids to overcome that.

He was a good student and mentioned that he had a college scholarship waiting for him after graduation. But the best thing baseball ever did was create the College Scholarship Program, which I explained in full to him. It is really a better guarantee for an education than the colleges can offer because their plan is year by year and if a player gets hurt, it's over, boom, just like that. But with baseball, it makes no difference if he gets released or gets hurt or whatever, that scholarship is in his contract and he gets his college paid for. We gave him a $100,000 bonus, which was good for an organization's first-round pick back in 1982, and that plus the scholarship looked good and he took it.

Bob Kipper and my son Mike both got signed by the California Angels in 1982, and as far as I know that was the first time they met, even though they both grew up in the Chicago area and both played high school baseball there. That happens all the time, where players don't meet if their teams don't play each other. So Mike and Bob Kipper went to the Northwest League together as rookies and roomed together. And those two were smart, too. Instead of renting an apartment and needing furniture and phone hookups and all that, they rented a hotel room by the week or something like that and got it all plus maid service. No phone deposits or any of that stuff.

The next year we took a kid from the southside of Chicago, a kid named Mark Doran that I found playing at the University of Wisconsin. I thought he had more tools than anybody, but I don't think he made it to the big leagues. That happens sometimes when a player doesn't stay focused on his goal. And I don't think he did. That happens to a lot of first- or second-year players when they're not careful, and it's too bad.

Erik Pappas was our organization's fourth number-one pick in a row signed by Nick Kamzic and me. He was a hell of a good prospect. A pitcher who went to the big leagues and even has a no-hitter under his belt. When we saw him play, he was great and we loved him. Then I went with the White Sox for two years and I signed Dan Matrick, Bob Wickman, and Mike Vogel.

Then came the Milwaukee Brewers. With them I signed Mike Matheny, Mark Loretta, a steal as a seventh round pick, and Tim Unroe.

Mark Loretta is what I like to call "my pride and joy." He was a gentleman, a real nice kid; you could talk to him. He was like one of the boys, know what I mean? We found him playing at Northwestern University at Evanston, Illinois. He wasn't drafted after his junior year and he had a hell of a junior year. After he got out of high school, the word was out among the scouts that he was a college-orientated guy and we all took a pass on him. So four years later as a senior in college, everybody figured he was going to be a hard sign and nobody drafted him after he had a great junior year. He played any position and did anything you wanted him to do. He was an average runner at best, but he was very smart. So we drafted him as a seventh-round pick and I got him $30,000. Thirty thousand dollars for a seventh round pick, a senior.

So he had a job offer with Wal-Mart in a management position I think, and he said he needed two thousand dollars more and he would sign. Well, it went back and forth with his dad and I finally said that the organization wasn't gong to give him any more money. "In fact," I said, "we don't really have to give him anything. Either he goes and plays for us or he goes to work."

Well, they thought it over and he finally signed. It was so silly. The kid had a chance to play ball and make millions down the road if he made it to the big leagues, and they were quibbling over two thousand dollars more. This went on and on, this back and forth, and I tried to get the organization to give him the money and finally they did just to put an end to it. So I called their house and asked Mark to meet me in Chicago at Joe's Restaurant to sign the contract and set his career in motion. So we met there, I bought his lunch and we talked and he signed. Some time later, we celebrated with a glass of Rizzo's Red Homemade Wine. And guess what? He made the big leagues in 1995 and is still playing today. A good career.

Mike Matheny turned out to be a happy accident for us. It was really something. I went and saw him play with my son, Mike, who was an area scout at that time. Actually, we went to watch somebody else that day at Michigan or one of those big-gun schools, and that's how we found him. Mike Matheny was like an afterthought. But after we saw him, I was with Milwaukee at the time, and I called Al Goldis, our scouting director, to tell him about the ballplayer were there to see. Wish I could remember who that was. It was a pitcher, I know that.

Anyway, Mike and I were talking and he said, "Dad, what about Matheny? Don't you like Matheny?"

I thought about it as long as it takes to snap your fingers. "Yeah, I like him," I told him, "but he's not in my area. I don't want to go over a scout's head and call the ballclub and say I saw this guy." But when I finally did call the ballclub, there was nothing in on him. Nobody ever put in a report or nothing about Mike Matheny.

My son said I should mention it to Al Goldis, so I did. My son said, "Dad, if they want you to write a report on him, write a report on him. At least you've got it in the office and if something comes up, you can at least say you've seen him and put down what you did." So I did. I liked the kid and said so in my report. I figured he was a good fifth-to-tenth round pick and good catching is hard to find. I didn't think he was going to hit that much, but defensively he had some pretty good tools. Sure enough, we wound up drafting him. And the kid who had that area called me up and he says, "I heard you wrote a report on him."

I say, "Yeah. Did you get to see him play?"

He says, "Yeah."

And I say, "Well, evidently you didn't like him then, huh?"

The kid says, "Well, I didn't watch him that well."

So I told him, "I wrote a report on him, so I guess you're probably going to have to go sign him."

Later he called me up. He didn't know what the hell to do. He was a scout, one of those young kids that probably never played, and he didn't know what to do. Not my problem. But anyway, we drafted him and the rest is history.

Tim Unroe, an infielder, was another special player I signed with the Brewers. I discovered him when he was a senior at St. Louis University. I went there because I heard he'd had a great junior year and nobody drafted him. Nobody. So we drafted him after his senior year and gave him something like a thousand dollars. He was a twenty-eighth round pick for the Brewers and was an all-star player throughout the minor leagues. He made it to the majors with Milwaukee and had a five- or six-year career. He's a real fine young man.

I signed Chris Burt as an outfield/pitcher. But his story didn't end so well. It's too bad because everybody feels bad when this happens. They sent him to the Midwest League and the Brewers development people overused him. He broke all league records for saves that year, pitched every day, and they blew his arm out and he was out of baseball. His arm was in such bad shape that he couldn't even wipe his tomata!

And then I signed a kid named Lyle Prempas, in the twenty-fifth round, a high school pitcher, about six foot-eleven. He had a bad arm in high school, but I knew the kid well because I played with his dad years ago. So we agreed to do a draft and follow on him to see how his arm improved. I got him into Trident Junior College. He pitched one year there and had a record of 17–2 or something like that. So we signed him after that for $125,000.

After that I became a major league scout, so that was the end of my scouting and signing amateur players. After Milwaukee I worked for the Yankees, Royals, Diamondbacks, Dodgers, and now I'm with Seattle. If I keep this up, pretty soon I'll have worked for all thirty clubs.

I've gotten some nice awards, too. I was named the Topps National Scout of the Month in 1994. And do you know who the player was? Tim Unroe. He was the player of the month in the Southern League, I think it was. See, when your player gets an award like that in the minor leagues, we get the same award. In 1989 the Pitch and Hit Club of Chicago gave me the Chicago Scout of the Year Award. That was real nice.

This year there is something new sponsored by the Topps Company and the Gold-

Phil Rizzo, center, with sons, Mike, the GM of the Washington Nationals (left), and Bernie celebrate his induction to the Professional Baseball Scouts Hall of Fame in August 2008. The plaque reads as follows: Phil Rizzo got his first taste of professional baseball at the tender age of 19, signing his first contract out of high school. Rizzo spent eight years playing minor league ball before making his transition into scouting. Rizzo's scouting career spanned forty plus years including stints with eight different Major League organizations. During his tenure as a scout he was responsible for the signing of numerous Major League players such as Bob Kipper, Erik Pappas, Bob Wickman, and Mark Loretta. In 1989 Rizzo was recognized as the recipient of The Pitch and Hit Club of Chicago and Scout of the Year Award (Rizzo family collection).

klang Group. They own six minor league clubs all over the place. They've set up an award called the Professional Baseball Scouts Hall of Fame. Professional baseball can't find room for us at Cooperstown, so these guys are giving scouts some recognition. I think they've been planning it for a long time because it all seems pretty organized.

I got this letter from them that says I'd be in the last group to be inducted in 2008 in August. The way I understand it, there's six ballparks and there will be a Professional Baseball Scouts Hall of Fame Wall somewhere in each one of them. I was inducted in the park of the St. Paul Saints. In other words, they're making a place for all the plaques on a wall in the outfield or something like the Yankees have in the outfield. Somebody said it could be a wall teams will build along a walkway someplace in their parks.

Topps said they also plan to have baseball cards for the scouts, just like the ballplayers have, and our statistics will be a list of players we signed and stuff like that. I'll send you one. I don't know if there's bubble gum in our cards or not. But if there is any, you can chew it! They said the only scouts eligible for this honor are the ones who have at least twenty years experience. Funny thing is, to most of us older guys, twenty years at it is really nothing.

Here's a letter I got from Jim Bowden of the Washington Nationals to congratulate me for being selected for this. It says,

> Dear Mr. Rizzo,
> It is my pleasure and honor to extend our sincere and heartfelt congratulations on this most significant occasion, that of your induction into the inaugural class of the Professional Baseball Scouts Hall of Fame.
> With incredible hard work and enormous talent you have earned respect throughout the sport at every level. Your contributions to spending forty-plus years are treasured. There's no award yet invented that can adequately repay what you and other members of this illustrious inaugural class has given our sport.
> Above all, of course, the most important contribution you have made is the gift of your son, Mike Rizzo, now assistant general manager of the Washington Nationals organization. It's our good fortune to be the beneficiaries of Mike's outstanding talent. Congratulations to you and your family on this memorial occasion.
> Best Wishes,
> Jim Bowden.

When I worked with the Diamondbacks, my son Mike was the scouting director and I worked for him. He used to send me to look at all the top high school and college guys. I was not amateur scouting like when I started. I was more like a special assistant to the GM.

These days I'm just a scout. I work for the GM, but the one who hired me got fired. I'm sort of a special consultant to the GM. When I was with the Dodgers, I was very instrumental in making the trade, getting Greg Maddux to get over with the Dodgers. I don't know what happened, but according to Ned Colletti, he wanted to go to San Diego because he has a home and his family there, and the next thing you know, this year he wasn't doing too good during the season and all of a sudden he was back with the Dodgers.

I've been in this business a long time. The draft started before I got there and then came the scouting bureau. Today the organizations and the bureau get long lists of names of players and their schools and their coach's name and all that. But where did all those names come from? Did they just jump out of the woodwork? Who's making those lists of names that makes their jobs easier? We never got none of that! We had to go out there and find them ourselves. That's what I call scouting, not the way it's done today. I don't know what to call it, but it sure ain't scouting!

Now you got these kids today, the new scouts, and they go out there with these lists, and I mean they don't know nothing about the game. Nothing! Ninety percent of them never played marbles! Guys who want to scout should at least have played the game to have an idea what a ballplayer goes through. They have to know about what obstacles you have to walk through before you become a player. There's physical and mental maturity, patience, a head for the game, and lots and lots of practice to name a few of them. There's knowledge of situational hitting or situational pitching to name some more. I'm not sure some of these newer kids even know the difference.

They can read books and they think they're learning how to scout. Heck, many of the scouts in my day probably didn't even know how to read. In our time many of the guys didn't complete high school because of the Depression and all that. We were on WPA. We got tickets to eat. We had no money. Relief. We had relief and the struggles that went along with living like that. But none of those kind of things have influenced the players today. I was the youngest of all the old-time scouts and they told me about things they had to do. Now I'm seventy-eight and they're all older than me. And the organizations tell them how lucky they are to be working for nothing. Well, that's a crock. Our mind alone, what we know about the game, should be worth something! But they don't even think of that.

Now I'm getting hot under the collar about it. See, I lost all respect for the game. Remember the scouts who signed Joe DiMaggio, Ted Williams and all the stars? Back then you found them, you hid them, you drove them around in your car so the other scouts from the other organizations couldn't get to them and sign them away from you. It was like a bidding war. A competition. And then they came up with the draft. And that's just a farce. It doesn't work the way we were told it was supposed to. I don't think the scouts today get it, and I don't think half of the people in baseball get it. Fans think all scouts do is sit there and watch ballgames. They don't get it. They have no idea of what it takes to play pro ball.

Today these fans don't even know about the minor leagues unless there's a team in their town. And even then they don't consider it professional baseball because it's not a major league team. In my day they had D, B, C, A, Double-A, and Triple-A, all the way up to the big leagues. And then there's open classification, which was the old Pacific Coast League. But they don't have that anymore. Most players in the Coast League didn't even want to go to the majors because they were making more money and everything was better there. The weather, week-long series, the competition was good, lots of former major league players at the twilight of their careers, you know, but they could still play pretty good. The fans supported that league and they knew it was professional baseball, just not the major leagues. Today the players don't want to go back down because they have so much money they don't have to. A lot of things are different today, and not for the better!

Everybody knows me by now and they know I speak my mind and I have no love lost for this game, believe me. I never made any money in this game my whole life. I did it because I loved to play it. I've loved it since 1936, when my mom gave my brother and me a Louisville Slugger bat. The game is in my blood. I love the game, but I hate the business of it.

Cecil Espy

(1935–)

Espy has a different story to tell. He was a part-time scout by choice who never played professional baseball at any level. In fact, he was well on his way to his dream of being a big league umpire when he was asked to scout for the St. Louis Cardinals in 1981. He spent his entire career with that organization and recently retired with twenty-five-plus years of service.

My story is different from the others for a couple reasons. I'm a part-time scout, hired that way and stayed that way by choice. Second, I'm a lot younger and only been scouting twenty-five years, and I never played minor league ball. I tried, but it just didn't happen. I played in high school and San Diego Junior College for awhile, and then went into the military. After I got out of the military the scout who really found me was Kent Parker. He was scouting for the Padres in the local area then. Did I mention San Diego has always been my home?

I also played with a couple of semipro clubs. Earl Wilson, a pitcher, and infielder Deron Johnson played there, too. We were all on the same ballclub. They wound up in the big leagues. I played there for two years and had a real good year and that's when Kent found me. I signed in '64, the last year before the draft came in.

So Kent Parker invited me to spring training with San Diego. At that time Harry Elliott was managing the club. I had a good spring there, but they had to release me because they hadn't made room for Cleveland's players. They had a working agreement with Cleveland at that time. Jimmy Reese was playing there at that time. He was a really nice guy and fought for me to make the team as the first baseman. Jimmy Reese went to Ralph Kiner, the general manager at the time, and said, "Hey, take a look at this kid. Don't release him. This guy can do all right at first base." And they said, "We'll see." That was the answer. Elliott had me catching, but Jimmy wanted me to go to first base. And tied up with this was another kid named Horace Tucker, a very good looking center fielder. So, to make room for Tucker, they released me. Some call it politics. And that's really what it was.

So I came home and said, "The heck with it. Rather than waste my time in the minor leagues for the next ten years, I might as well start some career and go to work." So I started umpiring. I did real well there and learned a lot doing that. I went to an umpire school conducted by the San Diego Baseball Association. That was in 1962.

I would've been a professional umpire. That was my goal when I started umping. I wanted to be a big league umpire. And I was on my way. The only thing that stopped me from becoming a professional umpire was that at the time my wife had a kidney problem and she was very sick and even on the kidney dialysis machine. I needed the medical benefits very badly and at that time the benefits as an umpire were pretty slim. So what I did was explain that I can't go now because my wife is very sick and I won't go without her. Well, I lost her. And I had two small kids and I couldn't go then because the kids were in school and I couldn't leave them. So I stayed as a minor league umpire.

Let me tell you an umpiring story that happened a few years later, after I decided to become a scout. This guy who is umpiring in the big leagues now is one I umpired with when I got started. His name is Kerwin Danley. He's a big black guy in the National League. He came out the same year as Tony Gwynn out of San Diego State. He got drafted out of high school but didn't sign and didn't get drafted out of college. I was staying at Lake Marina and he came to my house out there and asked to talk to me. He said, "I'm thinking about going into umpiring." Well, I looked him straight in the eye and got my serious voice, paused so he could take it all in, and I said, "Is this really what you want to do?"

And he said, "Yeah. I really want to get into it." He was real firm in the way he said it. So I said, "Okay, I'll tell you what. If you want to do it, you're at the right age, you're at the right time, and things are right because they really want some black umpires. You're right on time. So get out there and get going. Now, I'll tell you what. This is my last year because I'm getting into scouting. I'm going to turn all my gear over to you, I'm giving you everything I have to get you started. So, you young buck, you'd better carry the load and you'd better get to the big leagues. I wouldn't be giving it to you if I didn't think you could go all the way up there."

And he got started and moved right up in a hurry. Then he was interviewed on ESPN when he was getting ready to go to the big leagues. He was in the locker room for that. And I'll be darned if there's my shinguards. He was putting them on during the interview! I was so thrilled.

I umpired in the San Diego area that same year at the college level. And I did several college tournaments, all the way from regional to national. I worked a San Diego-Cal State Fullerton game when Jim Beeston was managing the San Diego State team. One of my friends who was a scout, Joe Henderson, approached me. He said, "Hey, man, come here a minute. I got a guy here who needs somebody to help him with his scouting for the Cardinals."

So I stepped out there and he introduced me to him. It was Angel Figueroa with the Cardinals. Angel said, "Hey, man, I need a man to help me scout in this area. I need help bad. Would you be interested in helping me out a little bit? I've got a lot of good reports on you."

I said, "I'll give you my number and if you give me a call we can get together." He called and he hired me as a part-time scout. So we talked and I asked him what he wanted me to do. He told me he wanted me to cover all of San Diego to Oceanside to Pomona back down to Lakeside and the entire area. It was a huge area and it was my area. I said okay and we worked that out. I was still umpiring that year, which gave me an edge because I could see the better pitching.

To make a long story short, they had Bud Black, and I was umpiring behind the plate the game when he set the record with nineteen strikeouts. He still holds that record for San Diego State. By the way, he's a big league manager now.

When I first started scouting, Freddie McAlister was in his first year as scouting director for the Cardinals and he taught me so much about scouting. He watched me, asked questions about why I was doing this or that or not doing this or that, and we talked about all of it. He knew what he was doing and I always respected him because of that.

And then they had another kid there named Mark Williamson. Freddie McAlister was in his first year as scouting director with the team the first year I went with them in '81 and we got into it about this guy here. This is a true story. He ended up with Baltimore. Mark was a right-handed pitcher, about 6'2", about 180. And I'll tell you, the kid had an engineering degree and was smart as a whip. I knew this about him because I'd had him down in Little League when I was coaching. Anyway, I told Freddie, "Listen, Freddie, this kid's got it all. He throws nothing but strikes. He takes command. And his ball is moving all the time. He has the best moving stuff on the ballclub." I kept telling him how much I liked this kid.

Freddie looked at him and said to me, "I hate that SOB! If that's all you're going to show me, I don't wanna see anymore of him. I don't like him." That's what he said to me. I would soon learn that he always said that. Anyway, that was my first meeting with Freddie and my first impression was that this guy doesn't know what he's doing. But what I have found out is that he was testing me. He was a great boss. He tried to always be fair to the scout and to the player he was looking at. And he'd tell you like it is and he'd tell it to your face. He won't tell you one thing then go behind your back and do other things. But after all the fuss he said, "I don't like him, but if you like him, you put him in. I may be wrong and you may be right. You take him. I don't want him."

Cecil Espy never played professional baseball. When he got into scouting, he was a professional umpire, hoping to become a major league umpire. Everyone knew he had a good eye for spotting talented players. In 1979 Angel Figueroa hired him to scout for the St. Louis Cardinals in his home area of San Diego. He chose a part-time rather than a full-time position and remained with the Redbirds for his entire twenty-five-plus-year career. His son, Cecil, enjoyed an eight-year major league career (Rhonda Yarbrough, daughter — Cecil Espy collection).

So I said I'd put him in, and Freddie said, "You do that. Don't show him to me no more." I put him and believe it or not, he didn't get taken. In fact, the truth be told, nobody took him. So I was the only donkey lying there.

But the way he'd played at San Diego State, Jim Dietz, the head coach there for many years, called Jack McKeon, GM of the Padres then, and said, "Jack, I got a great kid here who didn't get taken, so would you have a look at him and give him a job?"

Jack said, "Sure." And they just threw him into the mix there. It was part of the politics of the game, I'll do this favor for you and later you can do one for me.

He played, and boy did he work his way up. And McKeon had him playing for the Las Vegas Stars. I went down there to see him and Larry Bowa was managing the club there. I was scouting the Las Vegas area. So Bowa walked over to me and said, "Hey, you see anything you like down here?"

And I'll never forget this. I told him, "There's a kid here I almost got fired over, but I love the guy."

Bowa says, "Yeah? Who's that?"

And I say, "Mark Williamson." And he can tell by the look on my face that I'm dead serious and really supportive of this player.

Bowa says, "You ain't lying! This guy's something else. I don't understand why they don't like him." That year Williamson had an outstanding season at Las Vegas. Bowa was upset because the big team wouldn't even invite him up to be on the forty-man roster. They never called this kid up.

Bowa was, well, let's say he was agitated about it. He kept saying, "I just can't believe it. He's the best thing I have on this club."

What happened was that in the off-season, the Padres made a trade for Joe Carter. They got rid of Sandy Alomar, Jr., and a player to be named later. Anyway, later that same year, I think it was '84, I was in San Juan, Puerto Rico, when they were playing another Puerto Rican team. I was there to see Alomar and another kid named Boston and Carlos Baerga at third base. So when I came back, I told them Baerga was ready for the big leagues, but I wasn't too sure about third base, but he was ready.

When I was talking to Jack about it, he said they made the trade for Joe Carter and sent three players for him: Baerga, Alomar and Williamson. Oops, I'm wrong here, that wasn't the Williamson deal there. In the Williamson deal they got a little second baseman from Baltimore. Williamson went to spring training and made that ballclub and wound up with thirteen years in the big leagues.

Every time I run into Freddie, I have to ask him if he likes Williamson better now since he played thirteen years in the big leagues. We laugh about it.

Marty Keough was the West Coast scouting supervisor at the time. He had all the minor leagues, the West Coast, Arizona and some other areas. That was Marty. So he brought Freddie down because we were looking at David Wells and Sam Horn that year. We had Andy Hall and Steve Swain that year. We're talking about high first-round drafts that year. And we had another kid by the name of Mark Davis. But he wound up going to Stanford University. We had Tony Gwynn that year, and Bobby Meacham. Bobby was our first-round pick. It was a tough draft because there was a lot of good players out there at that time. But that's what makes it fun, too.

Another time when he came to town we went to a local high school. The coach there had everything all set up for us and ready to go. He was already pitching batting practice. Freddie says, "Who we going to see first?"

Sam Horn hit first, and I said, "He's going to be a high draft." So Horn stepped in and Freddie walked all the way out to center field. He said, "I'm the ball chaser." So Horn hit them to center field and Freddie picked them up and put them in the bucket. Marty was behind the backstop watching Horn take his swings. I was watching all this, and suddenly Freddie started waving at me and wanted me to come out there where he was.

So I put the balls in the bucket and ran out to center field. He says to me, "Sam Horn, I don't know about that big SOB." He always said that. "That big donkey took twenty-five cuts before he hit the ball."

"True," I said, "but look where he hit it. Over the 500 foot mark on that wall and I'll bet it's still flying. Freddie, you're the director and it's your call. But somebody's going to take him."

And Freddie looked up at me and looked right in my eyes, and I'll never forget this, he said he didn't know nothing about me. He's learning me and trying to figure me out. And that's how I got started. He was one of my best teachers, or mentor, I guess they say. He was always tough because he wanted his scouts to think for themselves, and to do that you got to know what to look for in players and how to scout them. He was no-nonsense in a nice but firm way.

Let me stop a minute and tell you what it means being a part-time scout. People who don't know about the scouting life don't realize what part-time scout means. They think we're not real scouts. I work 364 days a year. So I'm working part-time, and I'm working all year round. I don't get paid like part-time for just six months, I get paid all year round on the first and the fifteenth. The part time scout has his own area. I make reports on players that go to the front office. And I have a crosschecker come and look at players I'm high on. The only difference between the part-time and the full-time scouts is that they'll limit my work to a point. See, I don't have to be in the office for the full team reports like the full-time scouts do. They have to do reports on the whole team. I don't have to do that. If I see a player I like, that's the guy I make a report on. Just the ones I like.

And they may call and say, "Hey, go up to here or there to check out this kid and tell me what you think of him." And they expect me to do that soon. Then they may send me off in the complete opposite direction to do the same thing there. This happens all the time.

The full-time scouts are on the road all the time, but I'm not. Of course, having the territory I do helps with that, too. I am still on the road every day, but it's limited to my area so I can get home each night rather than living out of a suitcase like the full-timers do. I have more time with the family and doing other things.

Southern California has so many kids, so many schools, and so many games to see. We move from park to park. In other words, we go to one park and see what we want to see, and then go to the next park. You don't stay there. You're there to scout players and not watch ballgames. There's just too much work to do. I may see two or three games in an afternoon and a couple more at night just looking at this player or that one. So we could get to as many as three parks during a single game. That's true in my area where there's so many games happening all at once with only a few miles in between parks. And when we see the player, we have to make decisions about whether or not the guy can play. And you can tell. You can tell if he's got good instincts, if he's got a good arm action. You can tell if he's got a good approach on the ball and if he has good speed. I'm making it sound pretty easy, but you got to know about how the game is played to know what to look for and how to look for it.

I had three chances to go forward from being a part-time scout. First I had a chance to go with the Giants with George Genovese, who wanted me to work for him. It was about '91. I also had an opportunity to go with the Texas Rangers in 1994, and then I had a chance to go with Cincinnati Reds in 2000. But I like my job with the Cards, and the area they gave me was my home turf. Plus, I liked the vacation time with this job. As a full-time scout, you may only get a two-week vacation and that's it.

I have another story for you. This situation hurt me more than any other because we didn't get this player. I wanted this guy so doggone bad and I'll tell you, I told myself that I'd never get this close to another player as long as I'm scouting again.

There were two brothers. The one I really liked was Brian Giles. I just loved Brian Giles. There was me and another scout named Dennis Haren for the Los Angeles Dodgers. We looked at him more than any scouts in baseball. I must've looked at him two months, seen him at least fifteen times in high school. He went to Granite Eagle High School, and he did nothing but hit, run, throw, and I loved him. So I brought in Keough to look at him. I said, "Keough, I got a man you absolutely have to come and see." And I got the "Okay" from him, but it took him more than a month to get here. And the first thing he said to me was, "Angel Figueroa told me that the kid can't hit the ball up high in the letters because he's too muscle-bound, that it interferes with his bat speed on those high pitches."

I said, "Marty, if he can't hit that ball up high, you ought to fire me, because I'm telling you, he can hit that ball no matter where they pitch it. Just take a good look and you'll see what I mean. Oh yeah, Marty, take a good look. Angel don't work for us no more. He hired me, but he's moved on and is with Pittsburgh now. St. Louis isn't paying Angel to look at the kid. You're paying me to look at him! If you don't think I have no knowledge, then stop paying me and get rid of me. But at least take a look!"

So then he came in and wouldn't you know, Giles had a bad day that day. Everybody has a bad day, but I saw him over and over and over and he was a player! That kid could out-play most guys on any given day and the fans loved him because everything he did was exciting. Marty only saw him once and never came back.

And you know what happened? That kid went in the sixteenth round and he should've gone in no less than the second round. Gary Sullivan of the Cleveland Indians signed him in the sixteenth round for only $10,000. And look what a career he's still having.

And the same thing about his brother, Marcus. Marcus was put in right field, and he didn't run well, didn't throw well, and didn't have as good defensive instincts, but he could flat hit the ball. I got to be friends with his father with all the scouting I did for those two, and I told his father, "If you want him to get in the big leagues, get him out of right field and move him to second base and he may have a chance." Thank goodness somebody agreed with me because it gave him a chance at a big league career.

And Marcus and Brian are still playing this year [2008]. Between the two of them, they made millions and millions of dollars in this game. Of course, there's lots of players that offer a good contrast to that and sometimes the kid who gets nothing and plays hungry works his way into a good career, too.

Let me tell you one more. Now it's 1981 and Tony Gwynn was playing at Long Beach for San Diego State. This goes back to 1981 when Freddie and I were still getting used to each other.

So we were going to Hoover to see Mark Davis, my little cousin. His mother's dad was my mother's brother. So we get there and Freddie says, "Which one is Mark?"

"Here he is. He's standing right next to us."

Well, I never seen Freddie run so fast in my life. He took out his watch and ran over to the first base line and leaned over the fence. Mark stepped up to the plate and hit a rocket, a base hit right up the middle. "He took that wide turn at 4.2 flat!" Freddie said. "Whew! This boy can run! This is my man! Let's go." He hadn't even looked at the rest of his tools.

"Freddie, you haven't even looked at Tony Gwynn yet." So I kidded him, "Freddie, you know you're cheating, and you know you don't wanna pay nothing." I said, "Now look, you can get Mark, but it's going to cost a hundred thousand dollars tax-free. That's what he wants. Are you willing to pay that? If you are, then just go up there and I'll take you up to the house and introduce you to his dad and you can do it." The Cards ended up drafting him in the fifth round.

Then we went over to San Diego State to see them play Cal State Fullerton and he asked me, "Who do you think is the best player on the San Diego State team?"

I said, "Without a doubt, Tony Gwynn." So Angel turned around and said to me, and I'll never forget Angel saying this to me, he said, "Bullshit." And Freddie gave him a long, stern look.

Finally he pointed his finger right in his face and said, "Look, let me tell you something. I was not talking to you. You're sitting in front of us talking to Marty, so you talk to him. When I want your advice, I'll ask you for it." I always respected Freddie for this because he was talking to me, trying to find out what I thought and I told him. Tony Gwynn was the absolute best out there.

So then Freddie says to me, "Why do you think he's the best?" At that time he couldn't throw from left field to third base, but the kid could really hit and he could run the bases. His speed shocked me. And we talked about him a little while, and I told Freddie I thought he was a real hard worker before the games and you could see his determination out there. He wasn't pushing it. I don't mean that, because he was graceful.

I told Freddie, "Because of what he can do with that bat and because of all the work he does on his own time to improve the things he can't do as well as hit."

Now, Bobby Meacham was on that same team and he's the one the Cardinals took first that year. So when the game started, Meacham got a base on balls. Al Newman, who later went with Minnesota, was the number two hitter. Newman struck out. Tony Gwynn came up and hit a rocket right out of the ballpark. The second time up he hit another rocket out of the park that hit a telephone pole. "See, Freddie, that's why I like him. He's my number one man."

So then Freddie began to trust my judgment better.

Then we went to Grossmont High School. There must've been sixty scouts out there that day. They were watching a kid named Steve Swain from Grossmont and a kid from Silicon Valley, a catcher named Andy Hall. So me and Marty and Freddie went there. The whole place was flooded with scouts. He took me over on the third base side, and I'll never forget this, and Marty came over with him. All the rest of the scouts were on the first base side because these two guys were right-handed hitters and he wanted to clock them when they were going from home to first. From the right side we could also see their approach on the ball and all that.

Freddie put me on his left side and Marty on his right, and he said, "Marty, you go on back there with the other scouts, and Espy, you stay here with me." He was checking me to see if I knew what I was doing. In the beginning he did that a lot with all new guys. He wanted to know that if I send him a report from California to his office in St. Louis, he could count on what I said about the player and he wouldn't have to send Marty all the time or fly halfway across the country to check my judgment for himself.

He pulled out a yellow card and turned his shoulder to me where I couldn't see him and he put his card over to the right to block me out. He was grading the player and he kept marking on this card. A few seconds after he was finished, Marty popped right back up next to him. They must've had a sign or something. I didn't think about that right then, but Marty just popped right in there. I was wrong. He wasn't grading that player on the card, he was grading me and my comments about the player. Then he took out two yellow cards. He gave me one and gave Marty one. And he said, "Marty, I want you to grade out five players: Steve Swain, Andy Hall, David Wells, Sam Horn, and Mark Davis." Then he said, "Espy, I want you to do the same."

Okay. I filled mine out and gave it to him. He says to Marty, "Marty, why didn't you give David Wells something on his change?"

Marty says, "I didn't see him throw a change." If you don't see the guy throw a change, you have to give him a three. Anyway, Marty hadn't seen Wells' change, but I'd seen it a lot when he played out in the Pony League with me and my boys. So then he sent Marty back to the other side again and he started talking to me. And of all things, he said, "You know, I gave you a thousand dollar raise, didn't I?" and I said that he did. So Freddie says, "The reason I did that was because I didn't know anything about you. And I like to check my scouts to make sure that when I talk to them or call them and they give me an opinion about a player, I can take his word for it and I won't have to travel cross-country to double check him. Now there's no doubt in my mind." So here's what happened. Steve Swain was the number one draft for the Houston Astros. But when he looked at my card, I had zeroed him. Well, Freddie had zeroed him, too, but I didn't know it, and he asked me about that. He said, "Why'd you zero him out?"

"I'll tell you why Freddie. I watched this kid and I watched this kid. Look, this kid does not wanna play ball. He's just out here to see how far he can get in here. He wanted to play football, and if he's drafted for baseball, he's going to quit and go to football. I'm telling you, Freddie, don't fool with him."

And that's exactly what he did. He played two years. He played two years with Houston, first-round pick, then went to Oregon to play football, got all broke up and tried to come back to baseball but nobody would take him.

I know what Freddie likes and what he doesn't like. When it comes to first, second, third or fourth round picks, he likes power and college players. Freddie knew that meant a million-six right off the bat. But if you look at Freddie's record during his years as scouting director, you'll see that all of his first picks went to the big leagues.

See, the first four or five picks are usually picked solely by the scouting director. Yes, scouts find those guys for the boss to make decisions on, but then guys like me have the jobs of finding players to pick up farther down in the draft order. I remember Joe McDonald always tells his guys to look for a player that may have one tool nobody has seen yet. Like if a guy has a good arm but can't hit, then put him on the mound. If he has a strong arm, then let's see if we can make a pitcher out of him.

You know what? I had Sammy Sosa with the Texas Rangers in 1989 and a kid named Wilson Alvarez. I was in the clubhouse, this was in Double-A ball, he was pitching and they beat him up pretty good that night. So he came back to the clubhouse and he was hanging his head and you could see he was mad at himself for the outing he just had. And I told him, "Man, don't hang your head. You learned some things out there tonight and you need to think about them. Then you'll go out next time and do better and go on to have a good career in the big leagues. I know you're going to be a good big league player."

Then Sammy came to the club two days later, just a kid, not yet twenty years old, and a power hitter. I watched him a few days in batting practice and could see he was going to be a good hitter, but he showed no patience at the plate. He hit the ball out of sight. People who didn't know him or hadn't worked with him called him a skinny kid, but actually he was put together pretty good. He was broad in the chest and had a strong upper body. But his legs were skinny and the jersey was loose so it didn't show.

To make a long story short, Sammy and Wilson were both struggling, so they got sent down and a few days later they were both traded to the White Sox for Harold Baines. I just could not believe it. What a deal. And the next year they both made it to the big leagues. Both of them.

I have to talk to high school coaches all the time. But the thing is, when you talk to a high school coach, most of them don't even know when he has a prospect on his squad. He doesn't pay attention to the kid's potential, he's just looking to win baseball games for his school, and he keeps kids that can produce on the field all the time. I mean, it's just common sense from their point of view. The kids wanna play and coach wants to win. It works.

When scouts talk to college coaches these days, they're going to lie to you. They're not going to tell you the truth because they only want you to take players they can't use anymore. If there's a good player helping his team but he still could come back and play in his senior year or whatever, the coach isn't going to mention him because he can still play there and help his team. I had this happen this year to me. What's worse is that coaches who do that are risking players' careers. I mean, what if a kid gets hurt because he didn't get rested and then when a scout turns in a report, he has to say whatever disability he sees. It's just wrong.

This is how the game works. College coaches get paid to win, not to develop players or help them get scouted and drafted. Look at Coach Hill at the University of San Diego. In his third year there he took that team to the regional tournament and he's going to get that club to the nationals as soon as they get him some players.

Those coaches got to look out for their own jobs so they're only going to tell you what works in their own best interest. If they still need a certain player, they're not going to point him out to a scout. So for a lot of them, I don't even waste my time talking to them. I scout them myself and make my own decisions now.

It used to be that coaches would call scouts and say, "Hey, I got this great kid on my team and you should put him on your draft list." Then he'll give a list of stats or whatever. I don't ever do my scouting over the phone like that. I always want to see the kids for myself. The coach may draw my attention to a kid and I'll go see his team to catch a look, but I make my own decisions. No phone deals. Scouting is a lot like the lotto. Sometimes you win and sometimes you lose. But if you don't take any numbers, there ain't no way you're going to win, right? Well, scouting is just like that. You see players you like and you turn them in. Sometimes you're right and sometimes you're wrong. But you certainly can't win if you don't turn in no numbers.

Every scout knows who the top five pick are. That's easy. But scout for the guys who will be 40, 45, or 52. Find them. That's where the fun's at, and that's where the scouting skill comes in. You got to be able to see something you like in that kid and predict with some accuracy what his actual potential is.

Bird dogs are one thing I don't use, but lots of scouts do. It all depends on the area. I'm only part time in the San Diego area. But full-time scouts have to use bird dogs because their areas are huge and there ain't no way he can see them all. Bird dogs can help them. Now if a scout's smart, he'll train his bird dog a little as to what to look at and what to look for because most of them don't know a prospect when they see one. But they read all the papers and keep track of the guys getting their names in the papers. Then they are supposed to check them in person and get back to the scout.

Since I've been in the game, I've seen some changes that are really no surprise. The salaries are out of control at the big league level. They're spending so much money up there. So in comes the corporate owners with lots and lots of money. They're looking at every way they can to come up with that money. They cut back on front office people. So they let go all the experienced baseball men who have worked their way up to high salaries, and they're bringing in all the college kids. They may know stuff about business, but they don't know nothing about baseball.

Take a look at scouts now, all young college kids who probably never played or even seen minor league baseball. They don't have the background of the game. No more old veterans. Like with the Cardinals. The only veterans now are Freddie, Marty Keough, Marty Maier, who was scouting director for three years after Freddie left, me, and a handful of others. It used to be that all the scouts and front office personnel had a background in the game and we had baseball in our blood, as they used to say.

Eddie Creech came in for one year before going to the Dodgers as scouting director. I did have problems with Mo and Scotty, the young guys. They didn't know what the heck they were doing. Mo knows a lot about PR and computers and stuff, so they found a job for him. They could see there were problems, so Marty Maier came back as director and then they moved Mo to some special assignment job. It's hard for veterans to work for them young guys. That's no secret. How hard is it to see the veterans with all our expertise taking orders from the college kids like that? It's got to be very tough for those who have to do it. I never had to do that yet, but it's coming. We all know it is.

Money is another problem in this game. The problem with the money, well, there's two aspects of it. First is the agents. The players don't know how the system with agents works and they can fall into a lot of trouble if they aren't careful. First, you really don't need an agent out of high school and you really don't need one out of college. All you need to do is see what round you're drafted in.

Now a comment about agents. A lot of people in this game don't like them. I mean a whole lot of them. And it seems there's more agents out there all the time. Scott Boras is the best agent there is. If you can get him, you're going to get money. He's going to get you millions that you shouldn't have got. I'll tell you what. When I turn in the name of a player, the organization always asks if he has an agent. If I say he has an agent, they want to know who it is. If the kid's working with Boras, they often back off and don't even want to draft him because they know they'll have to pay money they wouldn't have to pay if he wasn't their agent.

I had a kid and they asked me who was his agent and when I said Steve Greenberg, they said that was no problem. I have a kid now we drafted in 2002 named Tabor Lee, younger brother of Travis Lee. Tabor was drafted in the third round. So you can just take the third round average to see what that round's worth and then ask for the same thing. He got his brother's agent, Scott Boras, so he'll probably wind up getting a million dollars in the third round because of that agent he has.

No high school guy drafted in the third round is going to get a million dollars, that's for sure. At least that used to be for sure. But now with all the agents stepping in, these kids are asking for that. And some even say they'll settle for $300,000 to sign. Give me a break. What they don't understand is that if a low round kid asks for that kind of money, no organization is going to sign him, so he should either not ask or prepare to go on to college ball. Baseball won't pay that for those lower round picks. Now some teams will do that, like the Yankees or the Mets or Atlanta, but most don't.

Here's how the Yankees do it. They got a kid out of high school in 1980 named Glenn Braggs. He played in the big leagues for awhile. The Yankees took him in the fortieth round and they offered him $40,000. Imagine! He turned them down and went to the University of Hawaii. He played there for four years and never got drafted during those years until he finished his degree. Then Milwaukee took him and he wound up in the big leagues in a couple of years, playing left field for them, and I think he stayed up for seven or eight years.

The Cardinals had a kid named Steve Sails who wanted $25,000 when Freddie was scouting director, and I'll never forget this. Freddie gave him ten. And said it was exactly right for him and he wasn't going to budge. But I waited two days and I called Freddie and asked for more money, maybe eight thousand, so we can sign him for eighteen.

Freddie said, "Offer him a penny and tell him that's our offer, and he'll sign."

You know, Freddie wouldn't give anymore money and we went back and he kept on begging and kept on begging, and we finally signed the kid for $20,000. That's how most ballclubs have to do it. Money is a factor to them.

Now you take the Yankees and George Steinbrenner. I love the guy because he puts pressure on you. If you're doing your job, then you got no problem with him. But if you're not doing your job with George, let me tell you something, you're not going to be there long.

And don't you ever walk into one of his meetings and tell him, "I like this kid but he's a tough sign." Don't ever say that to George. He going to let you know right away, "What do you mean, 'he's tough'?" A scout I know told me about this because it happened to him. George asked him if he liked the guy. When the scout said he did, George told him to go ahead and get his name on that contract, whatever it takes.

"Get out there and sign him!" George yelled. "But you better be right." And that's the way George does it.

The Cardinals don't work that way because they'll tell you right away, "Aw, no-no-no. That player's demands are way out of line. He's out of our market. We can't do anything with that."

Here's another example with the Padres. Reggie Waller was scouting director there and they took Troy Glaus, third baseman for the Angels, in the second round right out of Carlsbad High School. They offered him $250,000 and he turned them down and went to UCLA because he wanted more. They said they couldn't give him more. But if that had been the Yankees, they'd have gotten him at any price. Atlanta wanted him, too. We wanted him, too. But the Padres were down low in the draft that year so they got first pick at him. But they couldn't sign him because they didn't have the money.

Another thing that I've seen is that the Players' Union has become so powerful, too powerful if you ask me, and it's seriously hurting the game. Owners are afraid to not give players the big money today because they have to keep their teams competitive in order to stay in business. But if owners start refusing to pay the money, then they're afraid of collusion charges against them. So they got themselves in this financial mess and they don't know how to get out of it. Look at the ten-year salary they gave Alex Rodriguez at Texas and then with the Yankees. The fans jump all over the players for that, but the players aren't really accountable for things like that. It's the owners. It's a game to some of them to get the guy who's the biggest fish, the best catch, for that year. And some, like Steinbrenner, are willing to do it at any price.

Let's look at it. The fans bash the players over this when it's the owners. Would you or would I say, "No thanks," if they offered one of us a million or two dollars for the same job we're doing? No way! So the guy takes the money and then he's suddenly the greedy athlete, the guy who takes all the bad press and so forth.

A big change in the game now is the fact that everybody knows it's big business. A good example of that is to just take a look at all the Japanese players coming in now. They're getting nothing but big money. And, don't get me wrong, they can play, but they fill seats in the parks everywhere now because more ethnic fans come in to support those players. It's business. Many of them come right from Japan to the big leagues and they're not ready for the big leagues, but just them being there sells more tickets. That's the way the game is now. It's all about money.

Japanese baseball now is becoming just like the Dominican is with dormitories and instruction teams and all that all over the place. But you take a kid like Ichiro with Seattle who hits the ball all over the place, and I'm going to tell you something there, you go back fifteen years and with that style of hitting he never would've gotten a chance to play in the big leagues. Using the Japanese baseball teams like farm teams like they seem to be doing now saves the big leagues a lot of money in player development costs.

Now let's look at it the other way, too. You take American players and put them on Japanese clubs, and we're only allowed to put two of them on one team at a time. They put a limit because they're not going to let American players take over Japan. But the American system doesn't do that. And that along with the other stuff we talked about just goes to demonstrate that baseball is just a big business now. They're making money with the Japanese players now so they're going to go get them.

They could get Dominican players for nothing. They come in by the boatloads, and they don't give them money until they get to the big leagues. But when they do get to the big leagues, they got to pay them good. It's just business. They're using more of the Latin players than ever before because they are so talented, but they don't have to give them signing bonuses and a lot of stuff until they make the big leagues and that saves money.

Puerto Rico and the Dominican and all them foreign countries won't allow but two American players per team in our winter ball season because it's their regular season and it's to showcase their own players for their own fans. I think the Dominican carries four now. But no matter what the number is, it's still not an even thing between them and us in terms of numbers, if you know what I mean.

It's sad because baseball really isn't a sport anymore. It's strictly big business. Fans look at it as a sport, but the people in it look at it as strictly business, especially the owners.

How'd it all come to this? When they put free agency and arbitration in there, well, that's when the game started going backwards. And that's when all this out of control stuff began. Right now if you file for free agency after six years, you can go wherever you want to, to the highest bidder. And that's what the owners are trying to stop now.

See, arbitration goes through the Players' Union. A guy can't settle his contract amount. They go there and they base their season against others and arbitrators have to decide what kind of money the guy's worth. They base it on others who had similar years. They have arbitrators in there on the player's side and on the owner's side. They look at all the stats presented and if the player's season compares with the others, he comes out a winner. The decision from arbitration is binding and all parties agree in advance to accept it. That's what really hurts the owners. It gave the players too much power.

Now they're trying to get it out and it's too locked in. I don't know how they're going to get things straightened out now. They got themselves in a big mess now. I really don't see how they're going to do it because the players keep signing up for free agency and owners keep giving the players all the money. And the owners keep the problem going and making the problems bigger for themselves by passing out the money like that.

The first free agent was Pete Rose, when he left Cincinnati and went to Philadelphia for $800,000, which was a ton of money in the 1970s. A ton of money. That's for veteran free agents. A few years after that happened, the money for amateur free agents went out of control. George Steinbrenner started giving the million dollar contracts to them. He messed up all the college drafts and all the high school drafts. 'Cause once you start giving out money like that, there's no turning back.

And since they put in the DH rule, veteran free agents are really cleaning up. This rule put five extra years on their careers. That's another thing that's got baseball where it's at today. Players in the American League wouldn't give that up for nothing and they want to lock it in. The National League won't put it in because it costs too much and that's money they can save for other things. They don't wanna keep these guys when they're thirty-five to thirty-nine years old because they want to move on and get a younger player and save the money. But the American League wants that in there and now it's going to be hard to get it out. And now it's the best of all worlds for those players who get those contracts. They don't have to work too hard except for concentrating on their timing and keeping their legs in shape by riding those bikes. But their chance of injury is less. They do work hard and a lot of them go back and look at the film to see what they did wrong. So by doing all of that, he's earning that money. It's not a gift to him by any means.

In 1980, the year when my son signed, the number one draft in the country was Darryl Strawberry and all he got was $160,000. That's all he got. Jerry Harris was number two in the nation, signed by the Toronto Blue Jays, and you know what they gave him? Sixty thousand dollars. Then you look at 2002 and the highest pick in the nation gets ten million dollars to sign. I don't care who the kid's agent is, today the first pick in the nation is at least a ten million draft right there. So the result of it all is that I and other scouts hate to draft high school kids in the first ten rounds because they all want a bunch of money and they haven't proven themselves yet. Example. I drafted a high school player in the fifth round in 1980 named Reggie Harper. Me and Marty Keough gave him $55,000 for the fifth round. He's a good kid. He played three years with us and then quit. He could run just like Bake McBride. I mean really run. And he was swinging the bat very well for us. We were all surprised that he quit.

It's hard for us who have been in the game a long time to see things going in the direction they are. A lot of scouts are worried about the game's future. I hope they'll find some way out of the mess they've made. They always have in the past.

Bob Harrison
(1918–)

Harrison prides himself on the fact that he's one of the most senior scouts attending games. Night after night he can be found at Dodger Stadium or Angels Stadium, where he still works as a major league scout for the Seattle Mariners. He turns in more than 250 reports on players every year. He's an exception to the scouts' own rule that being a former player at any level in pro ball is a requisite for their job. In fact, he never pursued a pro baseball career. Instead he coached youth baseball and amateur teams in Long Beach, California, for several years and managed to take some of them to world championships.

In 1961 the expansion California Angels asked him to run their winter baseball program. When they offered him a full-time scouting job, he refused because he didn't want to leave his young family, but agreed to work as a part-time scout and keep his day job at the Naval Shipyard. In 1967 he became a full-time scout with the St. Louis Cardinals, where he stayed for ten years before being asked to join the Seattle Mariners at their inception.

He is credited with signing almost thirty players who made it to the major leagues, including Ed Crosby, Garry Templeton, Dave Henderson, Bob Stoddard, Jamie Allen, Bud Black, Al Chambers, Carlos Diaz, Darnell Coles, John Moses, Paul Serna, Ed Vande Berg, Matt Young, Mark Langston, Mike Moore, Rickey Nelson, Alvin Davis, Dave Hengel, Calvin Jones, Jim Bowie, and the pride of his "collection," Ken Griffey, Jr. His stories about some of these signs offer keen insight about how scouts do their jobs. Another source of pride for him is that his son R.J., also a baseball man, is the scouting director for the Tampa Bay Rays. In 2003 Bob Harrison was the recipient of the Scout of the Year Award, West Coast. He took his son and grandson to the presentation. The following day the threesome made their first trip to the Baseball Hall of Fame in Cooperstown. He mentioned that he was sorry they didn't have any recognition of baseball scouts there.

First of all, I didn't sign a professional baseball contract when I got out of school in 1938. I played baseball all the time. I was on every team. I played always. It was my love. But I never had any idea I was ever going to be good enough to be a major league player. I knew I was a good player because I was a good athlete and I played all sports. But I wanted to also learn a trade and learn to work. I wasn't going to go to college, I wasn't that type of a guy. I had an offer from Maco Construction Company to give me a job to start learning a trade if I would come and play baseball for them on their weekend team, which was semipro ball. I took that instead of going over to the tryout camps to start playing minor league ball. In those days, nobody offered you anything. It was just a chance to play.

So I did that and worked at that for a few years until I had to go into the service in World War II. I went into the navy for two years. But before I went in, I married my sweetheart. We were both very young, she was eighteen and I was nineteen or something like that. She was pregnant when I left to go into the service, and when I got out at the end of the war was the first time I saw my son, Frank, and he was almost two years old. I wanted to go to work because I'd learned a trade and I was a welder. I went to work at the naval shipyard.

While I was doing that I went to minor league games and still couldn't get the baseball out of my system, and so I started coaching youth baseball in Long Beach. I coached a team of thirteen- and fourteen-year-olds in 1959 that won a world championship. During that same period I also coached American Legion teams. I became very active in the youth program there. I continued to coach in that, and in 1965 I coached another team that won a world championship. Off of that team we had players who eventually went on into professional baseball: Jeff Burroughs, Craig Swan, and others.

In 1961, the Angels got a major league franchise and the scouts who first started in the organization came around to me and asked me if I'd run a winter program for young players and help them scout. I told them, "I can't quit my job. I'm now a supervisor at the Naval Shipyard. But I will work for you on the weekends." And that's the way I started my scouting career. I was a part-time scout with the Angels in 1961.

I'd been with the Angels through 1965 and the Cardinals offered me a little better job. In 1967, when I was an area scout here, they let me take the summer to coach a Connie Mack team because the city was begging me to come back to the youth program and help them. I took them to a world championship in 1967. That was the same year the Cardinals won the world championship and I'm wearing a World Series ring. After three world championship teams around here, I really didn't have the time to devote to that anymore and I just focused all my time to scouting and working in the area and running the Professional Scout Program in the Scout League.

That's how I got started scouting. Let's see, that was forty-eight years ago. I spent the first five years with the Angels as a part-time scout and kept my other job until the kids got up to where I could afford to work full-time in baseball. Even though I had a job where I could take off every afternoon and see all the amateur games and so forth, I couldn't leave town at that time. So in 1967 I went to work as a full-time scout with the Cardinals for ten years. Then when the Seattle Mariners got a franchise, they came to me and offered me a good contract for those times. They gave me a chance to put a club together in Seattle and be the western state supervisor. I stayed with the Mariners for fifteen years and worked my way to the top. I had charge of all the Latin American countries. It was quite a responsibility, much more of a job than people may think, and a wonderful challenge.

A point of pride is that I signed twenty-some guys that played in the big leagues and I had five different players that were voted to the American League Rookie All-Star Team over the years. In 1982 was the first one, Ed Vande Berg, who I signed as a college senior and he went to the big leagues in a hurry. In 1983, a college senior left-handed pitcher out of UCLA, Matt Young. In 1984, I signed Mark Langston, another left-handed pitcher I signed out of college. In that same year Alvin Davis, a first baseman, a college senior out of Arizona State who I'd been close to since he was in high school but he never would sign. He went on to college, and after he got his degree, he was drafted and I signed him. In 1974 a kid out of this area that I signed with the Cardinals went on to become the National League Rookie of the Year, Garry Templeton, who played about fifteen years in the major leagues. So I had a pretty good stretch of players that won awards.

Kiddingly, I always said when I'd leave the house after I signed the kids, "Well, go out and do a good job and make me a good scout." After all, a scout is only as good as the players he's signed. I was fortunate to have a lot of them.

When I was with the Mariners and we started the first year, it was before they had a team. They hired five or six of us

Bob Harrison is one of the veteran scouts who never played professional baseball. Turning ninety in 2008, he can still be found at most home games of the Angels and the Dodgers where he's still a major league scout for the Seattle Mariners, the team he's been with since its inception. He received the Baseball Scout of the Year, West Coast, award in 2003 (Bob Harrison collection).

to scout the other clubs for the rest of the summer. That was in 1976. The Cardinals wouldn't release me until the June draft that year. So after that I worked until the rest of the baseball season was over, looking at all organizations while looking for players for the expansion draft along with the other guys. Then in December or whenever it was, we went to New York and we had the expansion draft. I think the first pick we took was a player our GM, Lou Gorman, was more familiar with because he'd drafted him in the first round with Kansas City—Ruppert Jones. I think the player that I'm most proud that we picked up was probably our last choice in the draft, a player named Julio Cruz. He was with the Angels organization then, a kid playing in A ball. I told Lou, "Instead of using this pick on an old veteran, why don't we take a chance on a kid that I like? He's a kid I'd seen a lot in the Scout League and he can run and hit and is a second baseman. I think he's going to be quite a major league player." So we picked him and he played for the Mariners for quite a long time and won quite a few honors.

But as far as that goes, golly, there's so many stories of players, you know. And I'm really so proud of not only the first-round picks and the high round picks that I've signed, because they're expected to make it to the major leagues, but the ones that were lower, that were college seniors that you just take a chance on because you like what you see.

One of those was Bud Black, who is now the manager of the San Diego Padres. He was a college senior, a left-hand pitcher out of San Diego State, and I took him down low. He went on to pitch and win 150 games in the big leagues, pitched there for about fifteen years. Here was a guy you see something in and nobody else was really that interested, you know, and we took the chance on him.

And Ed Vande Berg was the same way. He was a kid that didn't even get to pitch much in college, but I'd seen him in summer ball and I'd seen him around and took a chance on him. He pitched nine years in the big leagues. Those are guys who got very little bonus, if any, and went on to have success in the major leagues. All of us love to remember the guys like that and the details of their signing. It's like remembering a job well done, if you know what I mean.

Even though I've had so many good players that's played in the major leagues, when I went in and made the deals and closed the signings after scouting Ken Griffey, Jr., that's an experience I'll always remember. When we had our meetings up here in Seattle, the scouting director was Roger Jongewaard. He'd been with us awhile. I'd brought him in there and recommended him for scouting director's job and he got it, and during the course of that year, our owner was a self-made billionaire. He was a guy who always invited me to breakfast at his country club. Even one time when we were flying in his private jet from Seattle, he encouraged me to be his general manager, a job I didn't want. So he came to me that year, and he said, "Bob, I understand you guys are going to take a high school kid up high. Why don't you take a college kid?" See, he didn't have a lot of patience and he wanted us to take somebody who could get there faster and all that. He said, "You have to convince Roger to take so and so."

And I said, "George, Roger's the scouting director. Now, when we make that selection, the rest of us are going to take the one that we think is the best. And we're not going to take a college guy if we don't think he's better than the others."

We had a pitcher out of Cal State Fullerton by the name of Mike Harkey, who went as the sixth pick in the first round with the Cubs. Well, he'd read so much about him because of the local school and he's from the Newport Beach area, and I told him that Harkey was on our list but there are some high school kids. We scouted Ken Griffey a lot. We had a first-year scout that year that we were breaking in who was in the area and I spent a lot of time with him. His name was Tom Mooney. We looked at Griffey and I really liked what I saw. I mean, I thought he was one of the best-looking high school players I'd seen and everything he did came so easy. It wasn't because his father was a major leaguer. It was the fact that he was a good player. When I talked to his coach in Cincinnati, he told me that of all the good players he's had come out of there, Ken Griffey, Jr., was the best he'd ever had. I had to agree with him. And he's had some good kids come out of there.

So when we went back to Seattle to put the draft together, we had Harkey up on the board along with Griffey, and I told Roger, "When George comes in this room, he's going to look on that board and if we have Harkey right up there with Junior, he's going to give us a bad time." So I said, "I want to change my grade and I want to grade Griffey higher than Harkey, when they're even at the time. Because he's going to question me because I've been here the longest."

And so when he came in, sure enough, that's exactly what he did. He walked around the draft room where we were preparing our lists and all that, and he asked, "Well, who are you going to take?"

"Well, we're going to take Griffey," I said.

He said, "You're going to take a high school kid? What about the college kid?"

"Well," I said, "we like Griffey best, but we're going to have to work out a deal and try to sign him. And if we can't sign him, then we'll go talk to Harkey."

He didn't like that too well, and he said, "All right, I'm going to tell you, you all agree that you want to take this kid. You better be right. I'm just telling you that." And he left the room.

This was a day or two before the draft and I told him, "Okay, I'll catch a flight to Cincinnati." And I did that.

And I called the kid back there, the area guy, to arrange a meeting so we could talk with Griffey. So I flew in there and they had a hotel room rented at the Clarion Hotel in Cincinnati, and he brought the boy and his mother over there. After his father finished his game in Atlanta, we flew him in and we sat in that room and I started talking to them about it. And I told them that we want to take him, that he'd be the first kid in the nation taken in this draft. I knew what an honor that would be for his father. Even though there was an attorney involved, and I'd met the attorney who had represented his dad and who was a good guy, his dad was doing the negotiating. I sat in that room and we talked and his dad said, "Now here's what we want. We want this and we want that, and we want that."

I told him we couldn't do that. I said, "Some of the things you're asking for are not legal. We can't do that. We can't do that. But here's what we have." At that time what we had was $150,000. Today they're getting four, five, six million. Anyway, it was a good bonus. And it's now about two o'clock in the morning and his dad says, "Well, as a family we have to go sit down and think about this."

I said, "Well, Ken, I have to know because if we can't sign your son, then I have to go on. I have another appointment tomorrow and we want a commitment prior to the draft." You can't do that now because the agents won't allow the kids to do that.

So Ken said, "I'll go home and we'll talk about it and I'll call you back." So we sat up until about three or four o'clock in the morning and the phone rings. He said, "Bob, if you could come up a little bit, we would talk about it." In the meantime, I'd called back to Seattle and talked to Chuck Armstrong, our president, and said, "Can we come up a little bit more?"

He said, "You can go another ten thousand if you want."

So I told the dad I had made the call and had permission to give him another ten thousand, which brought it up to a hundred-sixty thousand. And I looked at the kid and said, "We'll make you the number one pick in the nation." The kid was just seventeen years old and totally in awe. So the dad says, "Okay, Bob, we'll take it."

And I said, "Well, you know, Ken, I really don't like to do this. I once had a negotiation with a kid I had drafted and we agreed on things that night and I was coming back the next day and the writer was going to be there and the photographer to take pictures for the newspaper. And when I got over there, they'd changed their minds." That was when I signed Garry Templeton. And I said, "It took me another week to get that thing straightened out."

And he said, "No, Bob, you've got my word."

So I said, "That's good enough for me."

I'd been to the house another time when I went to meet the family and all that. The next morning we had breakfast with them, got the contracts all signed and made out, got on the flight and returned to Seattle. And the next day in the draft, we took him number one. As it turned out, the best part of the story is that Ken Griffey, Jr., turned out to be exactly what I thought he would be. You never say in your own mind that this is a guy who has a chance to be a Hall of Famer. But we say in our report that he has a chance to be an all-star. As it turns out, Junior's going to be elected to the Hall of Fame on the first vote, I just know it. It makes a scout proud. He did it himself, but his scout had a lot to do with his career because we monitored him as he went along, and you stay close to him until he no longer needs that.

There's been so many I've had that kind of experience with that I've been able to get signed prior to the draft, guys like Mike Moore, Spike Owen, different ones that were number one picks. I'd come back with the contracts and they'd announce it the next day. In fact, with Mike Moore, when he was our number one pick, a pitcher out of Oral Roberts that year, I got him to agree and I flew him and his family into Seattle while the game was going on that night. I left the game so the writers who wondered who we were going to take the next day wouldn't know. And I drove to the airport and picked up Mike, his mother and his girlfriend who came along and took them to the hotel room that night and signed him the next day. Those are the fun type things that you look back at. There were a lot of good experiences like that with the younger players.

Darnell Coles, as I said in an article one time, and Garry Templeton were probably the two best athletes I ever signed. They were football players. Darnell Coles was out of Southern California and was voted one of the top athletes to come out of that school. Ronnie Lott came out of there. Darnell had a scholarship for football and he had an agent representing him, and when I got him in the draft, I went down and had a meeting with his agent, who was operating out of Palm Springs, and he didn't let me talk to Darnell. They don't like us to talk to the kids for fear we'll influence them and they don't want the kids to say something like they're excited about signing or something to lead you to believe they're going to sign. The agent wants you to know that it's going to be hard to sign him unless you meet the price.

Well, I went down there and I met with them in Palm Springs and I came out of there feeling pretty good, except that he had asked for things that couldn't be done. He wanted money deferred. He wanted an assurance that he'd play at a certain level at a certain time and a certain salary.

And I said, "You can't do that stuff, unless you sign a major league contract. We're not signing a major league contract." We worked on that for awhile, and then I had another meeting with them down here in Southern California. I met with Darnell and his mother at that time; he didn't have a father. The agent was there and we got an agreement. Darnell's picture is up on the wall in my office here. I have pictures of twenty or so of my players that have gone to the major leagues framed on the wall in my office. Darnell always looked to me as almost like a father to him because I had to stay with him and kind of calm him down and different things throughout his career. I was so sorry when he was traded to Detroit. It really hurt me. He's the kind of player that is an asset to any team and when you get close to them you hate to see them leave.

This story's real interesting. I thought I knew Garry Templeton very well when I signed him because I'd watched him from the time he was in the ninth grade and I was an area scout. By the time he was in high school and playing all the time, he was running track and he was playing football and he was an All-American high school type guy. He had college scholarship offers from all over. His dad was always at the games. I thought I knew him very well because I'd been around him so long. I knew he'd gotten in trouble in school and the police had come in there one time. I went and talked to the principal and I found out it was just an argument between the blacks and the browns and the teacher got hit in the scuffle or whatever. I knew one time he got suspended from the baseball team. I found out that was for smoking a cigarette. I knew he wasn't involved in drugs and didn't have a police record. I thought I knew all about him. I knew he was basically a good kid who had some real baseball tools and I wanted to give him the opportunity to play.

And so when I made the appointment and went to his house, they wanted to bring the baseball coach as a kind of advisor. I told them to go ahead and do that because the baseball coach at the high school was a friend. When I go there, the first person to greet me was a big guy and he said, "I'm so-and-so and I'm representing the boy. I'm the agent."

So now when I got in there, the dad, the kid, and the agent were standing there and the mother was back in the kitchen. And I said, "I thought you said the coach was coming over and you weren't going to have someone representing you." He more or less tried to stare me down to show me he meant business, I guess. I waited for somebody to say something and we sat there thirty seconds or so and finally the agent stood up and said to me that he was responsible for that. And when the coach got there and found out there was somebody there, he said, "Well, you won't need me then," and he started to leave the house.

So I said, "No, no, I don't want you to leave."

And that's when this agent started in on me. He said, "You're not going to take advantage of a poor black kid. You're not going to do this and that."

And I said, "Now, wait a minute. I'm not here to take advantage of anybody. I'm here to talk to him about signing a professional baseball contract with the St. Louis Cardinals. That's why we drafted him."

The agent started demanding a lot of things. So the family finally called time out and said they wanted to go in the back room and talk. The agent and I were left sitting there in the front room just kind of looking at each other. So when the family came back out, they told the agent they did want him to leave. So he left. At that point I made an offer of forty thousand, which was a fair price for a first-round pick then. The dad didn't say anything, but Garry says, "Well, Mr. Harrison, I'm going to need more money than that. I'm going to sign. I'm not going to college. But I'd thought about fifty thousand." So we know better than to offer top dollar to the player right off the bat because we know they're going to negotiate and they're going to want more.

He says, "You know why I need the money? I got a little baby to support."

"You have a baby? Where's the baby?" I'd seen some people and stuff kind of peeking around the door and there was a lady with a little baby in her arms.

And he says, "That's my baby." I knew right then I was going to get the ten thousand. So I asked him, "Are you going to get married?" He said he was not going to get married, but that was his baby and he wanted to support it. So we talked a little bit longer and I could tell how sincere he was, it wasn't just an excuse to get more money. So we got the fifty thousand for him and got to the airport for his airline tickets and took him with his mom and dad to the airport, had dinner along the way, and he got on the plane and off to a nice career.

We were always taught to look out for our players every year, in the off-season when they got home and during the season when possible to make sure they take care of themselves and eat right and get enough rest and the like. That's the way I was brought up as a scout.

Dave Henderson was our first pick in 1977. When we took him in the draft, we were twenty-sixth that year, we were the expansion teams, Toronto and us. Henderson came out of a small community out of the Fresno area. It was a farming community. He was another good athlete. He played football and he had scholarships to go play football. I got to liking him a lot, and at the time it was Mel Didier's first year there as our scouting director. I took Mel in there and Mel liked him. He liked football players anyhow because he liked that mentality.

When it came time for the draft, I was in Seattle. We called his name off that we took Henderson, twenty-sixth in the first round, and Mel's wife drove me immediately to the Seattle airport because I was going to fly into Fresno to go in and start negotiating with him. When I got there, he was on the all-star team and they were having a workout that night. I went over in there and talked to the coach, who invited me to a pool party they were having afterward for the kids so I could see Dave. The coach was going to represent him, a guy by the name of Frank Ball. They were looking for fifty thousand or seventy-five thousand, which was unheard of, and I said, "They sent me in with thirty thousand."

But I stayed out there talking with the coach about trying to get more to make him a fair offer. I drove around Fresno and found a hotel for the night and they were having an all-star game the next day. I asked a secretary at the hotel if she'd type out the contract for me because I didn't have any of that with me, and she did. I went to the game, and after he'd graduated, I went to his house and signed him for fifty thousand. Dave was great. He went on to an outstanding career. After that I made him my part-time scout in that area and he worked for me for several years.

Baseball today is not the same. First of all, the quality of play at the major league level has really weakened. But that's due to expansion and everything. And the next thing I see that would take the interest away from me if I were an area scout now, I wouldn't be able to enjoy the privileges of meeting families and signing their children. Because nowadays if the kid is drafted very high, it's all done with agents. You don't get close. Prior to the draft before you take anybody, you have to get to know as much as you possibly can about a boy. You need to go in the house. You need to get close to the family. They all are going to say they want to sign, but you have to get a feeling for the mother and the father. You have to feel who's the most dominant between the two of them. Does the boy sound like he's ready? Does he feel right about what's ahead for him if he signs?

You have to have a good idea because you don't want any surprises, like after you take them and all of a sudden they don't want to talk to you. You have to go through the agent. What's changed the whole thing is money. There's so much money involved now in signing bonuses. It used to be that when I'd go out to look at a guy, take Mark Langston, for instance. He turned out to be a great pitcher. Nobody in our organization saw him but me. I just said, "Take Mark Langston on this round. He's one of my guys."

The old-time scouts, Joe Stephenson and I'm sure George Genovese, two of the older guys who were so successful, well, it used to be that when the Red Sox had somebody, they'd just call the scout and say, "What round do you want me to take him in?" And they respected the scout enough that they'd take him based on what he said. It was hard for me to accept later on that they had to have more opinions. But that was because we don't sign them for a few hundred thousand dollars anymore. Now we sign them for millions. And there's so much money involved that it's taken the enjoyment away from the scout being a big part of the signing. I enjoyed it so much. But you can't do that anymore. That would take the fun out of the amateur scouting for me.

The thing is, today we have so many more scouts, which is good, because they want more opinions. Like I'm doing major league work, and before they do anything, they look for several opinions about a player. Not just your opinion. I used to ask, "Why do they need another scout to look at a guy after I give them my opinion? Because I felt that my opinion was all they would need. Now some scouting directors want so many opinions, I would be totally confused if I were making the selection. See, I wouldn't want so many opinions. I'd maybe ask my top guy and one other and we'd look at it and make a decision. It's tough now.

The thing that's changed the whole thing is the money, the big signing bonuses. The biggest gamble in the draft I've always contended, and I think everybody would agree, is the high school pitcher. Because he's the one who's apt to get hurt. And when you take a high school pitcher in the first round and you give him three or four million dollars, you're taking a really big chance. It used to be back in the days when I was working with the families, in those days a first-round pick was getting thirty or forty thousand dollars on average, and I'd go in there and say, "Golly, I wish I had forty or fifty thousand dollars in the bank." Especially when I was eighteen years old.

But the whole risk is on the ballclub. The owners, what they're doing is competing against themselves on free agents. So they take guys and give them these contracts, like the Dodgers right now. They got Andruw Jones, who hasn't played, and they signed him for eighteen million dollars. It's all about the money they put into guys and it's all at the risk of the ballclub.

The big power agent, Scott Boras, and I know him very well, and Scott and I have negotiated some contracts. At one time Scott and my son RJ were teammates, so we go back a long way. I ran into Scott the other night at Angels Stadium. He's either there or at Dodgers Stadium with one of his guys, or he has players on one of the clubs that's coming in to play. I'm not involved in the free agent draft anymore. Bobby Fontaine is the scouting director and he does a great job, and he talks me into looking at some players for him before I go to spring training. Bobby tells me not to run all over the country looking at players anymore. I just scout the major leagues and stay home.

I've never missed a paycheck from 1961 till now and baseball has been very good to me. I suppose it's because I've been a good worker and have been pretty successful. I am respected by other scouts and general managers and they've kept me around. Although I hate spending time on the computer, I still put in over 250 reports or so of evaluation every year. That part of it I get tired of, but anyhow I'm still enjoying going to the park. We're having a lot of changes in Seattle, Bill Bavasi was let go and I guess they're having trouble deciding who will be the new general manager, and they fired the manager, Jim Riggleman, a great guy. So I'm going to wait and see how all of this shakes out before I decide if I'll say with it for next year.

If a new guy comes in who wants me to work and if they can work under my conditions, then we'll wait and see. I may retire, and how many jobs do you know about where you can work until you're looking at ninety or even older and remain productive? I've been pretty lucky. I know it's a two-way street. I've worked hard for baseball, which I've always loved, and the game has been very good to me for many years.

George Digby

(1917–)

Digby didn't play in the major leagues, although he was quite good at LSU until a back injury from wrestling ended all his athletic endeavors. After graduation he taught at Holy Cross High School in New Orleans and coached three championship baseball teams before the Red Sox recruited him as a scout. He covered the southern United States from 1944 through 1994, followed by ten years as a scouting consultant until he retired from the game in 2004. He spent his entire sixty-year career with the Boston Red Sox.

Some of the many players he signed include Milt Bolling, Bobby Killman, Bob Montgomery, Haywood Sullivan and his son Marc Sullivan, Reid Nichols, Jody Reed, Faye Throneberry, and future Hall of Famer Wade Boggs. To Digby, scouting was more than a job. It was his mission as a member of the baseball community.

In 1949, Digby saw eighteen-year-old Willie Mays play with the Birmingham Black Barons, and raved about him to Red Sox owner Tom Yawkey, saying that he was the greatest baseball talent he'd ever seen. Digby had done some checking and felt the Red Sox could sign him for five thousand dollars. He told Yawkey, and Larry Woodall was dispatched to evaluate Mays. Although it rained the entire time he was there and he never saw Mays play, Woodall turned in a report on him anyway, saying Willie Mays was not a Red Sox type of player. With that the organization passed. Today this is seen as a reflection of the racial posture of the organization that was the last in Major League Baseball to hire a Negro player.

Throughout his career George Digby was praised for his work ethic and commitment to his search for new talent. He was equally dedicated to mentoring new scouts coming along, including Mel Didier, who has the highest praise for him. He wrote a small book for the All Star Sports Books series called Baseball for Boys: Big League Tips from a Big League Baseball Scout.

He was one of the founders of the prestigious Florida Diamond Club in 1972 along with fellow scouts Birdie Tebbetts, Walt Widmeyer, Dale Jones and George Zuraw. It exists to promote amateur baseball in Florida and provides a showcase for these players in an annual weekend baseball series attended by scouts, coaches and others from the professional ranks. He lives in Nashville, and at age ninety-one and in frail health, he still keeps a close eye on the game he loves.

In his honor the Boston Red Sox established the George Digby Award for excellence in scouting. He received the Scout of the Year Award, East Coast, in 1985. And he was inducted into the Boston Red Sox Hall of Fame in November 2008.

I fell in love with the game at age eight when I was in New Orleans, Louisiana, picking up bats for Babe Ruth. And I just stuck right with it, first as a player and then I became a scout when I was twenty-six years old.

Here's how that came about. I played on three city and state championship teams in high school and I was supposed to be the best prospect. In fact, we had some big leaguers come from that high school team, Jesuit High School. Rusty Staub and Will Clark were among them. From there my dad wanted me to go to LSU because I had a full scholarship for basketball and baseball. I went and my first year there I injured my back on the wrestling mat. So when I did go to sign a contract to play baseball, nobody wanted me.

But I loved the game, so I went into coaching high school baseball. I coached three championship teams at Holy Cross. I had a ballplayer there that the Detroit Tigers wanted me to bring up to Detroit. This was 1944. So I took him up there and they were going to try to sign him. But the Red Sox happened to be in town and asked me if I'd arrange for them to see the boy pitch. They finally signed the kid and asked me if I'd be interested in going to work for them. I could do that and make twice as much money as I did as a high school coach. When I was twenty-six I began scouting in New Orleans. My territory consisted of six states. I was the first scout the Red Sox hired in the South. There weren't many scouts back in those days, 1944, during the war. Things were rationed and I couldn't get enough gasoline for my car so I had five different train routes that I used to get around my territory. It was a lot of travel and schedule organizing, but as I think back, I remember those times as the good old days.

Red Sox scout George Digby (R) and Gary Randall of the Major League Scouting Bureau discuss college players at Middle Tennessee State University in Murfreesboro, Tennessee, in the spring of 1996 in preparation for the June 4 draft. That year the Red Sox drafted 45 players, led by high school RHP Josh Garrett taken as their number one pick; they took no players from MTSU (George and Helen Digby collection).

BOSTON Red Sox

FENWAY PARK • BOSTON, MASSACHUSETTS 02215

(617) 267-9440

Dear

    Welcome to the Boston Red Sox. We are happy that you have chosen our organization to begin your career.

    Being new to professional baseball we have some information that will assist you as you are preparing to join one of our minor league clubs.

    First of all, we will provide you with transportation to your assigned club. Any reasonable expenses such as meals, limousine or cab fare to and from the airport will be reimbursed to you so please keep all receipts and turn them into the business manager.

    The ball club will have a reservation for you when you arrive at a nearby motel or hotel and they will pay for your first nights lodging. After that you are on your own expense. Many of the players who have living accommodations will help you find a place as soon as possible. Usually only one night at a motel or hotel is necessary.

    It is very important to know what equipment to bring with you. The following is a list of equipment you should have with you:

(1) Two pairs of spikes
(2) Two gloves (if possible)
(3) Two athletic supporters with cup jock
(4) Two or three sweatshirts
(5) One heavy jacket or windbreaker (especially if you are a pitcher)
(6) A traveling bag to carry all this equipment and that can be used on road trips.

    Concerning the equipment the ball club provides, they only supply you with sanitary socks, belts, and uniform which includes outside socks and cap.

    It's very important to bring a reasonable amount of clothes which should include at least a sportcoat or suit in case you have to attend a function representing the club. Remember you are now a professional and you should dress and act like one. Wherever you go you represent your club and the Boston Red Sox organization and baseball fans are aware of this.

    Last but not least, make sure you have enough money with you until you are paid by the club. You will be paid on the 1st and 15th of the month. When you arrive get in touch with your manager or coach or someone affiliated with the club to let them know you have arrived.

    Good luck and have a good season.

Sincerely

Edward M. Kasko, Director
Player Procurement

This is the letter George Digby and the Boston Red Sox sent to all newly signed players, including the fifty-plus he signed who made it to the major leagues. Some of them include Milt Bolling, Faye Throneberry, Mike Greenwell, Jody Reed, Dalton Jones, and future Hall of Famer Wade Boggs (George and Helen Digby collection).

It was a great experience for me. I scouted Charley Trippi during that time. We became great friends. He was an all-star football player and told me that if he signed to play baseball, he'd leave at the end of the season because football was his game. So I wrote a report on him just like I knew what was going on, and it worked out just as he said.

Things were a lot different before the draft. It was always fun to work with young players wanting to get into this game at the professional level and talking with their families and all that. It was fun competing with scouts from other organizations to find players out there that they may have missed. The whole thing was fun. I guess over the years I've sent about fifty players to the big leagues. Of course, that number includes everyone who ever played up there even if it's a pitcher who only pitched one game and so forth.

One of my first fellows to get to the big leagues was Milt Bolling, a kid I signed out of high school in 1948. He was only seventeen at the time. After his playing career he later became a scout for twenty-five years or so before he retired. In fact, he scouted some of my old territory in Alabama and the South.

The first time I saw him he was a skinny kid, tall, six-foot-two, playing shortstop. He was playing against Haywood Sullivan, a catcher, when Dothan, Alabama, played Mobile, Alabama, for the state championship in American Legion baseball. They were both under the age of nineteen according to the American Legion rules at the time, and they were both coming into their senior year in high school. Back in those days we did it differently. I signed him right out of high school and put him on a train to Roanoke, Virginia. And I said to the fella managing there, Mike Higgins, "Mike, this kid's train'll get in at 8:15 tonight and I want you to let the coach handle the night game tonight so you can meet him at the station. He's only seventeen and he's going to be a big league player."

Well, he got off to a terrible start, hitting only about a buck-fifty. I was writing him letters, telling him not to worry about that or even going down. And I looked in the record book and noticed that Enos Slaughter, the Hall of Famer, hit the same thing his first year and only .180 the second year.

Bolling had to go back to the same team for a second year and he wasn't hitting too good then, either. But he finally got up over .200. He played his first season in Boston in 1952, and probably would have been Rookie of the Year but he broke his ankle sliding into second base about two weeks before the season ended. It was a shame. The team was playing in old Comiskey Park. Bolling had hit a double, and as he slid into second base, his spikes caught and he broke his ankle. Harvey Kuenn beat him out for Rookie of the Year.

But Milt Bolling ended up playing shortstop for the Red Sox for many years. He played right next to the Hall of Famer, George Kell. Years later he told me that if I hadn't written him all those letters, he would have quit. So you know what he did after that? Every time after he signed a player, he wrote letters to see how they were progressing and helped them stay with it when they struggled.

But it's hard to do things that way these days because we don't get to work with the kids and their families like we did in the past. There's not that same sense of closeness.

Bibliography

Scout Interviews

Hugh Alexander
Gib Bodet
Ellis Clary
George Digby
Dick Egan
Cecil Espy
Jerry Gardner
Bob Harrison
George Kissell
Al LaMacchia
Fred McAlister
Jethro McIntyre
Bobby Mattick
Julian Mock
Phil Rizzo
Eddie Robinson
Gene Thompson
Dick Wilson

Books

Bjarkman, Peter. *The Baseball Scrapbook*. New York: Barnes & Noble, 1995.
Dragseth, P.J. *Go Pro Baseball Wise*. Chicago: MZD Publishing, 1999.
Lamb, David. *A Stolen Season*. New York: Random House, 1991.
Levine, Peter. *A.G. Spalding and the Rise of Baseball*. New York: Oxford University Press, 1985.
Reichler, Joseph, editorial consultant. *The Baseball Encyclopedia*. New York: Macmillan, 1969.
Snelling, Dennis. *Pacific Coast League: A Statistical History, 1903–1957*. Jefferson, N.C.: McFarland, 1995.
Werber, Bill, and Paul C. Rogers. *Memories of a Ballplayer*. Cleveland: Society of American Baseball Research, 2001.

Newspapers, Monthly Publications, Other Publications

Mazur, Roberta, director. Programs, Baseball Scout of the Year Banquet, 1984–2007.
Cummins, Jim, ed. *The Baseball Scout: A Newsletter For and About Baseball Scouting*. Self-published by Cummins. May 1997, September 1997, November 1997, February 1998, June 1999, and March 2000 issues.
Harris, Kevin. "Yoakum Plays Big Role for Chicago." *Sacramento Bee*, 18 May 2006, evening edition.

Online Sources

Baseball Almanac (http://www.baseball-almanac.com)
Baseball Reference (http://www.baseball-reference.com)
Baseball Reliquary (www.baseballreliquary.org)
Baseball America (http://www.baseballamerica.com)
Society for American Baseball Research (http://members.sabr.org)
Baseball Library (http://www.baseballlibrary.com)

Index

Aaron, Hank 69, 83 114, 118
Acker, Jim 128
Ackerman, Carl 183
Adams, Daniel "Doc" 5
Adams, Red 198
Advance scouts defined 8
Agent(s) 16, 73, 111, 121, 216–217, 226, 228
Ainge, Danny 116
Al LaMacchia Award 17
Alabama-Florida League 171
Alaska Goldpanners 140
Albuquerque Cardinals 43
Alexander, Doyle 19, 152
Alexander, Gary 144
Alexander, Hugh 16, 19–28
Alicea, Luis 176
Allen, Jamie 221
Allen, Mel 111
Almon, Bill 138
Alomar, Roberto 64
Alomar, Sandy 210
Alou, Jesus 151
Alou brothers 90
Alvarez, Wilson 214, 215
Amateur scouts defined 8
American Association 117, 129, 146, 171
American League 7, 107
American Legion (baseball) 39, 56, 124, 126, 188, 222
Anaheim Valencias 42
Anchorage Bucs 140
Anderson, Larry 89
Anderson, Sparkie 186
Angels, Anaheim-California–Los Angeles (American League) 31, 125, 151, 156, 187, 188, 199, 200, 202, 222
Angels, Los Angeles (Pacific Coast League) 75, 81, 103, 116, 117, 127, 139, 217
Ankiel, Rick 184
Anson, Cap 6
Aparicio, Luis 63
Area scout(s) 36
Arizona Diamondbacks 107, 169, 199, 205
Arizona-Mexico League 44
Arizona-Texas League 41, 43, 45

Arkansas Travelers 76, 77, 78, 105, 127
Arnold, Chris 144
Artesia Giants 150
Asheville Tourists 146
Associate scouts 32
Astroturf 50, 143
Atilee, Joe 184–185
Atlanta Braves 97, 101, 102, 103, 128, 133, 138, 198
Atlantic League 7
Autry, Gene 187
Averill, Earl 89
Avery, Steve 198

Baerga, Carlos 210
Bailey, Larkin 20
Baines, Harold 215
Baines, Joe 175
Bakersfield Bears 74, 85, 121
Balcena, Bobby 79, 80–81
Ball, Frank 228
Baltimore Orioles 6, 103, 116, 118, 125, 126, 137, 209
Barber, Red 111
Barfield, Jesse 125
Baseball Hall of Fame 3, 16
Baseball Scholarship Plan 112
Batavia Clippers 148
Bauman, Joe 155
Baumer, Jim 149–150
Baylor, Don 116, 125
Beauchamp, Jim 182
Becker, Joe 121
Beeston, Jim 208
Beeston, Paul 68, 119, 134
Belanger, Mark 125
Belcher, Tim 97
Bell, George 128
Bell, Kevin 189
Belz, Jim 173
Bench, Johnny 179
Benedict, Bruce 128, 138
Benson, Vern 172
Bergesch, Bill 87
Bernazard, Tony 116
Berra, Yogi 64, 89
Bice, DeWayne 144
Big Red Machine 40
Big State League 132, 199, 200

Biggio, Craig 64
Bird dog(s) 25, 31, 32, 52, 216
Birmingham Barons 116, 117, 130
Birmingham Black Barons 114, 213
Bisbee-Douglas Miners 43
Bishop, Bob 194
Black, Bud 208, 221, 224
Black Sox Scandal 197
Black Yankees 157
Blankenship, Cliff 7
Blauser, Jeff 180
Blue, Vida 195
Bodet, Gib 187–198
Bogard, Dick 32
Boggs, Tommy 138, 139
Boggs, Wade 231
Bolling, Milt 179, 231, 234
Bonds, Barry 32, 142, 162
Bonds, Bobby 142, 152–153
Bonilla, Bobby 143, 144
Bonus Rule 9, 31, 124
Booty, Josh 33
Boras, Scott 16, 111–114, 216–217, 229
Boston Red Caps 5
Boston Red Sox 9, 63, 95, 104, 119, 147, 157, 160, 178, 187, 231, 232, 233
Boston Somersets 6
Bottomley, Jim 145
Bowa, Larry 210
Bowden, Jim 205
Bowen, Joe 161, 162, 167, 168
Bowen, Rex 161, 162, 163, 167 168, 170
Bowers, Buzz 17
Bowie, Jim 221
Boyer, Kenny 181
Bradley, Bill 22
Bradley, George 97, 98
Bradley, Milton 129
Braggs, Glenn 217
Branson, Jeff 160
Bream, Sid 162
Brennan, Tommy 139
Briles, Nelson 31
Broglio, Ernie 60
Brooklyn Dodgers 3, 41
Brooklyn Robins 6

237

Brown, Chris 144
Brown, Joe 82, 155
Brown, Kevin 20, 35
Brown, Ollie 144
Brummer, Glenn 172, 173, 174
Bryant, Ron 89
Burdette, Lew 83
Burke, Joe 7
Burleson, Rick 189
Burlington-Graham Pirates 41
Burroughs, Jeff 222
Burt, Chris 203
Busch, Augie 26
Bystrom, Marty 19

California League 39, 74, 81–82, 83, 85, 104
Cambria, Joe "Papa Joe" 13, 69, 144
Campanis, Al 24, 70, 150, 195
Canadian Hall of Fame 116
Caracas, Venezuela 151, 155
Cardinals 26
Carew, Rod 69
Carlton, Steve 26, 31, 64
Carolina League 41, 126, 136
Carpenter, Bob 24
Carpenter, Chris 176
Carrithers, Don 144
Carrola, Marc 82
Carter, Gary 125
Carter, Glen 201
Carter, Joe 134, 135, 210
Castro, Angel 155
Castro, Dominic 80
Catalina Island 78
Cepeda, Orlando 90, 157
Cey, Ron 19, 89
Chambers, Al 221
Chandler, Happy 130
Chandler, Spud 68
Chapman, Ben 66, 147
Charlotte Hornets 62
Chase Field (Arizona Diamondbacks) 107
Chattanooga Lookouts 62, 148
Chicago Cubs 3, 72, 81, 82, 94, 107, 116, 117, 122, 125, 127, 132, 198, 224
Chicago White Sox 7, 28, 75, 80, 116, 117, 126, 173, 199, 215
Chicago White Stockings 5, 6
Christopher, Loyd 52, 85, 86, 101
Cincinnati Reds 5, 52, 81, 95, 106, 116, 117, 108, 125, 126, 127, 132, 143, 160, 161, 162, 163, 165, 212, 219, 224
Clark, Jack 144, 151, 189–191
Clark, Tony 99
Clark, Will 232
Clary, Ellis 25, 62
Clayton, Royce 144
Clear, Mark 189, 196

Clemens, Roger 58
Clemente, Roberto 155
Cleveland Blues 6
Cleveland Indians 20, 27, 68, 77, 107, 116, 118, 139, 147, 151, 167, 212
Clift, Harlond 62, 67, 86
Coast League *see* Pacific Coast League
Coleman, Paul 176, 177
Coleman, Vince 179, 182
Coles, Darnell 221, 226
Colletti, Ned 205
Columbus Clippers 142
Columbus Red Birds 171
Comiskey, Charles 6, 7
Connecticut State League 7
Contraction 170
Cook, Murray 97
Cooperstown 16
Cornutt, Terry 103
Corporate ownership 14, 123, 168
Cottier, Chuck 200
Counsell, Craig 29, 35
Covington, Wes 126
Cox, Bobby 101, 116, 126, 134
Creech, Eddie 216
Cromartie, Warren 116
Cronin, Hep 17
Crosby, Ed 221
Crosschecker(s) 36
Cruceta, Francisco 29
Cuban Stars 157
Cunningham, Joe 172
Curaçao 111
Currie, Clarence 7
Curtis, Al 105

D'Acquisto, John 144
Dahlgren, Babe 79, 80
Dalan, John 7
Dalkowski, Steve 76
Dalrymple, Abner 6
Danley, Kerwin 208
Danville Dans 199
Davenport, Jim 66
Davis, Alvin 221, 223
Davis, Brock 116
Davis, Chili 144, 151
Davis, Eric 162
Davis, Mark 210, 212–213
Davis, Red 152
Davis, Tom 103
Davis, Willie 39, 173
Deal, Cot 180
Deal, Ken 88
Dean, Dizzy 3, 75, 77, 105, 145
Dean, Paul 105
Dean, Tommy 19
Deer, Rob 144
Delancy, Bill 75
DelGreco, Bobby 155
Denver Bears 80, 147

Derrenger, Paul 109, 110
Designated hitter (DH) 107, 130, 170, 219
Detroit Tigers 6, 29, 31, 38, 97, 98, 99, 100, 101, 103, 147, 167, 176, 187, 188, 193, 226
Devine, Joe 117, 122
DeViveiros, Bernie 30
Diaz, Carlos 221
Dickey, Bill 64
Didier, Mel 125, 228, 231
Dierker, Larry 185
Dietz, Dick 209
Digby, George 178
DiMaggio, Joe 3, 117, 124, 205
Ditmar, Carl 127
Divine, Bing 173, 174, 175
Dodgers, Brooklyn 3, 41, 66, 70, 71, 88, 114, 129, 146
Dodgers, Los Angeles 74, 119, 136, 137, 139, 141, 144, 150, 151, 155, 158, 166, 187, 188, 194, 199, 203, 212, 216
Doerr, Bobby 76
Dombrowski, David 29, 34, 35, 38, 59
Donald, Atlee 68
Doran, Mark 201, 202
Doubleday, Abner 107
Downey, Tom 75
The Draft 12, 24, 25, 33, 34, 35, 37, 46, 113, 119, 120, 122, 125, 141, 142, 153, 166, 168, 178–179, 224–225, 228, 234
Dressen, Charlie 106, 107
Dressler, Rob 103
Drew, J.D. 64, 113
Drews, Karl 147
Drysdale, Don 71–72, 121
Dubuque Rabbits 7
Duffy, Hugh 6
Duluth Dukes 171
Dunedin Blue Jays 140
Dunne, Mike 176
DuVall 176
Dwyer, Jim 172

Easter, Luke 44
Easterly, Jamie 128
Ebbets Field 114
Egan, Dick 29–40
El Cerito Imperials 42
Elliott, Harry 207
Ellis, Dock 46
El Paso Texans 43, 151
Embree, Earl 76
Ericks, John 176
Espy, Cecil 207–220
Essick, Bill 117
Ethier, Andre 129
Evangeline League 199, 200
Evans, Dwight 189
Expansion 14, 34, 35, 111, 120, 143, 183, 223, 228

Index

Fazio, Ernie 116
Federal League 6
Feeney, Chub 54, 94
Figueroa, Angel 208, 212, 213
Finley, Charlie 12, 86, 87, 167
Fitzgerald, Eddie 84
Flavin, John 116
Flood, Curt 116, 126
Florence, Paul 68, 127
Flores, Jesse, Jr. 39, 44
Flores, Steve 181
Florida League 30
Florida Marlins 34, 99, 103
Florida State League 140, 199, 200
Fontaine, Bob 96, 99, 229
Ford, Whitey 89
Fort Lauderdale 30
Foster, George 144, 151, 152
Fowlkes, Alan 144
Fox, Charlie 90
Foxx, Jimmy 145
Free agency 34, 58
Free agent 46, 47, 130, 137
Fregosi, Jim 37, 134
Freitas, Tony 83, 104, 105
Fremont Green Sox 128
Frisch, Frankie 145
Fryman, Travis 98, 167, 168

Gagliano, Bill 185
Gaines, Joe 116
Galarraga, Armando 29
Galbraith, John 46
Gamboa, Tom 39, 98
Gandil, Chick 7
Garagiola, Joe 67, 84
Garcia, Dave 90, 151, 152
Gardner, Jerry 41–51, 102
Garrett, Greg 144
Garrett, Josh 232
Garrido, Gil 151
Garvey, Steve 19, 95
Gaskill Red 142
Gassaway, Doug 26
Gaston, Cito 133–134, 135, 139
Gazella, Mike 80
Gehrig, Lou 64, 79
Genovese, Frank (Chick) 90, 152, 157
Genovese, George 1, 71, 90, 91, 91, 92, 144–159, 211, 228
Gentile, Jim 38
Gettman, Jake 7
Giants, New York 3, 9, 22, 41, 70, 106, 107, 111, 114, 123, 187
Giants, San Francisco 66, 75, 89, 90, 91, 92, 95, 96, 101, 103, 107, 141, 142, 144, 151, 185, 152, 155, 156, 158, 173, 191, 195, 211
Gibson, Bob 186
Gibson, Josh 73
Gibson, Kirk 136–137

Gilbert, Andy 152
Gilbert, Dennis 158
Giles, Brian 212
Giles, Marcus 212
Giles, Warren C. 111
Gilhousen, Ross (Rosey) 78, 193, 194, 195
Gillick, Pat 65, 118, 119, 125–126, 132, 134, 140, 142, 143
Giordano, Tom 17
Gladden, Dan 155
Glaus, Troy 217
Glennon, Eddie 30
Goldis, Al 203
Goldklang Group 17, 199
Goldklang Group Professional Baseball Scouts Hall of Fame 205
Gonder, Jesse 116
Goodman, Billy 76
Gordon, Joe 86
Gorman, Lou 223
Gott, Jim 128
Grabarkewitz, Billy 19
Gray, Pete 76
Green, Dallas 24, 27, 28
Greenberg, Steve 217
Grich, Bobby 116, 125
Griffey, Ken, Jr. 221, 226
Griffith, Calvin 67, 68, 70, 124
Griffith, Clark 6, 148
Grimm, Charlie 122
Grove, Lefty 145
Gulf Coast League 59, 186
Gullickson, Bill 125
Gwynn, Tony 208, 210, 212–213

Haak, Howie 49, 144, 150
Hall, Andy 210, 213–214
Hall, Dick 154
Hamilton Red Wings 146
Hammond, Chris 160
Hands, Billy 76
Haney, Fred 83
Hanlon, Dick 31
Hansen, Dave 187, 195–196
Haren, Dennis 212
Harkey, Mike 224
Harper, Reggie 220
Harper, Tommy 60, 116, 125
Harr, Charlie 27
Harris, Bucky 147, 148
Harris, Jerry 219
Harris, Phil 48
Harrison, Bob 158, 221–230
Hart, Charlie 28
Hart, Jim Ray 90
Hartford Dark Blues 5
Hartsfield, Bob 158
Hashem, Tufie 80
Hastings Giants 114
Heaverlo, Dave 95, 103
Hemond, Roland 16, 17, 158

Hemus, Sollie 183
Henderson 221
Henderson, Dave 221, 228
Henderson, Joe 208
Henderson, Ken 144, 152
Henderson, Rickey 56
Hengel, Dave 221
Henrich, Bobby 116
Herman, Babe 76
Hernandez, Keith 64
Hernandez, Mario 80
Herzog, Whitey 119, 175, 191
Hill, Glenallen 116
Hill, Marc 172–173, 174
Hines, Bruce 201
Hobbie, Glen 31
Holder, Brooks 76
Hollandsworth, Todd 196–197
Hollis, Thurston 75
Hollywood Stars 45, 74, 75, 76–77, 78, 83, 127, 147
Holzemer, Mark 201
Hopper, Clay 145, 146
Horn, Sam 210, 214
Hornsby, Rogers 72
Hough, Charlie 35
Houston Astros 11, 118, 124, 134, 143, 175, 185
Houston Buffalos 171
Houston Colt .45's 11, 116
Howard, Frank 19, 37
Howsam, Bob 161
Hoy, William "Dummy" 7
Hubbell, Carl 54, 90, 94, 95, 111, 123, 152
Hudlin, Willis 76
Hudson, Johnny 26, 90
Hughes, Gary 96, 97, 102
Hulbert, William 5
Humorous Stories on the Ballfield 7
Hunt, Ken 116
Hurst, Bruce 31
Hutchinson, Freddie 126

Independent team(s) 22, 30, 130
Indianapolis Clowns 114
International League 171, 180

Jackson, Bo 32, 163
Jackson, Conor 59
Jackson, Larry 76
Jackson, Ransom 81
James, Dion 56
Japanese baseball 218
Jockety, Walt 60
Johnson, Deron 207
Johnson, Frank 144
Johnson, Jim 39
Johnson, Sandy 32
Jones, Calvin 221
Jones, Chipper 168
Jones, Dale 213
Jones, Dalton 178

Index

Jones, Hank 197
Jones, Rex 79
Jones, Ruppert 223
Jongewaard, Roger 98, 224
Jordan, Brian 25, 182
Joyce, Lon 17
June Draft 10, 12

Kaat, Jim 76
Kaline, Al 38
Kamzic, Nick 199, 200, 201, 202
Kansas City Athletics 85–86, 96, 99, 103
Kansas City Royals 187, 188, 193, 194, 195, 223
Keenan, John 25
Kelchner, Charles "Pop" 10
Kell, George 234
Keller, Hal 138
Kelly, Bill 81
Kelly, Kenny 180–181
Kelly, Mike 117
Kennedy, Bob 172
Keough, Marty 27, 141, 182, 210, 212, 213, 214, 215, 220
Kerr, Buddy 90, 152
Kerros, Eric 187, 194
Killebrew, Harmon 63
Killman, Bobby 231
Kinder, Ellis 76
Kiner, Ralph 207
King, Eric 144
Kingman, Dave 91, 144, 181
Kipper, Bob 201–202, 204
Kirkland, Willie 126
Kissell, George 10, 178, 179, 182
KITE League see KITTY League
KITTY League 41, 43, 45
Klaus, Richard (Richie) 152
Klein, Don 3
Klein, Joe 99
Klein, Ronnie 154
Kling, Johnny 7
Kluttz, Clyde 86
Knepper, Bob 89
Knickerbocker, Billy 76
Knudsen, Kurt 98
Kotchman, Tom 17
Koufax, Sandy 64
Krug, Marty 76
Kubski, Al 11, 193, 194
Kuehl, Karl 56
Kuenn, Harvey 234
Kutcher, Randy 144, 155

Lajoie, Bill 97, 99, 194
Lakey, Gordon 66
LaMacchia, Al 25, 26, 47, 65, 116, 125, 128–143; see also Al LaMacchia Award
LaMar, Chuck 46, 101–102, 103, 134
Landis, Jim 116

Landis, Kenesaw Mountain 130
Lane, Frank 28, 118, 126, 155, 174
Langstrom, Mark 228
Lanier, Max 153
Larham, Arlie 7
Lasorda, Tommy 28, 70, 91, 92, 102, 137, 197
Las Vegas Stars 210
Las Vegas Wranglers 42
Latin America (scouting in) 34, 119, 144
Latin American Scouting system 49
Lazzeri, Tony 147
Lee, Bill 189
Lee, Leron 56
Lee, Tabor 217
Lee, Travis 217
LeMaster, Johnnie 65–66
Lemke, Mark 35
Lexington Giants 153
Lezcano, Sixto 116, 125
Lillard, Gene 88
Lilly, Art 86, 193, 194
Lindeberg, Don 193
Lindeman, Jim 176
Lippitore, Ed 130
Lipski, Bob 31
Little Rock see Arkansas Travelers
Littlefield, Dick 155
Littlejohn, Dennis 144
Livesay, Bill 96
Lolich, Mickey 89
Long, Dale 84
Longhorn League 199, 200
Lopat, Eddie 65
Lopes, Davey 19
Loretta, Mark 202, 204
Los Angeles Dodgers 37
Louisville Grays 5
Lumpe, Jerry 38
Lurie, Bob 95, 96, 158
Lyke, Jim 93
Lynch, John 33
Lynchburg Cardinals 147
Lynn, Fred 189
Lyone, Al 88

Mack, Connie 145
Maddox, Garry 144, 152
Maddux, Greg 205
Madlock, Bill 180
Magrane, Joe 176
Mahler, Mickey 128, 138
Mahler, Rick 128, 138
Mahoney, Neil (T.) 187, 194
Maier, Marty 216
Major League Baseball 61
Major League Scouting Bureau 4, 9, 12, 14, 29, 31, 32, 39, 52, 57, 68, 120, 161, 183 184, 187, 232

Maloney, Jim 116, 118, 125
Mancuso, Gus 123, 145
Mantle, Mickey 27, 37, 124
Marichal, Juan 90, 157
Marine, Del 100
Marshall, Bill 92
Martin, Billy 56, 60
Martin, Joe 181
Martinez, Horatio 152
Mathaney, Mike 202, 203
Mathes, Joe 178
Mathews, Eddie 83
Matthews, Gary 144, 152
Matthews, Wid 88
Mattick, Bobby 17, 48, 116–127, 128, 132, 134, 139, 140
Mattick, Dan 202
Mattick, Wally 116, 121
Mattingly, Don 98
Maxvill, Dal 174, 182
Mayfield Clothiers baseball team 41
Mays, Willie 38, 60, 63, 90, 114, 124, 158, 231
Mazatlan Venados 153
Mazzone, Leo 101
McAlister, Fred (Freddie) 26, 27, 121, 141, 171–186, 209, 210, 213, 216
McAuliffe 37
McBride, Bake 26, 172, 173, 220
McCovey, Willie 3, 64, 126, 185
McCullough, Clyde 82, 84
McDonald, Joe 98, 99, 175
McFadden, Leon 116
McGee, Willie 176
McGraw, John 111
McGrew, Charlie 82
McIntyre, Jethro 52
McKechnie, Bill 106, 108, 109, 123
McKeon, Jack 209–210
McPhail, Larry 126
McWilliams, Larry 128, 138
Meacham, Bobby 176, 210, 213
Melvin, Doug 97
Menke, Dennis 140
Merullo, Lennie 12, 17, 198
Mexicali Aguilas 49, 74, 79–80, 155–156
Mexican League 153
Mexican Leagues 153–156
Mexico (scouting in) 144, 150
Meyer, Billy 84
Michigan State League 128
Midwest League 199, 200, 203
Miley, Mike 139
Miller, Bob 96
Miller, Jim 31
Miller, Kurt 35
Miller, Ox 62, 67
Milwaukee Braves 83, 93

Index

Milwaukee Brewers 116, 117, 126, 169, 202, 203, 217
"Minister of Trade" 25
Minneapolis Millers 117
Minnesota Twins 63, 68, 143, 151, 213
Minor, Harry 158
Mitchell, Cameron (actor) 103
Mitchell, Dale 19, 23
Mize, Johnny 145
Mock, Julian 160–170
Modesto Reds 74, 82, 83, 104
Moffitt, Randy 144
Molitor, Paul 134
Montague Ed (Eddie) 53–54, 89, 93
Montgomery, Bob 231
Montreal Expos 52, 56, 59, 97, 116, 118, 120, 125, 169, 187, 196
Mooney, Tom 224
Moore, Johnny 48
Moore, Mike 180, 226
Moran, Butch 81
Morgan, Joe 60
Moseby, Lloyd 128
Moses, John 221
Mullen, John 114
Municipal Baseball League 128
Munoz, Mike 187, 196
Murff, Red 142
Murphy, Dale 89, 95, 128, 138–139
Murphy, Johnny 88
Murray, Ray 152
Murray, Rich 144
Murtaugh, Danny 83, 84
Musial, Stan 64, 69, 145–146, 178
Myers, Otto 76
Myers, Randy 89

National Base Ball Players Association 5
National crosschecker 29
National League 5
The Natural (movie) 30
Negro Leagues 72, 114, 157
Nelson, Ricky 221
Nen, Robb 29, 35
New Jersey League 7
New Orleans Pelicans 82, 83
New York Cubans 114
New York Giants 3, 9, 22
New York Knickerbockers 5
New York Mets 3, 87, 98, 103, 135, 142
New York Mutuals 5
New York–Penn League 16, 30
New York Yankees 9, 30, 63, 79, 80, 88, 89, 96, 97, 98, 103, 117, 119, 126, 128, 137, 138, 142, 147, 160, 217, 218
Newfield, Marc 99

Newman, Al 213
Nichols, Reid 231
Niekro, Joe 180–181
Niggeling, Johnny 62, 67
Norfolk Tars 147
North Carolinas League 152
Northeast Arkansas League 128
Northern League 21, 112, 171
Northwest League 4, 7, 85, 202

Oakland Athletics 52, 85, 103, 137, 140
Oberkfell, Ken 172
Odom, Blue Moon 167
O'Doul, Lefty 77
Office, Roland 56
Ogden Reds 116
Ohio State League 128
Oldham 116
Olerud, John 89
Oliva, Tony 69
Olmstead, Al 172
Olson, Ray 76
Omaha Cardinals 171
O'Neil, Buck 72
Ontario Orioles 42, 74, 78, 79
Ontiveros, Steve 94–95, 103
Orella, Elmer 105
Overall, Orval 7
Owen, Spike 226

Pacheco, Tony 16
Pacific Coast League 3, 35, 39, 42, 74, 75, 77, 78, 81–82, 83, 85, 88, 116, 117, 122, 126, 127, 147, 150, 205
Paciorek, Tom 19
Pagan, Jose 157
Paige, Satchel 157
Palica, Erv 75
Pappas, Erik 201, 202, 204
Paragould Browns 128
Parker, Kent 207
Parsons, Casey 103
Partee, Roy 30, 88
Pascual, Camilo 69
Passeau, Claude 82
Patterson, Bob 29
Patterson, Pat 118
Paul, Gabe 118, 120, 123–124, 183
PCL *see* Pacific Coast League
Pena, Jim 144
Pena, Tony 176
Peninsula League 56
Penner, Ken 75
Pesky, Johnnie 76
Peters, Hank 85–86
Pettit, Paul 155
Pfleger, Roy 146
Philadelphia Athletics 5, 6, 145
Philadelphia Phillies 24, 66, 128, 132, 134, 138, 146, 183, 219

Phillips, Dee 30
Phillips, Lefty 121
Phoenix Stars 41, 44
Piazza, Mike 141, 187, 197
Piedmont League 77, 147
Pieretti, Clark 105
Pinson, Vada 60, 61, 116, 123, 125, 127
Pioneer League 77
Pittsburgh Crawfords 157
Pittsburgh Pirates 7, 42, 45, 47, 49, 50, 82, 83, 84, 104, 108, 128, 142, 143, 148, 150, 153, 154, 160, 163, 176
Plank 103
Player development 34
Players League 5
Players' Union 60, 123, 120, 218, 219
Plesac, Dan 180
Pocatello Chiefs 91
Pointer, Aaron 60
Poland, Hugh 152
Pompez, Alex 90, 152, 157
Porter, Darrell 116, 125
Porter, J.W. 124
Powles, George 53
Poza Rica Petroleros 153
Prempas, Lyle 203
Professional Baseball Scouts Hall of Fame 16, 205
Professional scout(s) 8, 36
Pusich, Evo 152–153, 189

Queen, Mel 116
Quinn, Bob 138
Quinn, John 114

Rabb, John 144
Radbourn, Charlie "Hoss" 7
Rader, Dave 94, 95, 103
Ramos, John 97
Ramos, Pedro 69
Ramsey, Mike 172
Randall, Gary 232
Raschi, Vic 147
Reagan, Danny 79, 88
Reed, Jody 231
Reese, Jimmy 207
Reese, PeeWee 141
Reese, Pokey 168
Reno Silver Sox 42
Revenue sharing 170
Reynolds, Allie 19
Reynolds, Bob 93, 103
Rhines, Billy "Bunker" 7
Richards, Paul 11, 118, 124, 126, 137–138
Richardson, Jeff 160
Richmond Braves 182
Rickey, Branch 4, 9, 13, 42, 49, 66, 82–84, 88, 105, 120, 122, 144, 145, 148, 149–150, 154–155, 157, 170, 178

Rigney, Bill 152
Riverside Dons 42
Rizzo, Mike 200, 202, 204
Rizzo, Phil 17, 199–206
Robb, Ray 29
Robello, Tony 30
Robertson, Andre 128
Robertson, Jax 98, 99, 101
Robinson, Brooks 63, 149, 155
Robinson, Eddie 11, 12, 13
Robinson, Frank 64, 116, 118, 123, 125, 127
Robinson, Jackie 4, 49, 52, 66, 157, 158
Robinson, Paul 201
Rodriguez, Leo 155
Roenicke, Gary 125, 190, 191
Rogers, Kenny 29
Root, Charlie 76
Rose, Pete 118, 165, 183, 197, 219
Roseboro, John 37
Rosen, Al 44, 71
Rosselli, Joe 144
Rowland, Donny 17
Royster, Jerry 56
Russell, Bill 19
Russo, Jim 16
Ruth, Babe 76, 80, 130, 154, 232
Ryan, Nolan 135–136, 141, 182
Ryerson, Gary 144

Sabathia, C.C. 59
Sails, Steve 217
St. Louis Brown Stockings 5
St. Louis Browns 62, 67, 69, 128, 129, 172
St. Louis Cardinals 42, 75, 98, 105, 108, 126, 128, 129, 130, 141, 143, 145, 155, 161, 171, 173, 175, 177, 178, 182, 183, 185, 207, 208, 209, 212, 217, 223
Sakata, Lenn 92
Salt Lake City Bees 77, 150, 155
San Antonio Missions 128
San Diego Baseball Association 207
San Diego Padres 29, 52, 107, 138, 209
San Francisco Seals 75, 77, 78, 105
San Jose Bees 52, 58
Sandberg, Ryne 89
Sanford, Mo 160
Santin, Rudy 17
Santo, Ron 89
Saucier, Kevin 12
Sauer, Hank 90, 152
Sawatski, Carl 199
Sax, Steve 197
Schalk, Ray 7

Schembecler, Bo 99
Schilling, Curt 134
Schmidt, Mike 63
Schofield, Dick 201
Schudlich, Bill 98
Schuerholz, John 102, 195
Schwarz, Jack 90, 91, 92, 94, 95, 114, 115, 151, 152
Scout League 187, 188, 189, 186, 223
Scout of the Year Award (recipients) 19, 106, 144, 171, 204
Scout of the Year Awards Program 16
Scully, Vin 71
Seals Stadium 3, 78
Seattle Mariners 118, 125, 132, 168, 180, 199, 221, 222, 223, 224, 228, 229
Seattle Pilots 116
Seeds, Bob 77
Selig, Bud 118
Shafer, Jack 93
Shannon, Walter (Wally) 125, 178
Sheehan, Tom 152
Shepard, Larry 155
Shirley, Bart 19
Silvey, George 172–173
Sisler, Dick 146
Sisler, George 84
Slapnicka, Cy 20
Slaughter, Enos 234
Sloan, Brad 17
Smith, Lonnie 138
Smith, Mike 160
Smith, Ozzie 35, 138, 191
Smith, Roy 173
Smoltz, John 98
Snider, Duke 75
Snyder, Paul 102
Sophomore League 150
Sosa, Sammy 214–215
South America (scouting in) 150
South Atlantic League 7
Southeastern Baseball Camp 160
Southern Association 62, 76, 82, 117
Southern League 7, 78, 148, 178, 199
Spahn, Warren 83
Speed, Horace 144
Springfield Cardinals 145
Sprinz, Joe 77
Stankey, Eddie 183
Stargell, Willie 60
Stassi, George "Moose" 79
Staub, Rusty 124, 178, 232
Steinbrenner, George 96, 97, 168, 217, 219
Steiner, Bill 77
Stengel, Casey 6, 89
Stenzel, Jake 6

Stephens, Vern 76
Stephenson, Joe 87, 228
Steveros, Harry 56
Stewart, Art 17
Stieb, Dave 125, 128, 139–140, 141
Stoddard, Bob 221
Stoneham, Horace 54, 95, 158
Stottlemyre, Mel 89
Stovall, George 7
Strawberry, Darryl 219
Street, Gabby 145
Stuart, Dick 104
Sukeforth, Clyde 144, 150
Sularz, Guy 144
Sullivan, Gary 212
Sullivan, Haywood 231, 234
Sullivan, Marc 231
Sullivan, Timothy Paul (TP; Ted) 6–7; *Humorous Stories on the Ballfield* 7
Sullivan's Alerts 6
Sunday, Billy 6
Sunset League 42, 74, 79
Sutton, Don 19
Sutton, Larry 6
Swain, Steve 210, 214
Swan, Craig 222

Tampa Bay (Devil) Rays 34, 47, 181
Taormina, Sal 3, 152
Taylor, Eddie 89, 92
Tebbetts, Birdie 126, 213
Temple Eagles 200
Templeton, Garry 191, 220, 223, 226–228
Texas League 7, 128, 171, 178, 186
Texas Rangers 11, 29, 99, 135, 138, 175, 211, 214
Thomas, Gorman 125
Thomasson, Gary 144
Thompson, Gene (Junior) 44, 90, 106–115
Thompson, Jason 187, 193–194
Thompson, Tommy 165
Thorpe, Jim 22
Thrift, Syd 143
Throneberry, Faye 231
Thurston, Hollis 48
Tincup, Ben 7
Tolan, Bobby 46
Toledo Mud Hens 129
Tomko, Brett 168
Topps Company, Inc. 16
Toronto Blue Jays 68, 116, 126, 128, 132, 219, 228
Trautmann, George 81
Tredway, Red 82
Trippi, Charley 234
Trocolor, Bob 114, 187
Tryout camp(s) 10, 39, 42, 49, 52, 75, 150, 162, 163–164, 178

Tucker, Horace 207
Tucson Cowboys 43
Turner, Jim 109
Twin Falls Cowboys 91–92

Unroe, Tim 202, 203, 204
Upshaw, Willie 128

Valentine, Bobby 135
Valentine, Ellis 125
Vance, Dazzy 6
Vande Berg, Ed 222, 224
Van Eck, Ollie 146
VanSlyke, Andy 143, 176
Varitek, Jason 111
Vera Cruz League 153
Virdon, Bill 155
Visalia Cubs 74, 82
Visalia Stars 41, 74
Vogel, Mike 202

Wade, Ben 195
Walker, Tyler 59
Walker, Wally 74
Waller, Reggie 217
Walters, Bucky 45, 109
Ward, John Montgomery 5
Warwick, Carl 19
Washington, Claudell 56
Washington Nationals 6
Washington Senators 7, 62, 67, 70, 128, 147, 148, 199, 200
Weaver, George "Buck" 7

Weiss, George 89, 126
Wellman, Brad 187, 194, 195
Wells, David 142, 210, 214
Wenatchee Oaks 42, 74, 85
Werber, Billy 106
Werle, Bill 44
West, Max 44
West Brighton Cardinals 144
West Texas–New Mexico League 42, 199, 200
Western Association 117, 145
Western International League 42, 74, 85
Western League 5, 7, 80, 105, 147, 171
Wheat, Zack 6
Whisenton, Larry 128
White, Ernie 145
Wichita Baseball Congress 128
Wickman, Bob 202, 204
Widmyer, Walt 231
Wiencek, Dick 56, 98, 193–194
Wiggins, Alan 196
Wight, Bill 60, 102, 147
Wilder, Dave 101, 102
Wilfong, Rob 99
Wilhoit, Joe 6
Williams, Donnie 25
Williams, Frank 95, 103
Williams, Matt 144
Williams, Ted 63, 70, 76, 100, 118, 178, 205
Williamson, Mark 209, 210

Willis, Dontrelle 59
Willoughby, Jim 95, 103
Wills, Maury 150
Wilmot, Walt 7
Wilson, Danny 168
Wilson, Dick 4, 74–105, 126–127
Wilson, Earl 207
Wilson, Henry 7
Wilson, Jim 31, 32
Wirth, Alan 144
Wise, Rick 26, 89
Witt, Bobby 35
Wolf, Wally 116
Wood, Kerry 184
Woodall, Larry 231
Woods, Tony 181
Worrell, Todd 141, 181–82
Wright, David 197
Wynn, Early 64
Wynn, Jimmy 56

Yoakum, David 158
Young, Dimitri 176

Zarilla, Al 86
Zeile, Todd 97
Zerba, Frank 146
Zuk, Bob 125
Zuraw, George 162, 163, 166, 213

www.ingramcontent.com/pod-product-compliance
Lightning Source LLC
Chambersburg PA
CBHW081550300426
44116CB00015B/2827